Automating Cyber Threat Intelligence: Tools and Techniques for Enhanced Security Posture

AUTOMATING CYBER THREAT INTELLIGENCE: TOOLS AND TECHNIQUES FOR ENHANCED SECURITY POSTURE

Edited by

Adele Kuzmiakova

ARCLER
PRESS

www.arclerpress.com

Automating Cyber Threat Intelligence: Tools and Techniques for Enhanced Security Posture

Adele Kuzmiakova

Arcler Press
4164 Lakeshore Road
Burlington, ON L7L 1A4
Canada
www.arclerpress.com
Email: orders@arclereducation.com

ISBN: 978-1-77956-421-4 (Hardcover)

ABOUT THE EDITOR

Adele Kuzmiakova is a machine learning engineer working at the intersection of machine learning, computer vision, and natural language processing. Adele attended Cornell University in New York, United States for her undergraduate studies. She studied engineering with a focus on applied math. Some of the deep learning problems Adele worked on include predicting air quality from public webcams, developing a real-time human movement tracking, using 3D computer vision to create 3D avatars from selfies in order to bring online clothes shopping closer to reality, and creating visual stories and photobooks from photos on mobile devices. She is also passionate about exchanging ideas and inspiring other people and acted as a workshop organizer at Women in Data Science conference in Geneva, Switzerland in 2022 and 2023.

TABLE OF CONTENTS

LIST OF FIGURES

LIST OF TABLES

PREFACE

In today's digital landscape, the concept of "Threat Intelligence," also known as "Cyber Threat Intelligence" (CTI), has become essential for organizations aiming to bolster their cybersecurity defenses. CTI encompasses detailed knowledge about potential cybersecurity threats targeting an organization to enable security teams to adopt a more proactive approach. As cyber-attacks continue to surge globally, organizations face significant challenges, notably the task of effectively collecting and automating the analysis of threat data.

The sheer volume of cyber threat information can be overwhelming for threat intelligence analysts, making it difficult to distinguish between genuine threats and false positives. This is where artificial intelligence (AI) becomes a crucial asset. AI technologies, particularly machine learning (ML) and deep learning (DL), offer transformative solutions for automating and refining various aspects of threat intelligence, including data collection, in-depth analysis, intelligent sharing, and advanced technological integration.

AI algorithms can analyze vast amounts of cyber threat data, drawing from both historical and current information to identify patterns and adapt to emerging threats. By processing and organizing data such as files, IP addresses, domain names, and URLs—elements often involved in cyber-attacks—AI provides a comprehensive understanding of present, past, and potential future threats. This capability enhances the ability of threat intelligence tools to deliver timely and actionable insights.

The integration of AI in threat intelligence aims to augment human capabilities by significantly improving the speed, accuracy, and efficiency of threat detection and response. AI-driven tools can rapidly process and analyze data, offering more precise and effective threat intelligence solutions. This automation not only streamlines the threat intelligence process but also enhances its overall effectiveness, allowing organizations to better anticipate and respond to cyber threats.

The textbook *Automating Cyber Threat Intelligence: Tools and Techniques for Enhanced Security Posture* provides a comprehensive guide to modern approaches and technologies in the field of cybersecurity. It is structured into ten detailed chapters, each focusing on critical aspects of cyber threat intelligence and its automation.

The first chapter introduces the fundamental concepts of cyber threat intelligence, laying the groundwork for understanding how threat intelligence enhances security measures and prepares organizations for potential cyber threats.

Following this, the book highlights the importance of information sharing in preventing and mitigating cyber incidents. It discusses various strategies to facilitate effective information exchange among entities, aiming to strengthen collective cybersecurity efforts.

Chapter three addresses the process of transforming raw data into actionable threat intelligence. It covers techniques for monitoring, logging, and analyzing network activities to extract meaningful insights that aid in identifying and responding to threats.

In the fourth chapter, the focus shifts to Threat Intelligence Platforms (TIPs). This section explores the role of TIPs in aggregating, analyzing, and disseminating threat data, emphasizing their significance in automating and streamlining threat intelligence processes.

The textbook then transitions to automated threat analysis in chapter five, examining tools and methods for automating the analysis of cyber threats, enabling faster and more accurate detection and response.

Chapter six centers on automating incident detection and response. It provides practical insights into how automation can enhance an organization's ability to detect and respond to security incidents efficiently.

Chapter seven discusses the significance of threat intelligence sharing and collaboration, emphasizing the benefits and challenges of collaborative approaches in strengthening the overall security posture.

Machine learning and artificial intelligence applications in threat intelligence are covered in chapter eight, highlighting how these advanced technologies contribute to more sophisticated threat detection and analysis.

The ninth chapter focuses on automated threat intelligence management, offering strategies for managing and operationalizing threat intelligence through automation.

The final chapter looks ahead to future trends and emerging technologies in the field, providing an outlook on how evolving technologies will shape the future of cyber threat intelligence and security practices.

This textbook is intended for cybersecurity professionals, IT managers, and researchers seeking to enhance their understanding of automated threat intelligence. It is also valuable for students in cybersecurity programs and anyone interested in advancing their knowledge of the latest tools and techniques in cyber threat analysis and management.

CHAPTER 1

INTRODUCTION TO CYBER THREAT INTELLIGENCE

Contents

INTRODUCTION

It is crucial to keep looking for ways to keep organizations secure in this increasingly connected world where everything seems to be connected to the internet due to the rise in cyberattacks worldwide. Successful cyber security requires effective cyber threat information dissemination for any organization that wants to remain secure. The efficient gathering of information regarding cyberthreats is known as cyber threat intelligence, or CTI. The problem still lies in figuring out how to use the massive amounts of threat data that are becoming available for intelligence purposes.

1.1. DEFINITION AND IMPORTANCE OF CYBER THREAT INTELLIGENCE

The process of taking disparate pieces of information about a cyberattack and deciphering its meaning and mechanism is known as cyber threat intelligence, or CTI. It aids in anticipating and averting cyberattacks. It is also known as threat intelligence and is a technique for alerting an organization based on data that has been gathered and examined from various sources. Malware, insider threats, social engineering, weak or stolen credentials, application vulnerabilities, incorrect configuration, and user error are common sources of data breaches. The process of protecting data, files, and infrastructure has evolved, and threat intelligence is a step in that direction. The development of information gathering from various sources to protect assets in an environment was prompted by the sophistication of attacks. Dealing with cyber-attacks in the modern era is strongly supported by the sharing of threat intelligence. According to his definition, CTI is process-oriented, risk-focused, adversary-based, and customized for a range of customers. It is adversary-based since it looks to determine the attackers' motives, goals, and tactics. The goal of CTI is to reduce the risk that important assets and infrastructure may be compromised by an attacker's actions while maintaining the integrity of business operations. The goal of CTI is to provide intelligence an edge over cybercriminals. Given this, threat intelligence ought to be knowledge of threats based on facts that influences decisions. It was mentioned that the goal of threat intelligence is to match the objectives of cyber security with business objectives.

Cyber threat intelligence cannot be fully defined unless it includes pertinent threat data that has been put through the necessary phases of gathering, analyzing, and processing to produce timely, actionable intelligence that supports decision-making.

The field of cyber threat intelligence, or CTI, is becoming more and more established, but it is still evolving quickly. But intelligence work itself is a historically and commercially very well-established field. There are numerous ways to define intelligence. Good definitions all agree that understanding that can aid in decision-making is the result of intelligence, regardless of the particular context in which they are applied.

The UK National Crime Agency (NCA) defines intelligence as "information that is received or collected to answer specific questions on who, what, where, when, how, and why."

According to the US Central Intelligence Agency (CIA), "intelligence is knowledge and foreknowledge of the world around us—the prelude to decision and action."

This means that data and information about adversaries' intent and ability to target system and information assets is processed and analyzed to create cyber threat intelligence, which is intended to lessen that threat. In order to implement an intelligence-led security strategy, it is necessary to comprehend fundamental ideas like risk and threat.

1.1.1. What is Threat Intelligence?

Information about possible or ongoing attacks against an organization is obtained from a variety of sources and referred to as threat intelligence, also known as CTI. The data is then utilized to reduce and mitigate cybersecurity risks after being examined, improved, and arranged. Threat intelligence's primary goal is to make organizations aware of the different threats they face from outside sources, including advanced persistent threats (APTs) and zero-day threats. Threat intelligence comprises comprehensive data and background on particular threats, including who is attacking, what their capabilities and motivations are, and what indicators of compromise (IOCs) they may have. Organizations can use this information to make well-informed decisions about how to defend against the most harmful attacks.

1.1.2. What Does Threat Intelligence Do?

Organizations can better understand the risks associated with various attack types and how to defend against them with the aid of threat intelligence and cyber threat tools. Cyber threat intelligence also aids in averting already-occurring attacks. The IT department of a company may choose to use a threat intelligence service or conduct its own research to obtain data and recommendations on recommended security procedures. Businesses using software-defined networking (SDN) can quickly reconfigure their network to protect against particular types of cyberattacks by utilizing threat intelligence.

1.1.3. Why Is Threat Intelligence Important?

Intelligence is defined as information that gives an organization decision support and potentially a strategic advantage in the military, business, or security domains. A more comprehensive security intelligence strategy includes threat intelligence. It covers information about safeguarding a company against both internal and external threats, as well as the procedures, guidelines, and instruments employed in data collection and analysis.

Improved understanding of the threat landscape, threat actors, and their most recent strategies, techniques, and procedures can be gained through the use of threat intelligence. It makes it possible for enterprises to set up security controls pro-actively in order to identify and stop advanced attacks and zero-day threats. To ensure that security is always up to date with the most recent information, many of these modifications can be automated (Figure 1.1).

Figure 1.1. *The basics of threat intelligence: What it does, why you need it and where it's headed.*

Source: https://cdn.ttgtmedia.com/rms/onlineImages/ism-threat_intelligence_101-f.png.

1.1.4. Intelligence-Led Security

In conventional security, employing an intelligence-led strategy has long been recognized as best practice. Without it, organizations will always have insufficient defense against threats because they are unaware of them.

Alternatively, they might attempt to counter every possible attack, which is an unworkable strategy that might also make it harder for the company to run efficiently. For instance, before attempting to implement suitable security measures, a business wishing to construct a facility in a potentially hostile area would first look for information on the threat posed by local bad actors. The same rule of thumb holds true for cyber security: before taking defensive action, you must comprehend your threat. The adoption of intelligence-led cyber security testing frameworks, like the Bank of England's CBEST program, is guided by this methodology.

These frameworks' cyber threat intelligence component makes sure that organizations are put to the test in terms of their capacity to stop, identify, and react to accurate, realistic, and current attacks. Although the Bank of England's CBEST program was the first of its kind, the idea has since spread to other regulated industries in the UK as well as other countries, particularly the financial sector. These new schemes include:

- **STAR (Simulated Targeted Attack and Response):** As a generic framework applicable in any sector
- **STAR-FS (Simulated Targeted Attack and Response for Financial Services)**: Specifically for smaller UK financial institutions (i.e. those that don't qualify for the CBEST framework)
- **TIBER-EU (Threat Intelligence-based Ethical Red-Teaming)**: For the European financial sector, and its various national derivative schemes (TIBER-BE, TIBER-DE, TIBER-DK, TIBER-FI etc.)
- **iCAST (Intelligence-led Cyber Attack Simulation Testing)** for Hong Kong's financial sector
- **GBEST** For UK government departments
- **AASE (Adversarial Attack Simulation Exercises):** For financial institutions in Singapore
- **FEER (Financial Entities Ethical Red Teaming):** In Saudi Arabia
- **CORIE (Cyber Operational Resilience Intelligence-led Exercises):** For financial institutions in Australia

1.1.5. Threat and Risk

Risk is often described as the product of threat, vulnerability, and impact. For enterprises to implement a risk-based strategy for cyber security, they must thus be aware of the dangers they confront. A threat is defined as an adversary's intention and ability to target an asset, usually a system or piece of information. Organizations can prepare for and defend themselves against threats by having intelligence about them. An organization has a far better chance of defending itself when it is able to respond to important questions about the threats it faces, such as who is likely to target what assets, where, when, how, and why. This is especially true in the realm of cyber security, where defense becomes a challenging task due to the quantity and variety of adversaries as well as the rapid evolution of attack methods (Figure 1.2).

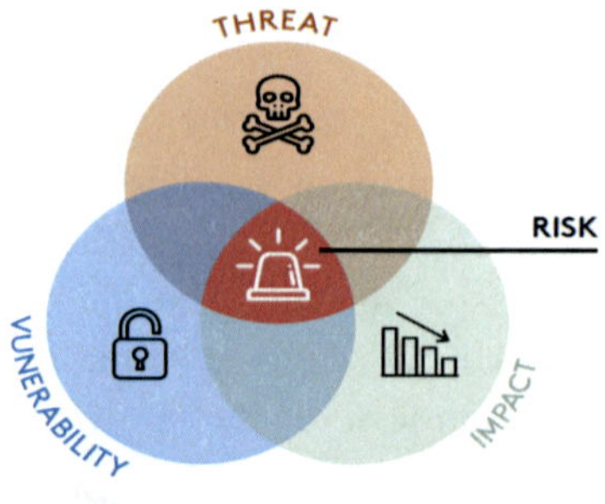

Figure 1.2. *Frequently, risk is defined as a combination of threat, vulnerability and impact.*

Source: https://www.crest-approved.org/wp-content/uploads/2022/04/CREST-Cyber-Threat-Intelligence.pdf.

Organizations can determine the probability of an incident happening by combining an evaluation of the maturity of their defenses with a thorough understanding of the threats they face. To determine the risk, this likelihood can be paired with an evaluation of the potential consequences of the event. This enables businesses to target the highest priority threats with their typically constrained security resources.

1.1.6. Data vs Information Versus Intelligence

There is a common mistake where data, information, and intelligence are used interchangeably.

- **Data:** Simple facts that are frequently available in large quantities are referred to as data. IP addresses and logs are common examples in the context of cyber security. Raw data has limited value on its own.
- **Information:** When this data is compiled to produce a useful output, such as a compilation of logs indicating an increase in suspicious activity, information is created.
- **Intelligence:** Processing and analyzing this data yields intelligence, which can then be applied to decision-making. In order to facilitate the development of incident mitigation strategies, the aggregated log data, for instance, is contextualized with previous incident reports pertaining to comparable activity.

An efficient model that illustrates this conversion of unprocessed data into final intelligence products is the Intelligence Cycle (Figure 1.3).

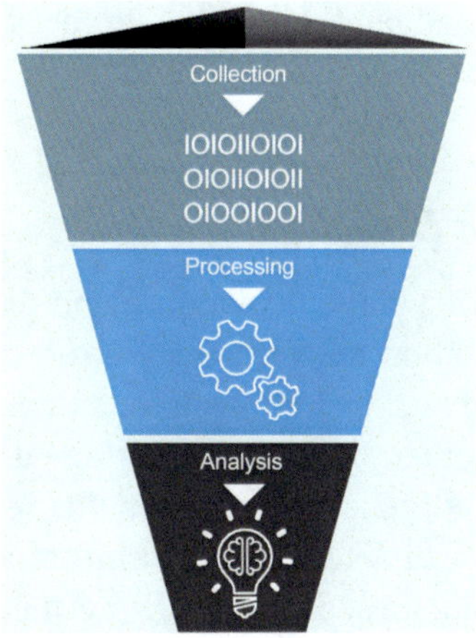

Figure 1.3. *Producing intelligence from raw data.*

Source: https://www.crest-approved.org/wp-content/uploads/2024/04/what-is-cti-how-is-it-used_2024-v2.pdf.

1.1.7. The Intelligence Cycle

The process of identifying, gathering, processing, analyzing, and disseminating raw data and information into finished intelligence for use by decision makers is described by the intelligence cycle, a conceptual model.

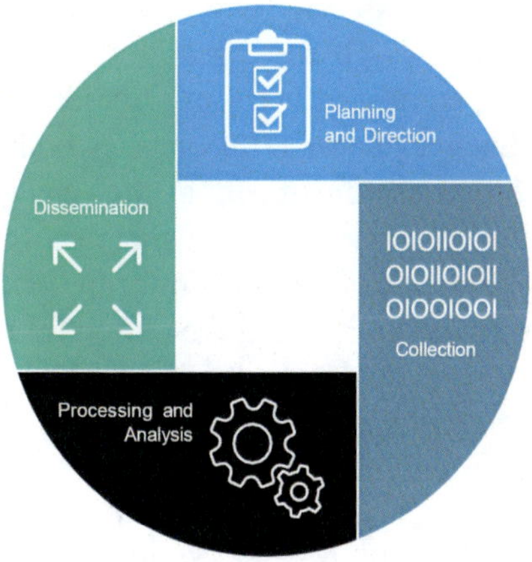

Figure 1.4. *The four phases of the intelligence cycle.*

Source: https://www.crest-approved.org/wp-content/uploads/2024/04/what-is-cti-how-is-it-used_2024-v2.pdf.

Activities can be directed and coordinated to effectively meet customer requirements if the process is followed and each stage's requirements are understood (Figure 1.4).

1.1.7.1. Planning and Direction

The intelligence cycle's first stage is planning and direction. It should involve a great deal of communication between the consumer and the producer and is used to coordinate intelligence operations to meet consumer requirements. The precise needs of the customer should be ascertained during this phase, which is also known as the intelligence requirements (IRs) or priority intelligence requirements (PIRs). One can determine what information is needed and how it should be gathered by using these IRs and PIRs. An intelligence collection plan (ICP) will frequently codify this output.

1.1.7.2. Collection

The process of collection entails obtaining the data and information most likely to satisfy specified requirements. Usually, this will entail gathering information from numerous sources. It can be challenging to determine which sources are most likely to yield the needed data, be trustworthy, and offer information that is easily accessed quickly. To help distinguish the signals from the noise, effective planning and guidance are needed.

1.1.7.3. Processing and Analysis

The third stage of the cycle is processing and analysis, where raw data and information are gathered, combined with information from other sources, and transformed into intelligence. During this phase, both human and machine capabilities must be focused on meeting the engagement's intelligence requirements while upholding intelligence principles. In order to evaluate the significance and ramifications of processed information, integrate it by fusing disparate data points to find patterns, and then interpret the significance of any newly developed knowledge, analysts usually employ a range of quantitative and qualitative analytical techniques. It is probable that analysts will employ various methods to guarantee impartial and precise evaluations that ought to be anticipatory and useful. This phase also involves evaluating the material collected and the source's credibility.

1.1.7.4. Dissemination

The timely delivery of finished intelligence products in a suitable format to the target audience is known as dissemination. When it comes to content delivery, the frequency of distribution should correspond with the duration of the content. For instance, operational content should be distributed regularly, while strategic content should be distributed less frequently. The intelligence cycle can restart by requesting input, improving current IRs, or creating new ones. Depending on whether processing and review are separated out from their respective parent phases of analysis and dissemination, the intelligence cycle usually consists of four or five main stages. The intelligence cycle is iterative in nature, regardless of the particular model used. To guarantee that the necessary information is processed and transmitted accurately and that the needs of the customer are always at the center of the process, every phase should include a feedback and review procedure.

The intelligence cycle rarely functions in real life according to the precise division of stages that the graphic portrays. Generally, during the delivery of a product or service, smaller, tighter cycles with independent feedback loops will be in place to make sure the delivery meets the requirements.

1.1.8. The Principles of Intelligence

The guidelines that intelligence processes and products should follow are summed up in the infographic below. The acronym CROSSCAT is frequently used to remember these ideas (Figure 1.5).

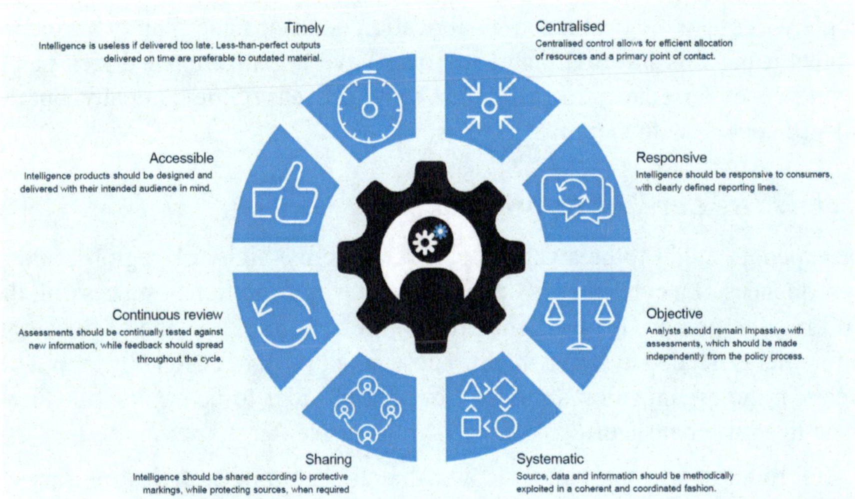

Figure 1.5. *The CROSSCAT principles of intelligence.*

Source: https://www.crest-approved.org/wp-content/uploads/2024/04/what-is-cti-how-is-it-used_2024-v2.pdf.

1.2. TYPES OF THREAT INTELLIGENCE

Threat intelligence comes in four flavors: tactical, operational, strategic, and technical. To create an extensive threat assessment, all four are necessary.

1.2.1. Strategic Threat Intelligence

Potential cyberattacks are outlined in this analysis along with any potential repercussions for stakeholders and non-technical audiences, as well as decision-makers. It is based on a thorough examination of new risks and global trends and is delivered as white papers, reports, and presentations. It is employed to provide a high-level picture of the threat landscape facing a company or an industry.

Who is targeting an organization and why is determined by strategic CTI.

1.2.1.1. Who Is This Information For?

Within an organization, high-level decision makers are presented with strategic threat intelligence. The executive board, C-level executives, and other decision-makers in charge of the organization's direction may be among them.

1.2.1.2. What Is This Information Used For?

People will make the best resource allocation decisions and plan cybersecurity budgets using this information. They may have organizational duties that go beyond the cybersecurity infrastructure to other areas of the company, but they will still consult with technical experts.

1.2.1.3. The Level of Information

These people ought to be aware of general patterns, high-risk regions, and the consequences of a cybersecurity attack. As long as a solution is successful, they don't need to comprehend the specifics of how it's implemented or the system requirements needed to stop a threat. These people will need to know about new threats in the organization's industry or area in order to determine whether to invest in additional security.

Information will take into account threats that your organization faces on a broader scale, not just those pertaining to the internal network. This could entail looking over your company's emails, social media accounts, website, and communications to make sure your brand integrity is maintained and your organization is safe from cyberattacks. These individuals may need updates on a quarterly or semi-annual basis because these decisions take time to implement.

1.2.1.4. What Type of Intelligence Is Gathered?

- New attack types;
- Economic and business impact of attacks and compromise;
- Regulatory and compliance legislation;
- Attack trends;
- Organizational vulnerabilities;
- Vulnerabilities and attacks on similar organizations.

1.2.1.5. Case Study

An organization's executive board will examine the cyber threat intelligence that has been compiled over the last three months at the end of the quarter. They can observe that 97% of malicious emails have been successfully blocked by the secure email gateway (SEG). This implies that the SEG is performing as intended. They may also observe, though, that there have been occasions in which attackers have tried to obtain access by means of MFA fatigue attacks.

In response, the board may choose to fund security awareness training (SAT) to make sure that every member of staff is knowledgeable about the potential dangers of a cyberattack and equipped to take the necessary precautions. In order to stop an MFA fatigue attack from occurring, they might also determine that the user should only receive a maximum of five MFA notifications before being locked out. The SOC team or IT managers who are able to implement this change will be informed of this directive.

1.2.2. Tactical Threat Intelligence

Threat actors' tactics, procedures, and techniques (TTPs) are disclosed by tactical intelligence. It is meant for people who are directly in charge of safeguarding data and IT resources. It offers information on potential attack vectors against an organization, including the most effective means of thwarting or mitigating the attacks. (Kime and Brian, 2016)

The goal of tactical CTI is to quickly identify a particular threat and provide you with the tools you need to react appropriately.

1.2.2.1. Who Is This Information For?

The format of tactical threat intelligence is intended to make it helpful to users who will be in charge of spotting and eliminating threats on a daily basis. These users will be security experts who have extensive understanding of both the threat remediation process and the application of cybersecurity solutions.

1.2.2.2. What Is This Information Used For?

Using tactical CTI, you can proactively address problems and cyber events on your network as they arise. Users can learn about malicious actors' TTPs by utilizing tactical intelligence. This data can be utilized to carry out remediation procedures and forecast the course of an attack.

Tactical intelligence will show the specific actions of an attack and point out ways to neutralize the danger. Rather than interfering with hypothetical, abstract risks, tactical intelligence performs much of the "groundwork" in resolving specific, identified threats.

1.2.2.3. The Level of Information

Indicators of compromise (IOCs), which are specific details about threats and compromised areas, are a valuable component of tactical intelligence. The information will be precise and limited to the devices and attack incidents that occur on your network. We'll discuss TTPs in terms of particular IP addresses and hardware. There will be code-level remediation.

1.2.2.4. What Type of Intelligence Is Gathered?

- Malware signatures;
- IP and URL blacklists;
- Traffic patterns;
- Log files;
- Credentials from APTs;
- Ransomware and Phishing campaign data.

1.2.2.5. Case Study

An alert notifies a SOC manager that a user's account has been automatically locked because of questionable behavior. The SOC can retrieve the specifics of this behavior and determine whether to look into the matter further or restore account access.

They observe that, despite having their regular office in New York, a user appears to have logged in from Berlin. Since this user has no business being in Berlin, the manager can deny access because it appears that the login was fraudulent. In order to prevent the compromise of a new password or other authentication method, they can reset user accounts in a secure manner.

1.2.3. Technical Threat Intelligence

The indicators that an attack is about to begin are the main topic of this information. These indicators include social engineering, spear phishing, baiting, and other forms of weaponization and delivery. Technical intelligence is a crucial tool for thwarting social engineering schemes. Although this kind of information is frequently combined with operational threat intelligence, it is dynamic since hackers constantly modify their strategies to capitalize on fresh developments and tricks.

1.2.4. Operational Threat Intelligence

This method gathers data from a range of sources, such as social media, chat rooms, antivirus logs, and historical events. It is employed to predict the type and timing of upcoming assaults. Automating the processing of hundreds of thousands of data points in multiple languages is a common application of data mining and machine learning. Operational intelligence is used by security and incident response teams to modify firewall rules, event detection rules, and access controls, among other configurations. Because the information gives a clearer idea of what to look for, it can also speed up response times. (Gerard and Johansen, 2020)

The main goal of operational CTI is to identify possible threats and assess the likelihood that they will have an impact on your company.

1.2.4.1. Who Is This Information For?

Network defense teams, or security managers, require this kind of information. Although these users will be somewhat aware of their threat landscape, they will still require a great deal of the specific, technical information about possible attacks. Intelligence must contextualize a particular attack within larger trends and elucidate attack mechanisms and intent.

1.2.4.2. What Is This Information Used For?

This information will be used to set up policies and make sure security solutions are properly suited to thwart likely-to-occur attacks. This data will offer useful insights that can be applied right now to improve your cybersecurity setup.

Every day, or at least every few days, intelligence will be updated and reviewed to make sure your cybersecurity infrastructure is operating as it should. This information can be used to recognize threats as they emerge and stop them from becoming attacks, as opposed to having to deal with ongoing attacks.

1.2.4.3. The Level of Information

The insights obtained from operational intelligence will guide the development of a cybersecurity defense plan. It will assist organizations in making sure that plans and policies are up to date and optimized to counter a wide variety of the most formidable threats. This information is intended for those in managerial positions, as they will be in charge of the threat hunters themselves. In order to find any flaws and stop such attacks, they will also try to compile and comprehend vulnerabilities.

1.2.4.4. What Type of Intelligence Is Gathered?

- Command and control channels;
- Details related to specific implementation of malware;
- File names;
- Malicious traffic;
- Suspicious IP addresses and domains;
- Tools used for attacks;
- URLs.

1.2.4.5. Case Study

A SOC team convenes first thing in the morning to evaluate the most recent intelligence and determine what modifications should be made. They can observe that a hostile actor has become involved with their EDR solution overnight. They can observe from the data that the attacker obtained access by using an out-of-date application. To shield users from this vulnerability, the SOC team can make sure that the most recent update (or patch) is installed on every device connected to the network. They may also choose to examine how the company uses that application and determine whether any security settings need to be changed. Maybe access should be restricted to privileged users or require MFA.

1.3. THREAT INTELLIGENCE LIFECYCLE

The process of gathering threat intelligence involves a number of steps, some of which are listed below.

1.3.1. Goals and Objectives

An organization must decide what it wants to accomplish by incorporating threat intelligence into its security solutions and strategy before choosing the appropriate threat intelligence sources and tools. Helping information security teams stop possible threats found during a threat modeling exercise will probably be the main objective. Getting intelligence information and instruments that can offer current guidance and notifications on threats deemed high risk and high impact is necessary for this. Making sure the appropriate strategic intelligence is gathered and supplied to C-level management is another crucial goal, as it keeps them informed about any modifications to the organization's threat landscape.

1.3.2. Data Collection

A company's threat intelligence program is built on logs from cloud services, security controls, and internal systems. However, gathering information from third-party threat data feeds is required to obtain insights into the most recent TTPs and industry-specific intelligence. These sources include data obtained from threat research reports, malicious IP addresses, social media platforms, hacker forums, and antivirus telemetry.

1.3.3. Data Processing

Automated processing is required to collect and arrange the raw data necessary to produce actionable threat intelligence. Manually adding metadata, correlating, aggregating, and filtering different kinds of data from different sources is not practical. Threat intelligence platforms and apps automate data collection and processing through machine learning, enabling them to continuously deliver information about threat actors' activities.

1.3.4. Analyze Data

In this step, questions like the when, why, and how of a suspicious event are answered by analyzing the processed data. This step would provide answers to questions about the timing of phishing incidents, the goals of their perpetrators, and the relationship and application of malicious domains and phishing emails.

1.3.5. Report Findings

Reports have to be customized for a particular audience in order to make it evident how the threats discussed impact their areas of responsibility. When feasible, reports should be disseminated to the larger community in order to enhance overall security operations (Figure 1.6).

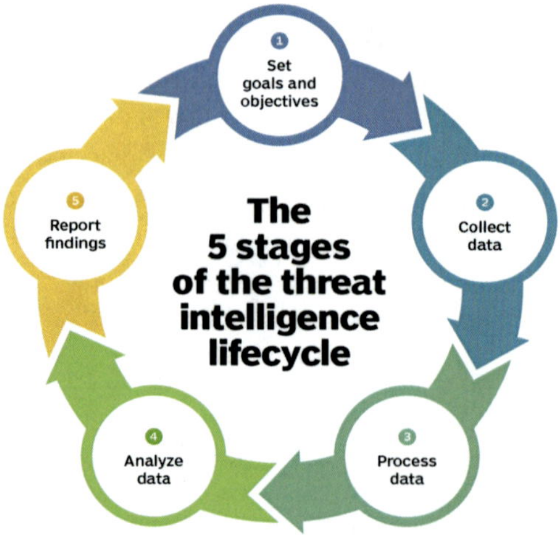

Figure 1.6. *The five stages of the threat intelligence lifecycle.*

Source: https://cdn.ttgtmedia.com/rms/onlineimages/whatis-5_stages_of_the_threat_intelligence_lifecycle-f.png.

1.4. DIFFERENT SOURCES OF INTELLIGENCE

Suppliers of cyber threat intelligence ought to utilize multiple data sources in order to offer a comprehensive, all-encompassing perspective on threats. Since the majority of organizations deal with a wide variety of adversaries, such as nation-states, cybercriminals, and hacktivists, their data and information sources must also be wide to meet the challenge.

The majority of sources are open in the sense that anyone with the necessary knowledge and tools can gather, process, and analyze the data they offer. In reality, though, systematic exploitation of many of these sources demands a level of capability and knowhow that tends to be concentrated in specialized CTI providers, even though a single person performing a CTI function may be able to gather some form of data and information from several of these sources.

Sources that CTI functions and providers frequently use are as follows.

1.4.1. Internal Sources

An essential source of data and information is an internal source, such as the output from an endpoint detection and response (EDR) tool, phishing filters, security information and event management (SIEM) tool output, and other logs covering system or network events. Processing these calls for cautious setup and will eventually necessitate the rejection of false positives. Knowing the threats that are truly present on a network—especially when those threats can be verified by outside sources—is crucial to comprehending the total threat that a given entity faces.

1.4.2. Atomic Indicators of Compromise

Hashes of malware samples linked to malicious campaigns, malicious domain names, and IP addresses (hosts) are the usual feeds that contain atomic indicators of compromise (IoCs). EDR and firewall systems have been processing large amounts of data automatically in recent years, alerting users when attempts are made to communicate with malicious infrastructure. It is mostly produced by malware variants that have been reverse engineered. IoCs have mistakenly been used interchangeably with CTI in the past, but they need more processing and analysis before they can be considered a stand-alone intelligence product.

1.4.3. Messaging Platforms

For threat actors, messaging platforms are an essential means of communication. They can also offer important information about the products and services that cybercriminals are trying to offer to one another. Due to their rich functionality and dynamic nature, platforms like Telegram experience high traffic volumes. Vendor shops or dedicated channels make it easier for illegal and sensitive material to be exchanged. The amount of collection resources needed to obtain and preserve access to the platform or conversation increases with the degree of privacy of the medium. Rather than depending solely on forums and marketplaces on the deep and dark webs, cybercriminal adversaries have been interacting with the community more and more in recent years through these specialized platforms as well as more direct, private means.

1.4.4. Deep Web

Threat intelligence services may find useful information from deep web forums and other websites that are hidden behind paywalls, login portals, or are not reachable through search engines. These websites are still a major means of communication for cybercriminals. These resources are especially helpful in determining what data or information about your company has been compromised and is available to possible enemies, such as information or credentials that have been leaked or even access that is for sale.

1.4.5. Dark Web

Marketplaces, stores, and other websites hosted on anonymity-focused networks like Tor or I2P are examples of dark web sources. Due to the phenomenon of double-extortion ransomware incidents, websites run by ransomware affiliates that publicize stolen data and advertise their victims have become more prevalent in recent years.

Though any CTI function can access these sources if they know where to look, more often than not, relevant sections of messaging platforms and the deep and dark web are scraped in bulk by specialized threat intelligence providers that offer access to the data as a service due to operational security and logistical considerations.

1.4.6. Social Media

Some threat actors use social media as a key component of their strategy, which makes it possible for CTI providers to get information straight from the source. Activists frequently seek attention, promote involvement, and declare their intention to pursue specific goals.

Criminals will use these platforms to talk to possible partners or customers of their goods and services, or to put more pressure on victims they are trying to extort. Social media will probably be used by threat intelligence services to gather data on the organization's attitude and spot accidental or malicious data leaks. Lastly, the cyber security community on social media sites like Twitter can also offer insightful information on emerging problems in a timely manner.

1.4.7. Code Repositories

Code repositories are becoming a more important source for CTI. The majority of threat actors no longer create their own malware; instead, they rely on frameworks like Cobalt Strike, which were first created for legitimate penetration testers, and proof-of-concept exploits released by security researchers on websites like GitHub. It is therefore essential to comprehend the tools and capabilities that threat actors can obtain through these sources in order to fully comprehend their capabilities. For CTI analysts, the release of a proof-of-concept exploit on GitHub during a vulnerability's lifecycle is frequently a crucial sign that more widespread exploitation is likely to occur.

1.4.8. Vulnerability Feeds

The use of vulnerability feeds and exploit databases as sources of CTI has increased due to threat actors' growing proficiency in swiftly taking advantage of newly discovered vulnerabilities. As CVEs (common vulnerabilities and exposures) are disclosed, CTI programs are evaluating them more and more to determine the possible effects on customers.

1.4.9. Geopolitical Developments

More than ever, geopolitical developments are a valuable source of information for comprehensive CTI services. A nation-state's likely priority technologies and sectors for cyber espionage operations can be inferred from its strategic economic development plans. Knowing how a state's goals translate into the possibility of disruptive cyberattacks during a geopolitical crisis helps determine which sectors need to get ready.

1.4.10. Media Coverage

The way that technology and security-related advancements are covered by the media will undoubtedly shape consumers' needs for intelligence. CTI operations should continue to concentrate on gathering data from primary sources whenever feasible. But it's also critical to recognize the forces that shape the public narrative surrounding cyber security, since these influence how the general public views this issue. Media outlets are also usually the first to report on statements from companies about security breaches they have experienced. This is especially significant in the current era of supply chain security and big game hunting ransomware.

1.4.11. Adversary Tracking

Threat actor groups' infrastructure, tools, and TTPs can be directly observed through adversary tracking. Finding trends in previous operations and taking advantage of operational security flaws to actively gather intelligence on adversary activity provides firsthand, fast, and unmatched insight into frequently sophisticated threat actors. But because of the resources needed, this source is usually only used by CTI providers and businesses that have a clear need.

1.4.12. Incident Response

Deep insight into threat actor activity can be gained through incident response and breach investigations, especially if the adversary has advanced through several stages of their operation. Though internal incident response capabilities can also reveal how an operation that affects the organization itself unfolded, specialized incident response firms can gather valuable insight into threat actor TTPs.

1.4.13. CTI Publications

Whitepapers and blog posts, which are primarily based on the first two categories, are examples of CTI publications that serve as important sources of potential intelligence. The threat landscape is extremely varied and global, and different providers have varying specializations, presences in different regions, and focuses. In addition, disparate methods and strategies lead to providers recognizing similar activity clusters, perceiving things differently, and increasingly referring to each other's reports. Because of this, there is no one source of truth for this category, and compiling information from these many sources can be very beneficial.

1.4.14. Human Intelligence

Human intelligence can be obtained from interaction with people through a number of the aforementioned channels; for instance, by interacting with someone to obtain knowledge that cannot be obtained from other sources. Threat intelligence providers should, however, only partake in this kind of activity within a well-defined framework and in the pursuit of particular intelligence requirements — in a morally and legally acceptable manner. It is imperative for providers to guarantee that their efforts to collect data from human sources adhere to legal frameworks like the General Data Protection Regulation (GDPR) and the Proceeds of Crime Act.

1.4.15. Malware Analysis

Through malware analysis, CTI analysts can extract information from binary data, such as IOCs, which they can use to inform tools, look into the purpose of an operation, or even attribute it. This ability has been made more widely available by websites like VirusTotal and analysis sandboxes, so even without a lot of reverse engineering knowledge, you can extract useful information from a file that you believe to be malicious.

1.4.16. Government Publications

In recent times, government publications have emerged as a reliable and frequent source of CTI. Unmatched visibility into nation-state activity is made possible by the roles played by intelligence services, national cyber security organizations, and computer emergency response teams (CERTs) in responding to incidents and gathering activity across various sectors. Intelligence services are able to link operations to actual enemies and employees. They're becoming more inclined to do so through indictments and public declarations, which sheds more light on how they operate.

1.4.17. Digital Risk Protection

Generally speaking, digital risk protection encompasses a wide range of sub-sources, including phishing sites, paste sites, expired certificates, compromised credentials, and other possible sources of information leakage that could jeopardize the operations or reputation of an organization.

1.4.18. Information Sharing Platforms

Platforms for exchanging information offer background and perspective on the activities of threat actors right now. These are typically divided along national or sectoral boundaries, such as:

- The UK National Cyber Security Centre's (NCSC) Cyber Security Information Sharing Partnership (CiSP);
- The Financial Services Information Sharing and Analysis Center (FS-ISAC);
- AlienVault's Open Threat Exchange (OTX), a crowd-sourced platform;
- US-CERT's (United States Computer Emergency Response Team) Automated Indicator Sharing (AIS) platform.

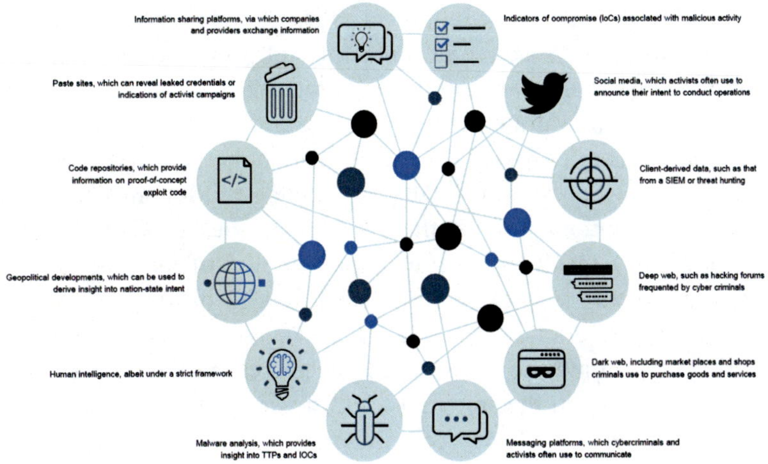

Figure 1.7. *A summary of different sources typically used by threat intelligence providers.*

Source: https://www.crest-approved.org/wp-content/uploads/2024/04/what-is-cti-how-is-it-used_2024-v2.pdf.

Effective CTI products and services should involve corroboration and fusing of material from multiple sources, as opposed to utilizing sources independently. A CTI program may be unable to fully utilize even a small number of these sources while still meeting the needs of its users for intelligence. This is not, however, the same as creating and sustaining a CTI program that meets consumers' needs for intelligence while methodically utilizing this entire spectrum of sources, in accordance with the CROSSCAT principles (Figure 1.7).\

1.5. CTI AND ITS EVOLUTION

Because CTI is the result of an analysis of adversaries' intentions, capabilities, and opportunities in cyberspace, it is extremely valuable to organizations. In order to fully comprehend the significance of gathering relevant data required for making decisions, we look at the early indicators of organizational threats. The Morris-worm was the first worm to proliferate over digital networks. It became one of the first cases to be publicly documented in 1988. It was a non-destructive worm that was launched from an MIT computer and spread to other internet-connected computers, slowing them down. It was also referred to as the internet worm. The formation of the Defense Advanced Research Projects Agency (DARPA) CERT to handle information sharing and address security and vulnerability issues with computers was one of the fallout from that incident. In order to be proactive in protecting infrastructure, security experts have continued to develop methods for gathering, analyzing, and creating tools. These are required in order to lessen losses and disturbances. When the Mandiant report was released in 2013, the CTI community began to grow and acquire significance. As of right now, CTI is being used more frequently and offers a variety of options to meet the needs of businesses. Organizations are embracing CTI as a result of a better understanding of its benefits. Despite having its roots in technology, some argue that CTI has used technology—rather than intelligence analysis and methodology—to address its problems. The gathering of accurate and useful intelligence presents the biggest challenge for CTI. It is ineffective if the amount of information obtained is not combined with action. The future of cyber security lies in collaboration, which is why CTI uses standards to guarantee the promptness of efforts. Organizations are now requesting automated data collection and strategy-level reports instead of just IoCs since CTI now addresses TTPs, threat behaviors, attack surface awareness, and strategic assessments. CTI integration, capabilities, technologies, and tools are all getting better. Instead of raw threat data, organizations are more interested in reports that can help with decision-making. Data processing and collection are becoming increasingly automated as businesses create their own intelligence needs. Since CTI is now a distinct field, this opens up more options in terms of careers and job roles. Organizations devoted to the study of CTI still exist today, and they continue to offer data on tools, methods, and information that are in style to improve threat intelligence.

1.6. THREAT INTELLIGENCE SHARING PLATFORMS

Threat intelligence is the methodical examination of both external and internal organizational threats. Information about cyberthreats that is not shared frequently results in breaches and the intelligence cycle failing. Sharing threat intelligence can enable organizations to better understand and address potential threats by leveraging their collective knowledge, expertise, and resources. This provides an advantage when making decisions about the methods, resources, and tactics to use. Sharing threat intelligence puts organizations in a better position to handle any threats that may result from access to information that has not yet been encountered. Most CTI-related organizations can be divided into three categories: those that generate intelligence, those that use intelligence that has been generated by others, and those that generate intelligence in addition to using intelligence that has been generated by others. Information overload, or having too much data without knowing where to begin or how to handle it, and information dearth, or having not enough data to make meaningful decisions, are the two challenges that come with gathering threat intelligence. Establishing sharing rules is necessary because inadequate data can result from non-disclosure of sensitive information, poor interoperability, and a lack of trust. The goals and objectives of information sharing, the identification of current internal sources of cyber threat intelligence, and the parameters of information sharing activities are a few examples of sharing rules.

Translating threat intelligence into proactive measures that protect organizations from attacks is where it becomes crucial for an organization. De Melo e Silva describes the relevance of standards and platforms. Time, effort, and expertise are all needed for the selection and processing of data into meaningful formats. The task of converting threat data into actionable intelligence and providing resources to support incident response falls to the Threat Intelligence Sharing Platform. It should be mentioned that defining the perimeter is necessary before incorporating Threat Intelligence into an organization's defense. Any CTI implementation's value lies in its ability to lessen threats unique to an organization. There are two types of Threat Intelligence Management Systems (TIMS): Content Aggregation and Threat Intelligence Management System. The former offers threat data feeds, while the latter uses the gathered data to generate business value. Tools exist to facilitate the sharing of threat intelligence. Security teams in organizations must be able to assess threats to their infrastructure effectively, which requires a combination of external and internal sources for threat intelligence to be translated into action. This combination is critical because it shortens the time between infection, detection, and remediation. Timely, accurate, relevant, and actionable intelligence are necessary for effective action. When used effectively, CTI can help achieve a number of goals, including stronger threat intelligence and reliable incident detection and response.

1.7. CTI TOOLS AND PROVIDERS

CTI is more in demand than ever. Long-form reports that provide a thorough overview of the threats are required by organizations. However, not every company has the resources on staff to deal with CTI. Many vendors use TSIP, which are software solutions that enable the exchange of data, information, and intelligence, in response to the rise in demand for CTI solutions. CTI solutions come in two flavors: open source and vendor-based. The market for CTI-related goods and services is a huge source of revenue for many vendors. The market for threat intelligence is expected to grow, which is important for businesses that are constantly searching for ways to identify potential security holes and cyberthreats. Providers equip decision-makers and organizations with the pertinent data they need to remain safe from harm. Suppliers can be divided into three categories: those offering comprehensive cyber threat intelligence, which is more expensive, and those providing threat data feeds or threat indicators. The majority of proprietary suppliers are based in China and the US. Among them are Singhand, Qihoo 360, Dell Security, FireEye, IsightPartners, and CrowdStrike. Kaspersky, Group-IB, Sophos, and Digital Shadows from Russia and England, respectively, are additional suppliers outside of these nations. IBM X-Force and Threat Tracer, S-ISAC, OASIS, Facebook Xchange, HP ThreatCentral, Checkpoint IntelliStore, and Alienvault OTX are a few other noteworthy providers. The term "open-source intelligence" (OSINT) describes the process of obtaining intelligence from publicly accessible sources, such as journals and social media platforms. Information and Event Management (SIEM), HoneyDB, Infosec - CERT-PA, Disassemblers, Stixify, JamesBrine, ThreatMiner, PhishTank, and VirusTotal are a few of the well-known open-source tools.

1.7.1. Threat Intelligence Tools

Organizations can use a variety of tools to gather information and implement threat intelligence into their current security operations. In addition to providing organizations with pertinent information about potential attack sources, threat intelligence services can also offer consulting services.

Some of the available tools include:

- Anomali ThreatStream compiles threat information from multiple sources and offers research instruments.
- A software as a service (SaaS) platform called Cyberint's Argos Digital Risk Protection Platform is made to examine an organization's attack surface as well as the cyberattacks that target its sector on the deep, dark, and open webs.
- Petabytes of data are gathered by Kaspersky Lab's Kaspersky Threat Intelligence to create threat intelligence feeds with useful information about cyberthreats and insights into the threats that are specific to certain industries.
- Digital Risk Protection from PhishLabs keeps an eye out for threats on social media, data leaks, brand impersonation, and account takeovers.
- The ThreatFusion Cyber Threat Intelligence module of SOCRadar collects information from the dark and deep webs. Security teams are notified about possible threats and threat actors aimed at a particular industry through intelligence feeds obtained from multiple sources.

1.8. CTI APPROACH

Sharing threat intelligence and creating space for proactive defense against intrusion attempts are the two main goals of CTI. Sharing the intelligence is the key to any CTI intervention. It is feasible to identify risks and take appropriate action when sufficient information is exchanged. When threats are clearly defined, their sources are located, expectations are set, concrete actions are outlined, and the data is presented in a standard, structured manner, threat intelligence becomes effective. An organization needs to create a plan before putting threat intelligence into action. One of the plan's objectives is to conduct an audit. The plan specifies the objectives for implementation as well as what needs to be secured. It also indicates the things that attackers are likely to target. These specifics aid in the creation of procedures and policies that guarantee its security and turn it into a document. The document functions as a checklist that directs the organization's incident response (IR) team's actions. This is due to the fact that keeping infrastructure safe requires catching breaches early on. Additionally, tracking breaches can be done in a variety of ways. At the tactical level, CTI can be used to manage patches, prioritize event response, thwart malicious activity with threat indicators, or carry out reaction and remediation.

1.8.1. Community-Based Approach

In a community-based approach, intelligence community members verify threat intelligence to guarantee its quality before disseminating it to other members. Among the requirements are:

- **Structured Threat Information Expression (STIX):** This is a standard language-based structured representation of threat intelligence. STIX is a language designed by MITRE that uses a structured format to specify, capture, categorize, and communicate threat information. The de facto standard for the exchange of structured threat intelligence is now STIX. The language is adaptable, machine-readable, and has automated forms. The versatility of STIX allows for a wide range of applications. The range of threat information that has been gathered, including observables, indicators, incidents, TTP, exploit targets, courses of action, threat actors, and campaigns, has led to its description as expressive. Strict policies for classification and trust, imprecise terminology use, and excessive flexibility are some of the drawbacks of STIX. It is also recognized to result in imprecise CTI expression.
- **Cyber Observable eXpression (CybOX):** An organized vocabulary for digital observables. A standardized language known as Cyber Observable Expression (CybOX) facilitates the systematic sharing and exchange of any observable, noteworthy event or cyber-related property. This can be thought of as a more advanced version of dealing with all Relational Database Transactions using a Structured Query Language (SQL). A common SQL format can be followed by all standard products built on relational databases, allowing data to be shared across various Intel platforms and products. In a similar vein, CybOX facilitates high-fidelity data exchange between various cyber-security systems regarding cyber observables (such as stateful measures, dynamic events, etc.). A wide range of pertinent cybersecurity tasks, such as threat assessment, malware characterization, operational event management, event logging, incident response, cyber forensics, and situational awareness, are supported by CybOX.
- **Common Vulnerabilities and Exposure (CVE):** The community-driven, publicly accessible data registry of known cybersecurity vulnerabilities is kept up to date by the worldwide, community-based CVE initiative (CVE List). It is the globally recognized benchmark for vulnerability identification.

- **Web Ontology Language (OWL):** A semantic web language intended to express intricate and rich knowledge about individual objects, collections of objects, and relationships between objects.
- **Trusted Automated eXchange of Indicator Information (TAXII):** The automated exchange of cyber threat intelligence is standardized by TAXII, a free and open transport mechanism.
- **Incident Object Description and Exchange Format (IODEF):** The purpose of the Incident Object Description Exchange Format (IODEF), as outlined in RFC 5070, is to enable the sharing of enhanced cybersecurity data among security specialists working for organizations. It offers a clear pattern for reliably embedding structured data, including XML and identifier-based data.
- **Real Time Inter-Network Defense (RID):** In order to enable the sharing of incident-handling data and integrate current detection, tracing, source identification, and mitigation mechanisms for a comprehensive incident-handling solution, Real-time Inter-network Defense, or RID, outlines a proactive approach to internetwork communication.
- **OpenIOC:** An expandable XML schema with technical features that reveal the methods of an attacker, a known threat, or additional proof of a compromise.

1.8.2. Risk-Based Approach

A framework that aims to comprehend the threats encountered is the risk-based approach. Risk is the result of combining impact, threat, and vulnerability. Many countries have tailored their frameworks to target particular industries and the types of threats they face. Red team exercises, which simulate actual attacks and assist government institutions in being proactive, are a major component of the framework. These tests are frequently conducted by independent providers in partnership with government institutions. CBEST was created by the Bank of England specifically for the UK financial industry. According to CREST, CBEST is a tool that helps identify potential risks to financial institutions by having stakeholders conduct simulated tests. The Threat Intelligence-Based Ethical Red team (TIBER-NL) is located in the Netherlands. Others in the UK include ATTEST for the aviation industry, GBEST for government agencies, and BEST for the telecommunications sector. TIBER-EU is used by the European financial sector.

1.8.3. Narrative-Based Approach

Reports that provide a detailed account of a sequence of events connected to an incident or intrusion are the basis for operationalizing narrative-based approach.

1.9. DIFFERENT TYPES OF CYBER THREAT INTELLIGENCE SERVICES

The term "cyber threat intelligence" covers a wide range of goods and services. These fall into two main categories: ongoing threat monitoring services and standalone deliverables.

1.9.1. Standalone Deliverables

Standalone deliverables include:

- Threat assessments that assist customers in comprehending the purpose and potential of threat actors to attack their company, a particular system, or a piece of information. Threat assessments can be used by a variety of audiences and formats, and they can be updated frequently. These range from the more tactical evaluations meant to guide controls and mitigation strategies to the more strategic ones meant for senior leadership consumption.
- Targeting reports, sometimes referred to as digital foot printing assessments, examine an organization's possible points of attack by utilizing reconnaissance tactics that are employed by skilled threat actors to gather and compile information about the target entity. A supply chain assessment of the company is becoming more and more one of these. They are intended to assist customers in comprehending the scope of their exposure and the ways in which an adversary might take advantage of it.
- Threat scenarios, which are frequently the result of the output from a threat assessment and a targeting report, describe possible attack paths against a specific system or asset within an organization. Plans for penetration testing are shaped by these kinds of situations.
- "X" BEST projects are intelligence-led security testing engagements mandated by regulators, and they are primarily based on the original CBEST framework for UK financial institutions. The aforementioned three deliverables are necessary for these schemes and help form the plans that penetration testing providers carry out during the subsequent project phase.
- Cyber threat intelligence providers can leverage their collection

capabilities to provide investigations and other smaller engagements. Finding out if private information has been leaked and is available on the deep and dark webs is one of the common use cases.

- Online Reconnaissance or VIP Exposure Reports, another name for person-focused and protective open-source intelligence reporting, are designed to detect and reduce possible threats to VIPs or executives. To give a summary of their possible exposure, the CTI provider will mimic the reconnaissance techniques employed by adversaries attempting CEO fraud or possibly more physical threat vectors.
- Briefings on particular events, problems, or study topics that are especially appropriate for senior staff members or people who are not normally familiar with cyber security.
- To help buyers become more adept at consuming threat intelligence or creating their own, providers can also offer consultancy, training, and capability building.

1.9.2. Continued Threat Monitoring Services

Continued threat monitoring services include:

- Subscriptions that are delivered through a specific portal and include reports are frequently incorporated into the security architecture of the customer. In addition to the ability to interact with the intelligence repository, conduct investigations, and integrate it into current processes, suppliers typically offer access to a consistent stream of up-to-date intelligence and timely reporting on pertinent incidents. Certain providers offer customized subscriptions that adhere to the intelligence cycle and furnish customized intelligence reports to fulfill the demands of an organization. These subscriptions may be supplemented on a recurring basis by elements of the aforementioned stand-alone products.
- By combining and correlating various feeds and subscriptions, Threat Intelligence Platforms (TIPs) enable users to pivot from different IOCs and carry out investigations.
- Data feeds are made up of unprocessed, raw, or uncontextualized data that the recipient organization will need to process. These may consist of information that can be enhanced by the user from the deep and dark webs, messaging platforms, or IOCs.

1.10. HOW IS CYBER THREAT INTELLIGENCE USED?

The use of cyber threat intelligence in an organization can be categorized into four primary areas in addition to the business functions listed below:

- **Predict:** Organizations can anticipate evolving threats with the aid of strategic threat intelligence and make appropriate plans to mitigate them before they become real.
- **Prevent:** Threat intelligence, such as malware signatures that can be used to update signature-based detection mechanisms, that can prevent incidents from happening in the first place.
- **Detect:** Intelligence that assists in identifying potential threats within a network, such as TTPs used in threat hunting exercises, or threats as they emerge.
- **Respond:** Information such as TTPs used by a threat actor once they are found on a network, which give instructions on the cybercriminal's next moves and how the victim should act, that can help guide a response to an incident already underway in order to lessen its scope or impact.

The type of material offered and the organization's maturity determine how much threat intelligence an organization can use. To gain insight into how to enhance an organization's capabilities, it can be helpful to conduct a separate exercise to evaluate the maturity of the organization with regard to producing, utilizing, and sharing cyber threat intelligence.

1.10.1. Security Operations Centre (SOC)

Processing and prioritizing a high volume of alerts from the assets it monitors falls under the purview of a SOC. Using security information and event management (SIEM) technologies, CTI should assist in assigning priority to incoming material. When choosing which incidents to escalate, which are already under control, or which are less important in light of the organization's threat model, CTI is also helpful.

1.10.2. IT Security Management

IT security departments can benefit from using tactical threat intelligence to prioritize implementing the right controls. For instance, a business is aware that it is highly vulnerable to extortionists who want to bring down its customer-facing portal through distributed denial of service (DDoS) attacks. The company can adjust and enhance its controls in response to tactical and operational intelligence about the extortionists' TTPs, including the particular protocols they target and the protocols they exploit.

1.10.3. Vulnerability Management

Even for organizations with specialized vulnerability management programs, prioritizing vulnerabilities for patching remains difficult due to the sheer volume of vulnerabilities in a typical estate. As was previously mentioned, CTI services can offer vital context about the possible threat to and effects of a CVE being exploited by utilizing a range of sources. This enables users to select which CVEs to prioritize beyond the conventional Common Vulnerability Scoring System (CVSS) rating.

1.10.4. Threat Hunting

CTI outputs can be used by more sophisticated users to proactively look for any indications of malicious activity or possible network or asset compromise. Hunting can be motivated by behavioral approaches, known IoCs, or hypotheses around specific TTPs.

1.10.5. Incident Response

Processes for responding to incidents require intelligence as well. Knowing which threat actors' TTPs and attack types are most likely to target the organization allows for the creation of "playbooks" that aid in directing the response to a breach, educating pertinent parties, and eventually reducing the impact. In addition, CTI aids in the removal of false positives, offers insightful context following an occurrence, and supports cleanup activities.

1.10.6. Supply Chain Cyber Risk

The application of CTI in third-party risk management (TPRM) programs has been prompted by the growing threat to supply chains. Customers can lower the amount of risk they personally bear by disclosing pertinent information to important partners and suppliers.

1.10.7. Intelligence-Led Security Testing

An increasingly important source of information for the penetration testing part of cyber resilience exercises is threat intelligence. Rather than adopting a compliance-based approach to security, critical assets are tested using real-world techniques thanks to threat assessments, targeting reports, and threat scenarios.

1.10.8. Strategy

An organization can benefit greatly from strategic intelligence when developing its security plan. You can create a countermeasure, like a threat hunting program, by recognizing larger patterns and changes in adversaries' behavior, such as the growing misuse of legal procedures and the usage of fileless malware. Budget allocation and the development of a long-term strategy, frequently at the board level, are made possible by taking a strategic approach to comprehending your cyber threats.

1.10.9. Risk Management

A more comprehensive risk assessment process can begin with the use of cyber threat intelligence. Threat intelligence can show the intention and ability of actors to target an organization's critical information and system assets, which are frequently referred to as critical functions in the context of regulator-mandated cyber resilience testing schemes. After determining the degree of risk to these assets through impact assessments, the proper remediation actions can be taken.

1.10.10. Tabletop Exercises

Using threat intelligence, scenarios can be created that include the most likely and severe incidents, for example. Scenarios can be used to create tabletop exercises in addition to helping to shape a penetration testing plan. These work especially well for involving the board and quickly and affordably evaluating readiness for specific situations.

1.10.11. Situational Awareness

Enhancing situational awareness about recent developments in the threat landscape throughout the organization is another common use case for CTI, albeit one that is broader in nature. While actionability should be the primary focus of all intelligence products and services, it's equally critical to contribute to a wider understanding of how cyber threats affect the organization and its personnel.

1.10.12. Training and Education

Information about the newest methods, such as social engineering or other advancements, can be crucial for staff education and training programs since threat actors will always use human weaknesses as an alternative to technical ones in security postures.

1.10.13. Compliance

Having a threat intelligence capability can also assist organizations in adhering to legal and regulatory requirements, such as the NIS Directive and the General Data Protection Regulation (GDPR). Businesses that must abide by the NIS Directive must approach cyber security from a risk-based perspective. GDPR-affected entities must assess the security of their data processing capabilities. Additionally, threat intelligence can help customers spot possible breaches early on.

1.10.14. Security Engineering

In certain situations, controls and security features that can be incorporated into products during the early stages of development can be informed by threat intelligence. "Secure by design" techniques must take into account information about threat actors and vectors that are most likely to target the technology.

1.10.15. Brand Monitoring

Departments that concentrate on brand and reputational monitoring may use intelligence pertaining to digital risk protection, for instance, if adversaries are attempting to mimic the organization's brand or deceive potential customers in any other way.

1.11. BENEFITS OF CYBER THREAT INTELLIGENCE

Benefits of cyber threat intelligence include the following:

- It enables businesses, agencies, or other entities to strengthen overall risk management, cyber security policies, and responses, as well as to build a proactive and strong cybersecurity posture. (Berndt, Anzel and Ophoff, Jacques, 2020)
- It drives momentum toward a proactive cybersecurity posture that is predictive, not simply reactive after a cyber-attack.
- It provides context and insights about active attacks and potential threats to aid decision making.
- It prevents data breaches from releasing sensitive information, thus preventing data loss.
- It reduces costs. Since data breaches are costs, reducing the risk of data breaches helps save money.

- It helps and provides instructions to institutions on how to implement security measures to protect against future attacks.
- It enables sharing of knowledge, skills and experiences among the cyber security community of practice and systems stakeholders.
- It facilitates the easier and more accurate identification of risks and threats, as well as delivery systems, infrastructure-wide indicators of compromise, and possible actors and motivators. (Shackleford, D., 2015)
- It helps in the detection of attacks during and before these stages.
- It provides indicators of actions taken during each stage of the attack.
- It communicates threat surfaces, attack vectors and malicious activities directed to both information technology and operational technology platforms.
- It serves as fact-based repository for evidence of both successful and unsuccessful cyber-attacks.
- It provides indicators for computer emergency response teams and incident response groups.

1.12. CYBER THREAT INTELLIGENCE: CHALLENGES AND OPPORTUNITIES

Cyber security and forensic experts must identify, evaluate, and counteract cyber threats almost instantly due to the rising frequency of cyberattacks. In actuality, responding to such a high volume of attacks in a timely manner is impossible without carefully examining the characteristics of each attack and implementing appropriate defensive measures; this is the essence of the idea of cyber threat intelligence. But without the help of artificial intelligence, machine learning, and sophisticated data mining techniques to gather, examine, and decipher evidence of cyberattacks, such intelligence would not be feasible.

Ensuring the security and privacy of personal and organizational data is the most difficult problem in the era of digital information technology and connected devices. The quantity and diversity of malware samples and cyberattacks have increased significantly in recent years, making it very challenging for forensic investigators and security analysts to identify and stop these kinds of attacks. The concept of "Threat Intelligence," which is defined as "the set of data collected, assessed and applied regarding security threats, threat actors, exploits, malware, vulnerabilities and compromise indicators," was developed by researchers to address this issue. In actuality, CTI was developed to assist security professionals in identifying signs of cyberattacks, obtaining details about the attack techniques, and subsequently reacting to the attack precisely and promptly. When a substantial amount of data is generated or collected from various security monitoring solutions, intelligent big-data analytical techniques are required to mine, interpret, and extract knowledge from the collected data. Here, an important challenge would be: How to provide such an intelligence? In this context, a number of issues arise and present fresh difficulties for the field, which we address below.

1.12.1. Cyber Threat Intelligence Challenges

Actually, cybercriminals use a variety of techniques to attack a victim in an attempt to (1) obtain the victim's private information (e.g. financial information); or (2) gain access to and take over the victim's computer in order to carry out additional malicious actions, like locking or encrypting the victim's computer (in the case of ransomware) or distributing malware (in the case of botnets). Even though various cyberattacks appear to use distinct methods of infiltration, their life cycles are essentially the same, ranging from reconnaissance of the target to carrying out malicious operations on the victim's computer or network.

1.12.1.1. Attack Vector Reconnaissance

Recognizing the attack vector and system weaknesses that cybercriminals might exploit is a significant challenge in defending against cyberattacks. In addition to the standard techniques that have been employed to trick victims (e.g., phishing) in order to carry out the actions that the attackers want, attackers have adopted more cunning and inventive techniques in recent years to target victims. These techniques include sending malicious software (malware) to the victim's computer in an unexpected format (such as Word or PDF files), taking advantage of 0-day vulnerabilities, and intruding on anonymous conversations to get in touch with threat actors. These sophisticated attacks include, for instance, the recent ransomware families with worm-like characteristics, which have compromised hundreds of people, businesses, and vital systems. The identification of the attacker and the attack's point of arrival is becoming an increasingly difficult problem due to these advancements in attack techniques.

1.12.1.2. Attack Indicator Reconnaissance

The use of sophisticated anti-forensics and evasion techniques by cybercriminals in their malicious code is another significant concern with the rise in cyberattacks. This renders conventional security assessment methods, such as traffic analysis and static malware analysis or CVSS (Common Vulnerability Scoring System), less effective. Furthermore, modern techniques in forensic investigation of exchanged and stored data are required due to the widespread adoption of new networking paradigms like software-defined networking (SDN), the Internet of Things (IoT), and cloud computing by organizations (e.g., using cloud resources for their big-data processing and storage).

1.12.2. Cyber Threat Intelligence Opportunities

The use of artificial intelligence and machine learning techniques to recognize, understand, learn from, and respond intelligently to sophisticated cyberattacks is being considered in the developing field of cyber threat intelligence. In order to give security professionals a way to identify cyber threat indicators, researchers have been considering various artificial intelligence techniques in recent years. The use of machine learning (ML) and data mining techniques in particular is on the rise because of their demonstrated effectiveness in network anomaly detection and malware analysis (both static and dynamic). In addition to the techniques that cyber defenders can employ to stop or identify cyberattacks, there are additional strategies that can be used to trick the attackers, like the deployment of honeypots. Under such mechanisms, security experts entice attackers with fictitious information or resources that appear genuine, all the while keeping an eye on the attackers' movements and proactively identifying the attack. It would be necessary to use a combination of these techniques to give security practitioners and analysts the most recent information.

1.13. AUTOMATING CYBER THREAT INTELLIGENCE

In today's connected world, cyber threats are a constant reality for organizations, and to safeguard their assets and reputation, they must remain ahead of the curve. Cyber threat intelligence, or CTI, is essential to this because it gives organizations the knowledge they need to foresee threats and take appropriate action in response. But it can be difficult to make sense of all the data produced by these threats due to their sheer volume, which is where CTI automation comes in.

Artificial Intelligence (AI), Machine Learning (ML), and Neuro-Linguistic Programming (NLP) technologies are used in CTI automation to simplify and improve the CTI process. Organizations can lessen the burden on their security teams, boost productivity, and guarantee that they have the most accurate and current information about the threat landscape by automating several stages of the CTI lifecycle, including collection, analysis, reporting, and management.

The ability to process massive amounts of data accurately and quickly is one of the main advantages of CTI automation. The collection and analysis of data from multiple sources can be time-consuming and labor-intensive with traditional manual CTI procedures. Organizations can more quickly and efficiently respond to threats by automating this process and identifying patterns and trends in the threat landscape (Figure 1.8).

Figure 1.8. *Automating cyber threat intelligence.*

Source: https://www.linkedin.com/pulse/future-here-automating-cyber-threat-intelligence-niels-groeneveld#:~:text=One%20of%20the%20key%20benefits,analyze%20data%20from%20various%20sources.

The capacity to recognize and rank threats according to the degree of risk they pose to the company is a major advantage of CTI automation. Organizations can use algorithms to assess a threat's possible impact and prioritize their response in accordance with that assessment by utilizing AI and ML technologies. Instead of squandering time and resources on less serious threats, this enables them to concentrate their efforts on the most urgent ones.

Another crucial component of CTI automation is visualization, which enables businesses to display their CTI data in a clear and useful manner. Organizations can swiftly spot trends and patterns in the threat landscape and decide how best to respond by utilizing interactive dashboards and other visualization tools.

In summary, the automation of CTI is the way of the future for cyber threat intelligence. Organizations can boost productivity, simplify their CTI procedures, and remain ahead of the curve in terms of cyber threat defense by utilizing the newest technologies. Organizations must adopt new technologies to stay ahead of the curve and constantly assess their CTI strategies as the threat landscape changes.

1.14. CYBER THREAT INTELLIGENCE PAST, PRESENT, AND FUTURE

1.14.1. How Has Cyber Threat Intelligence Developed Since the Initial Edition of this Guide?

The growing need for CTI goods and services is the first development that eventually propelled all others. Since these organizations already had established programs in 2019, the demand for threat intelligence has primarily come from businesses outside of the most experienced users, such as big financial institutions and other well-resourced businesses that face a disproportionately high threat. The adoption of CTI has been aided by a growing recognition of the benefits of an intelligence-led strategy for cyber security. The commercial market for CTI goods and services has expanded as a result of this rising demand. According to studies, the CTI market's value essentially doubled from US$5.5 billion in 2019 to $11.6 billion in 2021, and projections for 2027 are as high as $20.2 billion. Nevertheless, the fact that there is still a demand greater than there is supply for high-quality CTI practitioners, services, and products is also influencing CTI practice. Automation has received more attention as resources, including time, have become scarcer.

There are now new product classes that are made to take an automated feed of threat data and react appropriately. Examples of these products are Endpoint Detection and Response (EDR) and Security Orchestration, Automation and Response (SOAR). This has made it possible for analysts to shift from concentrating solely on data to the actual application of CTI, which is the analysis of threat intelligence to guide decision-making.

Organizations using CTI have more ability to utilize native sources of data and information when attempting to comprehend the threats they face thanks to the growing adoption of these and related technologies. For instance, businesses are now more likely than ever to monitor logs using features on their cloud-based security platforms in order to spot and look into suspicious activity. The rise in popularity and availability of open-source platforms and tools, which enable organizations without the means to work with a specialized provider to build their own CTI function and procedures, has made this transition easier. This trend, which has successfully contributed to the democratization of CTI capabilities along with the utilization of native datasets, is demonstrated by the increasing adoption of MISP and the OpenCTI platform.

The organization's overall cyber security architecture is integrating CTI functions and processes more and more as a result of these changes that have concentrated analytical capability. This is a step in the right direction away from a standalone role and toward a model where CTI can advise and guide a wide range of internal customers. The number of stakeholders in an organization has typically increased as a result of the removal of these silos and the shift toward tighter integration of CTI within the organization. Each stakeholder has unique requirements, feedback loops, and processes for refinement.

The widespread adoption of the MITRE ATTandCK framework has been a major factor in the integration of CTI. In addition to facilitating the translation of CTI products and services into numerous domains and use cases, including security testing and control evaluations, ATT&CK offers a common language for identifying and tracking the activity of threat actors.

The emergence of government agencies as intelligence providers is another significant development. The private sector continues to be the dominant force in public reporting of CTI content. But organizations like the US Cybersecurity and Infrastructure Security Agency (CISA), a number of national CERTs, and national security and intelligence agencies have become more involved in disseminating intelligence and enforcing related standards.

The idea that CTI is a public good has grown as a result of these advancements and the growing emphasis on openness and intelligence sharing. The 'Log4Shell' vulnerabilities serve as an example of how interconnected technology stacks are, and how supply chains are becoming more and more vulnerable. As a result of these changes, more and more sophisticated entities are sharing their knowledge and skills with less developed ones, believing that the increased security standards will ultimately benefit everyone.

1.14.2. What Next for Cyber Threat Intelligence?

It's probable that CTI services and products will be more deeply integrated with other business operations and cyber security measures. Even though we have listed a wide range of use cases, it is crucial that CTI products and services completely interact with other stakeholders in order to ascertain and meet their needs. Additionally, it is important to investigate how the CTI methodology and guiding principles can benefit the larger organization. In order to present a comprehensive, threat-led picture of the company, platforms are probably going to shift toward a "single pane of glass" strategy. The trend towards more efficient human-machine interaction should be supported by the growing sophistication and adoption levels of automated consumption and actioning of operational CTI outputs. For instance, as machine learning is used more often in platforms for processing and prioritizing alerts, it should become easier and more efficient for human analysts to be involved. Similarly, large language models and generative AI will be used more and more for repetitive tasks like report and summary generation. This might result in an organization having more room for proactive CTI use cases and concentrating more on the tasks that human analysts are capable of performing that machines cannot.

A company's ability to monitor and possibly exploit the quantity of available data sources will have a big impact on CTI. There will be a growing number of solutions available to track and create a more comprehensive baseline of user behavior so that unusual activity can be identified. These remedies aim to counter the ongoing trend that adversaries have adopted of "living off the land" and fileless malware.

Cyber security departments' regular operations will increasingly incorporate CTI products, which were previously thought of as stand-alone engagements. It is anticipated that intelligence-led security testing will become the industry standard for enhancing an organization's cyber resilience. This strategy is becoming more frequently available to more businesses across more industries.

Government agencies are probably going to have more and more impact on domestic CTI consumption. They intend to accomplish this by disclosing and releasing CTI. In particular, they will provide a wider range of commoditized tools and services to organizations that would not otherwise have the financial means to implement an intelligence-led strategy.

In order to encourage greater sharing of CTI products and services among pertinent industry verticals and interest groups, public-private engagement will also be crucial. This development will also be fueled by the growing importance of collective defense and the understanding of how threats to embedded technologies can pose systemic risks.

The growing professionalism of the CTI industry will serve as the foundation for these developments. There will be a steady increase in the standardization and codification of methodologies, the prevalence of accreditations and certifications, and the familiarity of career paths related to CTI. In order to meet the growing demand for CTI, the industry must mature more.

REFERENCES

1. Abu, M. S., Selamat, S. R., Ariffin, A., & Yusof, R. (2018). Cyber threat intelligence–issue and challenges. *Indonesian Journal of Electrical Engineering and Computer Science, 10*(1), 371–379.
2. Barnum, S. (2012). Standardizing cyber threat intelligence information with the Structured Threat Information eXpression (STIX). MITRE. https://www.mitre.org/publications/technical-papers/standardizing-cyber-threat-intelligence-information-with-the (accessed on 9 October 2024).
3. Berndt, A., & Ophoff, J. (2020). Exploring the value of a cyber threat intelligence function in an organization. In *IFIP World Conference on Information Security Education* (pp. 96–109). Springer, Cham.
4. Boukhtouta, A. (2016). On the generation of cyber threat intelligence: Malware and network traffic analyses. *Cyber Defense Magazine, 195.*
5. Bromander, S., Muller, L. P., Eian, M., & Jøsang, A. (2020). Examining the "known truths" in cyber threat intelligence–The case of STIX. In *International Conference on Cyber Warfare and Security* (pp. 493–XII). Academic Conferences International Limited.
6. Bromiley, M. (2016). Threat intelligence: What it is, and how to use it effectively. *SANS Institute InfoSec Reading Room*, *15*, 172.
7. Brown, R., & Lee, R. M. (2019). The evolution of cyber threat intelligence (CTI): 2019 SANS CTI survey. SANS Institute. https://www.sans.org/white-papers/38790/ (accessed on 9 October 2024).
8. Cascavilla, G., Tamburri, D. A., & Van Den Heuvel, W. (2021). Cybercrime threat intelligence: A systematic multi-vocal literature review. *Computers & Security, 105*, 102258. https://doi.org/10.1016/j.cose.2021.102258.
9. Conti, M., Dargahi, T., & Dehghantanha, A. (2018). Cyber threat intelligence: Challenges and opportunities. In *Cyber Threat Intelligence* (pp. 1–6). Springer, Cham.
10. Cranley, E. (2020). Cybercrime against healthcare groups 'worldwide' is on the rise during coronavirus pandemic, top UN official warns. *Business Insider*. https://www.businessinsider.com/top-unofficial-warned-of-cybercrime-spike-during-pandemic-2020-5?r=US&IR=T (accessed on 9 October 2024).
11. De Melo e Silva, A., Costa Gondim, J. J., de Oliveira Albuquerque, R., & García Villalba, L. J. (2020). A methodology to evaluate standards and platforms within cyber threat intelligence. *Future Internet, 12*(6), 108. http://dx.doi.org/10.3390/fi12060108.
12. Deibert, R. J., Rohozinski, R., Manchanda, A., Villeneuve, N., & Walton,

G. M. F. (2009). Tracking GhostNet: Investigating a cyber espionage network. Munk Centre for International Studies, University of Toronto.

13. Deliu, I., Leichter, C., & Franke, K. (2018). Collecting cyber threat intelligence from hacker forums via a two-stage, hybrid process using support vector machines and latent Dirichlet allocation. *2018 IEEE International Conference on Big Data (Big Data)* (pp. 5008–5013). https://doi.org/10.1109/BigData.2018.8622469.
14. Du, L., Fan, Y., Zhang, L., Wang, L., & Sun, T. (2020). A summary of the development of cyber security threat intelligence sharing. *International Journal of Digital Crime and Forensics, 12*(4), 54–67. http://doi.org/10.4018/IJDCF.2020100105.
15. Elmellas, J. (2016). Knowledge is power: The evolution of threat intelligence. *Computer Fraud & Security, 2016*(7), 5–9. https://doi.org/10.1016/S1361-3723(16)30051-3.
16. Friedman, J. (2015). Definitive guide to cyber threat intelligence. CyberEdge Group, LLC. https://cryptome.org/2015/09/cti-guide.pdf (accessed on 9 October 2024).
17. Giannetto, B., & Paganini, P. (2020). Mastering communication in cyber intelligence activities: A concise user guide. *Cyber Defense Magazine*.
18. Gragido, W. (2012). Understanding indicators of compromise (IoC) Part I. *RSA*. https://web.archive.org/web/20170914000000*/https://www.rsa.com (accessed on 9 October 2024).
19. Groš, S. (2020). Research directions in cyber threat intelligence. *arXiv preprint arXiv:2001.06616.*
20. Guitton, C. (2017). Foiling cyber attacks. *2017 International Conference on Cyber Security and Protection of Digital Services (Cyber Security)*, 1–7. https://doi.org/10.1109/CyberSecPODS.2017.8074853.
21. Hemsley, K., & Fisher, R. (2018). A history of cyber incidents and threats involving industrial control systems. In *12th International Conference on Critical Infrastructure Protection (ICCIP)* (pp. 215–242). Springer, Cham. https://doi.org/10.1007/978-3-030-04537-1_12.
22. Hoffmann, R., Napiórkowski, J., Protasowicki, T., & Stanik, J. (2020). Risk-based approach in the scope of cybersecurity threats and requirements. *Procedia Manufacturing, 44*, 655–662.
23. Hult, F., & Sivanesan, G. (2014). Introducing cyber. *Journal of Business Continuity & Emergency Planning, 7*(2), 97–102. https://www.ingentaconnect.com/content/hsp/jbcep/2014/00000007/00000002/art00002 (accessed on 9 October 2024).

24. Johansen, G. (2020). *Digital Forensics and Incident Response: Incident Response Techniques and Procedures to Respond to Modern Cyber Threats* (2nd ed.). Packt Publishing Ltd.
25. Johnson, C., Badger, L., Waltermire, D., Snyder, J., & Skorupka, C. (2016). Guide to cyber threat information sharing. *NIST Special Publication, 800*(150). https://doi.org/10.6028/nist.sp.800-150.
26. Kaplan, F. (2016). *Dark Territory: The Secret History of Cyber War*. Simon & Schuster.
27. Kime, B. (2016). Threat intelligence: Planning and direction. *SANS Institute*.
28. Le, D. B., Wang, D., Nasim, M., & Babar, A. (2019). Gathering cyber threat intelligence from Twitter using novelty classification. *arXiv preprint arXiv:1907.01755*.
29. Lehto, M. (2015). Phenomena in the cyber world. In *Cyber Security: Analytics, Technology and Automation* (pp. 3–29). Springer, Cham.
30. Luiijf, E., & Kernkamp, A. (2015). Sharing cyber security information. *Global Conference on CyberSpace 2015*. https://www.to2.nl (accessed on 9 October 2024).
31. Matilainen, J. (2020). Using cyber threat intelligence as a part of organizational cybersecurity. *University of Jyväskylä, 55*.
32. Mavroeidis, V., & Bromander, S. (2017). Cyber threat intelligence model: An evaluation of taxonomies, sharing standards, and ontologies within cyber threat intelligence. In *2017 European Intelligence and Security Informatics Conference (EISIC)* (pp. 91–98). IEEE.
33. Mittal, S. (2019). Knowledge for cyber threat intelligence. *University of Maryland, Baltimore County*.
34. Mutemwa, M., Mtsweni, J., & Mkhonto, N. (2017). Developing a cyber threat intelligence sharing platform for South African organizations. In *2017 Conference on Information Communication Technology and Society (ICTAS)* (pp. 1–6). IEEE.
35. Naughton, J. (2016). The evolution of the Internet: From military experiment to general purpose technology. *Journal of Cyber Policy, 1*(1), 5–28. https://doi.org/10.1080/23738871.2016.1157619.
36. Newsweek Staff. (1999). We're in the middle of a cyberwar. *Newsweek*. https://www.newsweek.com/were-middle-cyerwar-166196 (accessed on 9 October 2024).
37. Oosthoek, K., & Doerr, C. (2021). Cyber threat intelligence: A product without a process? *International Journal of Intelligence and*

CounterIntelligence, 34(2), 300–315. https://doi.org/10.1080/08850607.2020.1780062.

38. Phythian, M. (2013). *Understanding the Intelligence Cycle* (1st ed., pp. 23–30). Routledge.
39. Reddy, G. N., & Reddy, G. J. (2014). A study of cyber security challenges and its emerging trends on latest technologies. *arXiv preprint arXiv:1402.1842.*
40. Roberts, A. (2021). Cyber threat intelligence–What does it even mean? In *Cyber Threat Intelligence* (pp. 13–29). Apress. https://doi.org/10.1007/978-1-4842-7220-6_2.
41. Robertson, J., & Riley, M. (2014). Mysterious '08 Turkey pipeline blast opened new cyberwar era. *Bloomberg Business.*
42. Samtani, S., Abate, M., Benjamin, V., & Li, W. (2020). Cybersecurity as an industry: A cyber threat intelligence perspective. In T. Holt & A. Bossler (Eds.), *The Palgrave Handbook of International Cybercrime and Cyberdeviance* (pp. 191–214). Palgrave Macmillan. https://doi.org/10.1007/978-3-319-78440-3_8.
43. Samtani, S., Chinn, R., Chen, H., & Nunamaker Jr., J. F. (2017). Exploring emerging hacker assets and key hackers for proactive cyber threat intelligence. *Journal of Management Information Systems, 34*(4), 1023–1053. https://doi.org/10.1080/07421222.2017.1394049.
44. Sauerwein, C., Fischer, D., Rubsamen, M., Rosenberger, G., Stelzer, D., & Breu, R. (2021). From threat data to actionable intelligence: An exploratory analysis of the intelligence cycle implementation in cyber threat intelligence sharing platforms. *The 16th International Conference on Availability, Reliability and Security (ARES 2021), 85*, 1–9. https://doi.org/10.1145/3465481.3470048.
45. Schaberreiter, T., Kupfersberger, V., Rantos, K., Spyros, A., Papanikolaou, A., Ilioudis, C., & Quirchmayr, G. (2019). A quantitative evaluation of trust in the quality of cyber threat intelligence sources. In *Proceedings of the 14th International Conference on Availability, Reliability and Security* (pp. 1–10).
46. Shackleford, D. (2015). Who's using cyberthreat intelligence and how? *SANS Institute.* https://cdn-cybersecurity.att.com/docs/SANS-Cyber-Threat-Intelligence-Survey-2015.pdf (accessed on 9 October 2024).
47. Shackleford, D. (2017). Cyber threat intelligence uses, successes, and failures: The SANS 2017 CTI survey. *SANS Institute.*
48. Singh, S. (2018). Threat intelligence market worth $12.9 billion by

2023. *Markets and Markets*. https://www.marketsandmarkets.com/PressReleases/threat-intelligence-security.asp (accessed on 9 October 2024).

49. Skopik, F., Settanni, G., & Fiedler, R. (2016). A problem shared is a problem halved: A survey on the dimensions of collective cyber defense through security information sharing. *Computers & Security, 60*, 154–176.
50. Tounsi, W. (2019). *Cyber-Vigilance and Digital Trust: Cyber Security in The Era of Cloud Computing and IoT*. John Wiley & Sons.
51. Tounsi, W., & Rais, H. (2018). A survey on technical threat intelligence in the age of sophisticated cyber-attacks. *Computers & Security, 72*, 212–233. https://doi.org/10.1016/j.cose.2017.09.001.
52. Trifonov, R., Nakov, O., & Mladenov, V. (2018). Artificial intelligence in cyber threats intelligence. In *2018 International Conference on Intelligent and Innovative Computing Applications (ICONIC)* (pp. 1–4). IEEE. https://doi.org/10.1109/ICONIC.2018.8601235.
53. Vaidya, T. (2015). 2001–2013: Survey and analysis of major cyberattacks. *arXiv preprint arXiv:1507.06673*.
54. Wagner, T. D. (2019). Cyber threat intelligence for "things." *2019 International Conference on Cyber Situational Awareness, Data Analytics and Assessment (Cyber SA)*, 1–2. https://doi.org/10.1109/CyberSA.2019.8899384.
55. Wagner, T. D., Mahbub, K., Palomar, E., & Abdallah, A. E. (2019). Cyber threat intelligence sharing: Survey and research directions. *Computers & Security, 87*, 101589.
56. Warner, M. (2017). Intelligence in cyber-and cyber in intelligence. In F. N. Cate (Ed.), *Understanding Cyber Conflict: Fourteen Analogies* (pp. 17–29). Brookings Institution Press.
57. Win, K. M. N., & Thaw, Y. M. K. K. (2019). Information sharing of cyber threat intelligence with their issue and challenges. *International Journal of Trend in Scientific Research and Development, 3*(5), 878–880. https://doi.org/10.31142/ijtsrd26504.

CHAPTER 2

INFORMATION SHARING AND DIMENSIONS TO CIRCUMVENT INCIDENTS AND MITIGATE CYBER THREATS

Contents

INTRODUCTION

For our society to function properly, vital infrastructures like the power and telecommunications networks must be operational. But in recent times, cybersecurity issues have become more of a challenge for those who manage vital infrastructures (Langner, 2011). The surfaces and channels of attacks have grown dramatically as a result of growing network interdependencies and the use of standard information and communications technology (ICT) products (Rinaldi, 2004). To address this grave security issue, new strategies are needed. The sharing of network monitoring data and status information is one method that shows promise (Hernandez-Ardieta et al., 2013) of vital services with national authorities and strategic partners across organizational boundaries. The primary objective is to build a comprehensive situational awareness picture regarding possible threats and ongoing incidents. This is necessary in order to effectively prepare for and provide assistance during large-scale incidents. In a variety of cybersecurity scenarios, such as financially motivated cybercrimes, cyberwar, hacktivism, and terrorism, collaboration based on sharing threat information is thought to be effective. Depending on the circumstances, an attack's shape can vary. For example, cybercrime may use sophisticated persistent threats (APTs) to steal intellectual property, whereas cyberwar or cyberterrorism may use botnets to launch distributed denial-of-service (DDoS) attacks. Sharing information, however, gives victims the ability to launch coordinated and successful countermeasures and gives prospective targets early warning about how to safeguard their ICT infrastructures.

We contend that in addition to using targeted and coordinated countermeasures, we also need to use increasingly sophisticated, customized, and coordinated attacks. Conventional off-the-shelf (COTS) firewall and virus scanner systems don't seem to be able to keep out APTs well enough (Tankard, 2011). New attack types appear every day as a result of the networks of today's rapidly increasing complexity, the rise of zero-day exploit markets (Miller, 2007), and frequently overlooked vulnerabilities (such as out-of-date software or policies). As a result, a large number of Web-based knowledge bases and information security platforms have arisen. From there, users can get useful information about newly discovered threats, malware, and viruses that are spreading, as well as instructions on how to safeguard their infrastructure (for example, check out national Computer Emergence Response Teams (CERTs)). But frequently, this information lacks in-depth knowledge, is rather generic, and isn't tailored to any specific industry.

Such platforms need to offer professional users additional value in the form of sector-specific views, rich information, and experience reports in order to become more effective. Centrally coordinated national cybersecurity centers have been proposed by numerous standardization bodies, such as NIST (2014), ITU-T (2012), and ISO (2015). These centers are currently springing up all over the world.

Effective cybersecurity centers are challenging to set up, and frequently businesses, government agencies, and customer organizations lack the necessary skills to manage and utilize them. The difficulties stem from the need for extensive interdisciplinary research in cybersecurity information sharing. Even though the implementation of these systems is frequently limited to dealing with technical issues, standardization committees, social scientists, and economic experts face an equally important challenge. Questions about legal dependencies, regulatory compliance, the sharing-process design (i.e., who can share what and when in a corporate setting), and what can be learned from CERT implementations that are already in place, for instance, are all equally important.

2.1. THE DIMENSIONS OF INFORMATION SHARING

To achieve effective information sharing, many factors must be taken into account. We contend that the largest challenges encompass the various dimensions of technical, legal, regulatory, and organizational means, as opposed to being solely centered on the technical aspects as many others do. In this work, we conducted a thorough literature survey to find a sizable base corpus of literature and references. We then grouped the references based on their primary subjects. We employed this strategy, taking into consideration all the important dimensions that comprehensively capture the pertinent State-of-the-Art in the field of cybersecurity information sharing exclusively. But in the future, new dimensions might appear or gain significance. The dimensions of security information sharing, which need to be considered when setting up a large-scale organizational or even national cybersecurity center:

- **Efficient Cooperation and Coordination:** Experiences in the real world demonstrate the financial necessity of coordinated cyber defense, for example, because of the sophistication of attacks and the increased complexity and attack surfaces of systems. The primary means of achieving this coordinated cyber defense is information sharing. A vast array of shared information classes, such as indicators of compromise (IoCs), technical vulnerabilities, zero-day exploits, social engineering attacks, or critical service outages, are feasible for a broad spectrum of stakeholders.
- **Legal and Regulatory Landscape:** However, information sharing needs a legal foundation in order to be accepted by a significant

number of stakeholders. As a result, the US, the European Union, and a few of its Member States have started to draft a set of guidelines and regulations.

- **Standardization Efforts:** In order to facilitate the exchange of information, standards and specifications need to adhere to legal obligations. To begin this effort, a number of organizations, including NIST, ENISA, ETSI, and ISO, have already published documents. In the near future, these organizations will refine the current guidelines.
- **Regional and International Implementations:** Organizational measures and sharing structures must be implemented and integrated while keeping these standards and specifications in mind. CERTs and national cybersecurity centers have so far contributed significantly to this step.
- **Technology Integration in Organizations:** At some point, it will be necessary to choose and implement a set of technical sharing protocols and management tools. Here, it is crucial that the technological tools chosen are manageable and consistent with organizational procedures.

Following the complete adoption of information-sharing protocols, an ongoing assessment of their efficacy (e.g., in terms of identifying and thwarting novel threats, etc.) must be carried out and, if required, specific measures in the many dimensions reexamined in light of the results.

2.1.1. Efficient Cooperation and Coordination

A considerable number of new threat types have proliferated as a result of the increased use of information technology in contemporary critical infrastructures. These threats are worldwide in scope, and they are becoming more focused and intense as a result of new technological opportunities. There are mitigation measures in place to address these changing threats, but in order for technological solutions to be successful, cross-organizational and even cross-border collaboration is typically required.

2.1.1.1. Cyber Defense as a Joint Endeavor

Effective response mechanisms require international collaboration at the highest level. Digital borders are, in fact, ill-defined and do not line up with national boundaries. Furthermore, reports from recent publications demonstrate that threats like malware—and botnets in particular—no longer represent a personal problem for individuals, but rather a growing social and civic obligation that impacts every aspect of the digital society.

As stated by Helmbrecht et al. (2013), response mechanisms that comprise a multitude of well-established policy initiatives have existed since the inception of ICT development. Cyberattacks, on the other hand, pose a threat to the widespread adoption of ICT solutions by citizens. These attacks primarily target e-government services, online payment systems, and any other vital infrastructure that depends on computer networks. Last but not least, the growing use of ICT in fraud, war, terrorism, hacktivism, and vandalism lowers citizens' confidence in using it responsibly and puts them in ever-greater danger.

A confederation of nations must pursue ICT system security in a coherent manner that transcends national boundaries and is sustained over time. The primary European organization, ENISA, works to promote information, method, and result sharing among Member States while preventing work duplication in order to improve the convergence of efforts from those Member States. In order to help European institutions and Member States respond to threats to network and information security in a coordinated manner, one of ENISA's responsibilities is to facilitate such efforts.

By identifying technical standards, methodologies, procedures, and processes related to Computer Security Incident Coordination (CSIC), the NIST assists in the coordination of the current Computer Security Incident Response Teams (CSIRTs) when responding to computer security incidents. NIST offers guidelines on how multiple CSIRTs should collaborate when handling computer security incidents, as well as how CSIRTs can create mutual benefit with other organizations in a larger information-sharing community.

2.1.1.2. The Threat Landscape

The world of cyber threats is changing quickly. In cyberspace, creative ways to accomplish malicious goals are continuously emerging. Valuable data assets, including financial transaction records, product design blueprints, user credentials to sensitive systems, and other intellectual property, are being actively sought after by cybercriminals and some nation-states. To carry out sophisticated targeted attacks, attackers are equipped with the most recent zero-day vulnerabilities, top-notch toolkits, and social engineering strategies. These attacks evade conventional defenses by employing a number of stages and vectors to locate weak systems and private information.

The form, purpose, and sophistication of attacks have evolved from a few years ago. The new breed of threats uses sophisticated, zero-day malware to infect specific systems as well as mass-market malware meant to infect multiple systems. They make use of a variety of attack vectors, including email, application, and web-based attacks. Attacks of today target sensitive financial data, intellectual property, insider information, and valuable data assets. Typically, these attacks involve multiple stages in order to gain access to networks, propagate, and ultimately extract the valuable data.

Cybercriminals of the modern era are increasingly driven by social and political impulses in addition to economic ones. These days, international networks of linked activists and hacktivists, like Anonymous, are well recognized for their attacks on websites belonging to corporations, governments, and religious institutions.

It is essential to comprehend cyber threats and the deployment methodologies in order to design defense strategies that work. The elements that make up the dynamic landscape of cyber threats are getting more and more complicated. To fully capture the myriad facets of a cyber threat, a thorough examination of the documented cyber incidents is required. It is necessary to take into account attack strategies, threat agents, cyberthreats, and threat trends. Experts in cybersecurity who are evaluating threats to different systems and creating cybersecurity guidelines to protect sensitive data can benefit from this information. However, caution should always be used when interpreting such data—just because something has happened often in the past does not mean that it will happen again. Because of how quickly the landscape of cyber threats is changing, identifying trends early on is crucial.

Malicious URLs have replaced botnets as the preferred method of distributing malware for drive-by exploits since 2014. This is because URLs are more challenging for law enforcement to take down. One significant problem with code injection is that it can be used to attack widely used content management systems (CMSs). Popular CMSs are widely used, which increases their attack surface and attracts the attention of cybercriminals. An intriguing feature is the growing prevalence of P2P botnets, which are harder to identify and eliminate. Additionally, mining bitcoins, a "virtual currency," with the use of botnet infrastructures is a developing trend.

Within DoS attacks, domain name system (DNS) reflection attacks have become more common since the 2013 Spamhaus attack (Arstechnica, 2013). Additionally, there has been a reported rise in scareware and rogueware. The spread of ransomware and phony antivirus software to mobile platforms like Android is one factor contributing to this increase. Attacks using cyberespionage techniques have grown far beyond predictions (ENISA, 2013b). The public's outrage has been sparked by the recent revelation of several nationstate mass surveillance programs. Some of the most successful attacks were the result of identity theft, which used SMS-forwarders as a means of committing large-scale financial fraud. These attacks were based on well-known financial Trojans that target two-factor authentication and have been installed on mobile platforms (such as Zeus, SpyEye, and Citadel). Mobile devices are now experiencing search engine poisoning as well. These events led to the conclusion that attackers are always one step ahead and that it is frequently possible to wreak havoc by taking advantage of well-known and basic vulnerabilities.

Information sharing among organizations from these countries should continue, even though it may appear to be at odds with the methods used by some nation-states to conduct espionage on other nations. This is especially true for those with comparable infrastructures, which make them vulnerable to similar attacks or potentially appealing targets for attackers. The main takeaway from ENISA is that knowledge should be shared from the cybersecurity community to user groups in order to improve cyber defense. In order to achieve this, it is necessary to enable efficient information sharing among security experts as well as among all other stakeholders involved in critical ICT systems.

2.1.1.3. Incident Taxonomies

Security communities have developed a number of taxonomies over the past few years in order to distinguish and contrast events, incidents, and disclosed attacks in a unique way. The incident taxonomies currently in use were either specially created by individual CERTs (e.g. CERTs from Latvia and Hungary), or those that are globally and universally acknowledged. The so-called "Common Language" schema is one of the earliest, having been created at Sandia National Laboratories (Howard and Longstaff, 1998). Three key terms are defined in this taxonomy: incident, attack, and event. An event consists of information that is currently available about the attack target and the action that has been taken against it. The attack can be fully described once additional details, such as the tool used, the vulnerability that was exploited, and the outcome of the attack, are available. This taxonomy states that an incident can only be classified as described if the attack's source and goal are known in addition to the incident's details. This extensive taxonomy makes it possible to precisely identify and categorize incidents based on a number of factors. But it can be confusing and time-consuming; security specialists frequently aren't able to gather all the data needed to accurately describe an incident. As a result, this taxonomy is primarily used for theoretical purposes, research, and as a foundation for developing unique taxonomies.

2.1.1.4. Sharing Scenarios

In light of the current threat environment, there are numerous financial benefits to sharing in order to reduce security costs for each alliance member. In addition to P2P connections, a number of national initiatives envision the establishment of (national) cybersecurity centers that offer assistance and support upon request, particularly to critical infrastructure providers. In this work, we identified four scenarios that collectively highlight the high economic potential and the strong need for sharing. It is important to note that the concepts presented in this work have broader applicability than just information sharing between (non-ICT) CI organizations. This includes ICT network service providers, cybersecurity providers, and other infrastructure providers.

2.1.1.4.1. Sharing Information about Recent or Ongoing Incidents

This scenario allows information about ongoing incidents to be shared, such as service status, organizational impacts and consequences, and the attack vector (if known) or malfunctioning reasons along with an estimated recovery time. Although this information is deemed highly sensitive and may be exploited to damage an organization's reputation, it is a necessary precondition for facilitating assistance and support among parties, warning parties ahead of time, or helping partner organizations draw lessons from recent events. Three separate use cases are anticipated in this scenario are:

- Victim organizations notify a national cyber center with comprehensive information about the cyber incident.
- Critical-service organizations are notified by a national cyber center of incidents that have affected one or more of the federated organizations, either recently or currently.
- Within a confederation, organizations alert one another to significant service degradations brought on by ongoing incidents, with a focus on business customers.

2.1.1.4.2. Sharing Information about Service Dependencies

In this scenario, the impact of a (potential) service degradation or outage is better predicted by sharing static service dependencies. If services from various companies are interdependent, then this is especially pertinent for accurate risk assessment, for example a cloud provider's outage negatively affects the services of other businesses that rely on the cloud for back-end storage. In this scenario, the consumer of the service reports about the service dependencies in the following three cases:

- A national cyber center receives reports from organizations regarding the services that are essential to their operations.
- The national cyber center notifies federated organizations about service dependencies between other organizations.

- Federated companies keep each other informed about the dependencies between their services.

2.1.1.4.3. Sharing Information about the Technical Service Status

In this scenario, dynamic information about the technical status of services, e.g. their integrity, confidentiality, and availability are disclosed. Predictions for the necessary restore time are included in case of outages. Modeling or informing dependent organizations about the status of the service can be done with this information. In this scenario the provider of the service reports about the service status in one of the following three cases:

- Organizations inform the national cyber center about the status of the services they provide.
- The national cyber center informs organizations about other organizations' service status.
- Organizations inform one another about their service status.

2.1.1.4.4. Request Assistance of Organizations

An organization may ask the national cyber center's outside experts for assistance if it is unable to manage a cyber incident on its own. Furthermore, a national cyber center can request help from external organizations or individuals (e.g., if specific knowledge is needed but unavailable). Finally, a cyber center can serve as a middleman, bringing together the appropriate parties in a timely manner to address a cyber incident. We distinguish between two cases here:

- An organization asks for assistance from other organizations that might have dealt with similar issues in the past.
- The cyber center asks federated organizations for support for organizations facing a particular issue.

2.1.2. Legal and Regulatory Landscape

In recent years, CI cybersecurity has grown in importance and sensitivity on a global scale. The United States and the European Union are growing more cognizant of this issue, which has led to the publication of publications, guidelines, and directives that govern safe online environments for their respective Member States.

In order to guarantee a high standard of network and information security (NIS) throughout the Union, the European Commission and the High Representative of the Union for Foreign Affairs and Security Policy have released a cybersecurity strategy and commission directive (European Commission,

2016). The President of the United States signed Presidential Policy Directive (PPD)-21, "Critical Infrastructure Security and Resilience," and Executive Order (EO) 13636, "Improving Critical Infrastructure Cybersecurity," in February 2013.

The measures outlined in these directives will make critical infrastructure more resilient and secure against changing risks and threats. These documents demand the creation of a modern, comprehensive national framework that takes into account the growing significance of cybersecurity in protecting tangible assets.

The Cybersecurity Information Sharing Act of 2015, which makes it simple for businesses to share personal data with the government, particularly in cases of cybersecurity threats, further supports the provisions made by the EO regarding the defense of CIs against cyber threats. The bill establishes a mechanism for federal agencies to receive threat intelligence from private companies without mandating such information sharing. The main difference between the EO and the CISA is that:

- The EO focuses on the security of critical infrastructures in particular and states that exchanging threat intelligence is a prerequisite for achieving security.
- All manufacturing and technology companies should be able to use the CISA, which is solely focused on sharing security information.

Outside of the US and the EU, a number of smaller nations are now debating which crucial facets of Critical Information Infrastructure Protection (CIIP) should be governed by future directives and policies. Due to a lack of resources, Latin American nations like Uruguay, Argentina, Colombia, and Trinidad and Tobago are developing cybersecurity strategies that are primarily based on best practices and models that have been adopted from more developed nations.

A comprehensive overview of the cybersecurity policy environment in ten Asia-Pacific markets was provided by BSA-The Software Alliance and Galexia (2015). The study states that the markets included in the analysis have a history of being slow to develop national cybersecurity strategies and put the necessary legal frameworks in place for security and the protection of critical infrastructure. However, public and private stakeholders in the Asia-Pacific region are now working together to establish appropriate policy, legal, and operational frameworks; enhance collaboration with various relevant stakeholder communities; effectively share meaningful cybersecurity information; and prioritize the protection of critical infrastructures in order to strengthen the protection of critical infrastructure from cyber threats.

2.1.2.1. EU Cybersecurity Strategy: "An Open, Safe and Secure Cyberspace"

The tenets that the European Union plans to uphold for cybersecurity policy both domestically and globally are made clear by this strategy. In order to ensure safe access to the Internet for all, the European Commission (EC) has developed this document with the goal of addressing important issues like safeguarding fundamental rights, freedom of expression, personal data, and privacy; promoting a multistakeholder governance approach; raising awareness of the shared responsibilities of public authorities, the private sector, and individual citizens to protect themselves; and ensuring a coordinated response to strengthen cybersecurity. The plan identifies a number of strategic goals and initiatives that can improve the performance of the EU as a whole.

The establishment of the NIS directive (European Commission, 2016) and its planned implementation in all European Member States are particularly pertinent to the scope of this work. Each Member State must establish a functional CERT and approve a national and international NIS cooperation plan in accordance with the NIS directive. Coordination of prevention, detection, mitigation, and response to cyberattacks is found to be largely dependent on information sharing and mutual aid amongst the national NIS competent authorities. Both public and private participants in various fields (i.e., energy, transport, banking, public administration, etc.) are asked to carry out the necessary risk management and provide the national NIS competent authorities with the identified information. Events that significantly affect the ability to provide essential services must be reported to the same authorities, who will then share this information, if needed, with law enforcement and regulatory agencies that work together.

This strategy also places a high priority on combating cybercrime. In order to accomplish this, the EC is requested to assist the European Cybercrime Centre (EC3) in providing intelligence, analysis, forensic investigation, cooperation facilitation, and the establishment of channels for information sharing between the relevant authorities in the Member States, the private sector, and other stakeholders.

In addition, the mission of the Common Security and Defense Policy (CSDP) calls for the EC to create a framework for cyber defense policies to safeguard networks. A key goal of this mission is to implement threat analysis, information sharing, and dynamic risk management.

To address the intricacy of handling cyber incidents across the Union's interconnected networks, the strategy provides guidance to all relevant parties (law enforcement, CERTs, NIS competent authorities, and industry) regarding their respective roles and responsibilities at both the national and EU levels. The best people to handle cyber incident and attack response and prevention are national governments, who can also build relationships and networks with the private sector. At the same time, EU involvement is necessary for a national response to be effective.

2.1.2.2. EU Network Information Security Directive

A crucial element of the overall plan is the Network Information Security Directive, which mandates that all EU member states, important Internet facilitators, and operators of vital infrastructure—such as social networks, e-commerce platforms, and businesses providing banking, energy, transportation, and healthcare services—maintain a safe and reliable digital environment. The directive designates ENISA as a resource to offer knowledge and counsel to Member States and the Commission. By creating a cooperative network, ENISA should guarantee efficient and timely information exchange between the Commission and the Member States. A secure information-sharing infrastructure should be established within the cooperation network to facilitate the exchange of private and sensitive data. Only those Member States who can demonstrate that their processes, financial, human, and technical resources meet the strict security requirements will be granted access to the sharing infrastructure.

The Directive states that early warnings should only be issued within the network in the event of extremely serious incidents or risks that could have an impact on multiple Member States and necessitate coordination of the response at the Union level. Particular focus should be placed on maintaining unofficial but reliable channels of information exchange between market participants and between the public and private sectors during the notification process.

The Commission shall be empowered to adopt a Union NIS cooperation plan providing for:

- A definition of the format and procedures for the collection and sharing of compatible and comparable information on risks and incidents by competent authorities
- A definition of the procedures and the criteria for the assessment of the risk and incidents by the cooperation network

Events that lead to breaches of personal data and the exchange of information about risks and incidents within the cooperation network ought to necessitate the processing of personal data; in order to meet the legitimate public interest objectives under Article 7 of Directive 95/46/EC, the competent authorities must collaborate closely with personal data protection authorities.

2.1.2.3. U.S. White House Executive Order (EO 13636): Improving CI Cybersecurity

The cybersecurity of CI is strengthened by this Executive Order (EO), which was published on February 12, 2013, through increased information sharing and collaborative development and implementation of a cybersecurity practice framework with U.S industry partners. The EO fortifies the US government's alliances with operators and owners of vital infrastructure in order to combat cyber threats by:

- New information-sharing programs to provide both classified and unclassified threat and attack information to U.S. companies
- The development of a cybersecurity framework. The EO directs the NIST to lead the development of a framework of cybersecurity practices to reduce cyber risks to critical infrastructure

The EO mandates that high-quality, unclassified reports about cyberthreats be produced by federal agencies and shared with U.S. private sector organizations in a prompt manner to help these organizations defend against possible cyberattacks. Additionally, only critical infrastructure entities authorized to receive them should be the recipients of any classified reports that are created and distributed. It is necessary to set up a system for monitoring the creation, distribution, and removal of classified reports. Additionally, the EO broadens the scope of the Enhanced Cybersecurity Services program, facilitating the exchange of cyber threat intelligence in near real time to support participating critical infrastructure companies in their efforts to defend themselves online.

2.1.2.4. U.S. Presidential Policy Directive (PPD-21): Critical Infrastructure Security and Resilience

The national strategy for the security and resilience of critical infrastructure is updated by this directive. The three strategic imperatives listed below should be embraced in order to increase the security and resilience of the vital infrastructures in the United States.

- **Imperative 1:** Enhance the national unity of effort to fortify the security and resilience of critical infrastructure by streamlining and making clear the functional relationships throughout the Federal Government. It should be made easier for the federal government, operators, and owners of critical infrastructure to collaborate and share information. Two national critical infrastructure centers run by the Department of Homeland Security will be established as part of a redesigned framework: one for physical infrastructures and another for cyber infrastructures. They will act as hubs for partners in critical infrastructure to acquire integrated, actionable information and situational awareness.

- **Imperative 2:** Determine the baseline data and system requirements for the federal government to facilitate efficient information exchange. Secure and resilient critical infrastructures depend on effective information sharing between governments, operators, and owners of critical infrastructure. It should be made possible by the prompt sharing of threat and vulnerability data, along with data that permits the establishment of situational awareness during incidents. Thus, it is necessary to determine the requirements for redundant systems, system interoperability, and data and information formats and accessibility.
- **Imperative 3:** Establish an integration and analysis function to help guide decisions about critical infrastructures in operations and planning. The intersection of the two national centers should be the site of operational and strategic analysis of incidents, threats, and emerging risks (as identified in Strategic Imperative 1). It will be able to gather, evaluate, and combine threat streams, hazard, and vulnerability and consequence data to help prioritize resources and manage risks to critical infrastructure; predict cascade effects and interdependencies; suggest security and resilience measures for critical infrastructure before, during, and after an event or incident; and support incident management and restoration activities pertaining to critical infrastructure.

2.1.3. Standardization Efforts

When establishing information-sharing procedures, official recommendations from standardization bodies like NIST or ENISA are a great source of information.

2.1.3.1. ENISA: Proactive Detection of Network Security Incidents

In order to better understand how CERTs identify incidents, what resources and tools they use to find malicious activity, how to identify best practices and suggest actions to other CERTs, and how to assess challenges they encounter, ENISA conducted a study. Proactive Detection of Network Security Incidents presents the study's findings and provides recommendations to pertinent stakeholders on how to advance this process. The study found that some CERTs do not gather incident data about other constituencies or do not share this data with other CERTs, indicating that they are currently not making the most of all available external sources. The report looks at these and other flaws in the incident detection process from both a technical and a legal/organizational standpoint, and it makes one or more recommendations for each flaw that is found. They are directed at three different groups: (1) data providers, (2) data consumers, and (3) national or EU-level organizations.

The main recommendations for data providers center on ideas about how to connect with CERTs more effectively, better data formats and distribution strategies, and ways to enhance and enrich data quality. Data providers should create an easy-to-register process for clients, screen potential data recipients for eligibility, and connect with security institutions and communities in order to meet the stringent privacy requirements regarding shared information.

Data providers should adopt existing standards for sharing incident information, utilize standard data transportation methods such as HTTPS, SCP, or SFTP, and ensure the delivered data includes information that enables correlation between various sources (e.g., timestamps of events, Autonomous System Number (ASN), affected IP addresses or domain names, type of incident/exploit/malware, etc.). This approach attracts high-quality data sources and facilitates information sharing in commonly accepted formats. Providers should also grant clients access to information as soon as it becomes available, offer a thorough explanation of the procedures used to gather incident data, and include context and categorization.

ENISA (2011b) recommends that data providers add more metadata to incident information to improve data quality and provide insights into observed events. Additionally, strict filtering, verification, and data correlation are advised to reduce the occurrence of false positives. The report also states that data aging mechanisms must be implemented to remove data from blacklists while preserving data for offline analysis, historical reference, and research purposes.

An overview of how data consumers can obtain access to datasets is also provided in ENISA (2011b). The report offers recommendations for activities that CERTs can undertake to confirm the quality of data feeds, deploy new technologies, and improve the integration of external feeds with internal monitoring systems.

To facilitate data collection for services, the report suggests that organizations applying for access to data sources first identify which sources are most relevant to their needs. They should then install sensors in their networks or develop their own monitoring capabilities. Additionally, forming connections with security communities (e.g., APCERT, TF-CSIRT, FIRST) is advised to build trust and expedite the eligibility verification process for restricted data feeds. Lastly, when requesting services that involve installing sensors or sharing data, data consumers should be mindful of any potential legal implications.

Data consumers should put in place automation systems that enable the processing of incident data in accordance with best practices. Therefore, these systems should be able to handle a wide variety of data formats, store the data in a database that facilitates offline analysis, correlation, and visualization, and combine internal and external data. Verification of incoming data feeds must be ongoing. As a result, before feeding incident information into database or incident handling software, data consumers should establish standards and procedures for evaluating the caliber of the data sources and confirming incident details. To enhance the data and eliminate duplicate events, it is advised to correlate the data with external services. If a system for providing feedback is in place, data consumers ought to eventually use it to provide information that will help data providers raise the caliber of the services they provide.

Data-consumer CERTs are encouraged to implement their own monitoring mechanisms, such as sensor networks, client honeypot technologies, sandbox technologies, and passive DNS monitoring, since they may end up becoming data providers. Finally, initiatives that seek to strike a balance between the needs for security and privacy protection are highlighted, either at the EU or at the national level. These initiatives include encouraging the adoption of common formats and underutilized technologies and expanding the integration of statistical incident data. Additionally, studies in the field of data-leakage reporting are recommended.

2.1.3.2. ISO/IEC27010: Information Technology Security Techniques Information-Security Management for Inter-Sector and Inter-Organizational Communications

This international standard (ISO, 2015) offers general principles and guidelines for exchanging confidential information about IT security threats, vulnerabilities, and/or incidents amongst organizations or within an organization's community. For instance, when governments, businesses, law enforcement, and CERT-type organizations work together to investigate, evaluate, and resolve serious cyberattacks that affect multiple organizations and are frequently international or cross-jurisdictional. The goal of the standard is to facilitate the development of trust in the exchange and sharing of sensitive information, which will promote the expansion of information-sharing communities globally.

The standard requires the creation of communities for information sharing among its general recommendations. These communities need shared interests that specify the parameters of the sensitive information that is shared for them to be effective. Furthermore, it is important to specify the management responsibilities and organizational structures that apply to community information security management. Information that is shared within the community must be categorized according to its importance, necessity for the organization, sensitivity, legal requirements, and credibility. It is necessary to consistently ensure that shared information is adequately protected. Any information that could identify the source of the information exchange should be removed when anonymity is requested.

Developing, putting into place, and overseeing procedures that ensure a timely and secure flow of information is necessary in order for the parties involved in the information-sharing community to safely exchange sensitive information. Information should be distributed to the right parties through this process, with a reasonable guarantee that it won't be misused or improperly shared. Risk management, monitoring, and dissemination should all be a part of secure and resilient communications within the community.

Organizations operating in the same industry or with similar corporate goals can benefit the most from information sharing when it comes to exchanging sector-specific information security risk categories. Nonetheless, information sharing between sectors can be beneficial if a hierarchical structure or a geographic definition of communities is in place. Information-sharing communities should also specify the terms and conditions under which they will operate. These should include the goals of the community, the process for joining and leaving the community, the responsibilities of its members, the procedures and standards for discipline and expulsion, the guidelines for using shared information, and any legal or financial obligations.

An agreement for the exchange of information should outline the kinds of information (e.g. notifications, cautions and alerts, managing incidents, information requests, forecasts for the quality of service, etc.) that could be shared among community members to enable them to create and put into place suitable security measures for the degree of sensitivity of the shared information. If an appropriate technique of data filtering is not applied, sharing too much information may be just as harmful as sharing too little.

2.1.3.3. NIST: Framework for Improving CI Cybersecurity

The framework focuses on integrating cybersecurity risks into the organization's risk-management procedures and using business drivers to direct cybersecurity activities. It consists of three parts:

- The framework core;

- The framework profile;
- The framework implementation tiers.

The Framework Core is a collection of cybersecurity tasks, results, and useful sources that are shared by critical infrastructure industries. It offers thorough instructions for creating unique organizational profiles. From the executive level to the implementation/operations level, it presents industry standards, guidelines, and practices in a way that facilitates communication of cybersecurity activities and outcomes throughout the organization. Five continuous and concurrent functions make up the core of the framework: identify, protect, detect, respond, and recover. Together, these roles offer a high-level, strategic perspective of the cybersecurity risk life cycle inside an organization. After that, the framework core determines the fundamental key categories and subcategories for every function and pairs them with illustrative references, such as current practices, standards, and guidelines, for every subcategory.

Organizations can better match their cybersecurity efforts to their business needs, risk appetites, and available resources by defining profiles. A framework profile is a representation of the results chosen by an organization from the framework's categories and subcategories in accordance with its business needs. In a specific implementation scenario, the profile can be defined as the alignment of standards, guidelines, and practices with the framework core. Profiles can be used to compare a "current" profile with a "target" profile in order to find opportunities for strengthening cybersecurity posture. An organization can create a profile by going over all of the categories and subcategories and deciding which are most crucial based on business drivers and a risk assessment. They can then add more categories and subcategories as necessary to address the risks facing the organization. The current profile can then be used to support the setting of priorities and tracking of progress toward the target profile, taking into account other business requirements such as innovation and cost-effectiveness. Profiles can be used for internal or external communication within organizations, as well as for self-evaluations.

The tiers assist companies in comprehending the features of their cybersecurity risk management strategy. The framework's tiers give an organization's perspective on cybersecurity risk and the procedures in place to manage it context. Tiers indicate the extent to which cybersecurity risk management procedures used by an organization display the traits outlined in the framework (e.g., repeatable, adaptable, and conscious of danger and risk). The tiers, which range from partial (tier 1) to adaptive (tier 4), describe the various practices of an organization. These tiers show a progression from unstructured, reactive responses to risk-informed, agile approaches. An organization should take into account its current risk management procedures, the threat landscape, legal and regulatory requirements, business and mission objectives, and organizational constraints when choosing a tier.

The framework encompasses a methodology aimed at safeguarding civil liberties and individual privacy during cybersecurity operations carried out by critical infrastructure organizations. The framework can help organizations integrate privacy and civil liberties into a comprehensive cybersecurity program, even though processes and current needs will vary. Furthermore, by using the framework, organizations can enhance the security and resilience of critical infrastructure by implementing risk management best practices and principles. By compiling standards, guidelines, and practices that are currently being used successfully in the industry, the framework finally gives organization and structure to the various approaches to cybersecurity that are used today.

2.1.3.5. Recommendation ITU-T X.1500 Cybersecurity Information-Exchange Techniques

ITU-T X recommendation. The ITU-T (2012) standard, approved in April 2011, outlines methods for improving cybersecurity through the exchange of information that is coherent, comprehensive, global, timely, and assured (ITU-T, 2012). The cybersecurity information exchange (CYBEX) model is presented, and methods for enabling the sharing of cybersecurity information are covered. In order to support the significant activities and specification evolution taking place in multiple cybersecurity forums, the techniques include the structured global discovery and interoperability of cybersecurity information. The following basic functions make up the general cybersecurity information exchange model used in this recommendation. These functions can be extended as needed to enable guaranteed cybersecurity information exchanges, or they can be used separately or in combination as appropriate.

- Structuring cybersecurity information for exchange purposes;
- Identifying and discovering cybersecurity information and entities;
- Establishing trust and information exchange policy agreements between exchanging entities;
- Requesting and responding to cybersecurity information;
- Assuring the integrity of the cybersecurity information exchange.

Any two entities that want to exchange cybersecurity information must be able to understand each other's descriptions and structures, which should be consistent. In order to facilitate these exchanges, cybersecurity information is defined as structured data or knowledge about the following: the current state of cybersecurity-related hardware, software, or network-based systems, particularly vulnerabilities; forensic data pertaining to incidents or events; heuristics and signatures obtained from past events; cybersecurity entities involved; cybersecurity information exchange specifications (including modules, schemas, terms, and conditions) and assigned numbers; identities and assurance attributes of all cybersecurity information; and implementation requirements, guidelines, and practices.

2.2. REGIONAL AND INTERNATIONAL IMPLEMENTATIONS

A crucial component of each local cybersecurity ecosystem is CERTs. They maintain mailing lists to send out early warnings, gather data on emerging threats, and, in certain situations, offer assistance upon request. Within regions, CERT cooperation has shown to be the most successful. This makes sense because more frequent in-person meetings are encouraged by short travel distances and generally inexpensive expenses. The cultural backgrounds of the participating teams are similar, which facilitates common projects and eases social networking, which is another important factor. International cooperation is necessary, though, because cyber threats are worldwide in scope. As a result, CERTs have strong international connections with one another, and national cyber centers with strong connections are starting to emerge.

2.2.1. CERTs

- **Asia: APCERT:** APCERT is the platform for regional cross-border collaboration and information sharing. It was established during the inaugural Asia-Pacific Security Incident Response Coordination (APSIRC) meeting in Japan in March 2002 with the goal of enhancing working relationships between CERT neighbors across national borders. The APCERT agreement was accepted in February 2003 by 15 CERT teams representing the 12 Asia-Pacific economies. In order to improve the region's awareness and competency regarding computer security incidents, APCERT seeks to maintain a trusted network of computer security experts in the Asia-Pacific area. Additionally, it seeks to strengthen regional and international cooperation on information security in the Asia-Pacific area, foster collaborative research and development on topics of mutual interest to its members, support other CERTs in the area in conducting effective and efficient computer emergency response, and offer advice and/or recommendations to help address legal issues pertaining to information security and emergency response across regional boundaries.

- **Europe: TERENAs TF-CSIRT:** CERT teams concluded that it would not be feasible to establish a permanent, operational European CERT coordination center due to the disparate interests and needs of the various networks in Europe. Nonetheless, some teams have a shared interest in collaboration and advancement in particular fields. Some of the main common goals of this cooperation were to share statistical data about incidents so as to identify common trends, develop a European accreditation scheme, establish education and training, and support new teams. These efforts culminated in the formation of TF-CSIRT, a task force of TERENA, by the Euro-CERT group in May 2000.
- **Europe: NORDUnet CERT:** NORDUnet CERT is one of the regional CERT initiatives that seeks to improve coordination and incident handling amongst the nations of Northern Europe. NORDUnet CERT works with the Nordic national research networks to handle security incidents. NORDUnet CERT serves as the coordination point for all national CERTs in Denmark, Finland, Iceland, Norway, and Sweden, as it is the Nordic Internet highway connecting these countries' research and education networks. Every CERT is autonomous, functions within its own nation, and has the option to join international groups (TERENA TF-CSIRT, FIRST). However, those groups have created a peer network that doubles as a "Web of Trust.". Because NORDUnet CERT is a member of TF-CSIRT and FIRST, it also participates in international contacts.
- **South America:** To address two significant security issues, CERTs in the South American and Caribbean region have formed a working group under the auspices of CLARA (Cooperation of Advanced Networks in Latin America). The organization is focused on safeguarding REDClara's vital infrastructure. In the NRENs, it also addresses the formation of security working groups known as CLARA WG-CSIRT. In this context, the objectives of CLARA WG-CSIRT are as follows: (1) to create a security work framework for every NREN; (2) to encourage the formation of new working groups addressing security in Latin America and the region by means of member-focused training programs; and (3) to encourage the sharing of data and information regarding related issues, incident handling, etc.; (4) to encourage coordinated and timely responses to security incidents that arise on REDClara's and each NREN's infrastructure;

(5) to create a database of contact points in charge of security in each NREN; and (6) to collaborate with related initiatives, like TF-CSIRT and APCERT.

- **North America:** With the assistance of the CERT/CC team, the USCERT (United States Computer Emergency Readiness Team) in the country has arranged a number of CSIRT meetings that have brought together industry, government, academia, and product and security vendors as well as service providers. Additionally, the US government collaborates with the industry's Information Sharing and Analysis Centers (ISACs), holding meetings that are exclusive to groups that handle safeguarding the country's vital infrastructure. In particular, the Information Technology Information Sharing and Analysis Center (IT-ISAC) was founded as a reliable network of security experts from various IT-related businesses. Its mission is to safeguard the IT infrastructure by detecting threats and weaknesses in the infrastructure and exchanging best practices for promptly and effectively resolving them. The IT-ISAC's members can comprehend both physical and cyber threats thanks to its communication with other sector-specific ISACs. When combined, these services give users an up-to-date, comprehensive view of the IT infrastructure's security.

2.2.2. International Cooperations

Strong international cooperation and/or coordination among CERTs are essential for effective incident response. The goal of these partnerships is to more effectively combat the widespread nature of Internet security threats. Furthermore, a lot of CERT services rely heavily on working together with other teams that are spread out across the globe. Here, we provide a quick overview of the Forum for Incident Response and Security Teams' (FIRST) contribution to the development of the global CERT community. Finally, we report two cases of cross-regional cooperation: cooperation between Member States in the same organization that are from different regions, as well as some examples of sector cooperation initiatives.

2.2.2.1. First

The first is a 1990-founded organization whose mission is to improve incident response teams' coordination and communication. Currently, 286 teams from 61 different countries make up the FIRST membership. These teams come from a range of organizations, including the military, commercial, educational, and vendor sectors. Incident response teams can respond to security incidents by using resources, trusted communication between member teams, and best practices that are made available by membership in FIRST. Members of FIRST create and exchange technical knowledge, instruments, procedures, processes, and best practices. FIRST develops and disseminates best practices, fosters the growth of incident response teams and memberships from global organizations, and encourages the development of high-quality security products, policies, and services.

2.2.2.2. Sector Cooperation

The primary attributes of a sector-specific CERT are its constituency type and responsibilities. Similar duties and a common constituency serve as incentives for collaboration. Teams in the public or private sectors may affiliate and begin working together based on shared interests. An unofficial association of governmental CERTs is called the European Government CSIRTs group (EGC). This group's goal is to develop incident response techniques by utilizing member cooperation, given the similarity of their constituencies and problem sets. Members of EGC engage in a variety of activities to accomplish this goal. They create protocols for handling network security incidents, facilitate technology exchange and information sharing about IT security incidents, malicious code threats, and vulnerabilities, pinpoint areas of specialized knowledge and expertise that the group should share, pinpoint areas for cooperative research and development, and express shared perspectives with other initiatives and organizations. Additionally, EGC members collaborate with other worldwide CERT projects that address vulnerabilities and incident handling globally (for example, numerous EGC teams are part of FIRST and TF-CSIRT).

2.2.2.3. Cross-Regional Cooperation

Cross-regional collaboration between various groups and teams is typically predicated on the sharing of information and experiences during in-person gatherings. A prime example is the Central and Eastern European Networking Association (CEENet), an alliance of twenty-three national academic, scientific, and training institutions from Asia and Europe. The goal of CEENet is to coordinate the global facets of the networks for academics, researchers, and educators in Central and Eastern Europe as well as the surrounding nations. Since each member of this organization has experienced significant differences in ICT development, information sharing among those nations is essential to achieving an acceptable average level of ICT security throughout the entire region. The NATO Cooperative Cyber Defense Centre of Excellence is another instance of cross-regional cooperation (NATO CCD CoE). In Tallinn, Estonia, it is one of the NATO Centers of Excellence. The Center was founded on

May 14, 2008; it became an International Military Organization and was fully accredited by NATO. The goal of the international military organization known as NATO CCD CoE is to improve cyber defense capabilities, collaboration, and information sharing between NATO, its member countries, and its allies through research and development, education, lessons learned, and consultation. NATO CCD COE, among other things, creates manuals, guidelines, and recommendations for both domestic and international cybersecurity.

2.2.3. IT Crisis Management

In an effort to address cybersecurity concerns and provide cyber situational awareness, a few (primarily Western) nations have recently begun to set up IT crisis-management centers. When it comes to national cybersecurity for critical infrastructures, these centers are the primary information sources. They offer expertise and advice through services available on a 24/7 basis. A crisis management center needs to be able to accurately depict the nation's current state of IT security in addition to being a source of information. Thus, on the networks of the government and vital infrastructure, monitoring protocols are implemented. In order to maintain close communication with both domestic and foreign partners, close cooperation with the national CERT is typically established as well. Among the first nations in Europe to establish national IT crisis management centers were Germany and the Netherlands.

2.3. TECHNOLOGY INTEGRATION INTO ORGANIZATIONS

Internationally, national and governmental cybersecurity center establishment has advanced significantly in the last several years. Each of these organizations is at a different stage of development, and they must work together to coordinate national as well as cross-border responses to worldwide cyberattacks. Collaboration among numerous centers has yielded noticeable outcomes; TF-CSIRT, CEENET, North America CSIRT meeting, FIRST SIGs, and E-COAT are instances of best practices, code of conduct, legislation recommendations, etc. that have been developed obtained through successful international teamwork (ENISA, 2006), but there are still barriers to the easy sharing and exchange of security information. One of the primary obstacles impeding efficient exchange of information is technological. The most recent technological platforms, instruments, open protocols, and technology standards for exchanging and managing security information.

2.3.1. Open Web-Platforms and Open-Source Tools

Making data sharing amongst CERTs more effective is the goal of several initiatives. These programs, which are motivated by the interests of the "cyber community," are created by CERTs, NATO, or commercial enterprises. Since most initiatives are open source, they tend to be flexible and user-friendly, and some have already attracted strong user communities. Instead of recognizing and comprehending bigger events that comprise tiny individual attacks, CERTs are still frequently concentrated on finding and resolving a single incident.

Correlation has been shown to be helpful in improving understanding, removing false positives, and identifying duplicates—even in the case of straightforward cyber incidents. The process of comparing distinct events from various sensors and data sources to find patterns and relationships that allow the identification of events that are part of a single attack or serve as indicators of more widespread malicious activity is known as incident correlation. It makes an event's nature more understandable, lessens the amount of work required to handle incidents, and automates the classification and forwarding of incidents that are only pertinent to a specific constituency. Correlation can be used to process data from several tools on a network under observation or to obtain incident data from several external sources.

Enterprise-level correlation is carried out using SIEM (Security Information and Event Management) tools, which are already on the market. These tools analyze data obtained from various datasets. Open-source solutions are typically more difficult to maintain, but commercial solutions are frequently more expensive. To fully utilize all of the data feeds available to a CERT/CSIRT team in order to identify the cause of an incident, there is still no standard framework in place. Although they are still in their infancy, emerging solutions like Megatron and AbuseHelper that allow correlation of external services that provide incident data are becoming available. Many CERTs understand the need for these tools, but they are still underutilized.

2.3.1.1. Threat-Intelligence Sharing

Because highly sophisticated attacks of today attempt to evade known signatures and simultaneously exploit multiple vulnerabilities on different systems, it has become increasingly difficult to reliably detect security breaches using only traditional signature-based methods. Because human delay in intelligence sharing is eliminated by machine-digestible formats, organizations must exchange higher-level threat-intelligence data in order to promptly adapt their systems to new threats. Here is a review and comparison of some of the most widely used intelligence sharing tools.

A technical feature that characterizes a known threat, an attack technique, or other artifacts left by an intrusion is described in an extensible XML schema that makes up OpenIOC (Open Indicators of Compromise), an open framework for exchanging threat intelligence. Businesses that become members of the OpenIOC community have access to threat intelligence that is exchanged among over a thousand entities. To facilitate the documentation and classification of forensic artifacts of an intrusion detected on a host or network, an organization must populate a basic XML schema with pertinent information about the IoCs. Indeed, one of the main benefits of using OpenIOC is its simplicity. Given that utilities to parse and convert XML into other formats are simple to implement, further usage of OpenIOCs is straightforward. Conversely, OpenIOC is primarily used for file-based IoCs and is not widely used outside of Mandiant products. It also offers little support for network-based IoCs.

Another open-source program created by the NATO Computer Incident Response Capability (NCIRC) and the Belgian Defense CERT is the Malware Information Sharing Platform (MISP). MISP offers a central Internet of things database that is structured and contains both technical and nontechnical information about malware and attacks. Relationships between malware, events, and attributes are automatically established. Through the generation of IDS, OpenIOC, plain text, and XML outputs, it facilitates system integration. Information sharing between trust groups is enabled automatically. Additionally, subcommunities can be established to share specific data with specific parties.

2.3.1.2. Data Correlation Tools

It is advised that data providers use correlation techniques to get rid of duplicate data and false positives. Before sending the data to their constituencies, data consumers are strongly advised to put their own solutions for dataset verification into practice in order to help improve the quality of the data. While some organizations attempt to apply event correlation mechanisms on datasets they receive as well as the output produced by their own monitoring solutions, it is not an easy task to identify common patterns of behavior and relationships between incidents. After reviewing the most popular open-source data correlation tools, we divided them into three categories: incident handling tools with information correlation features, SIEM tools, and generic correlation tools.

2.3.2. Technical Standards and Protocols

Operator assistance from automated systems is required to perform incident analysis and take effective defensive actions. Human analysis alone is no longer sufficient to deal with the growing complexity of the threat landscape, the increasing frequency of cyber events, and the growing amount of data that needs to be handled in cyber threat intelligence and threat-information sharing. As a result, automation is increasingly being used to develop defensive capabilities. To ensure a satisfactory degree of interoperability amongst organizations, standardized, structured threat information representations are also necessary, considering the variety of architectures, products, and systems that are utilized as data sources for information-sharing systems. There are obvious benefits to exchanging information in both machine-readable and human-readable formats. Although machines are best suited for performing basic tasks like data collection, classification, and correlation, human analysts play a major role in the creation of intelligence information as they carry out analysis types that are typically not amenable to automation.

Critical infrastructure incident handling requires a two-stage process where incident data are first automatically collected, parsed, filtered, and then carefully examined by human experts to produce intelligence. By using human experts who can recognize, highlight, and analyze the most pertinent data, this approach dramatically lowers the chance of missing important security information (lowering the false positive rate) and takes advantage of machine learning techniques to process large amounts of raw data in an initial manner.

Additionally, the intelligence analyst must evaluate the fidelity based on the sources and techniques used to generate the threat information due to the varying quality of shared threat information. The necessity for expressive, adaptable, extensible, automatable, and human-readable structured representations of threat information is highlighted by all of these problems.

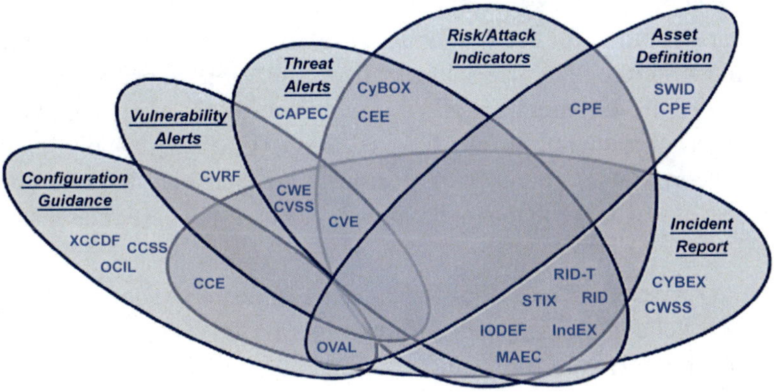

Figure 2.1. *Knowledge areas covered by the different existing standards.*

Source: https://www.researchgate.net/figure/Different-vulnerability-areas-covered-by-existing-standards-Skopik-2018_fig2_335064162.

Figure 2.1 provides an overview of current efforts by grouping concurrent standards into six knowledge areas: incident report (management), risk/attack indicators (intrusion detection), vulnerability alerts (analysis), threat alerts (analysis), and asset definition (inventory). The figure illustrates how certain standards are designed to be used in a particular area, while others cover a wider range of knowledge areas and offer a more comprehensive service. A number of the previously mentioned standards specify the format in which cyber threat data must be presented; they primarily rely on the sharing of IoCs. IoCs can be shared for the purpose of anticipating future attack attempts once they have been discovered through the process of incident response and computer forensics. Initiatives aim to standardize formats for IoC descriptions in order to achieve a more effective automated processing of these indicators.

2.3.2.1. OASIS Standards: STIX, TAXII, and Others

A technical committee of a US standardization organization, OASIS Cyber Threat Intelligence (CTI), supports several (community-driven) efforts to design standards for security-information sharing, including free and open source solutions for transport protocols and threat modeling. A standardized language for representing structured cyber threat information is called Structured Threat Information eXpression (STIX). With the STIX language, a broad range of use cases will be able to access comprehensive cyber threat information and adaptable mechanisms for handling it. The architecture of STIX includes a broad range of cyber threat information classes, such as cyber threat actors, adversary tactics, techniques, and procedures, exploit targets, courses of action, and indicators. An aggregate solution for each individual use case can be obtained by utilizing pre-existing structured languages like Cyber Observable Expression (CybOX), Malware Attribute Enumeration and Characterization (MAEC), and Common Attack Pattern Enumeration and Classification (CAPEC). Additionally, the language incorporates a number of flexibility mechanisms that allow for the independent use of some features, taking into account the particular use case in question.

A set of services and message-exchange mechanisms are defined by Trusted Automated eXchange of Indicator Information (TAXII). These are intended to be used for the detection, prevention, mitigation, and sharing of cyber threat information across organization and service boundaries. Organizations are able to share subsets of information with a chosen list of partners, improving their situational awareness regarding emerging threats. The recommended technique for automatically and securely exchanging data represented in the STIX language is TAXII. Use cases for TAXII include push and pull content distribution, private alerts and reports, public alerts or warnings, and the setup and administration of data sharing between parties. It has a modular architecture that supports a large number of different optional sharing models. Sharing models supported by TAXII include (but are not limited to):

- **Source-subscriber:** A single entity publishes information for a group of consumers.
- **P2P:** Direct relationships are established between a group of data consumers and producers. Every sharing transaction happens between people.
- **Hub-and-Spoke:** A collection of consumers and producers of data exchange information with one another. The data is routed to a central hub, which distributes it to each of the remaining spokes as needed.
- **Push or Pull Sharing:** Users of data can either request updates at their convenience (pull) or receive new data automatically (push).

2.3.2.2. IETF Standards: IODEF and RID

Two primary standards for describing (IODEF) and exchanging Real-time Internetwork Defense (RID) incident information were established by the Managed Incident Lightweight Exchange (MILE) IETF Working Group. The current RID and IODEF implementations are primarily restricted to the local exchange and technical description of IoCs; however, the standards are intended to facilitate large-scale sharing of complex incidents. An XML representation for exchanging incident information between administrative domains is provided by the Incident Object Description Exchange Format (IODEF) specification, which is outlined in RFC 5070. The data model includes details about hosts, networks, services that are operating on the systems, the impact of the activity, the attack technique and related forensic evidence, and methods for recording the workflow. Information about IODEF cybersecurity was intended to be transported via the RID protocol, which is outlined in RFC 6545. With a transport binding using HTTP/TLS, RID is adaptable enough to exchange other schemas or data models that are either independent of IODEF or embedded in it. For P2P models with higher security and privacy levels, RID is recommended.

2.3.3. Organizational Aspects of Tools Application

It should be noted that there is no "one size fits all" solution when it comes to tools. Powerful solutions typically require a significant amount of operating resources, which small and medium-sized businesses frequently cannot afford. On the other hand, protecting vital infrastructures is imperative. Every organization eventually needs to carefully evaluate the cost-benefit ratio. Overall, though, we can draw the conclusion that even for SMEs, some open-source solutions with sizable user bases can be implemented rather quickly and run at reasonable costs. In terms of standards, the OASIS standards are more powerful and have a larger community, but the IETF standards appear to be simpler to understand and implement. The release of STIX 2.0 and the choice to model artifacts in JSON rather than XML may hasten the adoption of technical standards and the desire to incorporate them into products.

2.4. CYBER INCIDENT INFORMATION-SHARING ASPECTS

Sharing information about cyber incidents is essential to bolstering group cybersecurity defenses. Organizations can obtain important insights that assist them in anticipating and mitigating potential risks by exchanging data on threats, vulnerabilities, and attack patterns. Sharing information facilitates cross-sector collaboration and allows for a more thorough understanding of the changing threat landscape. Additionally, it speeds up response times because timely threat intelligence dissemination enables organizations to take preventative action before an incident gets worse. Furthermore, information exchange fosters a feeling of camaraderie and confidence among participants, promoting a coordinated response to cyberthreats. Robust information-sharing mechanisms are crucial for mitigating the impact of incidents and protecting digital ecosystems as cyberattacks become more complex and frequent.

2.4.1. Public and Private Sector Cooperation

In order to improve capacities, resources, and procedures to handle cyber threats in critical infrastructures, public-private sector cooperation is encouraged by European and American regulations aimed at achieving cyber resilience. The U.S initiative (White House, 2013a) suggests growing the Enhanced Cybersecurity Services (ECS) information-sharing program (Department of Homeland Security, 2013) to allow critical infrastructure companies and governmental organizations to share cyber threat intelligence in almost real-time. The US government specifically hopes to enable the process of informing entities impacted by malicious cyber activity and to make it easier for businesses to share personal information with the authorities, particularly in cases of cybersecurity threats, by putting the CISA into effect. This bill contains privacy-related provisions that prohibit the sharing of data that is both known to be personally identifiable and unrelated to cybersecurity. These common cyber threat indicators may be used as evidence in crimes involving physical force as well as in the prosecution of cybercrimes. The European strategy (European Commission, 2013) aims to intensify the ongoing efforts to strengthen CIIP cooperation networks involving governments and private stakeholders by increasing international cooperation (e.g., by exchanging best practices, sharing early warnings, enabling joint incident management exercises, and so on). Moreover, by creating research and development initiatives and fostering closer ties between the EU's governments, businesses, and academic institutions, the EU encourages the improvement and eventual exploitation of the synergies between civilian and military approaches in safeguarding vital cyber assets. These documents do not specifically address information sharing regarding vulnerabilities impacting the ICT "supply chain". It is imperative that legal frameworks controlling the identification of potential threats, such as hardware back doors "built-in" by IT system manufacturers, be put in place.

2.4.2. International Cooperation

At the moment, the primary ways that incident-handling teams collaborate with one another globally are through periodic in-person meetings, conferences, mailing list subscriptions, and similar activities (ENISA, 2006). However, in order to achieve tighter and more comprehensive cooperation, more structured collaboration methods are needed. There are obstacles that restrict opportunities for cooperation or even prevent it altogether. International regulations that restrict the sharing and use of such information typically obstruct confidence between collaborating teams when handling sensitive data. Establishing a worthwhile degree of collaboration also has financial implications: while in-person interactions between interested parties are vital, they are not always inexpensive. Lack of service level agreements (SLAs) between cooperating entities frequently slows down team-to-team cooperation; the incident-handling process, for example, depends on strict request/response times that must be governed by shared regulations. Collaborating across borders requires teams to adhere to distinct legal frameworks. This problem affects the teams' service delivery and, in turn, how they handle specific types of attacks (ENISA, 2003). In particular, this relates to global collaboration. Furthermore, despite the fact that CERT teams were founded over 20 years ago, no established standard for CERT operations has been created or adopted. This severely hinders international cooperation and practically prevents information sharing.

While there are numerous barriers to cooperation amongst global stakeholders, it is advantageous to all parties involved. International cyber incident response teams that collaborate receive the greatest advantages when it comes to managing incidents together, managing projects, exchanging resources and information, and (social) networking. Possessing an ecosystem of global, interconnected sharing entities (governments, security agencies, providers of critical infrastructure, etc.), like the one put forth by Kaufmann and colleagues (2014), would in fact make it easier to acquire situational awareness and enable awareness of the present cybersecurity state of all the infrastructures under observation. This is the first action needed to handle incident response and cyber defense efficiently. Participating organizations can gain access to a wealth of pertinent security information that can be crucial in protecting against persistent cyber threats by being a part of these ecosystems. Resolved security issues, newly identified vulnerabilities, and any other pertinent information that is part of this shared knowledge are essential for safeguarding the infrastructures of the organizations and averting future incidents. Eventually, the variety of resources and skills within the sharing community will allow coordinated incident response methods to yield more effective outcomes.

2.4.3. Incident Information-Sharing Architecture

A common interoperable secure information-sharing infrastructure connects all Member States' national CERTs, which are in charge of managing incidents and national risks, according to the European directive (European Commission, 2016). This directive is important from an architectural perspective. Rather, the U.S plan calls for the DHS to run two national critical infrastructure centers, one for cyber and one for physical infrastructures. In order to provide situational awareness and integrated information to safeguard the physical and cyber aspects of critical infrastructure, they are meant to function in concert as focal points for stakeholders in that infrastructure.

While creating incident information-sharing architectures, P2P sharing models should also be considered, even though the previously mentioned approaches both advocate for centralized architectures. Previous research and studies on information sharing highlight the critical need for a more reactive infrastructure layout that can ensure high levels of responsiveness, availability, resilience, and trustworthiness from the sharing organization's point of view. Moreover, ad hoc incident response would be possible with the establishment of a P2P sharing infrastructure. Affected peers would be able to contact the most reliable and competent peers in the sharing network to request customized, anonymous security support in an emergency. A slowly reacting architecture could result from having a centralized entity handle the data collection, analysis, generation of incident, threat, and attack information, and distribution of indicators back to the sharing nodes. Moreover, the centrally collecting node would unavoidably become a single point of failure.

In addition, private businesses and organizations seem more inclined to divulge private information to reliable sources than to a single, centralized organization. This is evident from the examination of the collaboration amongst CERT teams. While there are existing and functioning regional and international CERT collaboration initiatives, an increasing number of sector cooperation groups have been established in recent times. Establishing P2P collaboration infrastructures and exchanging information with mutually trustworthy centers is a common practice among teams. However, this kind of approach increases the value and sensitivity of the shared information, necessitating a more dependable and secure communication infrastructure.

2.4.4. Data Collection, Information Analysis, and Intelligence Disclosure

When deploying their architecture, cyber defense centers should take various data-collection points into account. It is important to define and use interfaces that make it possible to gather unstructured data and open-source intelligence information. By combining information from "classic" data sources (such as CERTs' reports and indicators of compromise) with OSINT data, situational awareness can be attained more easily. The cybersecurity centers in Germany and the Netherlands that were the subject of this study already use this strategy, analyzing both open-source and proprietary data to stay up to date on the latest threats. As was already mentioned, gathering vast amounts of data necessitates more sophisticated analysis tools and techniques. Big data analytics methods should therefore be taken into consideration in order to aid in the creation of situational awareness (Maltby, 2011).

After data collection and analysis are complete, the process of sharing the data must be taken into account. High data transfer rates are ensured by automated sharing, but this also means that information is transmitted unsupervised. Serious liability issues could arise from this, and it might also be restricted by rules in global cooperative frameworks. Furthermore, there are times when sharing security information automatically isn't the best option because it might be too complicated, unclear, or doesn't fit into any existing model. Use free text reports that have been written, read, and interpreted by people in these situations. However, in order to conduct a thorough incident analysis, it is advisable to establish a combination of automated and manual information sharing whenever feasible.

Disclosing vulnerabilities, threats, and bugs to specific organizations is one of the primary goals of security information sharing. Such insights must be disclosed, and the process must be carefully planned. Publicly disclosing a vulnerability could put organizations at risk if a hot-fix or patch hasn't been released yet. Information exchange needs mutual trust between participants, and it won't work if it's done in full view of the public. Therefore, the sharing procedure should not start with the complete public disclosure of sensitive security information; instead, a responsible disclosure should be implemented. It is possible to make public sensitive and important information about vulnerabilities and bugs (as well as available exploits); however, in order to include a solution (bugfix, update, or configuration change) with the disclosure, the vendor must be notified in advance. In a similar vein, the U.S. Executive Order (White House, 2013a) requires authorized commercial service providers and operational implementers to receive access to sensitive and classified government-vetted cyber threat information. As a result, the DHS shares threat indicators with participating CSPs rather than CI entities directly.

2.4.5. Data Format and Exchange Protocols

Within the framework of the incident-sharing architecture among the expert centers, organizations, agencies, and owners and operators of critical infrastructure, the most important factors are the caliber and promptness of the information and intelligence shared. Sharing communities currently exchange indicators using a combination of proprietary and standard mechanisms; as this chapter explains, different protocols are used to exchange different types of data, depending on the size of the sharing system.

The European directive requires that the structure and protocols for the gathering and exchange of comparable and appropriate risk and incident data by the relevant authorities be specified in the Union's NIS cooperation plan. Similar to this, one of the objectives of the US PPD is to facilitate effective information exchange by identifying baseline data and system requirements, data formats, availability and accessibility, and the capacity to exchange different information classifications. The American Cybersecurity Information Sharing Act (CISA) "Receipt Procedures" outline the methods for obtaining, managing, and sharing shared information, including when the DHS Automated Indicator Sharing feature is in use. It explains how the national cybersecurity centers' protocols and standards, in addition to the STIX and TAXII specifications, are utilized by the DHS to acquire, filter, analyze, and distribute such information in real-time. These machine-to-machine specifications must be able to be used for communication by any entity taking part in the incident sharing capability. Furthermore, in order to facilitate sharing both within and across sectors, the US cybersecurity framework (NIST, 2014) promotes the development of standard approaches in the data exchange mechanism. Security automated technologies should be able to identify compromised systems, detect historical attacks in operational data archives, and assist in the detection of upcoming attacks when organizations share indicators.

REFERENCES

1. Abrams, L. C., Cross, R., Lesser, E., & Levin, D. Z. (2003). Nurturing interpersonal trust in knowledge-sharing networks. *Academy of Management Executive, 17*(4), 64–77.
2. Agrawal, R., Evfimievski, A., & Srikant, R. (2003). Information sharing across private databases. In *Proceedings of the 2003 ACM SIGMOD International Conference on Management of Data* (pp. 86–97). ACM. San Diego, CA. https://doi.org/10.1145/872757.872771.
3. Arora, A., Telang, R., & Xu, H. (2008). Optimal policy for software vulnerability disclosure. *Management Science, 54*(4), 642–656.
4. Arstechnica. (2013). Spamhaus DDoS grows to internet-threatening size. Retrieved from: http://arstechnica.com/security/2013/03/spamhaus-ddos-grows-to-internet-threatening-size/ (accessed on 9 October 2024).
5. BSA-The Software Alliance, & Galexia. (2015). Asia-Pacific cybersecurity dashboard—A path to a secure global cyberspace. Retrieved from: http://www.bsa.org/APACcybersecurity (accessed on 9 October 2024).
6. Clarke, R. (2011). China cyberassault on America. *Wall Street Journal.*
7. Dacey, R. (2003). Homeland security: Information sharing responsibilities, challenges, and key management issues. U.S. General Accounting Office. Retrieved from: https://books.google.at/books?id=R2n-PQAACAAJ (accessed on 9 October 2024).
8. D'Amico, A., Whitley, K., Tesone, D., O'Brien, B., & Roth, E. (2005). Achieving cyber defense situational awareness: A cognitive task analysis of information assurance analysts. In *Proceedings of the Human Factors and Ergonomics Society Annual Meeting* (Vol. 49, pp. 229–233). SAGE Publications. Orlando, FL.
9. Dandurand, L., & Serrano, O. (2013). Towards improved cyber security information sharing. In *Proceedings of the 5th International Conference on Cyber Conflict (CyCon 2013)* (pp. 1–16). IEEE. Tallinn, Estonia.
10. Denise, Z., & James, L. (2015). Cyber threat information sharing. Department of Homeland Security. Enhanced cybersecurity services program. Retrieved from: http://www.dhs.gov/sites/default/files/publications/ecs_final_factsheet_08182014.pdf (accessed on 9 October 2024).
11. ENISA. (2010). Incentives and challenges to information sharing. Retrieved from: https://www.enisa.europa.eu/news/enisa-news/incentives-challenges-for-cyber-security-information-sharing-in-europe-identified (accessed on 9 October 2024).

12. ENISA. (2013a). Detect, share, protect—Solutions for improving threat data exchange among CERTs. Retrieved from: https://www.enisa.europa.eu/activities/cert/support/data-sharing/detect-share-protect-solutions-for-improving-threat-data-exchange-among-certs/at_download/fullReport (accessed on 9 October 2024).
13. European Commission. (2016). Directive (EU) 2016/1148 of the European Parliament and of the Council of 6 July 2016 concerning measures for a high common level of security of network and information systems across the Union. Retrieved from: http://eur-lex.europa.eu/legal-content/EN/TXT/?uri=uriserv:OJ.L_.2016.194.01.0001.01.ENG&toc=OJ:L:2016:194:TOC (accessed on 9 October 2024).
14. Farwell, J. P., & Rohozinski, R. (2011). Stuxnet and the future of cyber war. *Survival, 53*(1), 23–40.
15. Fernandez Vazquez, D., Pastor Acosta, O., Brown, S., Reid, E., & Spirito, C. (2012). Conceptual framework for cyber defense information sharing within trust relationships. In *2012 4th International Conference on Cyber Conflict (CYCON)* (pp. 1–17). IEEE. Tallinn, Estonia.
16. Gal-Or, E., & Ghose, A. (2005). The economic incentives for sharing security information. *Information Systems Research, 16*(2), 186–208.
17. Golle, P., Leyton-Brown, K., Mironov, I., & Lillibridge, M. (2001). Incentives for sharing in peer-to-peer networks. In *Electronic Commerce* (pp. 75–87). Springer. Tampa, FL. http://dl.acm.org/citation.cfm?id=501193 (accessed on 9 October 2024).
18. Gordon, L. A., Loeb, M. P., & Lucyshyn, W. (2003). Sharing information on computer systems security: An economic analysis. *Journal of Accounting Public Policy, 22*(6), 461–485.
19. Harrison, K., & White, G. (2012). Information sharing requirements and framework needed for community cyber incident detection and response. In *2012 IEEE Conference on Technologies for Homeland Security (HST)* (pp. 463–469). IEEE.
20. Helmbrecht, U., Purser, S., Cooper, G., Ikonomou, D., Marinos, L., & Ouzounis, E. (2013). ENISA: Cybersecurity cooperation: Defending the digital frontline. Retrieved from: https://www.enisa.europa.eu/publications/cybersecurity-cooperation-defending-the-digital-frontline (accessed on 9 October 2024).
21. Herzog, S. (2011). Revisiting the Estonian cyber attacks: Digital threats and multinational responses. *Journal of Strategic Security, 4*(2), 4.
22. International Organization for Standardization (ISO). (2015). ISO/IEC 27010: Information technology—Security techniques—Information

security management for inter-sector and inter-organizational communications. Retrieved from: https://www.iso.org/standard/65109.html (accessed on 9 October 2024).

23. Kaufmann, H., Hutter, R., Skopik, F., & Mantere, M. (2014). A structural design for a pan-European early warning system for critical infrastructures. In *Elektrotechnik und Informationstechnik*. Springer.

24. Maltby, D. (2011). Big data analytics. In *Communication and Information in Society, Technology and Work* (Vol. 48). ASIST; Proceedings of the 74th ASIS&T Annual Meeting: Bridging the Gulf: Communication and Information in Society, Technology, and Work. New Orleans, LA, October 9–12, 2011. https://www.asist.org/events/annual-meeting/past/ (accessed on 9 October 2024).

25. Miller, C. (2007). The legitimate vulnerability market: The secretive world of 0-day exploit sales. In *Proceedings of the Workshop on the Economics of Information Security (WEIS)* (pp. 1–10). Pittsburgh, PA, June 7–8, 2007.

26. Parameswaran, M., Susarla, A., & Whinston, A. B. (2001). P2P networking: An information-sharing alternative. *Computer, 34*(7), 31–38.

27. Phillips, C. E., Jr., Ting, T., & Demurjian, S. A. (2002). Information sharing and security in dynamic coalitions. In *Proceedings of the Seventh ACM Symposium on Access Control Models and Technologies* (pp. 87–96). ACM. Monterey, CA. http://dl.acm.org/citation.cfm?id=507711&picked=prox (accessed on 9 October 2024).

28. Shepherd, S. (2003). Vulnerability disclosure: How do we define responsible disclosure? *GIAC SEC Practical Repository*. SANS Institute, *9*.

CHAPTER 3

FROM MONITORING LOGGING, AND NETWORK ANALYSIS TO THREAT INTELLIGENCE EXTRACTION

Contents

INTRODUCTION

Today's information and communication technologies are highly connected and important, which drives the need for a more coordinated approach to cybersecurity than is currently typical. We contend that one strategy essential to realizing a concerted push for cybersecurity is the sharing of threat intelligence between states and corporations.

It is essential that suggested solutions take into consideration the organization's and the state's current security installations in order to promote involvement and enhance acceptance. Furthermore, information sharing solutions must incorporate the current solutions. Two methods exist for this integration to take place. It is unrealistic to expect that all current monitoring solutions and processes will be changed to support cross-organizational information sharing, so the viability of data generated and monitored at the local level already needs to be carefully considered in order to produce shareable threat intelligence. Second, the information that is shared must facilitate the ongoing organizational procedures that are in place. This includes the automatic incorporation of shared data into technical solutions, such as intrusion detection systems' and security incident and event management (SIEM) installations' automatic import of threat intelligence. It also implies that procedures for incident response and operational security must be expanded.

3.1. AN OVERVIEW OF CONCEPTS IN CYBER THREAT INTELLIGENCE

To comprehend the efficient utilization of data produced and employed at the organizational level for security analysis within the framework of cyber threat intelligence, it is imperative to establish a common language for various facets of information that can be shared. Furthermore, using threat intelligence data requires an understanding of one specific crucial concept in particular: asset management.

3.1.1. Artifacts in Cyber Threat Intelligence

3.1.1.1. Observables

The lowest level of data used in threat intelligence is called an observable. Any measurable event or stateful property that can be found in the cyber domain is referred to by this term. A modification made to a file or a rule in an intrusion detection system (IDS) that is triggered are instances of event-based observables. Conversely, stateful properties consist of the value of a system variable, registry key, or hash value of a file on the system. Because of this, determining the nature of an event or property—that is, whether it is malevolent or benign—is impossible when it is categorized as observable. The elements of a system that can be measured or detected make up the set of observables in that particular system. The primary distinction between indicators and observables is this.

3.1.1.2. Indicator

An indicator is an observable that suggests that:

- A cyber attack is imminent.
- A cyber attack is currently present in the system.
- The system has been compromised at a previous point in time.

In this way, an indicator links malicious behavior to the states or events that are described by observables. The observable examples listed above can also serve as examples of indicators. A file's hash value can be used to determine whether or not the file it contains is known to be malicious software. Likewise, an ejected IDS rule is probably a sign of undesirable or malevolent system activity. Furthermore, it is possible to logically combine simple indicators to create more complex rules regarding a particular compromise.

3.1.2. Asset Management

Asset management is essential for an organization to filter information streams because cyber threat intelligence is shared in the form of indicators or threat intelligence reports. Not every organization or party will find value in all shared information. A software product's discovery of a new vulnerability only matters if the organization is using the product's vulnerable version. If so, in order to determine whether the suggested courses of action are feasible, it is imperative that you promptly identify all exposed instances as well as the dependent components. The corporate procedure known as IT asset management ensures that hardware and software components are visible and controllable. Both NIST and ISO have published standards and guidelines that offer a more comprehensive view of asset management, including the 19770 suite. Furthermore, formal procedures and checklists for designing and running IT services in accordance with the primary business needs are established by the Information Technology Infrastructure Library (ITIL), which serves as the foundation for the ISO/IEC 20000 standard on IT service management. Asset and Configuration Management as well as Software Asset Management are also included in these procedures. Best practices for IT governance and management are provided by ISACA through the Control Objectives for Information and Related Technologies framework. Their scope is comparable to that of the ISO/IEC 38500 on Corporate Governance for Information Technologies, which addresses the following six principles: Human behavior, Conformance, Performance, Strategy, Acquisition, and Responsibility in the governance of information technologies.

An overview of an asset's lifecycle and the duties that asset management must perform is provided in Figure 3.1. Be aware that IT systems contain a vast range of assets. These could be anything from services or software elements to actual network hardware. The general asset management approach is generally applicable, even though the management requirements for each type of asset vary. This chapter will not address the intricacy involved in planning and acquiring new assets. At this point, it should be mentioned that an asset's lifecycle begins long before it is actually deployed and doesn't finish until the consequences of its disposal are taken into account and lessened in the organization's remaining infrastructure.

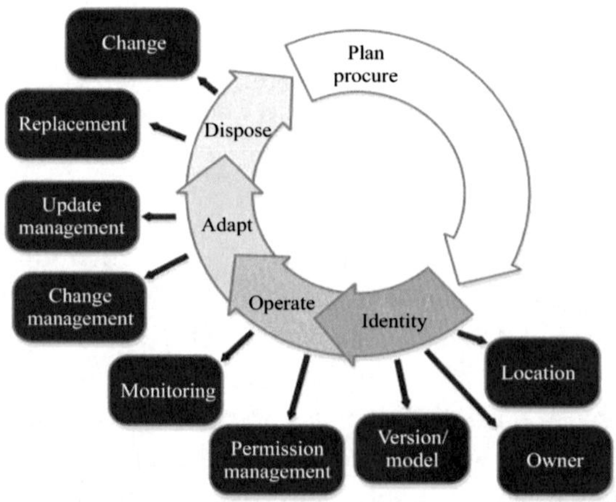

Figure 3.1. *IT asset life cycle.*

Source: Ivo Friedberg, Markus Wurzenberger, Abdullah Al Balushi, Boojoong Kang, From Monitoring, Logging, and Network Analysis to Threat Intelligence Extraction, ISBN 9781138031821.

3.1.2.1. Asset Identification

Correlation and collection of asset information are steps in the asset identification process. For further information, the reader is directed to NIST report IR 7693, which offers a formal specification of asset identification. Identification of assets fulfills the following objectives:

- **Identification:** In various organizational contexts, assets must be accurately identified. This is required in order to link monitoring data to the appropriate asset. This should not be confused with the lifecycle step for asset identification, which outlines how to gather this information about each asset.
- **Responsibility:** Every asset must have an owner who is in charge of overseeing its upkeep throughout its life and who can be held accountable for poor management.
- **Structured Access to Asset Information:** Every asset's properties must be kept and made available in a central database. This is required to evaluate the system's susceptibility to a recently received report or indicator as soon as possible.

Each asset should have the following data stored in order to meet these objectives such as:

- **Identifiers:** An asset has distinct identifiers and appears in various organizational contexts. Office PCs are physically identified by an inventory number, and they are given a location (such as a room number) to facilitate easy finding. It is also assigned an IP address within the company's network. Thus, if the PC's IP address is not saved as an extra identifier, it will be impossible to correlate traffic coming from the PC with the asset. To enable effective management, enough identifiers must be saved for every asset.
- **Owner:** Every asset within the organization must be possessed by a legitimate individual. Ensuring responsible operation and management of the asset is crucial. Furthermore, in an incident where the asset in question was mismanaged, only a real person can be held accountable.
- **Asset Information:** A central asset database should hold several properties for each asset, which can subsequently be filtered. It is crucial to react suitably and promptly to recently disclosed indicators. A list of computers running a software product is insufficient if a new exploit is discovered for a particular version of the product unless it also includes the installed version (and effective configuration) of each instance. In a similar vein, a network router vendor discovered an issue with several of the components that were sold. All impacted machines' model numbers are listed and made accessible to the public. But in order to compare the impacted model numbers in the public list with the internal list of the model numbers of the deployed devices, a company also needs this list. In the event that there isn't

a company-specific list of model numbers, it becomes inefficient to physically locate and verify each hardware device.

3.1.2.2. Asset Operation

The asset needs to be managed while it is in use after it has been correctly identified. There are two key components to this. One is making sure permissions are managed on time. The permissions people have given to assets should be updated in accordance with changes in project assignments or staff. The asset's owner bears the responsibility for maintaining its security. Observation is the second element. Since indicators are shared, it is necessary to constantly watch each asset's behavior for these indicators in order to ensure prompt incident response and attack attempt detection.

3.1.2.3. Asset Adaptation

Over an asset's lifetime, a variety of environmental changes necessitate adaptations. The following are the primary reasons for adaptations:

- New details regarding the asset come to light. For instance, mitigation techniques ought to be triggered by a CVE that details a software component vulnerability.
- The asset is available for updates. Organization-wide update policies that specify how updates must be handled should be in place for every kind of asset. Managing newly created user accounts and modified configurations falls under this as well.
- An associated asset is modified. Every asset communicates with every other asset. Typically, these exchanges are precisely defined to guarantee proper functioning. As such, in the event that one of the associated assets is modified, they must be assessed. For instance, interoperability restrictions might be broken by installing software updates in response to recently discovered vulnerabilities.

Consideration must be given to these adaptations in order to achieve secure asset operation. The modifications must also be accurately recorded in the asset database. You'll see that the database is configured at the start of the asset's operational phase, during the asset identification process. If it is not kept current, judgments about the organization's risk level will be made using information that is out of date.

3.1.2.4. Asset Disposal

The asset must be disposed of properly before it can be deleted from the asset database, which completes the asset life cycle. As was previously stated, assets are interdependent. Therefore, it's crucial to resolve all dependencies before removing an asset. Be aware that proper change management in the associated assets will be required for this. Because of the dependencies, assets are frequently replaced rather than removed completely. In this instance, a new asset is presented, which calls for its accurate identification in return. If relationships that were established for the previous asset can be carried over and updated for the replacement instead of starting from scratch, this process may be simpler. However, there is a chance that unmonitored assets that are still there will only be deleted from the asset management system. If it is not certain that a replacement can support every dependency, this is frequently the case. In this instance, the new replacement asset is used in parallel with the old asset. The old asset is eventually replaced, but it is never disposed of properly. Threat actors can take advantage of the unmonitored vulnerabilities that result from its availability and lack of management.

3.2. RAW MONITORING DATA: ORIGIN, STRUCTURE, AND INSIGHTS

Monitoring the state and behavior of systems is necessary to identify indicators and attacks. Different kinds of data elements are created during monitoring, and analysis tools then use this data to make inferences about the status of a system under observation. Understanding the data sources that the analysis techniques can access is essential to comprehending how exchanging cyber threat intelligence can enhance the general security of information and communications technology (ICT) infrastructures. Three sources of monitoring data are introduced in this section: file and process information, network traffic, and log data. Every type of data has information about it that is organized in an identical manner. Following a brief summary, the observables that are described by the relevant data are described. An explanation of the required monitoring infrastructure comes next. Lastly, common evasion strategies are discussed, which attackers use to conceal indicators from discovery. It's critical to comprehend how the monitoring infrastructure is installed in a functioning network in order to comprehend it.

3.2.1. Log Data

All processes that are executed in computer systems and ICT network environments leave automatically generated traces in log data. As a result, it protocols every event that takes place in these kinds of network infrastructures. Log data is typically presented in a text format that is readable by humans.

This facilitates access to the offered information. Unlike other data sources, like network packets, the information is accessible without requiring any pre-processing that takes a lot of time, computation, or resources. Log data is therefore a useful tool for cybersecurity analysis.

Several abstraction levels are involved in logging, including the data link layer (switch logs), the network and transport layer (firewall logs), and the application layer (web server logs, data base logs, mail server logs, etc.). The fact that security analysis typically uses only lower log levels—warning and error logs, for example—is one disadvantage of logging. Verbose logging-on information, however, is necessary to conduct a thorough analysis; this is frequently neglected. The task in question is resource-intensive and generates substantial amounts of data that require storage, potentially impacting the target systems' performance. Additionally, when collecting log data, organizations must guarantee the privacy of both their customers and employees. Sensitive information including IP addresses, machine fingerprints, user names, and machine names can be found in log data. When users inadvertently enter their passwords into the name field of a login dialogue rather than the password field, occasionally their passwords are visible in readable format.

3.2.1.1. Observables

Typically, a single protocolled event and a time stamp make up a single log line. The date and time of the logged event are contained in the time stamp. The information about the day, month, and year, along with the time the log line was generated, is dependent on how the logging is configured. An ICT network process, a network connection, or any other action performed by a user or a program are all described by the event. The event contains information about the location and reason for the log message's creation, whereas the time stamp contains information about when the log message was generated.

Log files contain protocoled events, such as observables of malicious activity occurring within a computer network. Log data contains observables of malicious program processes and network connections in addition to user activities. Depending on how the logging is set up, data regarding the sent and received content is also retained. Every log message is assigned a severity level between 0 and 7, which are emergency (0), alert (1), critical (2), error (3), warning (4), notice (5), informational (6), and debug (7), when the protocol standard syslog is used to generate log data. Different tiers of log messages are stored, depending on how the deployed logging is configured. Only events describing irregular system behavior and, consequently, security-related observables that result in program and system crashes are present in log messages between levels 0 and 3.

Higher severity log messages don't always contain security-relevant observables. As a result, in order to separate out the pertinent data describing security-relevant observables, like the following, security analysis tools are needed:

- **Application-Specific Observables:** which contain data unique to a monitored application and related to security. One log line from an SSH server may indicate a malicious event. For example, the log message may describe the login of a system administrator using an unknown IP address assigned to a suspicious location, such as a distant country from the last login location.
- **Environment-Specific Observables:** which describe system behavior that is only malicious for a specific ICT network environment. This may be a captured exchange of data between various hosts, like when a client computer connects to a Web server using a particular browser that is suspected of being used by malicious software.
- **Collective Observables:** which are described by a group of log lines. A malicious sequence of log lines, an anomalous frequency of a log line, or an anomalous number of log lines within a given time window can all result in a collective observable. These kinds of observables can be set off, for instance, by a malicious access pattern or a database dump that generates an unusually high number of queries.

Log data is a valuable source for observables, particularly for legacy systems and products with small market shares that are frequently not directly supported by security solution providers and vendors (e.g., SIEM vendors that provide parsers for well-known products).

3.2.1.2. Monitoring Infrastructure

Log files are often saved as plain text files by default. In the event of a system crash, this has the benefit of being easily accessible. The issue of log data accessibility being dependent on the availability of the database itself arises when utilizing a database format. The volume of generated log data is growing exponentially as a result of the growing digitization in recent years. For this reason, appropriate log management solutions are required—and not just in large-scale network settings. This volume of data needs to be handled by these. Log management includes the gathering, storing, and analysis of log data in addition to the searching and reporting of log data. For the majority of programming platforms, there exist so-called logging frameworks, which facilitate the incorporation of appropriate logging functionality in new software products. Three parts are typically needed for logging: a handler, a formatter, and a logger. It is the logger's responsibility to gather the data that needs to be logged. Usually, a different logger is defined for every class. The logger's configuration determines the final level of detail at which data is logged. It is possible to define this so-called severity level for every logger. The logging framework determines whether to log a message or not based on how the severity level is configured. Following the logger's transmission of the log data to the logging framework, the formatter receives the given object—typically represented as a binary object—and transforms it into a string for output. Ultimately, the handler shows the generated log line in a console, saves it to a file, or forwards it to another program while it watches for log messages at or above the specified level of severity.

Syslog is the widely used standard for sending log messages. The main benefit of the syslog protocol is its broad compatibility with various devices and network elements. Sending log messages to a centralized location—a so-called syslog server—is its main function.

Thus, syslog helps to set up centralized logging. Centralized logging streamlines the correlation of data gathered at various network locations and greatly eases log management. While the syslog standard has many benefits, it also has some disadvantages. To begin with, there is no standard for formatting messages in Syslog.

As a result, there is an inconsistent experience because each developer can specify their own format for log messages. By default, Syslog sends log messages across the network using the User Datagram Protocol (UDP). Due to packet loss and network congestion, log messages may be lost because UDP is a connectionless protocol. The Transmission Control Protocol is a more dependable protocol for sending log data (TCP).

3.2.1.3. Evasion Techniques

Although log data is crucial for identifying security breaches and intruders, an attacker may also utilize it to obtain information about an ICT network's infrastructure. To gain insight into the logging mechanisms in place, one should pay particular attention to the (stealthy) passive phase of advanced persistent threats. By manipulating the logs during the active phase, this information can then be used to conceal the attack. For instance, a hacker may turn off the database log to conceal a SQL-injection. As a result, safeguarding the logging against manipulation is vital. Digital signatures that can be appended to newly created log entries provide a straightforward solution; nevertheless, practical limitations in terms of space and processing power, as in sensor networks, may make this solution impractical. Therefore, it seems that effective yet portable safety precautions are required. In terms of security, centralized logging solutions are superior to decentralized logging solutions because: (1) only one node needs to be secured; and (2) in the event of an attacker taking over a Web server, they can only alter local log lines and not the centrally stored version because, when used in conjunction with a data diode, data only flows to the log server and no write operations are performed on old data.

3.2.1.4. Current Applications

There are many uses for data logging in the ICT industry. A crucial source of information for system monitoring, which includes knowledge and data acquisition, is log data. As such, system monitoring is necessary for system analysis and diagnostics. Logs are examined for their empirical and statistical characteristics in order to learn about alterations in the system's behavior. For example, log data can be used for error analysis in this course.

In the course of digital forensics, log data is also examined. Digital forensics is a broad field. It can be used to look into the source of an attack and learn more about the perpetrator and the attack's goal after it has been detected. Yet cybersecurity is not the only application for digital forensic analysis.

It can also be used to identify the causes of other system malfunctions, such as incorrect configuration or malfunctioning network components.

Log data can be used for real-time intrusion detection in addition to forensic analysis. Consequently, one can use signature-based detection techniques, which examine individual log lines to spot unusual and malicious system activity that could be brought on by malware or an attacker. Advanced persistent threats (APTs) are one type of targeted attack that can be detected using more advanced anomaly detection techniques, such as those that correlate log lines over time.

Database logs are useful for backing up and restoring database content in the event of a system failure or destruction due to unauthorized access. It is simpler to recover transactions and activities from log data that are saved in text format as opposed to corrupted binary files.

The effectiveness of implemented firewall rules can be verified using firewall logs. Additionally, they can offer details if application errors are caused by the firewall. Additionally, they can be used to identify malicious activity, such as repeated failed attempts to get past the firewall—a sign that an intrusion attempt has been made. Unusual outgoing connections may also be a sign that malware is being used to initiate an attack.

3.2.2. Network Traffic

3.2.2.1. Observables

Networks are created as IT systems are connected, allowing assets to communicate with one another. Network traffic is the manifestation of this communication, from which observables can be retrieved and contrasted with indicators. Packet-switched network protocols are typically used in corporate IT networks to transport traffic. These protocols divide the information bit stream into several packets, each of which is transmitted over the network separately. At the target, the entire information stream is then assembled again. Threat actors must use network communications during incidents to carry out different attack steps like exfiltration, lateral movement, and reconnaissance. Events that occur during the incident will either add new traffic or change already-existing network traffic, which can be identified using indicators and tracked using a variety of observables.

The payload is placed inside of a "envelope" to manage packet transmission. It is made up of a protocol header that is appended prior to the data and a tail that is appended subsequent to the data. The protocol header provides instructions on how the packet should be handled both during transmission and upon reception. This procedure is carried out several times in a layered manner to support various levels of abstraction for network operations, in order to manage the intricacy of data transmission. For this layered networking approach, the ISO OSI model as specified in ISO 7498 is the most widely used model. It outlines the seven levels that are utilized to transfer data between two applications. Each layer affixes an additional envelope around the packet as the data pass through it.

This implies that in order to reveal the network layer header, each router in the network discards layer one and layer two protocol data. Before the actual transmission begins, it selects the appropriate port to forward the packet on, modifies the protocol as needed (e.g., by changing IP addresses), and rewraps it into layers two and one.

The TCP/IP model, which is commonly used on the Internet, is an alternative to the ISO/OSI model. Only four layers are defined—Application, Transport, Internet, and Data Link—which partially addresses the functions of several layers in the ISO/OSI model.

There are two methods for keeping an eye on network activity. Only the information contained in the protocol envelopes is saved and examined during traffic flow monitoring. On the other hand, packet captures save the entire packet, including the payload and header data. Both the envelope and the payload of a packet contain observables. They are divided into four categories in this chapter: payload, general traffic, application-oriented, and transport-oriented observables. Payload observables necessitate access to the actual data, whereas transport-oriented and application-oriented observables are present in the protocol envelopes. Helper protocols, which are utilized implicitly by network components, or traffic occurrence analysis over time are sources of general traffic observables.

3.2.2.1.1. Transport-Oriented Observables

The packet envelopes that are introduced at layers 1-4 of the ISO/OSI model contain transport-oriented observables. The most often used observables in network traffic monitoring are those found in the packet headers. This section focuses on the Internet protocol suite, also known as TCP/IP, due to its widespread acceptance and use. It might have something to do with the OSI model, in which IP is the network layer protocol and TCP is the transport layer protocol. Combined, layers 5-7 form the application layer.

These protocol header fields contain a variety of transport-oriented observables. A network device reads the packet when it arrives and deciphers the IP header to determine how to handle and route it to reach its destination. The TCP header fields can be recorded and used as observables once the encapsulated protocol (in this case, TCP) can be interpreted. The source and destination IP addresses of a particular packet are examples of observables. Finding a botnet client on the network under observation is one way these observables can be used as indicators.

The packets with the questionable IP address in the source IP address field can be identified each time the malware establishes a connection with the command and control server. Monitoring network traffic to identify beaconing is another example. The malware periodically pings the C2 infrastructure to inform it that it is prepared to receive new commands after the host becomes infected for the first time.

Typically, this traffic uses well-known protocol ports that are probably not blocked by firewalls on active networks. But frequently, the traffic's destination port is unusual for normal traffic. This is because the traffic is frequently passed through a number of proxies that are not connected to the attackers. Benign services use these proxies on a regular basis. Therefore, it is necessary to route the malicious traffic to unbound ports that are not typically used. Lastly, port scans can be carried out using TCP and other protocols by using programs like nmap. The identified asset can be fingerprinted, for example, to determine its operating system, based on the specific settings in the response packets. The number of connection attempts and the range of ports that are probed can be analyzed as part of network traffic monitoring to identify this behavior. Packet header data has the drawback of being easily manipulated during an incident.

Depending on the protocol being used, the adversary may arbitrarily alter different parts of the header in order to avoid detection.

3.2.2.1.2. Application-Oriented Observables

Rather than using traditional transmission methods, the application layer protocols are in charge of higher level service functionality. Because of this, they frequently have important observables that can be used to identify when well-known application protocols are being used maliciously. The use of well-known protocols is highly advantageous for threat actors. Because so much legitimate traffic is sent using the same protocols, malicious traffic can be hidden more easily amongst it.

It is feasible to keep an eye on whether the corresponding underlying application is being used in the expected manner based on application layer observables. Probing may be an indication of the reconnaissance phase of an HTTP connection attempt made to a variety of popular paths in the administration section of popular content management systems (CMSs). These days, though, most people regard these brute-force attempts as typical noise on any machine that can be accessed over the Internet.

The header data in emails sent via SMTP serves as another illustration. They include the path taken by the mail between the sender and the recipient across several mail servers. Using this data, one can identify questionable paths between two email addresses, which may be a sign of a spoof message. Emails that seem to originate from the same office network (for example, from one employee to another within the same company) but appear to exit the domain before reentering it can be identified in this way.

3.2.2.1.3. Payload

The packet payload is another source of observables. A monitoring system can disassemble the data that is contained in the protocols to find harmful content. This feature is particularly useful in Intelligent Control Systems (ICSs) where assets communicate clear-text measurements and control actions. Indicators can be created with knowledge of the underlying physical system to identify malicious or inaccurate measurements or set points. Nonetheless, it can also be applied to conventional Internet applications.

The use of encryption techniques, particularly with the widespread adoption of SSL/TLS, makes payload analysis more challenging. From a security perspective, encryption must be promoted; however, adversaries also frequently use it to evade payload monitoring.

3.2.2.1.4. Traffic-Specific Observables

Networks that use packet switching are dynamically configured. This is the primary factor behind the modern Internet's success. It was initially intended to resist significant physical attacks. Network equipment and hosts use helper protocols to connect the network nodes and guarantee connectivity wherever possible in order to dynamically handle the network setup. These protocols continue to offer attack points in contemporary networks since they were created without consideration for IT security. Since they typically don't employ encryption, they can be easily used as observables and for reconnaissance.

Clients connecting to IP networks managed by DHCP use the Dynamic Host Configuration Protocol (DHCP). A time-limited DHCP lease is used by a DHCP server to grant clients a free IP address in response to their requests. Since DHCP lacks encryption, a malicious or infected network node may function as a rogue DHCP server. Consequently, it is possible for manipulated leases to be issued, which may result in a man-in-the-middle attack or a denial-of-service attack (invalid IP addresses preventing the client from connecting) (e.g., when the lease specifies a wrong DNS server for DNS lookups, which redirects HTTP traffic to malicious servers).

DHCP can also be used to identify newly connected hosts to a network. The packets under observation may reveal rogue machines transmitting erroneous DHCP leases or clients attempting to spoof DHCP requests in order to gain control of IP addresses.

When the IP address of a machine is known, the Address Resolution Protocol (ARP), which is not routed, is used to determine the MAC address of that machine inside the boundaries of a single network. This is significant because, more often than not, the TCP/IP information—rather than the link layer information (MAC)—is utilized to determine the intended recipient of a data stream. To reduce communication, IP to MAC mappings that are known once are kept in a local buffer. A broadcast request, also known as an ARP request, is sent to every machine in the local network when the mapping of an intended receiver is unknown. This request is received by all machines; however, only the machine that has an active interface with the requested IP address returns a response with its own MAC address.

Even with well-known flaws (like ARP cache poisoning), this protocol's broadcast feature makes it an excellent choice for keeping an eye on how computers behave within a network.

Control and error messages are used by the Internet Control Message Protocol (ICMP) to regulate IP traffic. Usually, networking hardware uses it directly without a user's help. On the other hand, ICMP in the user domain is demonstrated by the ping command and the trace route. The ICMP echo command is used by pings to find out if a host is reachable and available. In a similar vein, trace routes use host unreachable ICMP error messages and time-to-live exceeded in transit. Many switches filter ICMP messages because of their vulnerabilities. On the other hand, attackers frequently use them for reconnaissance, and network administrators use them for fault analysis.

It is also possible to find and use other patterns in a stream of network traffic as observables. One example of this would be a node's traffic load that deviates from typical traffic patterns. In a similar vein, traffic patterns among particular assets can be determined. An internal database server is not expected to receive the same volume of traffic as a public Webserver that is directed towards locations outside the company's boundaries. In the second scenario, a notable rise in data traffic leaving the business network may be a sign of data exfiltration.

3.2.2.2. Monitoring

Obtaining a comprehensive view of network traffic is a challenge in network traffic monitoring. Network switches are used in modern packet-switched networks to distribute packets to the designated recipients. Only the packets pertinent to each host are received by the hosts. One host cannot provide a whole picture, so host-level monitoring is helpful for error analysis but not for network monitoring. Monitoring network traffic at the network switches that stand between segregated subnetworks is the standard method instead. Monitoring is installed on the network switches between the different domains; for example, between the Corporate Network and the public Internet. Industrial network switches provide so-called mirroring ports. Every network packet seen on one switch port can be configured on the switch to send a copy of that packet out through the mirroring port. The traffic collection and analysis monitoring infrastructure is connected to this mirroring port. Port mirroring in Cisco systems is commonly known as Switched Port Analyzer (SPAN). The fact that network traffic is typically not fully monitored is one issue with port mirroring. Only broadcast traffic or traffic that crosses boundaries between segregated networks is recorded and examined. The switch's inability to handle traffic from multiple ports to a single mirroring port is the cause. Additionally, not every regular port has a mirroring port. The traffic that crosses network boundaries is typically the traffic that needs to be prioritized for monitoring.

In-line monitoring can be utilized if there are any more vital communication links in the subnetwork. A network bridge that receives all communication between two communication partners and has the ability to read and modify all traffic before forwarding it is used to carry out in-line monitoring. Additionally, intrusion prevention systems (IPSs), which require this kind of installation in order to actively intercept malicious traffic, are supported by this. In the event that an error or power outage causes an in-line monitoring system to shut down, there is a risk to connectivity. For this reason, bypass switches are used during installation. If a fault causes the connection to be lost, these special switches have the ability to detect the condition of the in-line system and forward traffic directly.

A lot of the time, helper protocols broadcast some commands. This indicates that all hosts within the subnet are able to view the packet. As a result, monitoring systems at the three locations—host-based, port-mirrored, or in-line monitoring—can also analyze it.

Network traffic is typically collected in two main formats, depending on the type of monitoring. Information about network traffic flow is the first kind. Initially created by Cisco under the name NetFlow, it was subsequently modified by other businesses. The router gathers and compiles data regarding various IP traffic flows. Version, Sequence Number, Input and Output Interface ID, timestamps for the flow's start and end times, the number of bytes and packets observed, IP header information (the source and destination IP addresses and port numbers are particularly crucial here), and a union of all TCP flags observed during the flow's lifetime are all contained in a NetFlow record. The flow records that are seen at the router are then erased there and forwarded via UDP to a collector. The collector should be placed close to the recording device in order to reduce the overhead caused by the newly added network traffic.

The second kind of network monitoring is packet captures. In this instance, the entire packet—that is, its payload and header information—is gathered, saved, and processed. Deep-packet inspection typically requires this method, which is carried out by wireshark and tcpdump. The same observables that are captured by flow records are also present in packet captures because the entire packet is stored. Nevertheless, because packet captures store a much larger amount of data, algorithms must be used to process the data and extract relevant observables.

3.2.2.3. Evasion Techniques

Adversaries can evade detection by disguising attack indicators in network traffic using a variety of techniques.

Since communication protocols (like HTTPS) are using encryption more frequently, encrypted traffic is becoming a common occurrence in traffic that is being monitored. Although encryption is a crucial component of security and privacy, adversaries frequently use it to thwart payload analysis. Only when a detection mechanism possesses a copy of the private key that was used for encryption can it examine the payload. Transport protocol packet headers, on the other hand, are typically unencryptable by an attacker because network equipment must be able to read them in order to guarantee proper delivery. On the other hand, the application layer protocols' header data cannot be tracked if the transport layer protocol encrypts it.

Fragmentation is another way to avoid payload inspection. The payload may be divided by the attacker into several tiny packets, each of which the IDS must reassemble in order to recognize the malicious payload. In an attempt to make the IDS's reassembling process more difficult, the attacker can then send packets out of order or introduce sporadic delays during transmission, hoping that the target machine will not reassemble while the IDS times out or fails. This is a reasonable assumption given that the traffic from several hosts is frequently handled by the IDS. To handle the complexity in time, therefore, shorter timeouts and simpler algorithms are required.

Encoding can be used, like encryption, to avoid being recognized by signatures. Hexadecimal-encoded ASCII strings, for instance, are accepted by Web servers. When the victim consents to the attack, signatures can be evaded if the intrusion detection system is not fully aware of all possible encoding scenarios.

Within the same class, there are several methods that take advantage of variations in the way that IDS and target host interpret encodings or packet structures. When data fragments are defined as overlapping, when the payload is reassembled, the IDS and the host may use different portions of the overlapping data. Similar to this, different operating systems treat particular protocol flags in different ways. The attacker may take advantage of these discrepancies between the protocol standard and the implementations.

Information about the sender and the intended recipient of a packet is contained in the packet headers. If the sender information is not verified, it is frequently possible to spoof the sender information using dummy data or the address of another machine in order to conceal the attacker's whereabouts within the network or to give the impression that the packet is coming from a legitimate machine. Helper protocols can also be used to hijack other machines' network configurations for covert purposes.

3.2.3. Files and Processes

The term "malware," which is short for "malicious software," describes computer programs that are intended to harm a system or carry out other undesirable tasks. Malware detection is crucial to computer system security because malicious software attempts to infiltrate networks, obtain private data, interfere with system functions, and harm the system itself. Malware attacks have not only targeted general ICT systems but also targeted ICSs, with the aim of gaining control over physical processes and causing significant physical harm.

For decades, computer scientists have extensively studied malware detection. Static analysis, dynamic analysis, and hybrid approaches are some of the detection techniques used. The process of analyzing a file's contents without actually running the file is known as static analysis. Runtime analysis is carried out by dynamic analysis, which launches the executable file, watches how it behaves, and looks into how the program impacts the host computer. This is conceivable since malware typically consists of one or more executable files with harmful content. Certain malware detection techniques employ hybrid approaches that integrate both analysis techniques to address the shortcomings of each.

Malware detection techniques monitor observables at the host machine, such as binary patterns, instructions, or system calls, in order to identify any malicious content or behavior.

3.2.3.1. Observables

Malware is identified using various observables depending on the analysis method. The observables that are most frequently used are listed below. But as new methods are discovered, new observables are discovered or the arrangement of observables to create indicators is changed.

3.2.3.1.1. Binary Patterns

Malicious files can be one or more and contain malicious content. Once the threat actor has compiled these files, they are typically saved as binaries. These binaries frequently include distinct code patterns that can be directly extracted or found in decoded data. Additional data, such as commands, the control server, or target locations, may also be included in malware. The extra data can be expressed as alphabet strings, which can then be utilized to create original patterns. Patterns are derived from malware's additional configuration and metadata, or from executable code. Sets of distinct patterns come together to create signatures, which are then used to identify the same malicious file in various places. Any new file or update to an existing file in the monitored memory space can then start the pattern analysis. These signatures can also be used by different organizations in their detection processes and shared as indicators (IoC).

Regrettably, in order to evade binary pattern-based malware detection, malware authors employ obfuscation techniques (such as code compression and encryption) and create variations of the same malware. Nevertheless, distinct binary patterns can be found and utilized to identify malware that is already known to exist, and obfuscation methods occasionally fall short of producing a sizable number of variants. For instance, the encrypted patterns stay the same or there aren't many encrypted patterns if the same encryption key or a small number of keys are used.

3.2.3.1.2. Operation Codes (Opcodes)

Since malware is a program, in addition to static binary analysis, executable code can be extracted and examined for malware. When it comes to things like instructions, functions, and system calls, executable code provides more insight into the program than does the binary. The program executes a series of instructions one after the other in order to accomplish its goal. Each instruction consists of exactly one opcode and, depending on the opcode, one or more operands. Opcodes are simple program operations like register and memory operations, but they also convey program behavior information. Malware detection techniques based on opcodes can employ frequency analysis, sequence analysis, or both.

Bilar predicted malware by comparing the opcode histograms of known malware and benign programs. In a similar vein, other techniques use opcode frequency and sequences to simulate malicious activity. Runwal and associates suggested using a graphical method to determine how similar the opcode sequence is. (Bilar, 2007)

It is necessary to convert a binary file into executable code and then extract the opcodes from the executable code in order to perform opcode analysis. Disassemblers can be used for the translation, and depending on the technique, various kinds of opcode information can be extracted. Debuggers, instrumentation techniques, operating system level tools, and opcode information can be extracted to circumvent obfuscation methods.

Dynamic methods examine how a program behaves while it is running. Information flow tracking, dynamic binary instrumentation, function call monitoring, and virtual machine inspection are some of the main dynamic techniques. While these methods may be able to identify malware that has been obfuscated as well as malware variants, they come with a high resource cost and significant overhead. These challenges frequently restrict malware detection to a static method (such as antivirus software or scanners); nevertheless, because of their known limitations, they can be easily circumvented.

3.2.3.1.3. System Calls

Basic and necessary operating system functions like memory access and network communication are handled by system calls. Creating a program without a system call is nearly impossible. It has been determined that system calls represent a potentially useful feature for malware detection when they are watched over. System call patterns offer useful details about a program's runtime operations that can be utilized to describe malevolent activity.

The system calls of a sample can be grouped using clustering techniques, such as the n-gram approach, to find malicious patterns. To detect malicious intent, another strategy is to classify the system calls according to shared operating system resources. An alternative method examines system call sequences that may signify a series of malicious actions (such as reading crucial files and transferring them via a socket). In order to distinguish between malicious and benign programs and to identify suspicious files, one can also utilize the frequency distribution of system calls.

Static analysis can be used to disassemble the executable code from the binary file and determine which system calls are used in a program. Debugging and instrumentation are two examples of dynamic analysis that can track system calls made during runtime. To get around more sophisticated obfuscation methods such as sandbox detection, researchers devised ways to watch how the program behaves in hardware. NumChecker examines hardware events such as total instructions, branches, returns, and floating point operations to identify malicious changes made to a kernel function (system call). Ozsoy and associates suggested utilizing architectural events (such as frequency of memory read/writes, frequency of opcodes, frequency of immediate branches taken, etc.) as the features and machine learning for malware classification in order to design a processor that is aware of malware. The aforementioned techniques all model the malicious behavior using low-level hardware features. Rahmatian and associates suggested host-based FPGA intrusion detection system that characterizes appropriate system behavior using system call sequences. The main limitations of this approach are as follows: Each program needs to be assisted by system calls-based FSM; it does not allow unknown programs to run; and FSM of system calls would be significantly large for complex programs, thus demanding large memory size. While these approaches are harder to circumvent by the attacker, they are also more cost intensive to implement and hard to deploy in an operational environment (Rahmatian et al., 2012).

3.2.3.1.4. Information Flow

While system call and opcode information concentrate on the actions of operations programs, program behavior analysis also considers the information (or data) that a particular program handles. In this instance, the analysis method is more concerned with the data itself than with how they are handled.

Programs can contain (or generate) data, or it can come from outside sources (such as input files, data transmission, and user actions). Programs can be traced for the data (or resources) they access, and correlations between data accesses can be found that may point to questionable activity. Rather than keeping an eye on every operation, it is possible to find hidden information by tracking the actions that programs take on data. One method of obfuscation is to insert bogus instructions in between legitimate ones. Nevertheless, the junk instructions can be eliminated by eliminating instructions that are unrelated to particular data. Both static and dynamic analysis allow for the tracing of information flow, but dynamic analysis is more resistant to obfuscation techniques.

Hardware can also employ similar strategies to get around particular obfuscation methods. Demme along with others suggested keeping an eye on lower level micro-architecture metrics like cache miss rate and instruction per cycle by using a hardware performance counter. Tang and associates used unsupervised machine learning to create baseline models of benign program execution in order to identify deviations brought about by malware exploitation.

3.2.3.2. Obfuscation Methods

Signatures are used in standard static solutions, like antivirus, scanners, and anti-malware programs, to detect malware. Malware can be identified by a distinct byte sequence, which can then be used to identify the same malware. Unfortunately, in order to evade signature detection, malware authors create variations of their original program using obfuscation techniques (such as code compression and encryption). In addition, extracting the signatures of every malware requires a significant amount of labor and time for signature generation.

Malware can first be "packed" or encrypted to evade signature detection (i.e., compressed). One benefit of encryption is that an encoded version of the code won't contain a signature that exists in the unencrypted version. The inability of the decryption code to be encrypted itself and the need for the code to eventually be decrypted are the drawbacks of encryption, according to the malware author. Thus, the signature could be the decryption code.

The next logical development in the arms race between malware authors and SD is polymorphic malware. There is no fixed decryption code that can be used as a signature because polymorphic malware morphs the decryption code. For every infection, a unique decryption code should ideally be created. It is challenging to detect polymorphic malware with robustness.

One term used to describe metamorphic malware is "body polymorphic". That is, metamorphic code morphs the entire malicious code, not just the decryption code. There won't be a common signature if the morphing is complete enough, so encryption won't be required. Metamorphic software can be created using a multitude of techniques. These strategies include code shuffling, register swapping, subroutine permutation, general code obfuscation, and equivalent instruction substitution. Advanced techniques, such as anti-virtual machine inspection and anti-debuggers, are employed by malware authors to conceal their malicious activity and ultimately evade detection. For instance, a malware employs anti-debugger strategies like anti-ptrace, anti-sigtrap, and anti-breakpoint to look for malware detectors on the host system. If it detects any, it leaves the system without causing any damage.

3.3. EVALUATION AND ANALYSIS OF MONITORING DATA TO DERIVE CYBER INCIDENT ALERTS

Observables can be layered with different analysis techniques for more successful detection. Five categories of analysis techniques are presented in this section: (1) stateful analysis, (2) cross-layer analysis, (3) anomaly detection, (4) signature-based analysis, and (5) ontologies. While anomaly detection is used to describe cross-layer analysis, rule-based analysis encompasses stateful analysis and signature-based analysis.

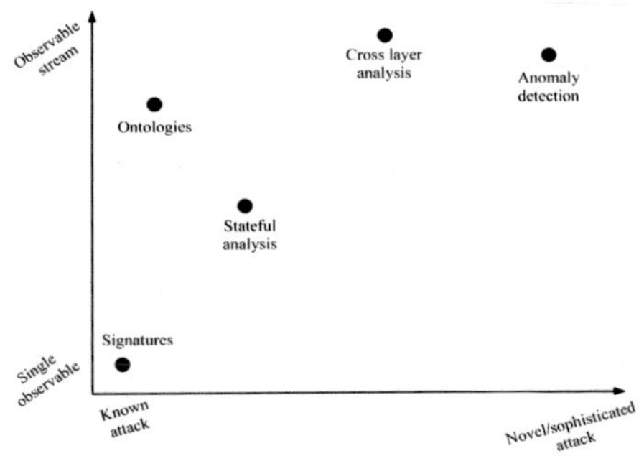

Figure 3.2. *Classification of the five analysis categories. The position on the plane indicates if a specific approach operates on single observables or a stream of observables. It further shows if a method is more suitable to detect known attacks or novel and highly sophisticated attacks.*

Source: Friedberg, I., Wurzenberger, M., Al Balushi, A., and Kang, B. (2017). From Monitoring, Logging, and Network Analysis to Threat Intelligence Extraction. In Collaborative Cyber Threat Intelligence (pp. 69-128).

Here, we outline broad ideas and potential integrations between each approach and information sharing frameworks. How each strategy can profit from shared information and how it can be used to produce new information that should be shared is a key question. The approaches are shown in Figure 3.2 on a plane, with one axis describing their requirements on the information that has been analyzed and another axis indicating whether each approach is better suited for detecting known attacks or new or extremely sophisticated attacks. It is evident that rule-based methods work better for identifying known attacks. On the other hand, methods for anomaly detection can be employed to obtain signs of new or unidentified attacks. Streams of observables allow for the classification of more complex situations and the use of more data. Conversely, in known attacks, more straightforward rule-based methods frequently yield more trustworthy outcomes.

3.3.1. Rule-Based Analysis

There are two concepts for establishing rule-based analysis:

- Black-listing;
- White-listing.

White-listing focuses on permitting pre-defined normal activities, whereas black-listing identifies pre-defined malicious activity.

3.3.1.1. Black-Listing

A black-listing rule looks for certain values in the data that is being watched. Black lists are used to identify particular IP addresses, port numbers, user names, or clients that shouldn't be present on a network belonging to a company. Black-list techniques have a significant flaw in that it is simple for attackers to get around security tools that use black-listing by avoiding the forbidden values. Although those methods are very good at stopping known attacks, it is hard to maintain them current, so those methods are open to unknown attacks that, for example, use zeroday exploits.

Common security solutions that use black-listing techniques include firewalls, antivirus software, and signature-based detection techniques. Black-listing rules are generally very effective against known attacks, which make up the majority of malicious activities, and they are relatively easy to set up and update. Because of this, they serve as a crucial foundation for security analysis, particularly in smaller businesses that lack the manpower and funding to implement sophisticated security measures. They are the recommended option for private use as well. Black lists need to be updated regularly to maintain an adequate level of protection for an ICT network infrastructure because blacklisting rules prohibit specific events, like the occurrence of malware signatures or communication on particular ports. Blacklisting techniques are typically based on centralized distribution mechanisms, where solution providers update their clients with predefined signatures and rules to detect new malware, because this is a resource-intensive task. Thus, those strategies benefit from Indicators of Compromise (IoC) that are automatically shared. The fact that rules to identify malware signatures don't need to be customized for a particular network infrastructure—rather, they should appear the same in all environments—benefits this process. But one disadvantage of such widely-used, general rules is that they can't identify unwanted behavior specific to an infrastructure, like when zero-day vulnerabilities are exploited.

3.3.1.2. White-Listing

White-listing, as opposed to black-listing, does not outright forbid any particular behaviors or values that are apparent in the monitored data. These methods permit a particular baseline of typical system behavior, which is known as the "ground truth". Data that is continuously gathered is then contrasted with the ground truth that has already been established. An attacker will find it more difficult to stay true to this ground truth because their actions typically generate network events and logs that deviate from the typical behavior of the system. Simple white-listing rules, or the ground truth model, can analyze individual events, like a single log line, and permit the use of only particular IP addresses, ports, or web browsers, among other things. They can also correlate multiple events. This means that a baseline of typical system behavior is permitted ("ground truth"), in contrast to black-listing techniques, which forbid certain system behavior. It is possible to obtain the model for this baseline of typical system behavior from data sources like network traffic and log data. Therefore, white-listing strategies aim to circumvent the disadvantage of black-listing, which is that an attacker may be able to circumvent the rules once they become aware of them. Furthermore, because white-listing techniques only permit standard user and system operations, they improve security against unknown attacks that leverage zero-day exploits or attack vectors that weren't considered when creating the rules.

3.3.1.3. Black Versus White-Listing

Black-listing security mechanisms are the cornerstone of an organization's cyber defenses. They do, however, modify their tactics and make their attacks more complex and organization-specific in order to evade detection by blacklist security techniques (for example, by employing customized malware with distinct signatures derived from toolkits).

Conversely, sophisticated anomaly detection systems that employ whitelisting techniques can identify minute variations in the system's operation and, consequently, indications of unidentified intrusions. Numerous attackers take advantage of flaws in various network layers and misuse distinct network regions as points of entry to execute a successful attack. It takes an appropriate synthesis of various approaches to counter sophisticated APTs. In order to detect unknown attacks, more sophisticated and intelligent white-listing solutions must be added to the widely used and simple-to-deploy black-listing techniques that are effective enough against known threats. Enterprise networks and ICT infrastructures are typically distinct systems with distinct applications. As a result, they take into consideration flexible solutions that can be tailored to those circumstances. White-listing techniques can be used to accomplish this, whereas black-listing relies on disseminating pre-made signatures that weren't created with a particular network in mind. Furthermore, the lack of regular rule updates from major vendors makes the application of black-listing problematic, particularly for older systems and systems with small market shares.

3.3.1.4. Sharing

The foundation of any effective security solution is rule-based analysis. White-listing strategies are about to become more significant, whereas black-listing strategies have been around for a while. Approaches that involve blacklisting can also benefit from this development. White-listing enables the observation of novel, as-yet-undiscovered attacks by detecting deviations from typical system behavior, without depending on the frequent updating of signatures. Observable IoCs can be defined in light of this. SIEM systems, or system information and event management, can be used to facilitate the processing of these IoCs in a useful way. By combining data from security solutions (firewalls, intrusion detection systems, etc.) with organizational context and publicly available open and external threat intelligence from vulnerability databases, mailing lists, and online platforms, SIEM systems are able to interpret alarms. Based on the IoC that was acquired from whitelisting approaches, all of this information can then be utilized to define signatures for black-listing approaches.

Alarms can also be correlated with data from risk management, configuration management, compliance management, and other sources using SIEM systems. The unique challenge here is to limit the massive amount of information without losing crucial insights by applying data fusion techniques appropriate to the network's use. When the proper combination of contextualization and data fusion techniques is used, detected alarms can be interpreted more precisely, which improves situational awareness.

3.3.2. Intrusion and Anomaly Detection

The methods for anomaly detection used in ICT network infrastructures for intrusion detection are the subject of the section that follows. The process of locating patterns in an ICT network that defy expected system behavior is known as anomaly detection.

Reasons for this anomalous system behavior that usually refers to malicious activities include the following:

- Invaders;
- Cyber attacks;
- Misconfiguration;
- System failures.

3.3.2.1. What Are Anomalies?

There are different types of anomalies that can indicate malicious system behavior:

- The most basic type is a point anomaly, also known as an outlier or an anomalous single event. A point anomaly is an element that is far apart from every other element in a two-dimensional space. This might be an unexpected IP address or login name on an ICT network.
- An event that is abnormal in one context but may be normal in another is called a contextual anomaly. This could be an unexpected timestamp or another anomalous event parameter in an ICT network. An example of a contextual anomaly would be an employee logging into their system outside of regular business hours, even though this would be typical during regular business hours.
- Typically, an anomalous frequency of a single, typically normal event is the source of a collective anomaly. This might be a database dump in an ICT network, brought on by a SQL-Injection. A significant amount of log lines referring to standard SQL queries are produced during a database dump. The single lines in this instance are typical, but their high frequency is not.

Simpler detection techniques discussed in earlier sections may also be able to identify anomalies that pertain to the types that have been described. However, as APTs try to remain under the radar, these kinds of anomalies are typically not the result of APTs. An advanced persistent threat (APT) is a specially designed and highly skilled attack that is hard to identify, typically targets a single target, and causes a lot of harm, like major financial loss, intellectual property theft, or compromised systems. Moreover, it is challenging to identify these kinds of attacks quickly—it typically takes months. Sequential anomalies are another kind of anomaly that can be found and reveal APTs.

A sequence of anomalous single events that are typically classified as normal is called a sequential anomaly. A sequential anomaly in an ICT network may result from breaking an access chain, for example. For instance, access to a standard database server is typically restricted to a Web server and a firewall. Therefore, if someone gained direct access to the database server without first visiting the Web server, that would be malicious.

3.3.1.2. Intrusion and Anomaly Detection Approaches

We go over various intrusion detection techniques, with a particular emphasis on anomaly detection. Statistical techniques and machine learning are typically employed in these methods. Tools for detecting anomalies can take in a variety of data formats, including textual log data and network traces. (Liao et al., 2013).

There are three general methods that are used in intrusion detection systems (IDS):

- Signature-based detection (SD);
- Stateful protocol analysis (SPA); and
- Anomaly-based detection (AD).
- SD detects attackers using predefined patterns and signatures. This approach is easy to use and efficient in identifying known attacks. The following are the method's shortcomings: attackers can avoid IDS based on SD because it is ineffective against unknown attacks or unknown variants of an attack. Additionally, because the attack landscape is constantly evolving, it is challenging to maintain the most recent versions of the signatures, which makes maintenance time-consuming.
- Predefined profiles that specify benign protocol activity are used by SPA. To ascertain whether protocols are being used appropriately, occurrences are compared to these profiles. IDSs that use SPA as a foundation monitor the status of application, transport, and network protocols. They rely on vendor support because they use universal profiles that the vendor developed.
- AD techniques pick up a baseline of typical system behavior, or "ground truth.". All occurrences are compared to this ground truth in order to identify unusual system behavior. Unlike SPA- and SD-

based IDS, AD-based methods enable the detection of unknown attacks. The often high false positive rate of AD-based intrusion detection systems is a disadvantage.

- Black-listing techniques can be applied to both SD and SPA since they make use of signatures and rules that characterize malicious events. In addition to being more adaptable, AD techniques can identify new and unidentified threats. They use white-listing techniques because they only allow standard system behavior. Even though SD and SPA are quite simple to implement, vendors who share signatures are typically needed for them to work. Conversely, AD-based methods are typically more difficult to set up but are more adaptable and can handle a variety of scenarios.

IDS techniques can be broadly divided into three categories based on the level at which the detection occurs: host-based IDS (HIDS), network-based IDS (NIDS), and hybrid or cross-layer IDS:

- **Host Level:** HIDS is the initial form of IDS and was invented for the purpose of securing military mainframe computers (Intrusion Detection System/ Intrusion Prevention System (IDS/IPS) Market (Host Based, Network Based, Wireless, On-Premise & Cloud Deployment, Appliances, Software, Professional Services)—Global Advancements Forecasts & Analysis. An intrusion detection system (IDS) of this type must be installed on each system (host) in the network that is to be watched, much like basic security solutions like antivirus software. Although HIDS offers detailed, high-level information about an attack and permits monitoring of a single host in great detail, it can also be rendered inoperable by certain types of attacks, such as denial-of-service (DoS) attacks, since once a system is compromised, so is HIDS.
- **Network Level:** A network's entire network's traffic is tracked and examined by NIDS. The best use case for NIDS would be to keep an eye on both incoming and outgoing traffic. Nevertheless, the network may become slower and a bottleneck may form as a result. One sensor node is enough for network-wide NIDS monitoring, and the compromise of one system in the network has no effect on the sensor's functionality. One of the main disadvantages of NIDS is that full monitoring cannot be ensured if the NIDS's band width is overloaded, as some network packets and potentially crucial data may be dropped.
- **Cross-Layer:** Hybrid intrusion detection systems and cross-layer anomaly detection techniques integrate various techniques. In

order to minimize their disadvantages and maximize their benefits, hybrid IDS typically offer a management framework that combines HIDS and NIDS. Cross-layer anomaly detection techniques seek to minimize the false alarm rate while simultaneously optimizing detection capability and making the most of the information that is available. As a result, anomaly detection can make use of a variety of data sources, including the textual log data and network traffic data discussed in earlier sections. Lightweight solutions that enable a high data throughput to enable real-time analysis and evaluation of the gathered data are made possible by the timely detection of intrusions and attacks.

3.3.1.3. Self-Learning and Adaptive Approaches

Black-listing has the limitation of only being able to identify known attack patterns. As a result, these methods take rule base updates by developers into consideration. Small businesses in particular cannot afford the staff members and resources needed to maintain their internal security solutions. As a result, they are dependent on the assistance of suppliers and their rule sets or pricey Managed Security Service Providers (MSSPs) who oversee the security solutions. As a result, the rule sets are not customized to the unique ICT network infrastructure and needs of a company.

Legacy systems or systems with small market shares that are a part of large companies' network infrastructures also pose a problem. Vendor support for these systems is frequently lacking, and they frequently lack adequate documentation. Because software developers in the past frequently neglected security, legacy systems are particularly ill-secured. Cyber physical systems (CPS) that connect and control devices in the energy and manufacturing sectors, like smart grids and supervisory control and data acquisition (SCADA) systems, have issues with legacy devices. Rules for identifying intrusions and attacks are frequently nonexistent due to a lack of documentation and maintenance support. However, these systems typically generate some logs, and network packets can be gathered to keep an eye on errors and the status of the system. Therefore, in order to secure these systems and adjust to the data that is available and the dynamic threat landscape, flexible anomaly detection techniques are needed.

Self-learning anomaly detection techniques are one way to address issues like missing signatures, inadequate vendor support, and difficulties brought on by a rapidly evolving threat landscape.

Generally, there are three methods for implementing self-learning features to build a baseline of normal system behavior that then serves as the "ground truth":

- **Unsupervised:** During a training phase, this method can learn to distinguish between malicious and normal system behavior without the need for labeled data. When the training is finished, it classifies any additional data provided based on the results.
- **Semi-supervised:** Also known as "one-class" classification, this technique is used when the training set only includes data that is devoid of anomalies.
- **Supervised:** A labeled training set with both legitimate and malicious data is needed for this technique.

There is no need for direct human involvement in the learning process when using these three approaches. The user must make sure that the training data for the other two methods is either accurately labeled or free of anomalies, whereas unsupervised self-learning operates completely independently of human influence. As such, the techniques that have been previously discussed fall into the category of unsupported self-learning approaches. There are certain difficulties when self-learning is done entirely on your own. Even though it's quite simple to provide training data for unsupervised self-learning and doesn't require any data pre-processing, these methods may come to accept malicious system behavior as the norm. Semi-supervised methods use training data free of anomalies in an attempt to circumvent this issue. The issue of obtaining training data that is assured to be anomaly free arises when these methods are applied. It is typically challenging to retrieve such a dataset from an operational productive system. It is also true that for self-learning based anomaly detection, the more data supplied in the training phase, the more precisely the system performs later on when an ICT network is being watched over. Supervised self-learning techniques offer the most accurate ground truth, but they require a lot of time and resources to provide training datasets that are appropriate for particular network environments. As a result, AD-based IDS that use supervised learning have the lowest false positive rate.

System administrators can affect the anomaly detection process through supported self-learning approaches, which can help prevent negative outcomes like teaching malicious behavior as normal and vice versa. This means, for example, that an administrator can determine whether an event is anomalous or a false alarm, allowing the event to be classified as normal system behavior going forward. This is useful when an event occurs for the first time and is therefore not part of normal system behavior. Moreover, self-learning can be employed to modify and maintain the baseline—which characterizes typical behavior—when new devices are added to or removed from a network or when updates affect the software that is being used. White-listing and self-learning anomaly detection systems can identify unknown attack patterns and adjust to changing circumstances, but they also frequently generate a high volume of false alarms. Developing cross-layer anomaly detection methods is a viable solution to that issue. In order to ascertain whether an anomaly occurred, data and alerts from multiple anomaly detection systems are aggregated and sorted.

3.3.1.3. Sharing

The previously discussed points apply to IDS as well, since black-listing techniques are part of SD and SPA and white-listing is implemented by AD. Furthermore, a victim of an attack can share comprehensive details about detected observables (like IoC) and the various actions the attacker took, as AD-based IDS are particularly well-suited for revealing modern, sophisticated attacks like APTs. Using this information, a CERT can advise which systems to monitor more closely or what kinds of anomalies to look for in order to quickly identify the attacker. Organizations can set up their AD systems to more carefully monitor impacted areas of their cyber infrastructure based on these so-called threat intelligence (TI). One way to do this would be to specifically search for anomalies in DNS query logs. This is because, despite the fact that a new botnet variant has emerged and the command and control server's IP address and URL are constantly changing, no reliable signatures are yet available to identify this threat. Therefore, it is recommended that organizations keep a closer eye than usual on their DNS logs. The sensitivity with which an anomaly detection system raises alarms can be configured dynamically. This would only increase the false positive rate (FPR) for those particular areas of the company's network, not add to the administrative burden of handling false alarms across the board, and guarantee a higher detection rate for real threats. Lastly, by exchanging tactics, techniques, and procedures (TTPs) and threat intelligence (TI), organizations can improve their cyber situational awareness and determine the best use of their limited monitoring resources (i.e., which systems, protocols, etc.). This is because the more log and network data they monitor and analyze in detail, the more human resources they require to determine whether the results are legitimate alarms or false positives.

3.3.3. Ontologies

3.3.3.1. What is an Ontology?

An ontology is a method of representing knowledge in a particular domain of interest that involves comprehending and expressing key concepts and their relationships. The term ontology originated in the field of metaphysics; a branch of philosophy concerned with the nature of existence. The term "machine intelligence" (AI) was first used by researchers in the mid-1970s because of its acknowledged use in mathematical logics and the creation of computational models that facilitate automated reasoning. An ontology is defined as "an explicit specification of conceptualization" in the context of computer and information sciences. It formally represents the knowledge within a domain as a set of concepts and their relationships to model the domain and support concept reasoning. (Gruber et al., 1993)

The main representational primitives used by an ontology to specify captured knowledge in the domain are:

- Classes are collections or abstracted groups that have a property in common that allows for a clear definition among all of its members. Anything within the domain, such as an explanation of a task, function, action, strategy, procedure, or object classification, can be considered a concept. In an ontology, for example, individuals or system groups within departments, roles, or processes could be specified as classes or subclasses. The common attributes listed in the root class can be inherited by the subclasses.
- Concrete objects in the domain, such as people, systems, attacks, or resources, are referred to as instances or individuals. These objects, such as John, Employee01, or ERPserver03, represent a particular person or system within the domain. It is possible to attach an instance to the class to which it belongs.
- The primary purposes of attributes and properties are to attach values to data or to describe potential relationships between classes. Data properties and object properties are the two categories of properties. Class relationships, such as the binary relationships between a subclass and a superclass, are represented by object properties. On the other hand, classes or individual members can have values and information attached to them via the data properties. These values may represent any information that was extracted from the input data or the raw packet features.
- A collection of claims and statements known as rules and axioms allow for the implicit information to be deduced from the known facts. To create sentences that are always true, the axioms are applied.
- Imagine a cyber-security scenario in which a hacker uses a database server's input validation vulnerability to launch a SQL injection attack and steal private data. In this instance, the ontology might define the primary classes of [Attack, Attacker, Vulnerability, Asset, Impact], with subcategories like attack types (like database, Web, and network attacks) added as subclasses of the attack class.

Additionally, the SQL injection is an example of a database attack class instance.

As a result, the connections between different classes that have been described are logical ones, much like when an attacker [exploits] a vulnerability.

3.3.3.2. Features of an Ontology

An ontological framework has various advantages for knowledge engineering and modeling in computer science, such as the following:

- **Formal Representation of Domain Knowledge:** An ontology is a formal representation of knowledge in a particular domain that is machine-readable and interpretable. As a result, machines can access and search information and its semantic meaning more effectively.
- **Flexibility on the Level of Information Abstraction:** Better information analysis is possible because the represented knowledge can be flexible expressed at different levels of granularity (abstraction). As a result, by employing the ontology data annotation capability, irrelevant attributes can be removed from the data while other attributes are added. This enables the creation of high-level perspectives of the overall security of the network and the synopsis of expected actions in intricate cyberattacks.
- **Interoperability on Heterogeneous Knowledge Sources:** The integration of heterogeneous data gathered from various sources and in various formats is made possible by an ontology. As a result, it closes the knowledge gap between technical and operational applications. For example, the raw data collected in the network may be associated with organizational policies and information about the physical environment. With the help of this feature, analysts may be able to investigate detected attacks with less manual effort and be able to eliminate false alarms that do not involve the necessary context.
- **Powerful Semantic-Level Search and Reasoning Capabilities:** An ontology is a formal representation of knowledge in a machine-interpretable format that facilitates powerful semantic-level functions, like reasoning over learned material to find logical connections between concepts or extrapolating information.
- **Extensibility and Reusability:** Because of their nature, ontologies can be reused in various contexts and perhaps even in different applications. An ontology typically seeks to provide community members with a common vocabulary that allows them to share

and integrate shared understandings of how a domain should be conceptualized. This makes it possible to analyze information automatically with less human intervention from non-expert users by reusing domain expertise and knowledge that has been captured.

An ontology can be very useful in many applications that need to automatically analyze large amounts of data and give meaning to the terms and relations used to describe the domain. This is because of the features that have been described. An ontology is a more sophisticated but adaptable solution than the conventional taxonomies used in the field; it enables its creator to better express relationship definitions between different pieces of information at different taxonomy levels and to capture domain knowledge. For instance, ontologies permit the definition of additional relationships among classes at other levels, whereas taxonomies only permit the definition of parent-child relationships. This enables the linking of all relevant data, even when it is spread across various contexts. Examples include mapping vulnerabilities, asset information, cyber-attack scenarios, and cyber-physical and human knowledge to instances of network packets in the dataset.

Kim and Lee's work provides a visualization of the ontological view on the real-world malware example, Stuxnet. It explains the relationships between the different components used in the Stuxnet attack scenario, such as the objectives of the attacker, the vulnerabilities that are exploited, the details of the assets, and related resources.

3.3.3.3. What are Ontologies used for?

The main applications of ontology approaches are in knowledge engineering and reasoning on datasets that allow one to solve a specific problem within a particular domain. Ontology has been used in many applications due to its strong features, which include data modeling, the incorporation of description logics, reasoning over data, and the representation of information in a machine-readable format. Ontologies have become increasingly popular among researchers across various disciplines in the past few years. This covers the application of ontology to data mining, intrusion detection and security event management, cyberattack classification and prediction, system modeling and simulation, and context management. A website repository (LOV4IoT) offers a comprehensive list of 303 real-world ontology examples across various domains, complete with source codes and related academic publications.

In general, the main objectives of ontologies as presented in the literature can be summarized as follows:

- To share a common understanding of concepts and information

within the domain among the members of a community and software agents (machines);
- To facilitate integration and interoperability on heterogeneous knowledge sources;
- To enable reuse of the domain knowledge;
- To automate the analysis of knowledge in the domain.

3.3.3.4. Ontology Design and Implementation

Rather than being a well-understood engineering procedure, ontological construction can be viewed as a crafting art. Diverse ontology structures can arise from the minds of different people. It is evident that a number of factors, including the activities followed, the level of domain expertise available, and the ontology's defined scope and role, could influence the quality of the produced ontology and its possible application. Clarity, coherence, extensibility, minimal ontological commitment (minimizing domain claims in ontology), and minimal encoding bias (encoding the information as independent from the used symbols as possible) are the five main design criteria for ontologies.

Moreover, there are a number of ontology development methodologies that offer a set of standards to follow throughout the ontology lifecycle. The most popular approaches include Ontolingua, KBSI IDEF5, TOVE, and IDEF5. In addition, a number of formal languages are available to encode the data needed for the ontology model. These include the Web Ontology Language (OWL and OWL2), the DARPA Agent Markup Language (DAML+OIL), the Resource Description Framework (RDF), the Frame Logic (Flogic), the Extensible Markup Language (XML), and the Knowledge Interchange Format (KIF). It is entirely up to the designer to decide which of the suggested approaches and languages best meets his needs; each has pros and cons.

3.3.3.5. Ontological Approaches for Cybersecurity Information Sharing

The task of exchanging information is difficult due to the vast amount of available data in the domain and its intricate nature. Furthermore, when integrating this data, interoperability problems arise because different tools, systems, and sensors may produce disparate pieces of information in disparate formats.

To make it easier to model threat intelligence and facilitate the sharing of cybersecurity information, several initiatives and standards have been put forth. These standards are commonly known as the Cybersecurity Information

Exchange Framework (CYBEX), Open Vulnerability and Assessment Language (OVAL), Incident Object Description Exchange Format (IODEF), Common Vulnerabilities and Exposures (CVE), Common Platform Enumeration (CPE), Common Configuration Enumeration (CCE), Common Attack Pattern Enumeration and Classification (CAPEC), and European Information Sharing and Alert System (EISAS). However, the adoption of disparate standards and formats for cybersecurity information frequently resulted in fragmented data and hampered interoperability. Additionally, attempts to map information to technical features in the dataset or integrate information from human knowledge or operational context may make this problem more apparent. For example, analyzing information about the involved processes and system configurations may be necessary for the detection of some cyber-attacks in many critical infrastructures, rather than relying solely on network packet traces.

Large volumes of heterogeneous data that need to be integrated, modeled, and analyzed are the primary obstacle facing current state-of-the-art cybersecurity event management and information exchange solutions. Furthermore, their capacity to identify sophisticated modern attacks like Stuxnet malware is being hindered by the lack of automated methods to deal with missing data, dynamic context information, and logical connections between disparate pieces of information. Consequently, current research endeavors aimed at resolving these concerns and enhancing cybersecurity analysis and data interchange via ontology are being documented. The ability to model large data flexibly while enabling the capture and integration of contextual information, the ability to extract the logical relationship among disparate information pieces, and reasoning capabilities to address data quality issues like missing or faulty data may be the main benefits of ontology-based systems. (Leenen and Meyer, 2015)

REFERENCES

1. Asgarli, E., & Burger, E. (2016). Semantic ontologies for cyber threat sharing standards. In *2016 IEEE Symposium on Technologies for Homeland Security (HST)* (pp. 1–6). Waltham, MA. https://doi.org/10.1109/THS.2016.7568896.
2. Bayer, U., Comparetti, P., Hlauschek, C., Kruegel, C., & Kirda, E. (2009). Scalable, behavior-based malware clustering. In *NDSS* (Vol. 9, pp. 8–11). San Diego, CA: Citeseer.
3. Bilar, D. (2007). Opcodes as predictors for malware. *International Journal of Electronic Security and Digital Forensics, 1*(2), 156–168. https://doi.org/10.1504/IJESDF.2007.016865.
4. Leenen, L., & Meyer, T. (2015). The use of semantic technologies in cyber defense. In *Proceedings of the 10th International Conference on Cyber Warfare and Security: ICCWS 2015* (p. 170). Academic Conferences Limited.
5. Liao, H. J., Lin, C. H. R., Lin, Y. C., & Tung, K. Y. (2013). Intrusion detection system: A comprehensive review. *Journal of Network and Computer Applications, 36*(1), 16–24. https://doi.org/10.1016/j.jnca.2012.09.004.
6. Lin, T. T. Y., & Siewiorek, D. P. (1990). Error log analysis: Statistical modeling and heuristic trend analysis. *IEEE Transactions on Reliability, 39*(4), 419–432.
7. Mundie, D. A., & Ruefle, R. (2012). Building an incident management body of knowledge. In *2012 Seventh International Conference on Availability, Reliability and Security* (pp. 507–513). Prague, Czech Republic, 20–24 August. https://doi.org/10.1109/ARES.2012.83.
8. Rahmatian, M., Kooti, H., Harris, I. G., & Bozorgzadeh, E. (2012). Hardware-assisted detection of malicious software in embedded systems. *IEEE Embedded Systems Letters, 4*(4), 94–97. https://doi.org/10.1109/LES.2012.2218630.
9. Runwal, N., Low, R. M., & Stamp, M. (2012). Opcode graph similarity and metamorphic detection. *Journal in Computer Virology, 8*(1, 2), 37–52. https://doi.org/10.1007/s11416-012-0160-5.
10. Sadighian, A., Fernandez, J. M., Lemay, A., & Zargar, S. T. (2014). ONTIDS: A highly flexible context-aware and ontology-based alert correlation framework. In *Foundations and Practice of Security* (pp. 161–177). Springer. https://doi.org/10.1007/978-3-319-05302-8_10.
11. Santos, I., Brezo, F., Nieves, J., Penya, Y. K., Sanz, B., Laorden, C., &

Bringas, P. G. (2010). IDEA: Opcode-sequence-based malware detection. In *Engineering Secure Software and Systems* (pp. 35–43). Springer, Berlin, Heidelberg. https://doi.org/10.1007/978-3-642-11747-3_3.

12. Sridhar, S., Hahn, A., & Govindarasu, M. (2012). Cyber-physical system security for the electric power grid. *Proceedings of the IEEE, 100*(1), 210–224. https://doi.org/10.1109/JPROC.2011.2165269.

13. Tsai, C. F., Hsu, Y. F., Lin, C. Y., & Lin, W. Y. (2009). Intrusion detection by machine learning: A review. *Expert Systems with Applications, 36*(10), 11994–12000. https://doi.org/10.1016/j.eswa.2009.05.029.

CHAPTER 4

THREAT INTELLIGENCE PLATFORMS (TIPS)

Contents

INTRODUCTION

Businesses must contend with a wide range of quickly changing cyberthreats. Cyber threat actors are always in the process of creating new instruments and strategies to get around the security measures that companies have put in place. A success could result in a data breach, ransomware infection, or other serious security incident that affects the company. Threat intelligence gives businesses insight into the newest attack campaigns and trends in the cyber threat landscape, allowing them to anticipate and avert attacks. But analysts find it challenging to manually process threat data and extract insights quickly enough to be useful due to the sheer amount of available data. Threat intelligence data collection, analysis, and distribution are all automated by a TIP. An organization can make sure that its defenses are utilizing the best data available to detect and thwart possible attacks by utilizing a TIP.

4.1. UNDERSTANDING BASICS OF THREAT INTELLIGENCE PLATFORMS (TIPS)

One of the most important tools in the cybersecurity toolbox of contemporary organizations is a threat intelligence platform (TIP). It offers essential capabilities for comprehending, foreseeing, and quickly and effectively addressing cyberthreats. With the cybersecurity landscape constantly changing, TIPs have become indispensable organizational tools. Security teams can identify, investigate, and respond to threats more effectively and accurately when they have access to information on known malware and other threats, which is made possible by TIPs. Instead of gathering and organizing data, it allows threat analysts to focus their time on data analysis and potential security threat research. Additionally, a TIP makes it simple for security and threat intelligence teams to communicate threat intelligence information to security systems and other stakeholders. TIPs can be implemented as on-premises or software-as-a-service (SaaS) solutions.

4.1.1. Purpose of a Threat Intelligence Platform

A few recurring problems in today's cybersecurity environment are large data volumes, a shortage of analysts, and increasingly sophisticated adversarial attacks. There is little interoperability among the many tools available in today's security infrastructures for managing this data. This means that managing systems will require an excruciating amount of engineering work, and time and resources that are already scarce will inevitably be wasted. Many businesses are opting to deploy a TIP in order to address these problems. Threat Intelligence Platforms are a useful tool for managing cyber threat intelligence and related entities, such as actors, campaigns, incidents, signatures, bulletins, and TTPs. They can be implemented as an on-premise or SaaS solution. Its ability to carry out four essential tasks defines it:

- Aggregation of intelligence from multiple sources;
- Curation, normalization, enrichment, and risk scoring of data;
- Integrations with existing security systems;
- Analysis and sharing of threat intelligence.

4.1.2. The Value of a Threat Intelligence Platform

Through the enhancement of security operations centers (SOCs) capabilities, threat intelligence platforms provide tremendous value. They compile threat information from multiple sources and convert it into useful insights. In contrast, threat intelligence and security teams benefit from a TIP when:

- Research, gathering, aggregating, and organizing threat intelligence data, as well as normalizing, de-duping, and enriching that data, should all be automated, streamlined, and made simpler.
- Track and promptly identify, confirm, and address possible security risks in real time.
- Learn important details about security risks, threats, attacks, and vulnerabilities—both past and present—as well as about threat adversaries' strategies, tactics, and procedures (TTPs).
- Establish procedures for reporting and responding to security incidents.
- Give other stakeholders access to threat intelligence information through dashboards, alerts, reports, etc.
- Provide security systems, including firewalls, endpoints, application programming interfaces (APIs), intrusion prevention systems (IPSs), and security information and event management (SIEM) solutions, with the most recent threat intelligence data on a regular basis.

4.1.3. How Threat Intelligence Works

The process of gathering threat intelligence in cybersecurity is dynamic and all-encompassing, with multiple stages that are essential to creating a strong defense against cyberattacks. It affects the way security operations centers (SOCs) function, beginning with data collection and continuing through to practical solutions.

4.1.3.1. Data Collection

The first step in threat intelligence is gathering information from various sources. Among them are open-source intelligence (OSINT) resources, which include information that is freely accessible via the Internet, discussion boards, social media, and specialist cybersecurity reports. Crucial internal sources include past incident reports, network traffic data, and server logs. An additional layer of data is available through subscription-based intelligence feeds, which provide perspectives from government agencies, research groups, and industry experts.

4.1.3.2. Data Analysis

After the data is gathered, it is analyzed to look for patterns (pattern recognition). This entails searching for patterns in cyberattacks, such as recurrent system vulnerabilities or comparable techniques employed by threat actors. Threat intelligence depends heavily on the ability to spot anomalies. Anomalies could be a sign of a security breach since they represent a departure from the norm, like strange network traffic. It's critical to comprehend the data's context. This entails determining which threats are real and which are false positives, as well as comprehending the implications of a threat within the particular context of the organization.

4.1.3.3. Conversion to Actionable Intelligence

After analysis, the data is transformed into useful intelligence. This entails condensing the massive amount of data into insights pertinent to the security posture of the company. By assisting companies in comprehending their threat landscape and making appropriate preparations, this intelligence supports strategic planning.

4.1.3.4. Real-time Processing and Response

SOCs can swiftly detect new threats thanks to real-time processing of threat data. A threat is dealt with more quickly the sooner it is identified.

4.1.3.5. Automated Responses

Threat intelligence platforms frequently have the ability to automate countermeasures against specific threats, like severing impacted systems or upgrading firewalls to block malicious IP addresses. The intelligence is also used to guide incident response plans, which include mitigating and recovering from attacks.

4.1.3.6. Continuous Improvement

Threat intelligence is an ongoing process rather than a one-time event. The knowledge gathered from threat analysis strengthens defenses and security plans. An ever-evolving and cyclical process, threat intelligence is essential to the cybersecurity ecosystem. It is the cornerstone of proactive cyber defense strategies because it gives SOCs the capacity to foresee, recognize, and take prompt, informal action in response to cyberthreats.

4.1.4. Types and Examples of Threat Intelligence

Threat intelligence is a broad field with many subtypes that address diverse cybersecurity requirements. Every category has a distinct function in offering an all-encompassing perspective of the cyberthreat environment.

4.1.4.1. Strategic Intelligence

A high-level perspective of the cybersecurity environment is provided by strategic intelligence, which focuses on long-term trends and insights. For the purpose of giving decision-makers and policy developers a more comprehensive understanding of threats, potential risks, and their effects on business or national security, this kind of intelligence is essential. Some instances are as follows:

- Global cyberthreat reports detail trends in cybercrime, nation-state activities, and advancements in cyber capabilities.
- Analysis of cybersecurity legislation and policy changes and their implications.
- Long-term risk assessments for industries or organizations.

4.1.4.2. Tactical Intelligence

The study of threat actors' TTPs is known as tactical intelligence. Understanding the tactics and methods of attackers is essential for incident responders and SOC teams. Some instances are as follows:

- Detailed analysis of attack patterns and methodologies used in recent cyberattacks.
- Information about specific hacking groups and their preferred methods, such as certain phishing attacks or exploits.
- Best practices and defensive strategies to counter specific TTPs.

4.1.4.3. Operational Intelligence

Operational intelligence focuses on targeted, active, or impending threats and attacks. This highly actionable and frequently time-sensitive intelligence is intended to help SOC teams respond to active threats. Some instances are as follows:

- Real-time alerts about ongoing cyberattack campaigns.
- Information about newly discovered vulnerabilities being actively exploited in the wild.
- Incident reports and breakdowns of recent data breaches or security incidents.

4.1.4.4. Technical Intelligence

The technical aspects of threats, such as malware signatures, IP addresses, and indicators of compromise (IoCs), are the focus of technical intelligence. Teams in charge of IT and security employ this kind of information to erect barriers and address particular technological risks. Some instances are as follows:

- Hash values of threat actors' IP addresses, malicious domain names, or malware files.
- An examination of the behavior of malware, the ways it spreads, and how to remove it.
- Updates and signatures to identify and stop known threats in intrusion prevention and antivirus software.
- Practical Applications:
  - **Technical Intelligence** would offer IoCs like malicious URLs or email addresses used in the campaign, whereas tactical intelligence might include information about a novel phishing technique.
  - **Malware Analysis:** Technical intelligence would cover reports on new malware variants, including their behavior, attack vectors, and impact, while operational intelligence would concentrate on the active campaigns that are currently using that malware.
  - **Emerging Hacking Trends:** Strategic intelligence assists companies in comprehending how these trends may affect their long-term security posture more broadly. Tactical intelligence, on the other hand, focuses on the potential applications of these trends in attacks against them.

When combined, these forms of threat intelligence enable organizations to comprehend and address cyberthreats on several fronts. Technical intelligence is useful in addressing particular threats and incidents, tactical and operational intelligence in daily security operations, and strategic intelligence in long-term planning and policy development.

4.1.5. Need for Threat Intelligence Platform (TIP) in an Organization

Manually compiling threat intelligence data is time-consuming because it often originates from hundreds of sources. This means that rather than depending solely on human analysts, a technical platform is required to handle this task in an automated, intelligent manner. To manually collect and analyze threat intelligence data from various sources, recognize and address potential security risks, and disseminate threat intelligence to other stakeholders, security and threat intelligence teams previously employed a number of tools and procedures (usually through email, spreadsheets or an online portal). This strategy is becoming less effective because:

- Businesses gather vast volumes of data in a variety of formats, including email, XML, JSON, CSV, PDF, and STIX/TAXII.
- Each year, the number and type of security threats (from malicious actors, malware, phishing, botnets, denial-of-service (DDoS) attacks, ransomware, etc.) continue to increase in scope and sophistication.
- Every day, millions of potential threat indicators are generated.
- To avoid extensive harm, businesses need to react to possible security threats far more quickly than in the past.

Teams that work in security and threat intelligence are frequently overloaded with false positives and noise. They consequently find it difficult to identify the data that is most pertinent and useful to their business. They also have trouble telling the difference between genuine and fictitious threats. They must therefore devote more time and energy to addressing the threats that actually represent a risk to their company.

4.1.6. Types of Threat Intelligence Data

Their threat intelligence platforms are reliant on the following categories of data. They guarantee that companies respond quickly to threats as they arise and take proactive measures to foresee and get ready for possible dangers down the road. This all-encompassing strategy is essential for preserving a strong cybersecurity posture in the constantly changing digital environment. Threat intelligence platforms help organizations stay ahead of the cybersecurity arms race by utilizing these kinds of data, guaranteeing a safer and more dependable digital environment.

- **Indicators of Compromise (IoCs):** IoCs are data points that raise the possibility of a system or network breach. They act as the warning signs or traces that an attacker has left behind. Unusual outgoing network traffic, suspicious changes to system files or registry entries, anomalies in the use of privileged user accounts, geolocation anomalies, IP addresses, URLs, and malware hashes are examples of common indicators of compromise (IoCs). IoCs are used to swiftly identify and look into breaches. They are used by security teams to search logs and other data sources for malicious activity.
- **Tactical Data:** This kind of intelligence focuses on the unique techniques used by threat actors. It describes the tools, techniques, and procedures (TTPs) that attackers employ as well as the attack vectors. Comprehending tactical data facilitates the configuration of security systems (such as intrusion detection systems and firewalls) to fend off particular attack techniques. Security professionals use tactical data to understand and anticipate attackers' techniques, allowing them to strengthen their defenses against these methods.
- **Strategic Intelligence:** An overview of the worldwide cybersecurity scene at a high level is given by strategic intelligence. It entails examining the causes, effects, and long-term patterns of cyberthreats. Understanding the geopolitical dimensions of cyberthreats, new trends in cyberthreats, modifications to cyberlaws, and changing cybercriminals' strategies are some examples of this. It helps policymakers create long-term security plans and policies. Organizations can anticipate and get ready for future threats by knowing broader trends.

4.1.7. Implementation of a Threat Intelligence Platform

A threat intelligence platform's implementation is a strategic process with multiple essential steps, all of which are necessary to guarantee the platform's efficacy and compatibility with the unique security requirements of an organization are:

- **Assessing Specific Intelligence Needs:** Establish Goals: Prior to taking any action, organizations need to assess their own threat environment and security goals. This entails determining which assets are most vulnerable to danger, which threats are most pertinent to the company, and the possible consequences of various threat scenarios. The primary emphasis ought to be on spotting, recognizing, and looking into possible attacks, security risks, and malevolent threat actors.

- **Choosing the Right Platform:** It is crucial to choose a threat intelligence platform that works well with the current security setup and integrates seamlessly. Data aggregation and analysis should be possible on the platform using formats that work with the company's current systems. The platform ought to be capable of integrating with current security systems, such as intrusion prevention systems, firewalls, and SIEM, and handling a wide range of data formats.
- **Training Personnel:** Training security staff in the technical aspects of the platform as well as how to interpret and act upon the intelligence provided is essential. This entails knowing how to rank threats according to their context. It is imperative to consistently furnish diverse teams within an organization with information pertaining to threats, thereby advocating for a multidisciplinary approach to threat intelligence.
- **Integrating the Platform:** It is recommended to integrate the threat intelligence platform with the current security tools and protocols. This entails establishing automated response workflows and making sure the platform improves current security operations rather than makes them more difficult. Including threat intelligence platforms into larger security operations, such as planning, monitoring, feedback, response, and remediation procedures, is one of the best practices. Additionally, automated enforcement and cross-team sharing of threat intelligence should be supported by the integration.
- **Continuous Evaluation and Improvement:** The way that threat intelligence is approached should also be constantly changing, just like the threat landscape. To guarantee that the threat intelligence platform continues to be effective against novel and emerging threats, this entails routinely reviewing and updating it. It is crucial to keep one step ahead of threat actors by automating security procedures and updating security systems. This requires constant learning and adaptation.

4.1.8. Practical Use Cases for Threat Intelligence

Not only is threat intelligence theoretical, but it's also an essential part of a program that applies in real-world scenarios to a variety of security domains. It offers crucial insights that enable enterprises to quickly manage and react to cyber threats, from security incident response and triage to security operations and threat hunting. Now let's go over the most common applications of threat intelligence.

4.1.8.1. Incident Response and Triage

Threat intelligence is crucial to incident response and triage. It helps assess the efficacy of incident response by enabling the measurement of important performance metrics like Mean Time To Detect (MTTD) and Mean Time To Respond (MTTR). Organizations can drastically cut response times by integrating threat intelligence with incident response, preserving data security and business continuity.

4.1.8.2. Security Operations and Threat Hunting

Threat intelligence is essential to the proactive detection and mitigation of sophisticated cyber threats (like advanced persistent threats) within security operations. By creating profiles for network applications and examining user and device data, artificial intelligence (AI) technologies and behavioral analytics improve the capacity to identify threats.

4.1.8.3. Vulnerability Management and Risk Analysis

An efficient threat intelligence program that incorporates operational intelligence is essential for vulnerability management. Organizations are able to prioritize patching and take proactive measures to address potential software vulnerabilities by using it to identify critical vulnerabilities that are being actively exploited.

4.1.8.4. Fraud Prevention

Preventing fraudulent uses of your data or brand is critical to maintaining the security of your organization. Deep insights into the strategies and objectives of threat actors are provided by integrating threat intelligence from both surface and subterranean sources. Additionally, you must of your brand or data.

4.1.8.5. Security Leadership

Security chiefs have to strike a balance between the need to defend against new threats and their limited resources. At the end of the day, threat intelligence is what all security professionals need to map the threat landscape, assess risk, and provide the necessary context for making timely, well-informed decisions.

4.1.8.6. Reducing Third-Party Risk

Traditional risk management techniques become inadequate when organizations digitize and increase data collection because they do not provide the necessary context for contemporary security challenges. Threat intelligence improves risk assessment and management by offering up-to-date insights into third-party threat environments.

Threat intelligence is essential for strong cybersecurity because it gives organizations the knowledge they need to foresee and counteract cyberthreats, improving their overall security posture. Through comprehension of the various types of threat intelligence, its lifecycle, and utilization of suitable tools and services, entities can proactively maintain an advantage over cyber threats.

4.2. KEY FEATURES TO CONSIDER IN A TIP

In today's sophisticated threat environment, a threat intelligence platform that relies only on indicators is insufficient as a security tool. Adversaries frequently alter their strategies, and gathered evidence won't reveal the actor's sophistication or motivations. Look for a solution that combines various threat intelligence sources and enables users to access, share, and navigate the information. Platforms for threat intelligence should combine and remove duplicate indicators from various sources. What gives security operations teams direction on what to do next, though, is actor and attack tactic enrichment. Additionally, a wide range of controls or detection tools, such as security analytics (SIEM, NBA), endpoint detection and response (EDR), next-generation firewalls (NGFW), vulnerability and asset management tools, and incident response workflows, should be integrated with the automated process of identifying new attack campaigns.

A TIP should have certain key capabilities, including the following:

4.2.1. Data Sources and Quality

The diversity and caliber of the data sources in a TIP should be your first point of concern. Multiple data sources, including open source, commercial, industry, government, and internal feeds, should be able to be ingested by a good TIP. To give you precise and useful intelligence, it should also be able to corroborate, enrich, and validate the data. Time and resources shouldn't be wasted on irrelevant noise, out-of-date information, or false positives.

4.2.2. Integration and Automation

The TIP's compatibility with your current security procedures and tools should be your second priority. An effective TIP ought to be able to integrate with your firewall, antivirus software, endpoint detection and response (EDR), security information and event management (SIEM), and other systems with ease. Additionally, it ought to be able to automate processes like reporting, enhancing, blocking, and alerting. By doing this, you can improve the efficacy and efficiency of your security while also saving time and lowering human error.

4.2.3. Analysis and Visualization

The capacity to meaningfully analyze and visualize data is the third quality you should search for in a TIP. Dashboards, charts, graphs, maps, and other tools that aid in understanding the background, significance, and patterns of the threats and actors should be available to you from a reliable TIP. Additionally, it ought to be able to accommodate several analysis levels, including tactical, operational, and strategic. You can make decisions, gather information, and interact with your stakeholders in this way.

4.2.4. Customization and Scalability

The TIP's ability to be scaled and tailored to your unique requirements and objectives should be your fourth feature to take into account. A good TIP should be flexible enough to fit your sector, organization, region, and industry. It should also be able to expand with your company and manage big data volumes. A platform that can't adapt to your changing needs or a one-size-fits-all solution should not be your only option.

4.2.5. User Experience and Support

The user experience and support that a TIP provides should be your fifth criteria. Easy to use, configure, and maintain is a must for a good TIP. It ought to offer you technical support, updates, documentation, and training as well. You don't want to deal with a vendor who doesn't care about your happiness or a complicated, glitchy, or out-of-date platform.

4.2.6. Cost and Value

The cost and value of the TIP is the sixth feature you should think about. A decent TIP should have transparent pricing and licensing procedures that are reasonable and adaptable. It should also show you how it helps you accomplish your security goals and give you a clear return on investment (ROI). You don't want to underinvest in a platform that falls short of your expectations or overspend on one that underlives its claims.

4.3. POPULAR TIPS

TIPs generate an alert feed for a security team that is prioritized and contextualized by analyzing internal log files and external threat feeds. TIPs provide improved and consolidated threat feeds, which complement other business security tools.

Here are the top threat intelligence platforms:

- IBM X-Force Exchange;
- Anomali ThreatStream;
- ThreatConnect Platform;
- Recorded Future;
- FireEye Threat Intelligence;
- Splunk Enterprise Security;
- Check Point ThreatCloud;
- CyberProof Defense Center;
- LookingGlass Cyber Solutions;
- Digital Shadows SearchLight.

4.3.1. IBM X-Force Exchange

With the cloud-based platform IBM X-Force Exchange, businesses can streamline compliance and create a strong data security program. Along with faster threat detection and response, access to IBM Watsonx's AI, and the capacity to create unique machine learning models, it offers all the necessary resources to outwit adversaries. Businesses can store and query structured data, manage infrastructure, environments, and deployments, run code on actual quantum systems, aggregate and analyze massive datasets, and run workloads on hybrid cloud infrastructure with IBM X-Force Exchange.

4.3.1.1. History

X-force was created by Internet Security Systems (ISS) in 1996. After ISS was purchased by IBM in 2006, the X-Force name was incorporated into IBM Security. In order to facilitate cooperative defense, the X-Force Exchange TIP was introduced in 2015 and makes available to the general public the vast amount of threat intelligence gathered by IBM X-Force.

4.3.1.2. Description

Through a cloud-based platform, IBM X-Force Exchange offers collaborative threat intelligence that helps security analysts investigate threat indicators and expedite attack responses. It provides information about:

- IP and URL reputation;
- Web applications;
- Malware;
- Vulnerabilities;
- Spam.

Once machine-generated intelligence and carefully selected human-generated insights from IBM X-Force researchers are made available through public case file collections on the most recent malware campaigns and threats, users can further augment their security insights with these resources. With the help of private groups and shared collections, users can work with peers to validate threats, create response plans, and fortify their current security solutions with threat intelligence obtained through open standards.

4.3.1.3. Markets and Use Cases

When IBM introduced the X-Force Exchange in 2015, it was reported that more than 1,000 organizations contributed to the threat database, which included five of the top 10 banks and six of the top 10 retailers worldwide. Additionally, IBM and Check Point announced sharing threat intelligence feeds in 2016. Organizations needing to support a streamlined security investigation process find X-Force Exchange appealing because it offers integrated workflow support through private groups and Collections. According to Dillingham, one retailer significantly shortened the length of their investigations by substituting X-Force Exchange for several threat intelligence feeds. This retailer is collecting threat intelligence through shared collections, freeing the security team to concentrate on using the information rather than on its collection methodology. On the other hand, external feeds can also be fed into an organization's X-Force Exchange dashboard if they wish to include more than one feed. After that, the TIP will compile a threat feed using data from all available sources.

4.3.1.4. Applicable Metrics

Because it is a cloud-based platform, X-Force Exchange can accommodate businesses of any size. Customers can ask as many questions as they want through the Advanced Threat Protection Feed or the platform itself each month. Usage-based billing is compatible with the X-Force Exchange Commercial API. As mentioned above, after a user submits their login credentials or API key for those feeds through the platform, more third-party threat intelligence feeds can be added to X-Force Exchange via the Threat Feed Manager.

4.3.1.5. Security Qualifications

The IBM X-Force Exchange can comply with international compliance standards, including ISO 27001, ISO 27017, ISO 27018, and the EU-US Privacy Shield and Swiss Privacy Shield frameworks, depending on the edition that is selected. X-Force Exchange functions as a threat intelligence platform that can supply automated threat feeds to other security systems that meet the necessary requirements, including firewalls and intrusion detection and prevention systems (IDS or IDPS).

4.3.1.6. Intelligence

Users can use machine-generated intelligence to improve their understanding of network security. IBM QRadar Advisor with Watson also uses threat intelligence from X-Force Exchange, enabling security analysts to take advantage of machine learning capabilities on the QRadar SIEM platform and QRadar SOAR (Security Orchestration, Automation and Response) product. Every threat intelligence that is generated is cross-correlated with pertinent sources that X-Force Exchange uses. This analysis is then automatically generated into reports that offer real-time visibility into other pertinent threat intelligence, activity history, geography, associated indicators, risk score, and categorization. Clients of X-Force IRIS (Incident Response and Threat Intelligence Services) can also obtain additional reports and Indicators of Compromise (also available for the Advanced Threat Protection Feed) from X-Force Exchange Commercial API and X-Force Exchange Enterprise API.

4.3.2. Anomali ThreatStream

Anomali ThreatStream is a platform for managing threat intelligence that automates the gathering, analysis, and conversion of unprocessed data into useful threat intelligence for security teams.

4.3.2.1. Company Description

Since its founding in 2013, Anomali has expanded to employ more than 250 people. It has multiple venture capital investors and is privately held. Its offices are located in Belfast, Dubai, Singapore, and Redwood City. In 2018, Anomali's series D funding brought in an additional $40 million, bringing the total amount of funding since launch to over $96.3million.

4.3.2.2. Description

Organizations are better equipped to identify, look into, and address current cybersecurity threats with the help of the Anomali suite of threat intelligence solutions. ThreatStream TIP enables security teams to swiftly comprehend and contain threats before they affect the entire network by aggregating and optimizing millions of threat indicators and integrating with internal infrastructure to detect new attacks and uncover existing breaches. These are some additional Anomali tools:

- Lens is a commercial product that employs Natural Language Processing (NLP) to scan unstructured data for threats.
- STAXX is a free tool to gather and share threat intelligence using STIX and TAXII standards for machine-readable information formatting.

Anomali offered a free, unconventional intelligence feed called Anomali Limo up until August 14, 2022. Anomali suggests that a replacement might be in the works, but he hasn't given any specifics yet. Anomali does, however, still offer safe threat sharing for threat sharing networks and ISACs. Features of Anomali ThreatStream consist of:

- Automated gathering of threat intelligence from hundreds of sources and formats, including open-source OSINT feeds, Anomali Labs, and information sharing and analysis centers (ISACs).
- Threat information is placed in context with pertinent actors, campaigns, and TTPs (tactical, technical, and procedural).
- Normalization, enrichment, de-duplication of data, and removal of false positives at scale.
- Threat intelligence scoring using machine learning (ML) algorithms to rate confidence in the score that reflects the severity of the threat.
- Global intelligence feed ROI optimizer to assess sources.
- Turnkey threat feed integration for security tools such as SIEMs, SOARs, firewalls, IPS, endpoints, etc.
- Security tool integration for inbound data ingestion and outbound response orchestration.
- Flexible integrations using RESTful API and SDKs.
- Workflows and functionalities to analyze and share data.
- Brand monitoring (automatic search for typosquatted domains & compromised credentials).
- Sandboxing (research malicious indicators directly within the ThreatStream platform).
- Extracting data from suspected phishing emails for immediate blocking.

- MITRE ATT&CK mapping of global threats.
- Visual link analysis to connect indicators to associated higher-level threat models.
- Integrated sandbox to investigate suspicious files.
- Share threat visibility and identification with more than 2,000 other organizations in ThreatStream Trusted Circles.
- Threat bulletins and other finished intelligence products for publishing reports to stakeholders.
- Flexible deployment options: cloud-native, virtual machine, on-premises private instance, or even ThreatStream AirGap – a completely stand-alone instance.

Commercial threat feeds and other apps from the Anomali App Store (some with trial periods) are examples of additional optional features. ThreatStream is "a central platform for collecting, managing, and sharing threat intelligence," according to Anomali. Organizations are guaranteed the ability to recognize and address threats specific to their environment through integration with common security solutions.

4.3.2.3. Markets and Use Cases

According to Anomali, it is beneficial for any organization looking to use threat intelligence in any vertical of the industry. The ThreatStream Platform from Anomali is utilized by numerous Fortune 100 businesses and banks.

4.3.2.4. Applicable Metrics

ThreatStream processes millions of Indicators of Compromise (IOCs) by consuming and analyzing structured and unstructured data from hundreds of threat intelligence feeds.

4.3.2.5. Intelligence

MACULA, a machine learning algorithm, is used by Anomali's ThreatStream platform to score and weight indicators and eliminate false positives. The ThreatStream platform automates data curation tasks that were previously done by hand. Additionally, it integrates with a variety of other security products, such as firewalls, SIEMs, endpoint software, and more. An organization can share threat visibility and identification with over 2,000 other participants through ThreatStream Trusted Circles. The Anomali App Marketplace offers premium threat feeds for purchase to organizations as well.

4.3.3. ThreatConnect Platform

ThreatConnect is a cloud-based solution that uses security orchestration, automation, and response (SOAR) capabilities to assist businesses in identifying and thwarting possible threats. Supervisors are able to keep track of everyday activities and get alerts about high-risk problems automatically. ThreatConnect includes a dashboard that enables businesses to create operational reports and obtain an actionable analytics overview of security events. Using pre-defined templates, managers can keep track of past trends and associate them with risks that have been identified. Through the commenting feature, users can also work with internal teams and obtain crowdsourced intelligence about potential threats. Integration with a number of third-party programs is made easier by ThreatConnect, including Cisco, Splunk, Slack, IBM Security, McAfee, and others. Pricing is available upon request, and support is offered online, over the phone, through email, and through documentation.

4.3.3.1. History

In 2011, Cyber Squared Inc. was established as the company. by Leigh Reichel, Andrew Pendergast, Richard Barger, and Adam Vincent. Following their $4 million series A funding in 2014, they changed their name to ThreatConnect, and in December 2015, they secured $16 million in series B funding. When the company connected Chinese government-sponsored organizations to the Anthem medical data breach, it garnered attention. Cybercrime expert Brian Krebs claims that ThreatConnect discovered domains that the group was using and that were purposefully similar to Anthem's legitimate domains. They also connected Russian-backed cyberespionage group Fancy Bear to Guccifer 2.0, the perpetrator of the 2016 DNC email leak. Additional cyberattacks that they linked to Fancy Bear targeted the World Anti-Doping Agency, which had just released a report regarding state-sponsored doping, as well as an organization looking into the Malaysia Airlines 17 disaster. ThreatConnect purchased Virginia-based Nehemiah Security, a software company, in September 2020.

4.3.3.2. Benefits

- Optimize operations by using orchestration and automated security processes;
- Get ahead of cyber attacks by leveraging threat intelligence;
- Gather artifacts from internal cases/incidents to turn into intel;
- Speed up the process for determining relevancy of IOCs;
- Prioritize security operations on business impact, threat landscape, and vulnerabilities;

- Data enrichment that ties into SecOps specific tools (bi-directional);
- Communication and collaboration tools for within the Security Operations Team;
- Maintain a chain of evidence or timelines of events;
- Time-saving when collecting artifacts from various sources;
- Measure/report MTTR, MTTD, and other KPIs of performance.

4.3.4. Recorded Future

Recorded Future gathers data from various sources and formats using sophisticated machine learning algorithms. It offers data cleansing, threat intelligence scoring, integration with incoming data ingestion, and orchestration of outgoing responses. Rapid threat detection and response are guaranteed by its real-time threat intelligence feeds.

4.3.5. FireEye Threat Intelligence

FireEye offers a platform for threat intelligence that is thorough and incorporates information from various sources. One of its unique selling points is its brand monitoring capability, which provides brand protection by automatically looking for typosquatted domains and compromised credentials.

4.3.6. Splunk Enterprise Security

The Splunk security information and event management (SIEM) solution is part of Splunk Enterprise Security (Splunk ES). It can assist you in leveraging security intelligence throughout the company and aggregating data to gain visibility. Simplified threat management, made possible by Splunk Enterprise Security, reduces risk and speeds up threat detection and response. You can implement incident response, support your security operations center (SOC), achieve continuous monitoring, and notify stakeholders about business risks with the aid of Splunk ES. The solution can be used in a variety of settings, including on-premises infrastructure, public and private clouds, and hybrid deployments. Software for Splunk ES is available when utilizing Splunk Enterprise. Additionally, Splunk Cloud users can access it as a cloud service.

4.3.6.1. How Splunk ES Can Help Organizations

Here are a few common use cases of Splunk Enterprise Security.

4.3.6.1.1. Continuously Monitor Security Posture

With the use of pre-made dashboards and Custom Glass Table views, Splunk ES assists in visualizing the security posture of your company. Static and dynamic thresholds, trending indicators, and security and performance metrics are some of these views. Additionally, Splunk ES provides a Use Case Library to speed up the identification of both known and unknown threats.

4.3.6.1.2. Prioritize and Act on Incidents

Splunk ES has a number of features that can help you streamline your incident response procedures. Centralized logs, pre-defined reports and correlations, alerts and incidents, correlations for particular views, and incident response workflows are among the noteworthy features.

4.3.6.1.3. Rapid Investigations

By providing ad hoc search capabilities in addition to static, dynamic, and visual correlations to aid in the detection of malicious activity, Splunk ES speeds up investigations. It enables you to rapidly build threat context by allowing you to explore and pivot on different fields from any data. When tracking an attacker's movements, you can use threat context to confirm evidence and find out more details.

4.3.6.1.4. Handle Multi-Step Investigations

Using Splunk ES, you can track down and examine breaches to find out what activities are connected to compromised systems. To learn more about the attack lifecycle, you can use the investigator journal, the investigation timeline, Splunk ES capabilities, and ad hoc searches.

4.3.6.2. Splunk Enterprise Security Features

4.3.6.2.1. Security Posture

Splunk Enterprise Security offers the following features to help you gain visibility into your security posture:

- **A Library of Security Posture Widgets**—you can add widgets to your dashboards or create your own.
- **View Security Events by Categories**—you can view events by location, source type, host, geography, and asset groupings.
- **Use KPIs to Assess Security Posture**—you can use KPIs to see trends and monitor your security posture.

4.3.6.2.2. Incident Review and Classification

For incident review and classification, Splunk Enterprise Security provides the following features:

- **Review:** Splunk ES allows you to view incidents as a single event or as a "roll-up" of related events. Additionally, it offers security teams an incident management workflow.
- **Classify:** With Splunk ES, you can assign incidents to team members, modify the criticality and status of incidents, and verify incidents.
- **Track:** For team metrics, Splunk ES audits, watches, and records status changes.

4.3.6.2.3. Endpoint Protection

The endpoint protection features offered by Splunk Enterprise Security include:

- **Endpoint Protection:** Splunk ES offers reports, searches, and a library of alerts for infrequent activity, malicious software (malware), and resource availability and utilization.
- **Prioritizing Threats:** Splunk ES assists with prioritizing threats and observing long-term patterns.
- **Integration:** Symantec Endpoint Protection, McAfee Endpoint Protection, IBM Proventia Desktop, and other endpoint security solutions can be integrated with Splunk ES.

4.3.6.2.4. Network Protection

You can monitor and identify events from a variety of network and security devices with the assistance of Splunk Enterprise Security's features. Searches, correlations, dashboards, reports, and alerts on network-based events are among the noteworthy features. The method uses statistical analysis on proxy data to explain behavioral outliers based on HTTP. It can assist you in identifying irregularities in a variety of components, such as intrusion detection sensors, routers, firewalls, data loss prevention (DLP) devices, load balancers, and wireless access points.

4.3.6.2.5. Threat Intelligence Framework

Splunk ES allows you to use threat feeds from multiple sources, which improves incident investigations. It is possible to weight feeds based on their relative values. It can also automatically gather, combine, and separate duplicate feeds. These are typical feeds:

- **Open Source Feeds**—available as flat files via an API service.
- **Subscription-Based Feeds**—available via TCP streaming.
- **Law Enforcement or Local Environment Feeds**—available through manual download.
- **Shared Threat Feeds**—available as OpenIOC or STIX documents via the TAXII protocol.

4.3.6.2.6. Risk-Based Analysis

You are able to rate the risk of assets, events, users, and behavior using Splunk Enterprise Security. You have the option of allocating points based on the value or relative importance of each component. Prioritizing security events and investigations can be aided by risk scores. Additionally, you can monitor component security status to comprehend and proactively manage business risk. These are the essential skills:

- **Index all Data Sources:** You can use all data with this solution without having to get vendor support or create custom connectors. Rapid access to, searching for, and analysis of data pertinent to the investigation is made possible by this degree of flexibility.
- **Scalability:** You can index hundreds of terabytes of data every day with this solution. Furthermore, it indexes data without using any schema, allowing you to search through terabytes of data quickly.
- **Flexible Dashboards:** The solution offers dashboards that are simple to construct or modify, allowing you to quickly produce a graphical representation of significant data or correlation. You can alter the view to see the organization's overall security posture and to see multiple dashboards on one screen.
- **Ad hoc Searches:** With the solution, you can quickly identify active attacks in the environment and choose the best course of action by conducting ad hoc searches.

4.3.6.3. How Does the Incident Review Process Work?

Let's examine the incident review procedure in more detail. You can filter and examine the data to prioritize security incidents using the Incident Review dashboard, which shows security events and their status. An "notable event" is a concept used by the dashboard. One or more data points that are correlated as belonging to the same security incident across multiple data sources are considered notable events. A noteworthy event could include, for instance, persistently unusual network usage, one or more attempts by unauthorized users to access a particular system, or hosts interacting with known malicious IP addresses.

Here is a sample workflow for triage of notable events:

- When reviewing the dashboard, an administrator or entry-level analyst uses sorting and filtering to find any newly noteworthy events.
- An event that needs to be investigated is assigned by the analyst to a Tier 1 analyst.
- The event's status is changed to In Progress by a Tier 1 analyst.
- Using the fields in the event object, the Tier 1 analyst gathers data regarding the incident. She logs her observations in the event's Comments section.
- The analyst can now perform adaptive response actions via actions available for the event.
- Once the event is fully investigated and remediation tasks are performed or escalated to other teams, the analyst changes the event's status to Resolved.
- The Tier 1 analyst assigns this event to a Tier 2 analyst for verification.
- The Tier 2 analyst validates the investigation and actions taken to resolve this issue, and then changes the issue's status to Closed.

4.3.6.4. Splunk Enterprise Security Pricing

Splunk Enterprise Security available pricing plans:

- **Workload Pricing:** The amount of compute capacity used by your analytics and search workloads determines the price of this plan. To help you manage how your entire capacity is used across various scenarios and Splunk capabilities, Splunk provides a number of licensing options.
- **Ingest Pricing:** This plan's volume consumption is determined by ingesting GB of data every day. By purchasing the next ingest level that is available, you can use more data. Existing clients can still choose this well-known pricing option.

4.3.6.5. Licensing Options for Splunk Enterprise Security

Splunk Enterprise Security provides term licenses that are time-limited. Although one-year terms are the norm, multi-year term license options are also offered. You can access and utilize Splunk Enterprise Security within the allotted time. At the conclusion of the term, you can either buy additional licenses or cease using the software.

4.3.7. Check Point ThreatCloud

Check Point ThreatCloud predicts, detects, and prevents threats by leveraging big data analytics, artificial intelligence, and machine learning. Its data cleansing capability ensures accuracy and relevance in threat data by removing false positives and duplicating data.

4.3.7.1. Check Point ThreatCloud Network

Check Point ThreatCloud is a constantly updated service built on a creative global network of threat sensors and organizations that work together to exchange threat intelligence and combat contemporary malware.

Consumers can receive protection updates with enhanced threat intelligence by sending their own threat data to the ThreatCloud. Clients who use the ThreatCloud network can gain from enhanced security and protection by utilizing the malware data that is gathered. Subsequently, the ThreatCloud can disseminate attack data, converting zero-day attacks into recognized signatures that the Anti-Virus Software Blade can stop. The most recent operating system environments and threat intelligence are sent to your network when you send files to the ThreatCloud service for emulation. By default, the ThreatCloud connection is enabled. This link provides a wealth of management functionalities. It is advised that it be turned on. You can alter the default setting to prevent this connection.

4.3.7.2. The ThreatCloud Intellistore

In addition to ThreatCloud, ThreatCloud Intellistore serves as a marketplace for threat intelligence, offering information from top cybersecurity providers. The data includes threat details such as IP addresses, domain names, URLs, command and control networks, DOS attacks, and more. Intellistore categorizes the available information feeds based on industries, geographies, and attack types, allowing you to select the feeds that best meet your needs. These feeds represent specialized intelligence that has been gathered and analyzed by vendors. ThreatCloud then converts this intelligence into Security Gateway-based defenses.

4.3.8. CyberProof Defense Center

CyberProof has sophisticated threat detection and response features, including the ability to extract data from dubious emails and block them right away (phishing response). Its platform easily combines with various security tools to improve defense capabilities all around.

4.3.9. LookingGlass Cyber Solutions

LookingGlass offers a machine learning-powered comprehensive threat intelligence platform. It provides a comprehensive approach to cyber threat management with threat intelligence scoring, automated data collection, data cleansing, and integration with security tools.

4.3.9.1. Description

To deliver up-to-date information on malware, malicious URLs, malicious entities, and indicators of compromise (IoCs), the LookingGlass scoutPrime tool integrates over 100 threat feeds. A global team of security analysts is adding to it by constantly improving the data feeds and giving clients insight into potential threats from the physical, digital, and third sectors. By using this TIP, analysts can provide guidance to stakeholders through customizable threat intelligence scoring, third-party risk monitoring, and a flexible analyst workflow. According to the company, "customers can take action on threat intelligence across the different stages of the attack life cycle with the help of prioritized, relevant, and timely insights."

Scoutprime also delivers the following features:

- Dynamic internet footprinting: monitor and analyze internet-accessible assets and networks to detect connections to known command-and-control nodes;
- Risk scoring and prioritization: a proprietary Threat Indicator Confidence score ranks threats based on the attack surface, an organization's environment, and threat landscape;
- Integration with additional tools such as geolocation, pDNS, Shodan, and WhoIs/Reverse WhoIs;
- Data aggregation: Aggregates, indexes, and normalizes data sources, proprietary indicators, and intelligence feeds;
- Real-time alerts available through email for new vulnerabilities, exceeded thresholds, and workflow triggers;
- Relationship monitoring classifies assets into groups and subgroups to monitor and develop categorized risk profiles;
- APIs and integrations export threat intelligence to security appliances;

- Reporting: Unlimited automated and on-demand management reports and scorecards.

4.3.9.2. Markets and Use Cases

All verticals can use LookingGlass, but third-party risk monitoring is where it will be most widely adopted. Originating in the National Security Agency, LookingGlass is primarily being adopted by the defense, energy, financial, and government sectors.

4.3.9.3. Applicable Metrics

LookingGlass ScoutPrime expands to accommodate the needs of the world's top 50 corporations. Threat intelligence is produced by gathering, ingesting, aggregating, normalizing, enriching, and analyzing threat data from more than 140 sources.

4.3.10. Digital Shadows Searchlight

A UK-based provider of cyber threat intelligence, Digital Shadows assists customers in locating private information that may be accessible via mobile, cloud, and social media platforms. The Digital Shadows Searchlight analysis platform gives you access to both your attackers' profile and your digital footprint. Through an "attacker's eye view" analysis of the organization, cyber situational awareness can help prevent, detect, and contain cyber-related incidents by warning you about potential threats, instances of compromised brand integrity, or loss of sensitive data. By leveraging SearchLight's extensive database of cyberthreats, Digital Shadows' professional services offerings offer a suite of solutions that significantly improve an organization's cyber situational awareness at the tactical, operational, and strategic levels.

REFERENCES

1. Adewopo, V., Gonen, B., & Adewopo, F. (2020). Exploring open source information for cyber threat intelligence. In *2020 IEEE International Conference on Big Data (Big Data)* (pp. 2232–2241).
2. Bing, C. (2016). This cyber startup is flying under the radar with a monster valuation. *DC Inno*.
3. Burger, E. W., Goodman, M. D., Kampanakis, P., & Zhu, K. A. (2014). Taxonomy model for cyber threat intelligence information exchange technologies. In *Proceedings of the 2014 ACM Workshop on Information Sharing & Collaborative Security* (pp. 51–60). ACM.
4. Caltagirone, S. (n.d.). Diamond model of intrusion analysis–A summary. ActiveResponse.org. Retrieved from: http://www.activeresponse.org/wp-content/uploads/2013/07/diamond_summary.pdf (accessed on 9 October 2024).
5. Camh, J. (2014). State governments & the future of cyber security regulation. *Information Week Bank Systems and Technology*. Retrieved from: http://www.banktech.com/compliance/state-governments-and-the-future-of-cyber-security-regulation/d/d-id/1279216 (accessed on 9 October 2024).
6. Du, P. Y., et al. (2018). Identifying, collecting, and presenting hacker community data: Forums, IRC, carding shops, and DNMs. In *2018 IEEE International Conference on Intelligence and Security Informatics (ISI)* (pp. 70–75).
7. Fung, B. (2014). Washington is making it easier for businesses to swap notes on hackers. *The Washington Post*. Retrieved from: https://www.washingtonpost.com/news/the-switch/wp/2014/04/10/washington-is-making-it-easier-for-businesses-to-swap-notes-on-hackers/ (accessed on 9 October 2024).
8. Guarascio, M., Ritacco, E., Biondo, D., Mammoli, R., & Toma, A. (2017). Integrating a framework for discovering alternative app stores in a mobile app monitoring platform. In *NFMCP 2017* (Vol. 10785, LNCS).
9. Heimdal Security Blog. (2022). Top 7 open source threat intelligence platforms that you can choose in 2022. https://heimdalsecurity.com/blog/open-source-threat-intelligence-platform-tip/ (accessed on 9 October 2024).
10. Holland, R. (2014). Actionable intelligence, meet Terry Tate, office linebacker. Forrester Research. Retrieved from: http://blogs.forrester.com/rick_holland/14-02-11-actionable_intelligence_meet_terry_tate_office_linebacker (accessed on 9 October 2024).

11. Hutchins, E. M., Cloppert, M. J., & Amin, R. M. (2009). Intelligence-driven computer network defense informed by analysis of adversary campaigns and intrusion kill chains. Lockheed Martin Corporation. Retrieved from: http://www.lockheedmartin.com/content/dam/lockheed/data/corporate/documents/LM-White-Paper-IntelDriven-Defense.pdf (accessed on 9 October 2024).

12. Krebs, B. (2016). Anthem breach may have started in April 2014. *Krebs On Security*.

13. Lewis, J. A. (2014). Cyber threat and response–Combating advanced attacks and cyber espionage. Center for Strategic and International Studies. Retrieved from: http://csis.org/files/publication/140313_FireEye_WhitePaper_Final.pdf (accessed on 9 October 2024).

14. Lockheed Martin. (n.d.). The Cyber Kill Chain. Lockheed Martin. Retrieved from: https://www.lockheedmartin.com/en-us/capabilities/cyber/cyber-kill-chain.html (accessed on 9 October 2024).

15. Mandiant. (n.d.). *APT1: Exposing One of China's Cyber Espionage Units*. FireEye. Retrieved from: https://www.fireeye.com/content/dam/fireeyewww/services/pdfs/mandiant-apt1-report.pdf (accessed on 9 October 2024).

16. Mukaram, A. (2014). Cyber threat landscape: Forecast. Recorded Future. Retrieved from: https://www.recordedfuture.com/cyber-threat-landscape-forecast/ (accessed on 9 October 2024).

17. Nakashima, E. (2015). Security firm finds link between China and Anthem hack. *The Washington Post*.

18. O'Donnell, C. (2016). Threat intelligence startup ThreatConnect closes $16M investment round and makes strategic move within Arlington. *Arlington Economic Development*.

19. Overly, S. (2014). Cybersecurity firm Cyber Squared raises $4 million, changes name to ThreatConnect. *The Washington Post*.

20. Robinson, T. (2016). ThreatConnect: Guccifer 2.0 likely persona for Russian-linked propagandists, PR operatives leaking info to media. *SC Magazine*. Haymarket Media Group.

21. Rothstein, E. (2015). Shirlington startup helping big companies prevent hacking. *ARLnow - Arlington, VA Local News & Community*.

22. Sauerwein, C., Fischer, D., Rubsamen, M., Rosenberger, G., Stelzer, D., & Breu, R. (2021). From threat data to actionable intelligence: An exploratory analysis of the intelligence cycle implementation in cyber

threat intelligence sharing platforms. In *The 16th International Conference on Availability, Reliability, and Security (ARES 2021)*.

23. Schwartz, E. H. (2014). Virginia cybersecurity startup Cyber Squared gets $4M and a name change. *The Capital*.
24. Thielman, S. (2016). Same Russian hackers likely breached Olympic drug-testing agency and DNC. *The Guardian*.

CHAPTER 5

AUTOMATED THREAT ANALYSIS

Contents

INTRODUCTION

Security teams must prioritize and handle a plethora of potential threats, and automating threat analysis is essential to this process. Threat analysis is a laborious process that many teams find themselves having to manually navigate through various tools, evaluate the findings of each analysis, identify any secondary artifacts, and then combine the data to create insights for remedial action.

This manual method wastes analyst cycles and results in slower response times. Security teams are always playing catch-up as threat actors exploit vulnerabilities and adapt to security measures, which is exacerbated by understaffed teams. The time it takes to conduct a thorough investigation and provide the prompt response required in the face of emerging cyberthreats highlights the inefficiency of manual threat analysis. Using cutting-edge software tools and algorithms, automated threat analysis is a novel approach to cybersecurity that speeds up alert triage by rapidly determining related forensics, verdicts, and scores.

By automating threat analysis in your company with Splunk Attack Analyzer and Splunk SOAR, you can accomplish the following goals: Recognize and evaluate possible security risks without requiring a lot of human involvement. Handle phishing attacks well, as they are the most common attack vector for many organizations. Analyze data faster and at a scale not possible for human analysts. Stay up to date on new tactics, techniques, and procedures (TTPs) so that deep analysis can be performed automatically, something that traditional tools cannot support due to their architecture. Even in situations where analysts are in short supply, automate the analysis of suspected malware and phishing emails. React to threats with greater efficiency and speed.

5.1. CYBER THREAT ANALYSIS

Effective cyber threat analysis is essential to cybersecurity. It is a crucial process that includes locating, examining, and assessing possible threats in order to preserve the integrity of our digital environments.

It's critical for companies utilizing Software as a Service (SaaS) platforms to understand and apply efficient threat analysis techniques, especially for those in the cyber threat intelligence space. Since threat intelligence is typically viewed as a security technology with a "low ROI," many security teams completely forego CTI programs. At Flare, we think this perspective is essentially false. The foundation of a security program can be provided by threat intelligence.

5.1.1. Understanding Cyber Threat Analysis: The Basics and Importance

The increasing use of technology for both personal and organizational purposes raises serious concerns about cybersecurity. Cyber threat analysis is a crucial part of comprehensive cybersecurity measures. Cyber threat analysis is a process that entails the identification, assessment, and comprehension of potential cyber threats that could harm a system, network, or organization. So, what is it, and why is it important? To assess and rank possible threats, it integrates elements of forensics, security intelligence, and data analysis. This assessment considers the potential impact of a given threat in addition to its likelihood of occurring. Organizations must remain ahead of potential risks as cyber threats continue to evolve in sophistication and complexity. Reactive actions are frequently expensive and can irreversibly harm a company's reputation once a threat has materialized. On the other hand, proactive steps like cyber threat analysis assist in foreseeing and reducing risks before they have a chance to cause major damage.

Cyber threat analysis is the key to effective cybersecurity through:

- Identifying patterns of suspicious behavior;
- Discovering security gaps;
- Predicting likely future attacks based on historical data;
- Discovering threat actors targeting your organization on the dark web;
- Understanding the methods employed by potential threat actors.

In a world where cyber threats are not a matter of 'if', but 'when', mastering the art and science of cyber threat analysis becomes vital for any organization navigating the digital environment.

5.1.2. Components of Effective Cyber Threat Analysis

Many essential elements are included in a thorough and efficient cyber threat analysis process. By combining all of these, security teams are better equipped to respond quickly and forcefully to threats that affect their organization.

Here are the five core components that shape a robust cyber threat analysis:

5.1.2.1. Threat Intelligence Gathering

Obtaining information regarding possible threats is the first step in the analysis process. Numerous sources, such as industry reports, open-source intelligence (OSINT), commercial threat intelligence feeds, and internal system logs, may provide this data. In order to identify potential threat patterns and indicators of compromise (IoCs), the goal is to compile as much pertinent data as possible. Not only does large data collection constitute the foundation of threat intelligence, but also the ability to identify new sources for data collection, contextualize data, and—above all—extrapolate actionable security information from intricate technical events. Stealer logs are a serious new threat that allows malicious actors to get around 2FA and MFA controls. For instance, a company that has been gathering the same intelligence for the past five years will have missed their introduction. Another striking illustration is the introduction of Telegram as a significant player in the ecosystem of cybercrime. By excluding this vital source of data, teams that solely gather from Tor sites risk missing out on a ton of context and valuable intelligence.

5.1.2.2. Threat Evaluation

After the data has been collected, evaluation is necessary. Understanding the nature of the threat data that has been gathered, as well as the tactics, techniques, and procedures (TTPs) that threat actors use, is part of this phase. Organizations are able to organize their response efforts according to the likelihood and potential severity of each threat. It is crucial to have teams with training who can not only analyze technical data but also translate that information into business terms and perform risk-based analysis. Although many organizations have excellent technical teams, they frequently fall short when it comes to communicating risk information.

5.1.2.3. Contextual Analysis

Every organization is not at the same risk from every threat. In the contextual analysis stage, you will learn how a specific threat fits into your unique organizational environment.

This could involve considering your:

- Industry sector;
- The nature of your data;
- Your digital infrastructure;
- Even geopolitical factors.

Comprehending the threat's context in relation to your business's larger framework is crucial. Context plays a crucial role in threat intelligence. For illustration, consider this piece of information out of context: "North Korea launches dozens of missiles amid soaring tensions." You would understandably be extremely concerned if you read that news headline without knowing anything about North Korea's past actions, the location of the missile launches, or any other info. On the other hand, your level of concern would probably drop if you were informed that this has happened previously, that they launched them into the sea, and that nobody was hurt.

5.1.2.4. Predictive Analysis

Predictive analysis is the next step after having a solid understanding of potential threats and their significance to your organization. Predictive analysis employs machine learning algorithms and historical data to identify potential future threats. It's a proactive approach that gives organizations the ability to get ready for and even stop possible attacks. If you have a lot of data, predictive analytics can be very helpful.

5.1.2.5. Threat Mitigation Strategy Development

The creation of mitigation strategies is the last step in an efficient cyber threat analysis process. Security teams can create a plan to safeguard the digital assets of their company using the gathered information and predictive analysis. This could include any number of things.

- Strengthening security protocols;
- Applying software patches;
- Implementing more advanced cybersecurity technologies.

You can make sure that your company stays ahead of emerging cyber threats by incorporating these essential elements into your cyber threat analysis. It takes more than just responding to cyberthreats to effectively and strategically handle them. It's priceless to have the assurance that you're ready for anything the digital world may throw at you.

5.1.3. Step-by-Step Guide: Executing Cyber Threat Analysis

A proactive strategy that supports your company's cybersecurity measures is cyber threat analysis. Understanding, foreseeing, and mitigating possible threats before they have a chance to cause harm is the aim. To do this successfully, take into consideration the following detailed instructions:

5.1.3.1. Identify Potential Threats

This involves gathering threat intelligence from a variety of sources like

- Log files;
- Threat intelligence feeds;

- Industry reports.

Gather as much data as you can about possible threats, paying particular attention to their signatures, or indicators of compromise (IoCs). This step frequently entails automating the gathering of threat intelligence through the use of specialized software tools.

5.1.3.2. Analyze Collected Intelligence

As soon as the data is collected, begin analyzing it to identify any possible risks. Search the data for trends and connections, and note the TTPs (tactical, technical, and procedural) that criminal actors are employing. By doing this, you can better grasp the threats facing your company and the risks they pose.

5.1.3.3. Evaluate the Relevance of Threats

Every organization has unique vulnerabilities. Evaluate how the identified threats might impact your specific context, including your:

- Industry;
- Data sensitivity;
- Digital infrastructure.

This step requires an in-depth understanding of your organization's unique digital environment and potential vulnerabilities.

5.1.3.4. Prioritize Threats

Sort the threats in order of possible impact and probability of occurrence based on your assessment. Setting priorities makes it easier to concentrate your security efforts and guarantees that the biggest threats are dealt with first.

5.1.3.5. Predict Future Threats

Anticipate upcoming cyberthreats by using the analysis. This entails evaluating past data, present trends, and developing technologies. Patterns that may point to potential future cyberthreats can be found with the help of predictive analytics tools.

5.1.3.6. Develop Mitigation Strategies

With a clear understanding of your threat landscape, you can then create strategies to mitigate identified threats. This involves:

- Remedying identified vulnerabilities

- Strengthening your defense systems
- Formulating response protocols in the event of a security breach

5.1.3.7. Implement and Review

Lastly, put the strategies into practice while regularly assessing their efficacy. It's critical to maintain dynamic and adaptable threat analysis and mitigation strategies because cyber threats are always changing. It's important to regularly review and update your strategies to make sure you're ready for any new threats.

Effective cyber threat analysis is a continuous process. It's a cycle of:

- Collecting data;
- Analyzing it;
- Predicting threats;
- Developing, implementing, and reviewing strategies.

This ongoing process ensures that your cybersecurity measures stay robust and up-to-date in the face of an ever-evolving threat landscape.

5.1.4. Leveraging SaaS Platforms for Advanced Cyber Threat Analysis

SaaS (Software as a Service) platforms have become invaluable allies for organizations as they battle an ever-growing digital threat landscape. The sophisticated tools and services offered by these platforms can greatly improve the effectiveness of cyber threat analysis. They are important in the following ways:

5.1.4.1. Automated Data Collection

Large-scale data collection from multiple sources, including network logs, cloud environments, and external threat intelligence feeds, can be automated by SaaS platforms. This enables businesses to compile an extensive set of data that serves as the foundation for a thorough and precise threat analysis.

5.1.4.2. Sophisticated Analysis Tools

SaaS platforms are able to conduct in-depth analyses of the gathered data by utilizing cutting-edge technologies like artificial intelligence and machine learning. They are able to spot trends, pick up on abnormalities, and highlight possible dangers that might go unnoticed otherwise. This makes threat detection more accurate and thorough.

5.1.4.3. Contextual Insights

These platforms are able to assess the significance of threats based on an organization's specific digital environment and risk factors by integrating contextual intelligence. By having this contextual understanding, businesses can make sure that the threats that are most pertinent to their specific situation are prioritized and addressed.

5.1.4.4. Real-Time Monitoring

SaaS platforms offer ongoing, in-the-moment digital asset monitoring for businesses. This makes it possible to identify any suspicious activity right away and respond quickly to stop any serious harm from happening.

5.1.4.5. Scalability

SaaS platforms adapt to an organization's changing needs. These systems can offer strong threat analysis capabilities even as a company's digital environment develops, guaranteeing that cybersecurity precautions are effective no matter how big the company.

5.1.4.6. Integration Capabilities

By combining SaaS platforms with pre-existing security infrastructures and tools, threat detection and analysis can be done in a unified and coordinated manner. This gives an organization's security posture a thorough overview and helps to eliminate potential blind spots.

5.1.4.7. Continuous Updates

Businesses can take advantage of frequent updates and improvements with SaaS platforms. SaaS providers update their platforms in response to emerging tactics and methods used by cybercriminals in order to counter evolving cybersecurity threats.

Cyber threat analysis using a SaaS platform can offer enterprises advanced, scalable, and real-time cybersecurity solutions. These platforms help businesses stay ahead of potential cyber threats and effectively safeguard their vital digital assets by streamlining the process of threat analysis and improving its efficacy. But selecting the best platform requires giving careful thought to the unique requirements of your company, the features that the platform offers, and how well it works with the security infrastructure that you already have in place.

5.1.5. Types of Threats Found in a Threat Analysis

An accurate and thorough cybersecurity threat analysis can uncover 3 main types of threats, which we'll go over one by one.

5.1.5.1. Accidental Threats

Unfortunately, one of the primary causes of cyberattacks nowadays is human error. This includes any mishap that could expose the infrastructure of a company, as well as incorrectly configuring security protocols. In addition to being unintentional, these mistakes could also be caused by insufficient compliance procedures and staff training. Through the implementation of threat analysis, organizations can identify and address inadvertent vulnerabilities prior to their being exploited by malevolent actors.

5.1.5.2. Intentional Threats

Malicious actions carried out by nefarious groups inside the company with the aim of gaining access to and profiting from the company's confidential information are referred to as intentional threats. They certainly cause the most harm, despite being less common.

5.1.5.3. External Threats

Attacks by externally motivated malicious entities are the most frequent threats that an organization must deal with. Known as "black-hat hackers," these criminals prey on businesses, authorities, organizations, or even private citizens who possess sensitive data. Their methods mostly revolve around taking advantage of holes in an organization's infrastructure. Even though there have been significant improvements in safeguarding an organization from these kinds of threats, they remain dangerous due to their growing frequency and quick adaptation to different defenses.

5.1.6. Benefits of Threat Analysis in Cyber Security?

It is imperative for any business, regardless of size, to remain ahead of malevolent threats. Points of vulnerability have grown as data has become more decentralized. Therefore, as part of threat analysis, it is essential to comprehend and evaluate an organization's infrastructure and patch all known exploits used in order to stay one step ahead of cyber threats. These are the top three benefits of using a threat analysis approach; let's examine them.

5.1.6.1. Continual Updates to Threat Modeling

Developing current and effective threat models is one of the most important components of a strong cybersecurity strategy. The purpose of threat models is to offer comprehensive and in-depth analysis of contemporary cyberthreats. Furthermore, threat models are quickly changing to keep up with the rapid expansion of the modern digital landscape. Therefore, it becomes essential to update threat models on a regular basis in order to remain safe from the most advanced threats ever created.

5.1.6.2. Reduce Attack Surface

An organization's attack surface is significantly reduced when it invests in a strong threat analysis approach.

This is a result of threat analysis providing them with an exhaustive list of all threats that have been identified. Furthermore, after thoroughly patching all points of exploit that these threats use, it becomes much easier to reduce the effective attack surface because the majority of similar threats are based on the same exploit.

5.1.6.3. Up-to-Date Risk Profile

An organization's security infrastructure can be greatly improved by maintaining an up-to-date risk profile, which is a security attribute that is produced through continuous analysis and classification of threats using an internal repository or risk management system.

This profile can help an organization's risk mitigation strategy get better over time and be used to conduct internal audits of security policies and procedures. All of this affects businesses greatly when they try to enhance their security infrastructure.

5.1.7. Phases of Threat Analysis Process

Threat analysis processes can be carried out in a variety of ways within an organization, but they should be structured to ensure that the entirety of the infrastructure is examined and yield repeatable results based on industry standards. But regardless of the method, at a core level, they all share four main components:

5.1.7.1. Scope

The scope of the analysis defines threat, asset or software, and threat environment that will be covered under that analysis.

5.1.7.2. Data Collection

In order to transform data into valuable insights that can direct threat assessments, a threat analyst needs unrestricted access to the information. The information can be stored in system logs for later review or it can be investigated and extracted. Examples of information sources include open-source internet searches, malware reverse engineering, firewall logs, reported exploitations, intrusion incidents, internal policies and procedures, logs and warnings, system configuration data, and other sources.

5.1.7.3. Threat Analysis

The real threat analysis process begins at this point. The threat analyst begins by testing and analyzing the data gathered in the earlier stages using security tools to identify potential risk areas. The organization will determine the possibility that a threat will be found and the potential consequences of its successful deployment for each one that has been identified. These potential effects fall into the categories of those that have an impact on the infrastructure or data integrity, confidentiality, and availability of the organization.

5.1.7.4. Mitigation and Acceptance

The business must choose which vulnerabilities will be fixed right away and which will have to wait after all threats have been identified. This acceptance may be explained, among other things, by the high expense or difficulty of protecting against that threat or the low probability of recurrence. Whatever the outcome, all actions and decisions must be approved by the executives of the organization, who also have to publicly state their agreement with the resolution.

5.1.8. Approaches to Cyber Threat Analysis (Methodology)

The following are various potential approaches for performing cyber threat analysis:

5.1.8.1. Threat Metrics

An organization can detect and record patterns in system behavior and recognize abnormalities when they occur by maintaining a record of security metrics. It can also be used to establish a connection between some unusual metrics and potential consequences. Adopting a systematic approach to identifying, evaluating, and disclosing risks has various benefits, even though its influence is minimal in comparison to alternative methods. Primarily, it facilitates data-driven choices about security measures, investments, and the rationale behind system modifications. The number of intrusions or attacks that occur each month is a prime illustration of a quantitative cybermetric. These figures may demonstrate the ability and intent of the enemy if they are accumulated over time.

5.1.8.2. Threat Models

Let's go into a little more detail now that we have reviewed threat models in brief previously. Threat models are designed only to quantify a threat's potential harm to a system. Threat agents that pose a risk to your infrastructure are identified, replicated, and used to perform an extensive software architecture analysis. A deeper comprehension and the discovery of significant system components are made possible by this process. The degree of threat posed by an organization cannot be determined solely by metrics. To identify and reduce risks, a more comprehensive security strategy would combine measurements with a methodical technique (like threat modeling).

5.1.8.3. The Generic Threat Matrix

This approach makes it simpler to completely characterize the threats and their severity by utilizing threat attributes and their risk level to do so. For the purpose of efficient threat management, analysts can perform unbiased analysis much more easily by grouping these threats into different levels.

5.1.9. Conduct Cyber Threat Analysis

Let us proceed to examine the process of conducting cyber threat analysis. As previously mentioned, these five steps do offer some general ideas that are fundamental to any cyber threat analysis, even though the specific methodology may vary depending on the organization.

5.1.9.1. Step 1: Identify All Network Assets

Finding and compiling a complete inventory of all endpoints and network assets is the first stage in performing a cyber threat analysis. This is typically accomplished by consulting the digital inventory list. At this point, a network architecture diagram that shows the connectivity and communication between each asset, process, and entry point is also very helpful.

5.1.9.2. Step 2: Collect Data From Network Traffic Monitoring

These malicious entities regularly scan the organization's network for any potential points of vulnerability because the majority of malware establishes connections with its assets through the network. Typically, they concentrate on TCP/UDP listening ports, such as SMTP, HTTP, FTP, and proxy servers. You can record these requests that are sent over the company network and assist with traffic monitoring by setting up network monitoring and network threat analysis.

5.1.9.3. Step 3: Trigger

Trigger, the third phase in the cyber threat analysis process, directs cyber security experts to a particular area of the system or network that they believe may be compromised. Using a variety of cutting-edge detection techniques, that portion of the system is fully monitored to spot any unusual behavior that could point to malicious activity. Proactive hunting often starts with a thought about a new threat. A hypothesis outlines possible environmental consequences or threats and the most effective methods for locating them. Start looking for indicators of compromise, assess environmental factors, and incorporate industry experience to create the most successful threat hunts.

5.1.9.4. Step 4: Investigation

Using multiple technologies, including Endpoint Detection and Response (EDR), the threat analyst conducts a thorough investigation into a suspected attack or compromised system during the investigation phase. Until the investigation is judged pointless or a complete picture of the dangerous threat is found, the investigation is carried out.

5.1.9.5. Step 5: Response and Resolution

Threats are identified and reduced with the help of automated systems. Malware files can be eliminated, altered or deleted files can be restored to their original state, firewall and intrusion prevention rules can be updated, security updates can be installed, and system configurations can be changed. Subsequent teams receive the information collected during the investigation phase and use it for additional responses, prioritization, analysis, and storage in preparation for the resolution phase. The information gathered is used to predict patterns, rank vulnerabilities and address them, and improve security protocols. Throughout this process, cyber threat analysts gather as much information as they can from the available data regarding the tactics, goals, and behaviors of an attacker. In order to eliminate current vulnerabilities, predict future security, and find patterns in an organization's security environment, they also assess data that has been collected.

5.1.10. Difference between Threat Analysis and Risk Analysis

Despite the fact that these two terms have different meanings, they are frequently used synonymously, which is incorrect. Threat analysis has been thoroughly discussed; now, let's quickly review risk analysis to better understand their distinctions. Similar to a threat analysis, a risk analysis looks for security holes in an organization's system and infrastructure. These could include risks related to data recovery, hardware operations, personnel skill sets, business continuity, and disaster recovery. It is, however, a more proactive method of protecting IT systems. Since anything could potentially disrupt operations, these risk assessments need to assess risk holistically. Threat analyses assess problems as they arise or are attempted, while risk assessments look at a wider range of scenarios to find potential issues and the degree of potential harm.

5.1.11. Cyber Threat Analysis Tools

Using a cyber-threat intelligence tool, the necessary data can be gathered to perform cyber threat analysis. You can think about the following threat intelligence analysis tools for efficient threat mitigation, but the one you select will depend on the particular requirements of your company and the ecosystem in which you operate.

5.1.11.1. Cisco Umbrella

Cisco Umbrella, arguably the most well-liked product on this list, is a cloud-based solution that uses threat intelligence to secure the endpoints, remote workers, and office locations of your company.

5.1.11.2. DeCYFI

CYFIRMA, a cybersecurity company based in Singapore, created DeCYFIR, a cyber threat intelligence tool and threat analysis software that can be used to identify and interpret threats straight from the sites where hackers are active.

5.1.11.3. Echosec

Using data from social media and the dark web, Echosec is an open-source intelligence cyber analysis platform that can shield your company from threats that haven't even surfaced yet.

5.1.11.4. GreyNoise

While processing threat intelligence data, GreyNoise—developed by a US-based startup—reduces false positives. A security analyst might miss the information it gathers, which is referred to as "noise."

5.2. TECHNIQUES FOR AUTOMATED THREAT MODELING

A proactive method for assessing cybersecurity risks is threat modeling. It entails identifying possible risks and creating procedures or tests to find and stop those risks. This entails categorizing threats, determining their potential effects on systems, and putting the proper countermeasures in place. Threat intelligence, asset identification, mitigation capabilities, risk assessment, and threat mapping are the five steps that make up a typical threat modeling process. These all offer various perspectives and levels of visibility into the security posture of the company. Security teams can employ the following eight primary approaches for threat modeling: hTMM, STRIDE, PASTA, VAST, Trike, CVSS, Attack Trees, and Security Cards. Every one of these approaches offers a unique approach to evaluating the risks posed to the IT resources of the company.

The importance of security has grown in the digital age as more and more data is kept in electronic form and as more devices are linked to the internet. Regulations imposing security requirements are now necessary to ensure security due to the widespread adoption of these systems. The use of threat modeling and risk analysis approaches, which enable the security administrator to gather (in an approximate manner) information on security issues from the outset of the system life cycle, is advised by best practices when it comes to addressing security. In addition to being widely accepted by the scientific community, the use of threat modeling processes is becoming more and more common.

If you have the necessary time and energy and can persuade your organization of the significance of this approach, these techniques and methodologies are an effective approach to both system and threat modeling. But with everything being code-based these days and everything being continuous, development teams have a lot of pressure to produce more in less time. As a result, security procedures that once took up more than a few minutes of developer time but were deemed necessary evils are now being dropped because they are deemed to be too expensive. That puts those who prioritize security in a challenging situation. How do you maintain high security standards and the attention to detail required to create a well-engineered system? Do you try to persuade your organization to bite the bullet and be more rigorous in applying security engineering practices, or do you try to get as much done as you can with your limited resources, knowing that the quality of your results (and, by extension, the security of the end product) may suffer?

Reducing the amount of time, you have to spend building system and threat models by hand and using automation to help you meet the demands of the security team and the business is one way to enable good security engineering.

Although the human component of a threat modeling exercise is undoubtedly significant, a computer can easily construct and analyze system models; you will still need to provide the input. Automation can help with question answering in addition to helping with model design. For instance, you can use a program to determine whether data flow A between endpoints X and Y exposes your vital data to the legendary Eve or not.

5.2.1. Why Automate Threat Modeling?

Let's face it—threat modeling the traditional way is hard, for many reasons:

- To perform threat modeling effectively, one must be able to identify a system's vulnerabilities, which requires a unique and highly specialized talent. This calls for preparation (reading this or other threat modeling primers, for example), as well as a fair dose of cynicism and critical thinking about the possibilities and the state of affairs (including how things might go wrong).
- There is a great deal to learn, and doing so will call for a wide range of experiences and knowledge. Security personnel must always be learning as their system becomes more complex or as changes are made (like the digital transformation that many businesses are undergoing these days). These changes in technologies result in an increasing number of vulnerabilities as new threats and weaknesses are discovered and new attack vectors are developed.
- There are lots of options available. This covers threat modeling and analysis tools and techniques, as well as modeled representations and methods for documenting, mitigating, or managing findings.
- Convincing stakeholders that threat modeling is important can be difficult, in part because of the following:
  - Everyone is busy (as mentioned previously).
  - Not every member of the development team is familiar with the system as intended or as specified. The two may not always match—what is implemented and what is designed do not always match what was specified. It can be difficult to find the right people who can accurately describe the current state of the system that is being studied.
  - Not every coder or architect is fully aware of the project they are working on, and not every team member will be cross-versed in every other area outside of small, tightly knit groups. This development approach is known as the Three Blind Men and the Elephant.

  - Some team members (hopefully, only a small number) have less-than-perfect intentions, meaning they may be defensive or provide intentionally misleading statements).
- You might be able to read the code, but that only gives you a portion of the story. Reading code could have cost you the opportunity to prevent design flaws that could have been more serious and that coding could not have prevented. Deriving the overlaying design solely from code can also be challenging at times.
- A system model takes time and work to create. Furthermore, it takes time to maintain a system model because nothing is static. When a system is implemented, its requirements will change, and you must update the system model accordingly. This means that a system's design will also change.

These are some of the explanations for why some stalwarts in the security community have voiced reservations about threat modeling's applicability as a defensive tactic throughout the development life cycle. And these are difficult reasons, to be honest. The complexity of systems and a program's relative incapacity to perform pattern recognition—a task that the human brain is better at—make automation challenging. The challenge lies in communicating the system in a form that a computer can comprehend without actually developing the system. Thus, two related methods are available: Threat modeling with code (also known as threat modeling in code): Utilizing a computer program to interpret and process input data in order to identify threats or vulnerabilities. Threat modeling from code involves writing computer code in a programming language or in a newly defined domain-specific language (DSL) that, when executed, results in analysis of threats being performed on a model that represents the input data provided.

Both strategies may work as long as the GIGO issue is fixed. The quality of your input (the description of the system and its characteristics) for the automation must directly correlate with the outcomes you obtain. Both approaches also demand that the analysis's algorithms and rules be "correct," meaning that a given set of inputs must produce legitimate and defensible outputs. Implementing either way can do away with the requirement for specialized skills to decipher system models and comprehend data, elements, and interconnections in order to spot potential security concerns. Naturally, this does mean that the language or framework needs to support this analysis and be properly programmed to do it. First, we will discuss how to build a machine-readable system model. Next, we will go over the theories behind each kind of automated threat modeling and offer both open-source and commercial projects that put them into practice. We use these ideas later in the chapter (and in the following chapter) to provide details on additional evolutionary threat modeling approaches that aim to function in the quickly evolving DevOps and CI/CD landscape.

Threat modeling is essentially dependent on input in the form of data that is encoded or contains enough information to be analyzed; this data allows you to identify threats. In threat modeling, when code is used instead of human intelligence, you specify the system to be assessed (e.g., the flows, entities, or event sequences that comprise a system, as well as the metadata required to facilitate analysis and recording of results); the application then renders and analyzes the system representation to generate output, and it may also render the representation as diagrams.

5.2.2. Threat Modeling from Code

By processing machine-readable system information, threat modeling from code produces output related to threats, vulnerabilities, and weaknesses. Since these kinds of applications require input data for interpretation, it must be robust to unexpected input. It accomplishes this by using a database or set of rules that specify what it should be searching for. Put another way, threat modeling from code is an approach that uses interpretation to build a system model that can be used to generate threats. When discussing Threatspec, for example, threat modeling from code is also known as threat modeling in code.

5.2.2.1. How It Works

When you employ threat modeling from code, data that describes a system model, its components, and their attributes are analyzed using a program (code) that is machine-readable. Utilizing a taxonomy of threats and weaknesses, detection criteria, and input system model and data interpretation, the program aims to:

(1) identify possible findings; and

(2) produce results that are human-interpretable. A text document or report in the form of a PDF will typically be the output.

5.2.2.1.1. Threatspec

Development teams and security professionals alike can benefit from the open-source project Threatspec. It gives you an easy way to record threat information with code so you can create reports or documentation that helps you make well-informed risk decisions. Threatspec is authored and maintained by Fraser Scott at *https://threatspec.org*.

Some of the benefits of using Threatspec include the following:

- Brings security to coders by using code annotations (with which they are probably familiar);
- Allows the organization to define a common lexicon of threats and other structures for development teams to use;
- Facilitates the security discussion of threat modeling and analysis;
- Automatically generates detailed and useful documentation, including diagrams and code snippets.

However, despite being a great tool for enabling programmers to add threat information to their code and thereby integrating security into the development process, Threatspec has a few drawbacks that should be considered. It may indicate that the design is already finalized because the tool initially requires code to exist or be created along with annotations. Different from threat modeling, but still very valuable, the development team's primary task in this instance is producing security documentation. Essentially, threat modeling "shifts right," which is not the right direction, for these kinds of projects.

Yet, it is evident from the Threatspec documentation that environments that have adopted the everything-as-code philosophy, like DevOps, are the most fruitful places to use the tool. The debate over whether to prioritize code development over design is moot in those situations. Additionally, Threatspec has added the ability to document annotations and threats without the need for code by putting the data into parsable plain-text files. For teams with a more structured development life cycle or that adhere to stricter systems engineering practices, this might help allay some of their potential worries. Expert knowledge is required by the development team, second. What constitutes a threat and how to describe it needs to be explained by an expert to the team. Accordingly, you are unable to directly address the scalability issue. According to the tool's documentation, this strategy is well-suited for talks or supervised drills between the security team and development team. However, this also introduces the security expert bottleneck, which makes scalability even more difficult. This obstacle might be addressed by providing development teams with extensive training, or by integrating security into the group from the outset. This would enable discussions to take place closer to the writing of code.

You can obtain Threatspec from GitHub at *https://oreil.ly/NGTI8*. It requires Python 3 and Graphviz to run and generate reports. The creator/maintainer of Threatspec is active in the security community, especially the OWASP Threat Modeling working group and in the Threatspec Slack, and encourages contributions and feedback on the tool.

5.2.2.1.2. ThreatPlaybook

The open source project ThreatPlaybook was created by the we45 team, under the direction of Abhay Bhargav. "DevSecOps framework [for] collaborative Threat Modeling to Application Security Test Automation" is how it is marketed. It is designed with development teams in mind, offering a practical means of recording threat intelligence and promoting automation in the identification and verification of security vulnerabilities. There is no V2 release of ThreatPlaybook; there is only a stable release (V1) and a beta release (V3). ThreatPlaybook supports test orchestration for vulnerability verification using GraphQL in MongoDB and YAML-based descriptions of use cases and threats with descriptive constructs. It also provides a good report generator, a comprehensive API, and a competent client application. It offers two choices for test automation integrations: its own Test Orchestration Framework functionality in V3 and the original Robot Framework Libraries. According to the documentation, ThreatPlaybook integrates well with OWASP Zed Attack Proxy, PortSwigger's Burp Suite, and npm-audit through the Robot Framework. ThreatPlaybook is available for download via Python's pip program or from GitHub at https://oreil.ly/Z2DZd. Good, if a little sparse, documentation and videos on how to install, configure, and use ThreatPlaybook can be found on a companion website.

5.2.3. Why is Threat Modeling Important?

- **Risk Mitigation:** In order to mitigate risk, threat modeling is essential. Organizations can mitigate risks and eliminate potential threats by proactively identifying them before they can be exploited. Compared to responding to a breach or attack after it has already occurred, this is far more economical. Furthermore, organizations can create more secure systems and applications from the beginning by knowing the possible attack vectors.
- **Enhanced Security Awareness:** Not all aspects of threat modeling are technical. Significant human analysis and decision-making are also involved. Teams can grow a security-focused culture within the organization and improve their security awareness by participating in threat modeling. By using threat modeling, they can inform their teams about possible threats and countermeasures to be taken.
- **Easier Compliance:** There are stringent cybersecurity compliance requirements across numerous industries and jurisdictions. These specifications frequently call for continual risk assessment, process optimization, and a thorough threat analysis. Threat modeling offers

a methodical and documented approach to threat analysis, which can assist organizations in meeting these compliance requirements. In addition, a thorough threat model documentation can prove due diligence in the case of a security incident. It can demonstrate that companies have taken appropriate action to find and eliminate possible security risks to their systems.

- **Cost-Effective Security:** One economical method of securing systems is threat modeling. Organizations can prevent the expensive consequences of security breaches and data loss by detecting threats early on. Moreover, organizations can guarantee the highest level of security for their investment by allocating resources to the most critical risks.

5.2.4. Advantages of Threat Modeling

- **Detect Problems Early in the SDLC:** Organizations can avert expensive and time-consuming fixes later in the development process by detecting possible threats and vulnerabilities at the design stage. Organizations can integrate security from the ground up instead of trying to patch it on as a last-minute solution thanks to this proactive approach. Developers have the chance to fix possible problems in their code by recognizing them early on. By doing this, software may become more secure and costly, disruptive patches or updates may not be necessary in the future. Put simply, threat modeling can assist in transforming security from a reactive to a proactive process.
- **Evaluate New Forms of Attack:** With the ongoing evolution of cybersecurity, new threats and attack vectors keep appearing. Threat modeling offers an organized method for locating and evaluating these ever-evolving threats, enabling organizations to stay one step ahead of them. Organizations can keep up with the most recent security threats and vulnerabilities by routinely updating their threat models. In order to stay ahead of the latest attacks, they can use this to modify their security plans and defenses in response to the shifting threat landscape.
- **Identify Security Requirements:** Organizations can identify the security controls they need to implement to safeguard their assets by comprehending potential system threats and the potential consequences of failing to maintain a strong security posture. To guarantee that the system is constructed with security in mind from the beginning, these security requirements should be integrated into the system design and development process. Systems may become

more secure as a result, and businesses may be able to prevent expensive and disruptive security breaches. Establishing channels of communication between IT, Security, and Development is crucial for business continuity and disaster recovery scenario building, though, since security is frequently overlooked.

- **Map Assets, Threat Agents, and Controls:** Security leadership and risk teams can improve their comprehension of what needs to be protected, who could attempt an attack, and how to defend it by developing a comprehensive model of the fundamental components of the most important business systems throughout the company. Controls over the web interface, APIs, and back-end databases, for example, need to be given top priority if the company operates a transactional website. It may be crucial for a manufacturing company to maintain service accounts and ICS operational while limiting all external access. By concentrating on the most important assets and threats, organizations can use this understanding to help them prioritize their security efforts and resources. In order to help organizations make sure they are adequately safeguarding their systems and data; it can also offer a clear implementation roadmap for security controls.

5.2.5. Threat Modeling Process

Threat modeling should involve a number of procedures and elements. If one of these elements is absent, models may be incomplete and risks may not be adequately addressed.

5.2.5.1. Apply Threat Intelligence

This section contains details on various threat types, impacted systems, detection techniques, processes and tools for taking advantage of vulnerabilities, and attacker motivations. This is a continuous process that should, whenever possible, be automated by security tools. Security researchers frequently gather threat intelligence data and disseminate it via open databases, proprietary software, or security messaging channels. It improves knowledge of potential dangers and guides countermeasures.

5.2.5.2. Identify Assets

To maintain a secure posture, teams require a real-time inventory of the parts, credentials, and data that are being used, as well as the location of those assets and the security measures that are in place. Security teams can monitor the final state of passwords and permissions and track assets with known vulnerabilities with the aid of this inventory. Security teams can see when assets change thanks to a real-time inventory. For instance, receiving notifications when assets are added with or without permission, as this may indicate a security risk. An inactive user or service account that has become active out of the blue could also be a sign of danger.

5.2.5.3. Identify Mitigation Capabilities

In addition to an organization's processes and security knowledge, mitigation capabilities can also refer to technology used to protect against, identify, and address specific types of threats. Determining whether they require more resources to counter a threat will be made easier by evaluating their current capabilities.

An organization can be first protected against traditional malware threats if it has enterprise-grade antivirus or endpoint protection, for instance. After that, they can decide whether to make more investments, like correlating current antivirus signals with additional detection tools.

5.2.5.4. Assess Risks

Vulnerability profiles as well as asset inventories are correlated with threat intelligence in risk assessments. Teams need these tools to develop a plan for addressing vulnerabilities and to comprehend the current state of their systems. System and solution active testing is another possible component of risk assessments.

Application security testing and software composition analysis, for instance, ensure that the applications operating on those systems are as secure as current information will allow. Penetration testing is used to confirm security measures and patching levels are effective in hardening systems.

5.2.5.5. Perform Threat Mapping

Following a potential threat's path through an organization's systems is known as threat mapping. It aids teams in anticipating where defenses can be applied or layered more successfully by simulating how attackers might move from resource to resource.

There is a more efficient model for illustrating the organization's current security posture in reports for compliance, where specific security mitigations and logs can be mapped against the most relevant use cases that challenge the business.

5.2.6. Threat Modeling Methodologies and Techniques

Security teams can use a variety of methodologies when performing threat modeling. Depending on the kinds of threats being modeled and the intended use, an organization can choose the best model for its needs.

5.2.6.1. STRIDE Threat Modeling

Microsoft engineers developed the STRIDE threat model, which is intended to direct the process of identifying potential threats within a system. It is utilized in conjunction with a target system model. It works best for assessing individual systems because of this. The threats it covers are represented by the acronym STRIDE, which is as follows:

- **Spoofing:** A user or program pretends to be another;
- **Tampering:** Attackers modify components or code;
- **Repudiation:** Threat events are not logged or monitored;
- **Information Disclosure:** Data is leaked or exposed;
- **Denial of Service (DoS):** Services or components are overloaded with traffic to prevent legitimate use;
- **Elevation of Privilege:** Attackers grant themselves additional privileges to gain greater control over a system.

5.2.6.2. Process for Attack Simulation and Threat Analysis (PASTA)

The seven-step PASTA methodology is centered on the attacker. It is intended to link technological requirements with business objectives. The steps of PASTA help teams to dynamically recognize, quantify, and rank threats. In a PASTA threat model, the steps are:

- Define business objectives;
- Define the technical scope of assets and components;
- Application decomposition and identify application controls;
- Threat analysis based on threat intelligence;
- Vulnerability detection;
- Attack enumeration and modeling;
- Risk analysis and development of countermeasures.

5.2.6.3. Common Vulnerability Scoring System (CVSS)

Utilized for known vulnerabilities, the CVSS is a standardized threat scoring system. Under the Forum of Incident Response and Security Teams (FIRST), it is maintained and developed by the National Institute of Standards and Technology (NIST). When known vulnerabilities are released, CVSS assigns security scores to them. This aids security teams in evaluating threats, determining consequences, setting patching priorities, and identifying countermeasures already in place. Security experts can also use it to reliably evaluate and implement threat intelligence that has been gathered by others. Due to the length of time since the vulnerability was first discovered, CVSS assigns a score to both the intrinsic characteristics of a threat and the effects of the risk factor. Security teams can specifically alter risk scores according to system configurations with the help of these measures.

5.2.6.4. Visual, Agile, and Simple Threat (VAST)

The ThreatModeler platform is the foundation for the automated threat modeling technique known as Visual, Agile, and Simple Threat (VAST). To maintain scalability and produce dependable, actionable results, large enterprises integrate VAST throughout their entire infrastructure. Teams can identify different infrastructure and operational concerns with the aid of VAST, which can be integrated into the DevOps lifecycle. Creating two different kinds of threat models is necessary for implementing VAST.

- **Application Threat Model:** It uses a process-flow diagram to represent the architectural aspect of the threat
- **Operational Threat Model:** It uses a data-flow diagram to represent the threat from the attacker's perspective

5.2.6.5. Trike

Threat modeling approaches are used in the Trike security audit framework to manage risk and defense. An analyst lists the system's actors, assets, rules, and actions after Trike defines it in order to create a requirement model. The actors are represented by rows in a step matrix created by Trike, where columns are the assets. Each matrix cell contains a rule tree, in which the analyst indicates whether an action is permitted, prohibited, or permitted with restrictions. The four parts of each matrix cell correspond to the possible actions (create, read, update, and delete). Following the definition of the requirements, Strike creates a data-flow diagram that maps each element to the proper actors and assets. Denial of service (DoS) and privilege escalation threats are detected by the analyst using the diagram. With each CRUD action and actor, Trike rates the likelihood of an attack using a five-point scale. Furthermore, it assesses actors according to the degree of permission they give for every action (never, sometimes, or always).

5.2.6.6. Attack Trees

Attack trees are diagrams that show the possible routes an attack could take within a system. These diagrams show potential paths as branches and attack goals as a root. In order to create trees for threat modeling, one tree is created for each attacker goal for a single system. Among the most traditional and popular threat modeling methods is this one. This type of methodology is frequently applied in internal data flow reviews when assessing vendor risk and system interoperability (web, CRM, back-end data, etc.). Although it was formerly employed alone, it is now commonly used in conjunction with other methodologies such as STRIDE, PASTA, and CVSS.

5.2.6.7. Security Cards

Rather than using formal threat modeling techniques, the Security Cards methodology is based on brainstorming and creative thinking. Its purpose is to assist security teams in anticipating and responding to unusual or rare attacks. Security teams can improve their understanding of threats and threat modeling techniques by using this methodology. The methodology employs a deck of 42 cards to assist analysts in responding to inquiries regarding potential future attacks, including who might launch an attack, what their potential motivation might be, which systems they might target, and how they might carry it out. Analysts can simulate potential attacks and think through how the organization might respond by dealing the cards in a manner similar to a tabletop game.

5.2.6.8. Hybrid Threat Modeling Method (hTMM)

hTMM is a methodology developed by Security Equipment Inc. (SEI) that combines two other methodologies:

- **Security Quality Requirements Engineering (SQUARE):** A methodology designed to elicit, categorize and prioritize security requirements
- **Persona Non Grata (PnG):** A methodology that focuses on uncovering ways a system can be abused to meet an attacker's goals

hTMM is designed to enable threat modeling which accounts for all possible threats, produces zero false positives, provides consistent results, and is cost-effective.

It works by applying Security Cards, eliminating unlikely PnGs, summarizing results, and formally assessing risk using SQUARE.

5.2.7. Threat Modeling Practices

Here are a few critical practices that can help security teams practice threat modeling more effectively.

5.2.7.1. Understand the System Architecture

A thorough understanding of the system's operation, architecture, and interoperability is necessary for threat modeling. A thorough understanding of the data flows and system architecture can aid in locating possible attack points. For example, data leakage or unauthorized access may be possible if the system interacts with other systems. Similar to this, security teams can find potential risks to sensitive data by comprehending how data flows through the system. Additionally, knowing the system architecture can aid in spotting possible weaknesses. An attack vector could be, for example, the system's reliance on a specific component with known vulnerabilities. Furthermore, as new vulnerabilities or attacker tools for internally-used tools become public, e.g., similar to when the ransomware SamSam used JBossAS, also known as JexBoss, a popular debugging and scanning tool among developers.

5.2.7.2. Use an Ecosystem of Tools

There are many different tools available that can assist with various aspects of threat modeling. Organizations should adopt tools that can:

- **Automate Threat Identification:** With the use of these tools, the system can be scanned to find known vulnerabilities that an attacker might exploit.
- **Help with Risk Assessment:** These tools aid in prioritizing which threats to address first by analyzing the possible impact and likelihood of a threat.
- **Help with Mitigation Strategies:** These tools can help with developing policies or user education initiatives, as well as with putting technical solutions like intrusion detection systems and encryption into practice.

5.2.7.3. Document and Communicate Findings

The threats that have been identified, the risks that are connected with them, and the suggested mitigation techniques must all be noted clearly. Making a record of the threat modeling process through documentation of findings can be helpful in the future or in the event that questions come up. Additionally, it guarantees that the dangers that have been identified and the countermeasures taken will not be overlooked or forgotten. Sharing research results is equally important. All pertinent parties, including developers, management, and even users, must be informed of the findings. Ensuring that all individuals are cognizant of potential hazards and comprehend the necessary actions to alleviate them is the consequence of this. In order to comprehend the flow of data and the exposure of potential compromise, conducting a risk exposure exercise may require system and tool owners from numerous teams, including security, marketing, and sales.

5.2.7.4. Foster Collaboration and Knowledge Sharing

Threat modeling is a collaborative effort involving multiple stakeholders, including developers, security experts, users, and management. It should not be performed in a siloed manner. Collaborating with others can guarantee that all possible risks are recognized and taken into account. It can also aid in making sure that the suggested mitigation techniques are workable and efficient. By learning from the achievements and mistakes of others within the company, knowledge sharing can enhance the threat modeling process' overall efficacy.

5.3. THREAT DETECTION AND RESPONSE

The process of detecting potentially harmful activity on a network and then developing a suitable countermeasure to eliminate or lessen the threat before it can take advantage of any existing vulnerabilities is known as threat detection and response. Threat detection is a complex concept that has many applications in an organization's security program. When something or someone gets past their defensive and preventative technologies and poses a threat, even the best security programs need to prepare for the worst-case scenarios. Combining human and technological resources to address a breach is known as detection and response. A robust program for threat detection and response integrates people, procedures, and technology to identify compromise indicators as soon as feasible and take necessary countermeasures. In order to detect possible threats instantly, Automated Threat Detection makes use of cutting-edge AI and machine learning technologies. This innovation guarantees proactive security measures and reduces vulnerabilities before they can be exploited, enabling businesses to stay one step ahead of the competition.

5.3.1. Detecting Threats

Rapidity is of the essence when it comes to threat detection and mitigation. In order to prevent attackers from having enough time to trawl through sensitive data, security programs need to be able to identify threats fast and effectively. Ideally, a company's defensive programs can neutralize most known threats, so they should be prepared to combat them. These dangers are regarded as established dangers. An organization seeks to identify additional "unknown" threats, though. This indicates that the organization isn't familiar with them, which could be due to the attacker's use of novel techniques or technological tools. Since even the most effective defenses can occasionally be overcome by known threats, the majority of security organizations actively search their environment for both known and unknown threats. So how can a company make an effort to identify threats that are known and unknown?

5.3.2. Leveraging Threat Intelligence

Threat intelligence is the process of identifying threats by comparing enterprise data with signature data from previously observed attacks. Because of this, it is especially good at identifying known threats—as opposed to unknown ones. Threats classified as known are identifiable due to the fact that the malware or the attacker's infrastructure has been linked to malicious activity.

Unknown threats are ones that haven't been discovered in the wild or are always evolving, but threat intelligence indicates that threat actors may be focusing on a particular industry vertical, a broad range of weak credentials, or susceptible assets. User behavior analytics (UBA) play a critical role in promptly detecting unusual activity on your network, which may point to an unidentified threat. UBA tools create a baseline for normal behavior in a particular environment, then use analytics (or, in some situations, machine learning) to identify and notify users when their behavior deviates from the baseline.

The different strategies, methods, and procedures TTPs that hackers use to access your company network can be identified by using attacker behavior analytics (ABA). Threats to privacy and security TTPs include malware, cryptojacking, and the exfiltration of private data. An attacker has the opportunity to tunnel deeper into your environment every second they are not detected during a breach. If you want to make sure that your security operations center (SOC) is informed about possible threats as early in the attack chain as possible, combining UBAs and ABAs is a tremendous place to start.

5.3.3. Responding to Security Incidents

Getting support and alignment from stakeholders before launching the framework is one of the most important parts of putting an effective incident response framework into place. When there is vital work that needs to be done, nobody enjoys surprises or questions that are asked after the fact. Essential questions for incident response consist of:

- Do teams know who is responsible at each phase of incident response?
- Is the proper chain of communications well understood?
- Do team members know when and how to escalate issues as needed?

The impact of a breach is reduced and smooth operations are ensured, even in high-stress breach scenarios, with an excellent incident response plan and playbook. Some things to think about when you're first starting out are as follows:

- **Defining Roles and Duties for Handling Incidents:** These responsibilities, including contact information and backups, should be documented in a readily accessible channel.
- **Considering Who to Loop in:** When determining which cross-functional or outside parties, like your board, customers, legal, or PR, should be informed and when, go beyond the IT and security departments. Responses will go more smoothly and expectations will be fulfilled if everyone involved in the communication process is aware of who is responsible for what and how it should be done.

5.3.4. What Should a Robust Threat Detection Program Employ?

- Data from network events, such as authentication, network access, and logs from vital systems, are aggregated using security event threat detection technology.
- To comprehend network traffic patterns and keep an eye on network and internet traffic, employ network threat detection technology.
- Technology for endpoint threat detection can offer comprehensive details about potentially harmful activities on user computers, in addition to any forensic or behavioral data that can help with threat investigations.
- Penetration tests, in addition to other preventative controls, to understand detection telemetry and coordinate a response.

5.3.5. A Proactive Threat Detection Program

To elaborate further on the importance of telemetry and taking the initiative in threat response, it's critical to realize that there is no one-size-fits-all solution. Rather, an array of instruments functions as a protective barrier encircling the whole attack surface of an enterprise, attempting to apprehend potential threats prior to their development into significant issues.

5.3.5.1. Setting Attacker Traps with Honeypots

An attacker may find certain targets too alluring to resist. Knowing this, security teams set traps in the hopes that a potential attacker would fall for the ruse. An example of a honeypot target in the context of an organization's network would be a target that appears to house network services that would be particularly alluring to an attacker. These so-called "honey credentials" seem to have the user rights that an attacker would require to access private networks or information. An alert is set off when an attacker attempts to take advantage of this bait, alerting the security team to potentially suspicious activity on the network that warrants further investigation. Find out more about the various kinds of deception technology.

5.3.5.2. Threat Hunting

By actively searching their own network, endpoints, and security technology, security analysts can find threats or attackers who may be lurking there as of yet undiscovered, as opposed to waiting for a threat to materialize in the organization's network. In most cases, seasoned security and threat analysts use this sophisticated method. A security team can keep an eye on the safety of the company's important assets, personnel, and data by utilizing a mix of these proactive defensive techniques. Their likelihood of promptly identifying and reducing a threat will also rise.

5.3.6. Use of AI in Threat Intelligence

An increasing number of organizations are discovering that artificial intelligence (AI) can be a potent ally in digital risk management as they battle the growing complexity and sophistication of cyber threats. The various uses of AI in threat intelligence are examined in this section, with an emphasis on how automated procedures improve the efficacy and efficiency of cybersecurity defenses.

- **Automated Threat Detection:** AI is very good at spotting patterns and anomalies that point to possible dangers. AI-powered automated threat detection systems are able to recognize suspicious activity instantly, facilitating quick response and mitigation.
- **Behavioral Analytics:** AI is used to detect anomalies from typical patterns by analyzing user behavior. This plays a crucial role in identifying advanced persistent threats (APTs) or insider threats that may escape detection through conventional methods.
- **Natural Language Processing:** Natural language processing improves the efficiency of sifting through enormous volumes of textual data. AI systems can interpret unstructured data sources and

extract useful information, enhancing threat intelligence's overall effectiveness.

- **Threat Hunting Assistance:** AI can be a force multiplier for human analysts when it comes to threat hunting. By helping to sort through massive datasets and find hidden threats, AI algorithms free up analysts to concentrate on more strategically important cybersecurity tasks.
- **Cyber Threat Intelligence Sharing:** AI makes it easier for organizations to share threat intelligence in a seamless manner. Automated systems have the ability to anonymize and instantly share pertinent threat information, forming a group defense against common enemies.
- **Predictive Analytics:** Organizations can foresee possible threats by utilizing AI's predictive capabilities, which are based on historical data and emerging trends. By taking a proactive stance, organizations can lessen the impact of potential cyberattacks by implementing preventive measures.
- **Automated Response and Mitigation:** AI is capable of automating mitigation and response plans in addition to detection. Artificial intelligence-driven automation shortens the window of vulnerability by speeding up incident response processes like isolating compromised systems and deploying countermeasures.

5.3.7. Challenges and Risks of AI in Threat Intelligence

Organizations must use caution and judgment when choosing appropriate domains for the deployment of AI models, even in light of the exciting opportunities that arise from integrating AI into security operations. Not every application will benefit from AI models' efficacy in producing the most accurate or ideal results. Diverse artificial intelligence methodologies are linked to inherent risks and limitations that account for this variability, including:

- **Bias in Training Data:** It is possible for AI models to unintentionally absorb and maintain biases found in their algorithms or training data, which could lead to inaccurate or misleading threat assessments. This raises a serious issue by highlighting the need for careful observation and mitigating measures to deal with skewed results.
- **Limited Data Availability:** AI models cannot function unless large amounts of high-quality data are available. However, the sensitive nature of the data or difficulties in its collection and analysis lead to a lack of available data in the field of cyber threat intelligence. This

restriction highlights the need for creative methods to improve the accessibility of data.

- **Adversarial Attacks:** A significant risk are adversarial attacks, which include efforts to trick or manipulate AI models in order to generate false or misleading output. In the field of cyber defense, for example, attackers might use deception techniques to trick AI models and avoid detection. Resilience of AI-driven threat intelligence is heavily dependent on countermeasures against adversarial attacks.
- **Over-Reliance on Artificial Intelligence:** Over-reliance on AI models by organizations to gather cyber threat intelligence poses a serious risk and may lead to an illusion of security. Artificial intelligence (AI) models are powerful instruments, but their application needs human supervision and knowledge as well. Advanced threat investigations will profit from the combination of AI power and human judgment when a balanced strategy is implemented.

REFERENCES

1. AbuEmera, E. A., ElZouka, H. A., & Saad, A. A. (2022). Security framework for identifying threats in smart manufacturing systems using STRIDE approach. In *2022 2nd International Conference on Consumer Electronics and Computer Engineering (ICCECE)* (pp. 605–612). https://doi.org/10.1109/ICCECE54139.2022.9712770.
2. Almubairik, N. A., & Wills, G. (2016). Automated penetration testing based on a threat model. In *2016 11th International Conference for Internet Technology and Secured Transactions (ICITST)* (pp. 413–414). https://doi.org/10.1109/ICITST.2016.7856742.
3. Althar, R. R., Samanta, D., Kaur, M., Singh, D., & Lee, H. N. (2022). Automated risk management based on software security vulnerabilities management. *IEEE Access*, *10*, 90597–90608. https://doi.org/10.1109/ACCESS.2022.3185069.
4. Alwaheidi, M. K. S., & Islam, S. (2022). Data-driven threat analysis for ensuring security in cloud-enabled systems. *Sensors*, *22*(15). https://doi.org/10.3390/s22155726.
5. Ansari, M. T. J., Pandey, D., & Alenezi, M. (2022). STORE: Security threat-oriented requirements engineering methodology. *Journal of King Saud University - Computer and Information Sciences*, *34*(2), 191–203.
6. Asif, M. R. A., Hasan, K. F., Islam, M. Z., & Khondoker, R. (2021). STRIDE-based cybersecurity threat modeling for IoT-enabled precision agriculture systems. In *2021 3rd International Conference on Sustainable Technologies for Industry 4.0 (STI)* (pp. 1–6). https://doi.org/10.1109/STI53101.2021.9732597
7. Bernsmed, K., Cruzes, D., Jaatun, M., & Iovan, M. (2021). Adopting threat modeling in agile software development projects. *Journal of Systems and Software*, *183*, 111090. https://doi.org/10.1016/j.jss.2021.111090
8. Brown, S., Fox, S., Hewage, C., & Khan, I. (2022). Threat modeling of cyber-physical systems: A real case study based on a window cleaning business. *SN Computer Science*, *3*. https://doi.org/10.1007/s42979-022-01021-3
9. Casola, V., De Benedictis, A., Mazzocca, C., & Montanari, R. (2021). Toward automated threat modeling of edge computing systems. In *2021 IEEE International Conference on Cyber Security and Resilience (CSR)* (pp. 135–140). https://doi.org/10.1109/CSR51186.2021.9527937.
10. Casola, V., De Benedictis, A., Rak, M., & Villano, U. (2019). Toward the automation of threat modeling and risk assessment in IoT systems. *Internet of Things*, *7*.

11. Chen, H. (2019). Determining information security threats for an IoT-based energy internet by adopting software engineering and risk management approaches. *Inventions*, *4*, 53. https://doi.org/10.3390/inventions4030053.
12. Chen, Y. T. (2018). Modeling information security threats for smart grid applications using software engineering and risk management. In *2018 IEEE International Conference on Smart Energy Grid Engineering (SEGE)* (pp. 128–132). https://doi.org/10.1109/SEGE.2018.8499431.
13. Danielis, P., Beckmann, M., & Skodzik, J. (2020). An ISO-compliant test procedure for technical risk analyses of IoT systems based on STRIDE. In *2020 IEEE 44th Annual Computers, Software, and Applications Conference (COMPSAC)* (pp. 499–504). https://doi.org/10.1109/COMPSAC48688.2020.0-203.
14. Ding, J., Atif, Y., Andler, S., Lindström, B., & Jeusfeld, M. (2017). CPS-based threat modeling for critical infrastructure protection. *ACM SIGMETRICS Performance Evaluation Review*, *45*, 129–132. https://doi.org/10.1145/3152042.3152080.
15. Dominic, D., Chhawri, S., Eustice, R., Ma, D., & Weimerskirch, A. (2016). Risk assessment for cooperative automated driving. In *Proceedings of the ACM Conference* (pp. 47–58). https://doi.org/10.1145/2994487.2994499.
16. Fabbri, S., Silva, C., Hernandes, E., Octaviano, F., Di Thommazo, A., & Belgamo, A. (2016). Improvements in the START tool to better support the systematic review process. In *Proceedings of the 20th International Conference on Evaluation and Assessment in Software Engineering (EASE '16)*. Association for Computing Machinery. https://doi.org/10.1145/2915970.2916013.
17. Faily, S. (2018). *Designing Usable and Secure Software with IRIS and CAIRIS*. Springer Cham.
18. Ficco, M., Granata, D., Rak, M., & Salzillo, G. (2021). Threat modeling of edge-based IoT applications. In *International Conference on the Quality of Information and Communications Technology* (pp. 282–296). Springer.
19. Frydman, M., Ruiz, G., Heymann, E., César, E., & Miller, B. P. (2014). Automating risk analysis of software design models. *The Scientific World Journal*, *2014*. https://doi.org/10.1155/2014/328602.
20. Goodwin, M. (2020). OWASP Threat Dragon. Retrieved from: https://github.com/owasp/threat-dragon/releases (accessed on 9 October 2024).
21. Granata, D., & Rak, M. (2021). Design and development of a technique for the automation of the risk analysis process in IT security. In *Proceedings of the 11th International Conference on Cloud Computing*

and Services Science–CLOSER (pp. 87–98). SciTePress. https://doi.org/10.5220/0010455200870098.

22. Granata, D., Rak, M., & Salzillo, G. (2022). Automated threat modeling approaches: Comparison of open-source tools. In A. Vallecillo, J. Visser, & R. Pérez-Castillo (Eds.), *Quality of Information and Communications Technology* (pp. 250–265). Cham: Springer.
23. Granata, D., Rak, M., Salzillo, G., & Barbato, U. (2021). Security in IoT pairing & authentication protocols: A threat model and case study analysis. *CEUR Workshop Proceedings*, *2490*, 207–218.

CHAPTER 6

INCIDENT DETECTION AND RESPONSE AUTOMATION

Contents

INTRODUCTION

In contemporary cybersecurity, incident detection and response automation, which makes use of technology to improve the efficacy and efficiency of managing security incidents, represents a revolutionary strategy. In order to detect, analyze, and respond to possible threats with the least amount of human intervention, this automation makes use of sophisticated tools and algorithms. Organizations can mitigate potential damage more quickly by cutting down on the time between incident detection and response by incorporating automated systems into their security infrastructure.

Advanced threat detection technologies, like Intrusion Detection Systems (IDS) and Security Information and Event Management (SIEM) systems, which continuously monitor network traffic, system behavior, and other pertinent data, are the first steps in the automation process. These tools detect anomalies or patterns suggestive of malicious activity using behavioral analytics, machine learning, and predefined rules. Without waiting for human input, automated systems are capable of producing alerts and initiating predetermined response actions upon detection of a potential threat. The ability of incident response automation to quickly and accurately handle massive volumes of data and alerts is one of its main benefits. Compared to human analysts, automated systems can process and analyze data much more quickly, eliminating false positives and giving priority to real threats. Instead of getting bogged down in repetitive duties, this capability frees up security teams to concentrate on more intricate and strategic aspects of incident management.

Implementing patches to fix vulnerabilities or isolating impacted systems are examples of automated response actions. Malicious IP addresses can also be blocked. For instance, an automated system can quickly isolate the compromised computers from the network to stop the malware from spreading if it detects a ransomware attack. Similar to this, automation can ensure complete and accurate records by streamlining the process of creating incident reports and recording the response actions made. Automation has advantages, but it also has drawbacks that need to be carefully considered in order to avoid overusing it or running the risk of having automated responses that are inaccurate. To minimize false positives and adjust to changing threats, automation rules and algorithms must be updated and adjusted on a regular basis. To make sure that automated systems are in line with the security policies and response plans of the company, regular reviews and modifications are required.

Automation of incident detection and response improves an organization's capacity to respond to security incidents quickly and efficiently. Organizations can minimize potential damage, speed up response times, and free up security teams to focus on more strategic matters by automating routine detection and response tasks. However, to guarantee automated systems' efficacy and alignment with overarching security objectives, meticulous management and continuous improvement are imperative.

6.1. OVERVIEW OF INCIDENT DETECTION

In the fields of cybersecurity and operational management, incident detection is essential. It is concerned with spotting and handling unfavorable situations that might jeopardize the availability, confidentiality, or integrity of systems and data. The first step in the process is to continuously monitor networks and systems for anomalies that might indicate impending incidents. Intrusion detection systems (IDS), security information and event management (SIEM) systems, and advanced analytics driven by machine learning and artificial intelligence are just a few of the tools and methods used to accomplish this monitoring.

The foundation of a successful incident detection strategy is the establishment of a baseline of typical system behavior, from which deviations may be assessed. This baseline is important because it aids in identifying threats that are real from benign irregularities. For example, an abrupt increase in network traffic could indicate the presence of a Distributed Denial of Service (DDoS) attack, or it could just be the result of an increase in activity from legitimate users. It takes advanced analysis to distinguish between these situations, and it frequently entails combining data from several sources.

Early incident detection reduces potential damage by enabling quicker response and mitigation. Organizations use a layered approach that combines anomaly-based and signature-based detection techniques to improve early detection. Known patterns or indicators of malicious activity, such as particular malware strains or attack vectors, are the basis for signature-based detection. Anomaly-based detection, on the other hand, looks for departures from predetermined baselines that might point to new or unidentified threats.

When these strategies are combined, a greater range of possible incidents can be covered. Threat intelligence plays a crucial role in incident detection as well, offering important context and insights into new threats and attack patterns. Through the integration of threat intelligence feeds, organizations can remain up to date on the most recent strategies, tactics, and procedures employed by adversaries, thereby enhancing their capacity to identify and address emerging threats. This proactive strategy improves the overall security posture and enables more accurate detection system tuning.

To expedite the process, incident detection also makes use of automated tools and technologies. Because automation can quickly analyze large volumes of data and generate alerts for suspicious activities, it can significantly reduce the time required to identify and respond to incidents. Automation must be properly controlled, though, to prevent producing false positives, which can overburden security teams and take resources away from actual threats.

A thorough understanding of the network architecture, application landscape, and user behavior of the organization's IT environment is necessary for effective incident detection. To keep up with evolving threat vectors and environmental changes, detection systems require regular updates and tuning. Furthermore, having clear incident response protocols guarantees that, in the event that an incident is discovered, it can be quickly handled in accordance with established protocols, reducing its impact on the company.

The process of detecting incidents is complex and includes baseline analysis, ongoing monitoring, advanced tool usage, and threat intelligence. Through the implementation of automated solutions and a range of detection methods, organizations can improve their capacity to detect and address possible incidents. This proactive strategy is vital for preserving overall operational resilience in the face of changing threats, as well as for protecting important assets.

6.1.1. Incident Response Automation

Using AI, machine learning, and pre-configured workflows to automatically detect, investigate, and resolve issues with the least amount of human intervention is known as incident response automation. The idea is to increase production readiness by automating monotonous tasks so that teams can react to different IT issues more quickly and effectively.

Some ways to automate incident responses include:

- **Alert Triaging and Routing:** By using predefined rules and machine learning algorithms, the incident management system can automatically assess the severity of alerts, filter out false positives, and route incidents to the appropriate response teams or on-call responders.
- **Containment and Remediation:** Automated incident response tools can execute predefined containment actions immediately upon detection of a threat. This may include automatically isolating affected systems, revoking compromised credentials, or deploying patches.
- **Compliance and Audit Logging:** The incident management workflow can be configured to automatically capture and store all actions taken during an incident, ensuring a complete audit trail without burdening responders with manual documentation tasks.

- **Security Testing and Scanning:** Automated security scanning tools can continuously monitor systems for vulnerabilities, misconfigurations, or potential threats and proactively identify and address security issues.
- **Recovery and Reporting:** Automation can assist in the recovery process by executing predefined run-books for system restoration and data recovery. Additionally, automated reporting tools can generate comprehensive incident reports.

To ensure a smooth integration into the architecture, the automation for these processes can be incorporated into the current development workflows and incident response process, which includes monitoring dashboards and CI/CD pipelines. Organizations can greatly cut down on response times, reduce human error, and free up their technical teams to work on higher-value, more complex tasks by implementing automation. To be more precise, automation and continuous integration/deployment were cited by 50% of the surveyed engineering leaders as essential to their production readiness.

6.1.2. Incident Response Automation Use Cases

Automation can significantly speed up incident responses in the following scenarios:

- **Time-Critical Incidents:** For major outages or security breaches where every minute counts, automation can execute containment actions immediately, such as isolating affected systems or rolling back problematic code changes.
- **Routine Incidents:** Low-priority issues that occur frequently can be partially or fully automated to eliminate toil and free up developers to focus on higher-impact work. For example, automatically restarting services or clearing disk space when certain thresholds are exceeded.
- **Data Collection and Analysis:** Automation can help centralize data from multiple monitoring tools, filter out irrelevant alerts, and correlate events to provide a cohesive picture of the incident. This automation layer can help developers quickly pinpoint root causes.

6.1.2.1. What are Security Incidents?

Any digital or physical breach that jeopardizes the availability, confidentiality, or integrity of an organization's information systems or sensitive data is referred to as a security incident, or security event. Security incidents can vary in nature from deliberate cyberattacks carried out by hackers or unapproved users to inadvertent security policy violations committed by authorized users with valid credentials.

Some of the most common security incidents include:

- Ransomware;
- Phishing and social engineering;
- DDoS attacks;
- Supply chain attacks;
- Insider threats.

Let's explore in detail:

- **Ransomware:** It is a type of malicious software, or malware, that locks up a victim's data or computing device and threatens to keep it locked—or worse—unless the victim pays the attacker a ransom.
- **Phishing and Social Engineering:** Phishing attacks refer to electronic or verbal communications that aim to deceive the target into disclosing private information, downloading malevolent software, transferring funds or assets to unapproved parties, or performing any other detrimental action.
- **Phishing Scammers:** Create phishing messages that appear and sound authentic, sometimes even posing as correspondence from a person the recipient knows directly. The most expensive and second most frequent cause of data breaches is phishing. It's also the most prevalent type of social engineering attack, which leverages vulnerabilities in human nature instead of digital security to obtain unauthorized access to private or confidential company information.
- **DDoS Attacks:** In a distributed denial-of-service (DDoS) attack, hackers gain remote control of large numbers of computers and use them to overwhelm a target organization's network or servers with traffic, making those resources unavailable to legitimate users.
- **Supply Chain Attacks:** Cyberattacks known as "supply chain attacks" gain access to a target organization by targeting its suppliers. This can be done by distributing malware through a vendor's services or by stealing confidential information from a supplier's systems. Cybercriminals used a vulnerability in Kaseya's VSA platform in July 2021 to trick customers into downloading ransomware masquerading as an official software update. Despite the growing frequency of supply chain attacks, only 32% of organizations have incident response plans ready for this specific cyberthreat.
- **Insider Threats:** They come in two varieties. Employees, partners, or other authorized users who purposefully jeopardize the information security of an organization are known as malicious

insiders. Authorized users who inadvertently violate security best practices—such as by using weak passwords or storing private information in unsecure locations—are known as negligent insiders.

6.1.3. How does Incident Response Automation Work?

The incident response automation automates some incident management tasks by using pre-written rules, scripts, and integrations. We will discuss the crucial roles that development teams and security teams play in these stages.

6.1.3.1. Define and Integrate

Developing the automation strategy and incorporating it into the current workflows is the first step in the incident management process. Security teams create a thorough incident response plan, identifying laborious manual tasks that are best suited for automation. These plans are frequently developed in light of past incidents or recurring problems. For each use case, security and development teams draft playbooks and runbooks that describe automated procedures step-by-step and guarantee alignment with SLAs, cybersecurity, and engineering best practices.

It is up to teams to decide which systems to integrate with. Using a security information and event management (SIEM) tool is one choice. Although they are frequently employed to notify users of security issues, they also play a crucial role in streamlining and improving the incident response procedure. SIEM platforms are useful tools for both reactive incident management and proactive security monitoring because of their capacity to deliver thorough, real-time insights.

Systems are configured by engineers to absorb and correlate log data from multiple sources. They then create alert rules based on suspicious behavior patterns or known indicators of compromise. Systems that are more advanced and automated can perform predictive analysis on their own. Based on past data and present system behavior, machine learning models can anticipate possible incidents and enable proactive responses.

6.1.3.2. Trigger and Analyze

During this stage, logs and alerts from multiple sources are continuously monitored by the incident management system to look for possible critical incidents. When specified rules are met, the incident response procedure begins. Alerts are sent by the system to various APIs, webhooks, developer-written scripts, and pre-made automation playbooks.

Triage is started by automated incident response tools as soon as an alert is raised. The scripts identify the incident's nature and possible severity, laying the groundwork for the proper course of action. The system can automatically start predefined containment actions for known issues based on this preliminary assessment, while escalating more complex or unique incidents for human review.

6.1.3.3. Respond and Contain

During this crucial stage, the automation platform performs pre-planned containment measures, like blocking suspicious IP addresses or quarantining devices, in accordance with the triage results. By providing dashboards and real-time notifications, the incident management system informs security teams and enables human intervention in intricate situations. Certain fixes that are normally performed by the on-call personnel, like resource scaling, automated rollbacks to stable versions, and service restarts, can be programmed into systems to be applied automatically.

In more advanced solutions, artificial intelligence (AI)-based tools can learn from previous events to suggest or automatically apply the best course of action for each particular circumstance. When there isn't a stable version to fall back on, engineering teams frequently still need to step in and handle non-trivial issues by rolling back changes and changing configurations, for example. In between a fully automated and a fully manual approach, they might use playbooks with predefined actions to quickly address common issues while minimizing downtime.

6.1.3.4. Recover and Report

Following the first automated containment steps, the incident moves into its lifecycle's recovery and reporting stage. In this instance, security teams investigate the event thoroughly, pinpoint the underlying cause, and put effective remediation plans into action using a more hands-on approach. Using the incident management system to track progress and coordinate efforts, team members use a combination of manual and automated tasks during this phase.

Since many of the response and contain actions are hasty and insufficient, engineers are essential in helping to restore the affected systems to a more permanent fix during the recovery phase. They can minimize downtime by restoring systems quickly by executing runbooks. When an incident is caused by code bugs, engineers create and implement patches throughout the infrastructure.

6.1.3.5. Refine and Improve

Continuous improvement is the focus of the incident management process's last phase. Teams from development and security work together to assess how well the automated incident response is working. They assess critical metrics to determine how well their incident management workflow is working, including mean time to detection (MTTD), mean time to resolution (MTTR), and overall response times.

The incident management system's post-incident reports, which point out any shortcomings or potential areas for improvement, offer insightful information about how well automated actions performed. Team members make necessary adjustments to automation playbooks, rules, and scripts, as well as refine and update their incident response plan, in light of these findings. For newly emerging use cases, they might modify the prioritization algorithms or develop fresh templates.

6.1.4. Benefits of Incident Management Automation

Implementing incident response automation offers significant advantages over traditional manual approaches. These benefits include:

- **Faster Incident Resolution:** Automation can significantly reduce the time from incident detection to recovery by eliminating manual toil and executing pre-approved actions in seconds. The faster incidents are resolved, the lower the impact to customers and the business.
- **Reduced Alert Fatigue:** Automation filters out noise and only involves developers for relevant, high-priority issues. This minimizes burnout and helps devs stay focused.
- **Improved Code Quality:** With routine incidents and rollbacks automated, developers can spend more time proactively optimizing code and infrastructure for resilience.
- **Enhanced Collaboration:** Incident response automation is a collaborative effort between security, development, and operations teams. Implementing it provides an opportunity to define clear processes and improve cross-team visibility.
- **Proactive Security:** Automated security scanning and testing helps identify vulnerabilities early in the development process, reducing the risk of major incidents.

6.1.5. Best Practices for Incident Response Automation

There are difficulties in putting incident response automation into practice. Insufficient expertise in automation technologies and integration techniques frequently results in inadequate implementations or an unmanageable dependence on outside consultants for teams. Furthermore, it is technically difficult to have a consistent incident response across larger systems because organizations usually use a variety of tools and platforms throughout their infrastructure.

To overcome these hurdles and effectively automate incident response processes, consider the following best practices:

- **Start Small and Scale Up:** The best place to start when automating your systems is by focusing on straightforward, low-risk tasks. Scorecards can be used to pinpoint manual tasks that are ready for automation as well as bottlenecks. Building trust in the automation system throughout the organization and facilitating easier change management are two benefits of gradually extending your automation efforts to more complex scenarios.
- **Focus on High-Value Tasks:** Prioritize automating tasks that will have the biggest impact on reducing incident response times or freeing up valuable resources. You can demonstrate quick wins and build momentum for your automation initiatives, starting with repetitive, time-consuming processes prone to human error.
- **User Training:** Spend money on thorough training courses for each team member participating in the incident management procedure. Make sure that employees, whether technical or not, are aware of how the automation functions, when to rely on it, and when human intervention is required. Frequent instruction and practical experience can enhance system adoption by fostering system confidence.
- **Version Control and Code Reusability:** Robust version control procedures and culture for automation scripts and playbooks facilitate simple change tracking, rollbacks when necessary, and team member cooperation. Reducing development time and enhancing consistency across your automation efforts can be achieved by writing modular, reusable code components that are easily adaptable to various scenarios.
- **Error Handling and Logging:** In addition to helping with troubleshooting, robust error handling and thorough logging also supply important data for audits and ongoing improvement

initiatives. Put in place thorough error-catching procedures and make sure that every automated action is fully recorded.

- **Testing and Continuous Improvement:** Make sure your automated workflows function as intended under a variety of circumstances by testing and reviewing them on a regular basis. You may enhance and broaden your automation capabilities by incorporating user feedback, real-world incident lessons, and a culture of continuous improvement.
- **Metrics and Monitoring:** Create precise metrics to gauge how well your incident management automation is working. Review these metrics on a regular basis to pinpoint areas that need work and convince stakeholders of the benefits of automation.

6.1.6. Incident Response Technologies

As previously mentioned, incident response plans usually include the security solutions that incident response teams should have in place to carry out or automate key incident response workflows, such as gathering and correlating security data, detecting incidents in real-time, and responding to in-progress attacks. These plans also outline the steps that CSIRTs should take in the event of a security incident.

Some of the most commonly used incident response technologies include:

- **SIEM (Security Information and Event Management):** SIEM collects and correlates security event data from networked devices as well as from various internal security tools (such as firewalls, vulnerability scanners, and threat intelligence feeds). Through indicators of real threats from the massive volume of notifications these tools generate, SIEM can aid incident response teams in combating "alert fatigue."
- **SOAR (Security Orchestration, Automation, and Response):** SOAR enables security teams to define playbooks—formalized workflows that coordinate different security operations and tools in response to security incidents—and to automate portions of these workflows where possible.
- **EDR (Endpoint Detection and Response):** EDR software is intended to automatically defend end users, endpoint devices, and IT assets within an organization from cyberthreats that evade detection by antivirus software and other conventional endpoint security tools. All network endpoints have their data continuously collected by EDR, which then analyzes it in real time to look for signs of known

or suspected cyberthreats. EDR can then take automatic action to stop or lessen the damage that threats it finds cause.

- **XDR (Extended Detection and Response):** XDR is a cybersecurity technology that creates a single, central enterprise system for threat prevention, detection, and response by combining security tools, control points, data and telemetry sources, and analytics across the hybrid IT environment (endpoints, networks, private and public clouds). XDR is a still-emerging technology that, by breaking down tool silos and automating response throughout the entire cyberthreat kill chain, has the potential to help security operations centers (SOCs) and extended security teams accomplish more with less resources.
- **UEBA (User and Entity Behavior Analytics):** (UEBA) detects unusual and possibly harmful user and device behavior using automation, machine learning algorithms, and behavioral analytics. Because insider threats resemble legitimate network traffic, UEBA is useful in detecting malicious insiders or hackers who use compromised insider credentials to avoid detection by other security tools. UEBA features are frequently found in SIEM, EDR, and XDR packages.
- **ASM (Attack Surface Management):** The continuous identification, analysis, remediation, and monitoring of vulnerabilities and possible attack vectors across all the assets in an organization's attack surface are automated by ASM solutions. ASM can map relationships between assets and reveal network assets that were previously unmonitored.

6.2. INTEGRATING THREAT INTELLIGENCE WITH SECURITY INFORMATION AND EVENT MANAGEMENT (SIEM) SYSTEMS

An important development in cybersecurity is the integration of threat intelligence with Security Information and Event Management (SIEM) systems, which improves the capacity to identify, evaluate, and counter threats more successfully. Through this integration, businesses can use outside data about new threats, weaknesses, and attack trends in conjunction with their current SIEM frameworks to implement more intelligent and preventative security measures.

A SIEM system's primary function is to compile and correlate data from a variety of sources across the network, servers, and applications that make up an organization's IT environment. It gathers event and log data, examines it to find possible security issues, and sends out alerts when it detects unusual activity. Even though SIEM systems are excellent at tracking and evaluating internal data, integrating threat intelligence feeds with them can greatly increase their efficacy.

Threat intelligence furnishes contextual data regarding nascent and established threats, encompassing indicators of compromise (IoCs), adversarial tactics, techniques, and procedures (TTPs), and patterns in cyberattack tactics. Organizations can obtain current information on recognized threats by integrating threat intelligence into a SIEM system. This improves the SIEM's capacity to recognize and rank possible security incidents.

Better detection capabilities are one of the main advantages of this integration. SIEM systems receive comprehensive information about known malicious IP addresses, domains, file hashes, and other indicators from threat intelligence feeds. The correlation rules and algorithms of the SIEM can be improved and enhanced with the help of this external data. To improve its detection of related activities or payloads across the network, the SIEM system can be updated, for instance, if a threat intelligence feed discovers a new strain of ransomware.

As a result, the SIEM system improves its ability to recognize pertinent threats and lower false positives. Enhanced incident response is an additional benefit. SIEM systems can deliver more contextualized alerts with integrated threat intelligence, assisting security teams in quickly determining the nature and extent of an attack. For example, threat intelligence can offer background information on whether suspicious network traffic that sets off an alert is linked to a known threat actor or campaign.

Responders to incidents can use this context to prioritize their response efforts, make better decisions, and adjust their course of action. Moreover, proactive threat hunting is made easier by the integration of threat intelligence with SIEM systems. Security analysts can proactively look for indications of malicious activity that might not have triggered alerts by using threat intelligence to create queries and searches within the SIEM. By taking a proactive stance, risks are recognized and reduced before they have a chance to do serious damage.

However, cautious management is necessary for a successful integration. Businesses need to make sure the threat intelligence feeds they use are consistent, pertinent, and up to date. They also need to modify their correlation rules and SIEM configurations to effectively incorporate threat intelligence without flooding the system with too much data or producing too many alerts.

Threat intelligence, when integrated with SIEM systems, improves cybersecurity by offering current information on emerging threats and useful external context. Proactive threat hunting, enhanced detection accuracy, and enhanced incident response are all made possible by this integration. Through the utilization of SIEM systems' internal data and threat intelligence's external insights, organizations can fortify their overall security posture and enhance their ability to fend off dynamic cyber threats.

6.2.1. Security Information and Event Management (SIEM) Integration

Integration of SIEM systems with additional security and network technologies and tools is known as SIEM integration. Organizations can obtain comprehensive visibility into potential threats by configuring the operational and infrastructure elements of the IT environment to feed log data and alerts into a SIEM system. Security teams can then perform data aggregation, correlation, and analysis, which gives them the ability to stop intrusions before any damage is done, counteract malicious activity, and improve security posture as a whole.

The process of integrating SIEM systems into an organization's overall cybersecurity infrastructure aims to improve the monitoring, analysis, and response to security threats. SIEM systems provide a centralized view of security-related data by aggregating and analyzing log and event data from various sources throughout an IT environment. In order to ensure that SIEM systems complement and improve current security measures, their effective integration necessitates a strategic approach.

- **Centralized Data Aggregation and Correlation:** SIEM systems are essential for gathering and combining log and event data from a variety of sources, such as servers, security appliances, network devices, and apps. Through integration, a centralized repository of security data can be created by configuring SIEM to receive data from these various sources. SIEM systems are capable of detecting patterns and anomalies that could point to security incidents by combining data from various sources. For instance, in order to identify possible brute-force attacks or compromised credentials, SIEM can correlate unsuccessful login attempts with subsequent successful logins.
- **Enhanced Threat Detection:** Enhancing threat detection requires integrating threat intelligence feeds with SIEM systems. Threat intelligence offers current details on known threats, such as threat actor profiles, attack methods, and indicators of compromise (IoCs). Through the integration of this intelligence into the SIEM system, entities can augment their capacity for detection. To improve the

ability to quickly identify and address phishing attacks, SIEM can be set up to generate alerts, for instance, if a threat intelligence feed discovers a new phishing domain. This will allow for the detection of traffic to the domain within the network.

- **Streamlined Incident Response:** For effective incident response, integration with other security tools and systems is essential. Security orchestration, automation, and response (SOAR) platforms and SIEM systems can be integrated to automate response actions according to predefined rules. For example, if SIEM notices anomalous behavior suggestive of malware infection, it can initiate an automated reaction, like severing the connection to the compromised system or blocking questionable IP addresses. This integration helps contain threats faster, decreases manual labor, and streamlines the response process.
- **Operational Efficiency and Scalability:** Making sure the SIEM system can grow with the organization's expanding data and security needs is another essential component of effective integration. This entails making sure the performance of the SIEM system doesn't degrade and setting up data gathering methods to manage growing volumes of log data. Furthermore, SIEM systems can monitor and analyze data from cloud environments thanks to integration with cloud services and infrastructure, guaranteeing thorough coverage across on-premises and cloud-based resources.
- **Customization and Tuning:** Customizing and fine-tuning the system to the unique requirements and threat landscape of the organization is crucial for maximizing the effectiveness of SIEM integration. This entails setting up dashboards, correlation rules, and alert thresholds in accordance with the security goals and policies of the company. To keep up with changing threats and modifications in the IT environment, regular updates and modifications are required.
- **Compliance and Reporting:** SIEM integration can also support regulatory compliance by facilitating the collection, storage, and analysis of data required for compliance reporting. SIEM systems can generate reports and logs that demonstrate adherence to various standards and regulations, such as GDPR, HIPAA, or PCI-DSS.

The centralization of data aggregation, enhanced threat detection, expedited incident response, and compliance support are some of the ways that SIEM integration strengthens an organization's security posture. To guarantee that SIEM systems offer optimal protection against dynamic cyber threats, careful configuration, tuning, and collaboration with other security tools are necessary for effective integration.

6.2.2. How Does SIEM Integration Work?

Finding data sources, gathering logs, standardizing data into a common format, generating alerts, correlating events, storing data, offering analysis tools, and integrating with other security tools are all steps in the SIEM integration process.

SIEM systems locate and gather security-related information from servers, endpoints, apps, databases, and network devices. To enable uniform comparison and analysis, the gathered data is subsequently normalized into a standard format.

SIEM software analyzes events from many sources and compares them to find trends that point to a security breach or a problem with compliance. The SIEM generates an alert set to alert the relevant personnel or start automated response mechanisms when it detects a possible security event.

Data is stored by SIEM systems in order to facilitate compliance reporting, forensics, and historical analysis. They also offer reporting tools to satisfy compliance requirements and analysis tools for security analysts to look into alerts. In order to enhance the data and raise the accuracy of event correlation, SIEM systems frequently interface with other security tools.

Security orchestration, automation, and response (SOAR) tools can be integrated with some SIEM solutions to automate specific incident types' responses, like isolating an infected endpoint from the network. On the basis of incident response results and security analyst feedback, the SIEM system is continuously improved. In the long run, this lowers false positives and increases the accuracy of event correlation.

By centralizing security management, SIEM integration gives businesses control and oversight over their infrastructure. An organization's capacity to recognize, comprehend, and react quickly and efficiently to security threats is improved by this integration.

6.2.3. Key Considerations before SIEM Integration

Several key considerations should be considered before integrating third-party tools with a SIEM system to ensure the integration is successful and adds value to existing security operations.

These considerations include:

- **Compatibility:** Make sure the third-party tool can work with your SIEM platform.

- **Data Quality:** Check if the data provided by the third-party tool is accurate and relevant to your organization's security needs.
- **Scalability:** Consider whether the third-party tool can handle large amounts of data as your organization grows.
- **Performance:** Assess the potential impact of integrating the tool on the performance of your SIEM system.
- **Security:** Verify that integrating the tool does not introduce new security risks.
- **Compliance:** Make sure the third-party tool complies with relevant regulations and standards.
- **Vendor Support:** Check if the vendor provides sufficient support and if there is a community around the tool you can contact for help.
- **Cost:** Evaluate the tool's integration cost, including licensing fees and additional infrastructure.
- **Maintenance:** Consider the maintenance requirements for the integrated solution.
- **Ease of Integration:** Assess how easy integrating the third-party tool with your SIEM is.
- **Centralized Management:** Ensure the integrated solution allows for centralized management within the SIEM.
- **Incident Response:** Understand how the third-party tool fits into the incident response workflow.
- **Customization:** Determine if the tool allows for customization to meet your organization's specific requirements.

By thoroughly considering these factors, organizations can make informed decisions that align with their security strategies and maximize the effectiveness of their SIEM systems through third-party integrations.

6.2.4. Security Information and Event Management Tools

There are a number of security information and event management solutions on the market. Arcsight ESM, IBM QRadar and Splunk are among the most popular.

6.2.4.1. ArcSight

ArcSight collects and analyzes log data from an enterprise's security technologies, operating systems and applications. Once a malicious threat is detected, the system alerts security personnel. ArcSight can also start an automatic reaction to stop the malicious activity. Another feature is the ability to integrate third-party threat intelligence feeds for more accurate threat detection.

6.2.4.2. IBM QRadar

IBM QRadar collects log data from sources in an enterprise's information system, including network devices, operating systems, applications and user activities. The QRadar SIEM analyzes log data in real-time, enabling users to quickly identify and stop attacks. QRadar can also collect log events and network flow data from cloud-based applications. This SIEM also supports threat intelligence feeds.

6.2.4.3. Splunk

Splunk Enterprise Security provides real-time threat monitoring, rapid investigations using visual correlations and investigative analysis to trace the dynamic activities associated with advanced security threats.

The Splunk SIEM is available as locally installed software or as a cloud service. It supports threat intelligence feed integration from third-party apps.

6.2.5. What are the Benefits of SIEM Integration?

An organization can obtain a more thorough understanding of its security posture by automating and optimizing the process of gathering and evaluating security data from multiple sources within its IT environment. As a result, the organization is better equipped to recognize security threats and incidents and respond to them. SIEM systems can provide a more accurate picture of the security environment and identify potential threats that individual security tools might miss by analyzing data from multiple sources.

Furthermore, by lowering the amount of false positives and false negatives, enterprises can improve the overall accuracy and efficacy of their security operations by integrating multiple security technologies.

The benefits of this integration are multifaceted:

- **Real-time Analysis:** By integrating real-time data feeds, SIEM can immediately analyze security events as they occur, enabling quicker identification of potential threats.
- **Advanced Correlation:** Integration allows SIEM to correlate events across different systems and applications, identifying complex attack patterns that might be overlooked if data sources remained siloed.
- **Automation of Security Processes:** Integrating with incident response platforms and automation tools enables SIEM to initiate

responses to threats without manual intervention, increasing the speed and efficiency of the security operations.

- **Consistent and Normalized Data:** Integration ensures that data from various sources is normalized into a consistent format, simplifying analysis and reducing the likelihood of interpretation errors.
- **Enhanced Visibility and Context:** Integrating with identity and access management systems and threat intelligence feeds provides additional context to security events, aiding in more accurate threat assessment.
- **Streamlined Compliance:** Integration with regulatory compliance frameworks allows SIEM to automate generating reports and logs necessary for compliance audits, saving time and resources.
- **Scalability:** As an organization grows, integration capabilities allow SIEM systems to easily expand and manage the increased volume and variety of security data.
- **Reduced Operational Overhead:** With integration, SIEM reduces the need for manual collection and analysis of security data, allowing security personnel to focus on strategic tasks rather than routine operations.
- **Better Incident Management:** Integration with ticketing systems and workflow tools helps track incident response processes from detection to resolution, ensuring accountability and documentation.

6.2.6. Fundamentals of SIEM Integration

SIEM integration focuses on aggregating log data from various entities such as servers, endpoints, and network devices. This consolidation is essential for providing a comprehensive view of an organization's security posture, facilitating the detection of patterns and anomalies indicative of potential security events:

- **Data Collection and Event Correlation:** Organizations use sensors and loggers throughout their infrastructure to collect data. Their SIEM systems analyze this data using advanced event correlation techniques, algorithms, and rules to identify indicators of cyber threats.
- **Proactive Threat Detection with Behavioral Analytics:** Modern SIEM systems incorporate proactive threat detection methods, leveraging machine learning and behavioral analytics to identify risks before they escalate into security breaches. These systems

constantly analyze behaviors to detect deviations from the norm, which could signal malicious activity.

- **Real-Time Alerts and Dashboard Visualization:** Real-time alerts and dashboards are essential to a SIEM system for maintaining situational awareness of an organization's security status. These dashboards present critical information in an accessible format, enabling quick assessment and action on security incidents as they arise.
- **Integration with Existing Security Frameworks:** SIEM solutions can be integrated easily with existing security systems, meaning organizations can use their current investments to enhance their security with SIEM technology. This technology improves the capabilities of intrusion detection systems and vulnerability management tools.
- **Automated Incident Response:** Automated incident response is a key feature of SIEM integration. When a threat is detected, the SIEM system can quickly take action to neutralize it before it can harm organizational operations. This is done through pre-configured actions that help mitigate the threat without delay.

6.2.7. SIEM and Threat Intelligence: Stay Current on Trending Threats

Keeping up with emerging threats and strengthening an organization's overall cybersecurity posture require integrating threat intelligence with SIEM systems. Through this integration, a strong defense against new and evolving threats is created by fusing the contextual and up-to-date insights of threat intelligence with the real-time monitoring and data aggregation capabilities of SIEM.

- **Enhanced Threat Detection with Threat Intelligence:** Critical information about novel and developing threats is provided by threat intelligence, which also includes threat actor profiles, attack tactics, techniques, and procedures (TTPs), and indicators of compromise (IoCs). Organizations can enhance their capacity to identify and address threats by incorporating this intelligence into a SIEM system. Threat intelligence feeds, for example, may contain information about recently identified malware signatures or malicious IP addresses. When these feeds are incorporated into the SIEM system, the SIEM can identify indicators of comparable threats within the organization's network by correlating this external data with internal logs and events. The SIEM can identify complex or unusual attack patterns that might otherwise go undetected thanks to this enhanced data.

- **Real-Time Updates and Contextual Awareness:** Threat environments are ever-changing, with new weaknesses and methods of attack appearing on a regular basis. By incorporating threat intelligence into SIEM systems, security teams can be guaranteed to have access to the most recent data. The SIEM system can be updated to identify relevant indicators and modify its detection rules in response, for instance, if threat intelligence sources report a new phishing campaign or a zero-day exploit targeting particular software. The ability to update in real-time enables organizations to promptly modify their security protocols and responses, thereby helping them stay ahead of emerging threats.
- **Improved Incident Prioritization and Response:** Improving incident prioritization is one of the main advantages of combining threat intelligence with SIEM. When SIEM systems have access to contextual data from threat intelligence, they are able to deliver alerts that are more precise and useful. Threat intelligence, for example, can assist in determining whether unusual network activity detected by the SIEM is associated with a known threat actor or current attack trends. Because of this context, security teams are able to focus resources on the most critical incidents and lower the risk of potential damage by prioritizing their response efforts based on the threat's relevance and severity.
- **Proactive Threat Hunting:** Additionally, integration helps with proactive threat hunting. Threat intelligence is a useful tool that security analysts can use to direct their searches and investigations within the SIEM system. For example, analysts can proactively look for indications of exploitation attempts or related indicators within their environment if threat intelligence indicates an increase in attacks targeting a particular software vulnerability. By taking a proactive stance, risks are recognized and reduced before they have a chance to do serious damage.
- **Automation and Efficiency:** Processes for threat detection and response can be streamlined by automating the integration of threat intelligence into SIEM systems. The requirement for manual intervention can be decreased by configuring automated updates from threat intelligence feeds to modify SIEM rules and alerts in real-time. In addition, automation makes it easier to apply fresh

threat intelligence quickly, preserving the SIEM system's efficacy against emerging threats.

- **Challenges and Considerations:** Although there are many benefits to integrating threat intelligence with SIEM systems, there are drawbacks as well. Threat intelligence feeds must be relevant and of high quality, as outdated or low-quality intelligence can result in erroneous alerts and the waste of valuable resources. Companies need to control the amount of alerts that the SIEM system generates in order to prevent alert fatigue and guarantee prompt and efficient responses. To remain effective, threat intelligence integration and SIEM rule tuning and calibration must be done on a regular basis.

Organizations can improve incident prioritization, contextual awareness, and threat detection by integrating threat intelligence with SIEM systems. By enabling security teams to adjust their defenses in real-time and stay up to date on emerging threats, this integration helps them improve their overall cybersecurity posture and resistance to changing threats.

Figure 6.1. *SIEM and threat intelligence: Stay current on trending threats.*

Source: https://www.ibm.com/blog/wp-content/uploads/2023/08/d67c48b0-19cc-469d-90b32643463ad4f8.blog-lead-space-40x21-1-1200x630.jpg.

Organizations face a growing array of cybersecurity threats, with the average cost of a data breach expected to reach an all-time high of USD $4.45 million in 2023. These dangers, which may lead to data breaches, can include ransomware attacks, phishing scams, and insider threats. Businesses must use cutting-edge security measures to safeguard their sensitive data and digital assets as cybercriminals become more skilled and diverse in their tactics. Threat intelligence and SIEM solutions are two essential components of the modern cybersecurity toolbox. Through the utilization of these resources, organizations can remain up to date on emerging threats and take proactive measures to thwart possible attacks and adversaries (Figure 6.1).

Solutions for SIEM are essential for preserving an organization's cybersecurity posture. They gather and examine enormous volumes of security-related data from different sources inside the IT infrastructure of an organization. Real-time data collection, correlation, and analysis are performed on event log data from users, endpoints, apps, data sources, cloud workloads, networks, and security hardware and software like firewalls and antivirus programs. SIEM solutions are capable of offering an all-encompassing perspective of an organization's security status by centralizing and aggregating this data. Data and insights containing in-depth knowledge about cybersecurity threats aimed at an organization are known as threat intelligence. It entails gathering, analyzing, and disseminating data regarding existing and prospective cybersecurity risks.

This data may include software or system vulnerabilities, indicators of compromise (IoCs), and cybercriminals' tactics, techniques, and procedures (TTPs). Teams dedicated to threat intelligence continuously keep an eye on a variety of sources, such as malware samples, forums, and dark web marketplaces, in order to give organizations early warning about new threats. Threat intelligence, according to Gartner research, can improve security teams' detection and response capabilities by shortening investigation times, improving alert quality, and providing coverage for the most recent threats and attackers.

6.2.8. The Synergy between SIEM and Threat Intelligence

SIEM solutions are built to perform rule matching on log data from many sources. With the integration of threat intelligence, SIEM solutions can stay one step ahead of emerging threats and advisories. Let's explore some benefits of incorporating threat intelligence within a SIEM platform:

- **Real-Time Threat Detection:** Integrating Threat Intelligence feeds into a SIEM solution enhances its capabilities. By cross-referencing internal data with external threat intelligence, organizations can identify patterns and anomalies that might otherwise go unnoticed. This enables faster detection of vulnerabilities, new malware strains, or targeted attacks.
- **Proactive Defense:** Threat hunting is key to effective cybersecurity. Instead of reacting to threats after they've caused damage, organizations can use SIEM and Threat Intelligence to identify threat actors that may already be lurking in an environment and thwart attacks before they continue. By staying informed about evolving tactics and vulnerabilities, organizations can adjust their

threat hunting techniques to find and counter threats before they materialize.

- **Improved Incident Response:** When a security incident occurs, the combined power of SIEM and Threat intelligence is invaluable. SIEM solutions provide a timeline of events leading up to the breach, while Threat Intelligence supplies insights into the attacker's TTPs and associated IOCs that can accelerate the investigation. This aids in incident response, containment, and recovery efforts.

6.3. AUTOMATION OF INCIDENT DETECTION AND RESPONSE WORKFLOWS

One major development in cybersecurity is the automation of incident detection and response workflows, which helps organizations respond to security threats more quickly, accurately, and efficiently. By utilizing cutting-edge technologies and established protocols, this automation helps to minimize the possible impact of threats and reduce the need for manual intervention in the detection, analysis, and response to security incidents.

- **Automated Detection:** Automation begins with the detection phase, where systems are equipped to identify potential security incidents using predefined rules and advanced algorithms. Modern Security Information and Event Management (SIEM) systems, for example, can analyze vast amounts of log and event data in real-time to detect anomalies and suspicious activities. Automation enhances this process by employing machine learning and behavioral analytics to recognize patterns indicative of potential threats, even those not yet known. For instance, automated systems can identify unusual patterns in network traffic or abnormal user behavior that may suggest an attack or compromise, generating alerts without requiring human oversight.
- **Automated Analysis:** Automation makes it easier to quickly analyze potential incidents and ascertain the type and gravity of threats they pose. Integration with threat intelligence feeds, which offer contextual data about known threats, vulnerabilities, and attack methods, is how this is accomplished. Automated systems have the ability to quickly determine whether an alert is a real threat by correlating data from multiple sources, including system logs, network traffic, and threat intelligence. Automation can, for instance, validate a threat and evaluate its impact if an alert suggests

a possible malware infection by cross-referencing it with known malware signatures and current threat intelligence.

- **Automated Response:** Automation helps the response phase a lot by allowing for the quick and precise execution of predetermined actions. Workflows for automated responses may involve implementing patches to fix vulnerabilities, blocking malicious IP addresses, or isolating impacted systems. An automated system, for example, can quickly respond to an intrusion attempt by disconnecting the impacted device from the network, containing the threat and averting additional harm. In addition, automated systems can update firewall rules or run pre-written remediation scripts in response to threats they detect, making sure that the reaction is uniform and compliant with organizational policies.
- **Efficiency and Speed:** The main benefit of automating workflows for incident detection and response is the notable boost in speed and efficiency. The time between detection and containment can be shortened by using automated systems, which can process and respond to incidents far faster than human analysts. In order to reduce the harm caused by security incidents and lessen their influence on business operations, a prompt response is essential. Security teams' manual workload is also lessened by automation, freeing them up to concentrate on more difficult jobs and strategic projects.
- **Integration and Coordination:** Security orchestration, automation, and response (SOAR) platforms, endpoint detection and response (EDR) programs, SIEMs, and other security tools and systems must all be seamlessly integrated for automation to be effective. Organizations can make sure that automated responses are thorough and well-coordinated throughout the whole security infrastructure by coordinating these systems. For instance, integrating with SOAR platforms enables the automation of incident management responsibilities like ticketing and team communications, as well as the coordination of intricate response workflows.
- **Challenges and Considerations:** Automation in incident detection and response has advantages, but it also has drawbacks. Automated systems need to be configured carefully to prevent false positives, which can cause alert fatigue and needless actions. To keep automated responses accurate and effective in the face of changing threats, automation rules and algorithms must be updated and fine-tuned on a regular basis. Organizations also need to strike a balance between

automation and human oversight when dealing with circumstances that call for complex decision-making or nuanced judgment.

Automation of workflows for incident detection and response improves an organization's capacity to effectively and efficiently handle security risks. Through the utilization of automated systems for identification, evaluation, and reaction, establishments can enhance their security stance, minimize reaction times, and enhance their defenses against constantly changing cyber hazards. To guarantee that automation enhances and complements overall security operations, however, successful implementation necessitates cautious management and integration with other security tools.

6.3.1. How Automated Incident Response Works

Cyber threat intelligence and data from inside your own company power incident response automation. Large amounts of data are ingested, coordinated, and analyzed by it to provide insights that enable it to handle and mitigate emergencies far faster than any human.

The tools from which an automated incident response platform might draw data include:

- Network and application logs;
- Intrusion prevention and intrusion detection systems;
- External threat intelligence;
- Identity and Access Management (IAM) tools;
- Endpoint protection tools;
- Data feeds from SIEM/SOAR;
- Third-party sources such as vendors and business partners.

An incident response automation solution then leverages this data to achieve three things:

- Differentiate false positives from genuine threats;
- Prioritize alerts based on risk, severity, and impact;
- Identify the potential origin point of any malicious software or threat actor.

6.4. CASE STUDIES OF AUTOMATED INCIDENT RESPONSE SOLUTIONS (SOAR PLATFORMS)

Organizations' approach to managing security incidents is being completely transformed by automated incident response solutions, especially Security

Orchestration, Automation, and Response (SOAR) platforms. To automate and coordinate incident response workflows, SOAR platforms integrate with current security tools like SIEM systems, endpoint detection and response (EDR) programs, and threat intelligence feeds. This integration streamlines complicated procedures and automates repetitive tasks to increase the speed and effectiveness of responding to threats.

Critical incident response tasks like threat analysis, alert triage, and remediation actions are automated by SOAR platforms. For example, the SOAR platform can automatically collect pertinent information upon detection of a potential security incident, correlate it with threat intelligence, and carry out pre-programmed response actions, like isolating compromised systems or blocking malicious IP addresses. This greatly minimizes possible harm by cutting the response time from hours to minutes.

Because SOAR platforms handle routine tasks and lessen alert fatigue, they also help security teams work less and be less burdened. While the SOAR platform manages automated responses and produces comprehensive reports for additional analysis, security analysts can concentrate on more strategic and complex tasks. Additionally, by using pre-written playbooks, SOAR platforms facilitate repeatable and consistent incident handling, guaranteeing that responses follow best practices and organizational policies.

All things considered, SOAR platforms improve an organization's capacity to respond swiftly and decisively to security incidents, bolstering overall resilience and lessening the effect of cyberattacks. Organizations can achieve enhanced efficiency, quicker reaction times, and a more proactive approach to incident management by utilizing automation and orchestration.

6.4.1. Case Study of Healthcare Provider: Streamlining Ransomware Incident Management

- **Background:** A major healthcare provider faced challenges in managing ransomware attacks, which posed a significant risk due to the sensitivity of patient data. The organization needed a solution to respond more effectively and minimize downtime.
- **Solution:** The healthcare provider deployed a SOAR platform designed to orchestrate and automate responses to ransomware incidents. The platform was integrated with endpoint detection and response (EDR) solutions, network monitoring tools, and backup systems.

6.4.1.1. Implementation

- **Automated Containment and Isolation:** Upon detecting ransomware activity, the SOAR platform automatically isolated affected endpoints from the network to prevent lateral movement.
- **Automated Backup Restoration:** The platform triggered automated processes to restore data from backups, reducing recovery time.
- **Playbooks for Ransomware:** Custom response playbooks were created to guide automated actions and ensure consistent handling of ransomware incidents.

6.4.1.2. Results

- **Reduced Downtime:** Automation significantly reduced system downtime by enabling rapid containment and recovery.
- **Minimized Data Loss:** Automated backup restoration ensured minimal data loss and expedited recovery processes.
- **Improved Incident Handling:** The structured response playbooks ensured a consistent and effective approach to managing ransomware incidents.

6.4.2. Incident Response Automation and Security Orchestration with SOAR

The basics of incident response, and introduce a new category of tools—SOAR—which make incident response more efficient, more effective and more manageable at scale.

6.4.2.1. What is Incident Response?

- **Reactive Incident Response:** Incident response is an organizational process that allows security teams to contain security incidents or cyber attacks, prevent or control damages. Incident response also allows teams to handle the aftermath of the attack—recovery, remediating security holes exposed by the attack, forensics, communication and auditing. This is known as reactive incident response.
- **Proactive Incident Response:** Many security incidents are only discovered weeks or months after they took place—while some are never discovered. Many organizations are developing proactive incident response capabilities. This involves actively searching corporate systems for signs of a cyber attack.

- **Threat Hunting:** Threat hunting is the core activity of proactive incident response, which is carried out by skilled security analysts. It typically involves querying security data using a Security Information and Event System (SIEM), and running vulnerability scans or penetration tests against organizational systems. The objective is to discover suspicious activity or anomalies that represent a security incident.

6.4.2.2. What is Case Management?

Case management involves collecting, distributing and analyzing data tied to specific security incidents, to allow teams to effectively respond.

Case management solutions help security staff:

- Open a case for a confirmed security incident;
- Quickly aggregate all relevant data into a digital representation of the case;
- Enable fast prioritization of cases for response;
- Investigate and add information to the case;
- Record activity in the aftermath of an attack and close the case.

6.4.3. Key SOAR Capabilities

SOAR tools provide the following four capabilities that help Security Operation Centers (SOC) respond to incidents more effectively.

6.4.3.1. Orchestration

Orchestration is the ability to coordinate decision making, and automate responsive actions based on an assessment of risks and environment states.

SOAR tools can do this by integrating with other security solutions in a way that lets them "pull" data and also "push" proactive actions. SOAR provides a generic interface, allowing analysts to define actions on security tools and IT systems without being experts in those systems or their APIs.

An example of orchestration: Process a suspicious email

- A SOAR tool can investigate whether the sender has a bad reputation, via threat intelligence, and use DNS tools to confirm the origin.
- The tool can automatically extract hyperlinks and validate them via URL reputation, detonate the links in a secure environment, or run attachments in a sandbox.
- Then, if an incident is confirmed, a playbook is run. The playbook

looks in the email system to find all messages from the same sender or with the same links or attachments and quarantines them.

6.4.3.2. Automation

Automation, which is machine-driven action execution on security tools and IT systems as part of an incident response, is related to orchestration. Security teams can establish a decision-making workflow, with enforcement, status tracking, and auditing capabilities, using SOAR tools. Security playbooks are the foundation of automation, and analysts can write them in Python or a graphical user interface (GUI).

An example of an Automation playbook: Exabeam's malware playbook.

- The SOAR tool scans the malware file and detonates the file in a sandbox using external services.
- The SOAR tool checks the file against reputation services such as Virus Total for accuracy.
- The SOAR tool identifies the geolocation of the source or originating IP address.
- The system notifies the user about the malware and a post-analysis cleanup is performed.

6.4.3.3. Incident Management and Collaboration

This SOAR capability helps security teams manage security incidents, collaborate and share data to resolve the incident efficiently.

- **Alert Processing and Triage:** A SOAR tool gathers and analyzes security data, typically taken from the SIEM, correlates data to identify priority and criticality, and automatically generates incidents for investigation. The incident already includes relevant context information, allowing analysts to investigate further. This removes the need for a human to notice the relevant security data, identify it as a security incident and manually set up an incident in the system.
- **Journaling and Evidentiary Support:** A SOAR tool provides an investigation timeline to collect and store artifacts of the security incident, for current and future analysis. Artifacts may relate to known attacker's activities, which may be carried out over an extended period. Additional artifacts can be pulled in to investigate if they are related to the ongoing incident.
- **Case Management:** The tool can record actions and decisions made by the security team, making them visible to the entire organization,

as well as external auditors. Over time, the SOAR tool creates an organizational knowledge base of tribal knowledge—threats, incidents, historical responses and decisions and their outcomes.

- **Management of Threat Intelligence:** A SOAR tools brings in threat data from open-source databases, industry leaders, coordinated response organizations, and commercial threat intelligence providers. The SOAR tool attaches the relevant threat information to specific incidents, and makes threat intelligence easily accessible to analysts as they are investigating an incident.

6.4.4. Dashboards and Reporting

SOAR tools are not only responsible for coordinating and automating incident response, but also for enabling central measurement of SOC activity.

SOAR tools generate reports and dashboards including:

- **Analyst-Level Reporting:** On activity by each analyst, such as number and types of incidents, mean time to detect and respond per analyst, and so on.
- **SOC Manager Reports:** Reporting on the number of analysts, incidents handled per analyst, and mean time for specific stages of incident response process, to identify bottlenecks.
- **CISO-Level Reports:** Alignment of risks with IT metrics to see the impact of incidents on business performance and regulations; measuring efficiently by looking at MTTD and MTTR across the entire organization, and reduction of labor through automation.

6.4.4.1. How Does SOAR Fit in with SIEM?

SOAR tools work closely with SIEM, the SOC's central information system. SOAR tools leverage the integration with SIEM to:

- Receive alerts and additional security data to identify security incidents;
- Draw in data required for analysts to further investigate an incident;
- Assist analysts in proactive incident response and threat hunting, which relies on querying and exploring cross-organization data.

6.4.5. SOAR as Part of Next-Gen SIEM Solutions

The next-generation SIEM solution needs to have a native component with advanced threat defense capabilities, workflow and orchestration, automated and manual case management, and the ability to handle and respond to detected incidents. According to Gartner, SOAR should be an integrated component of the SIEM, even though SOAR tools are developing as a distinct category.

The Security Intelligence Platform from Exbeam is an illustration of this new hybrid. Exabeam is a SIEM system that uses user entity behavioral analytics and advanced analytics. It is built on cutting edge data lake technology.

In addition, Exabeam comes with two components that provide full SOAR functionality:

- **Exabeam Incident Responder:** Provides security case management, integration with third-party tools, centralized security orchestration, and automated incident response via security response playbooks.
- **Exabeam Threat Hunter:** A point-and-click interface that lets SOC analysts quickly perform searches to identify patterns in vast amounts of historic security data. It also provides access to complete incident timelines for past and present security incidents.

REFERENCES

1. Pearce, J. M. (2014). Introduction to open-source hardware for science. In *Chapter 1–Introduction to Open-Source Hardware for Science* (pp. 1–11). Boston: Elsevier.
2. Roberts, S. J., & Brown, R. (2017). *Intelligence-Driven Incident Response: Outwitting the Adversary*. Google Books.
3. Shiller, R. J. (2019). Automation and artificial intelligence replace almost all jobs. In *Narrative Economics: How Stories go Viral and Drive Major Economic Events* (pp. 196–211). Princeton University Press.
4. Trevathan, V. L. (2006). *A Guide to the Automation Body of Knowledge* (2nd ed.). Research Triangle Park, NC: International Society of Automation.
5. Walker, M. J. (2012). *The Programmable Logic Controller: Its Prehistory, Emergence and Application* (Doctoral dissertation, The Open University).

CHAPTER 7

THREAT INTELLIGENCE SHARING AND COLLABORATION

Contents

INTRODUCTION

Contemporary cybersecurity strategies necessitate the sharing and collaboration of threat intelligence in order to protect organizations from ever-more-sophisticated cyberattacks. Cyber threats are not limited to a single organization in today's interconnected world; they frequently entail intricately planned attacks that can target numerous industries or even entire countries. In order to effectively combat these threats, organizations need to move past siloed defense mechanisms and adopt cooperative initiatives involving threat intelligence sharing. Threat intelligence is the term used to describe the gathering, evaluating, and sharing of data regarding possible or actual cyberthreats. Data on threat actors, their tactics, techniques, and procedures (TTPs), and indicators of compromise (IOCs)—which aid in identifying malicious activity—can all be included in this intelligence. Organizations that pool this intelligence are better able to anticipate, identify, and address threats as a group. Organizations can find patterns, anticipate future attacks, and create stronger defenses by combining their resources and insights.

Sharing threat intelligence is not without its difficulties, though. Concerns about data privacy, the possibility of disclosing private information, and the requirement for partner trust must all be managed by organizations. Establishing frameworks that protect the integrity and confidentiality of the shared data while also encouraging teamwork is necessary for effective threat intelligence sharing. Public-private partnerships and platforms such as Information Sharing and Analysis Centers (ISACs) are essential in fostering this kind of cooperation because they provide safe spaces where businesses can share data without jeopardizing security.

7.1. THREAT INTELLIGENCE SHARING

Cybercrime is rampant in today's world. Businesses fight a never-ending battle against a wide range of threat actors to safeguard enormous digital vaults containing highly valuable and sensitive data. In 2022, the global average cost of a data breach was $4,035 million. Companies can be devastated and demoralized by data breaches. In today's fiercely competitive business environment, the majority of organizations find it difficult to recover following a big data breach.

Organizations across the globe are faced with increasing cybersecurity complexities due to a number of factors, including a sharp rise in cloud infrastructures, the adoption of agile methodologies and pipelines, and highly skilled cybercriminals. Companies today take great care to safeguard their proprietary knowledge, industry- and region-specific insights, and business intelligence. But given the current state of cyber threats, attitudes toward some forms of intelligence must shift. Organizations should exchange threat intelligence with one another. Sharing threat intelligence can strengthen an organization's, a government's, a vendor's, a client's, an industry's, or a region's cybersecurity posture. Exchanging threat intelligence is crucial in thwarting crafty cybercriminals. Businesses cannot afford to cut themselves off from the larger community. Sharing threat intelligence is a potent means of guaranteeing strong cyber defense.

7.1.1. Different Types of Threat Intelligence Sharing

Primary threat intelligence sharing entails entities exchanging first-hand information. This includes direct cybersecurity threats that are gathered, examined, and disseminated by entities involved in a network of threat intelligence sharing. Sharing primary threat intelligence enables organizations to react to security threats almost instantly.

Sharing threat information that has been acquired, examined, and distributed by a third party is known as secondary threat intelligence sharing. It might contain intelligence feeds, reports, and briefs from governmental agencies, business associations, or commercial threat intelligence providers, for instance. Although this threat intelligence is typically broader in nature, it can nonetheless offer insightful information about more generalized threat trends and enemy tactics. Organizations combine both to create a strong cybersecurity strategy.

7.1.2. Advantages of Threat Intelligence Sharing

- **Optimized IT Resources:** Businesses are usually burdened by the hefty (and occasionally concealed) costs associated with cybersecurity. Businesses can correctly identify threats and choose comprehensive yet affordable countermeasures by exchanging threat knowledge. This can free up IT budgets for further investment and innovation while also significantly reducing the overall cybersecurity costs for businesses. By exchanging cyber threat intelligence, businesses can also optimize the performance of their current security teams.
- **Powerful Digital Engine:** Around the world, a lot of companies have turned their attention to the digital sector. Although there are many benefits, sharing threat information can help businesses lessen the risks that cloud apps and infrastructures will inevitably face. It looks like a bright but complicated technological future, and only businesses with the strongest and most secure digital anchors and security postures will be able to navigate it.

- **Robust Cybersecurity Posture:** Data is today's most valuable resource, and exchanging threat intelligence helps companies stop data breaches. In order to defend against even the most serious cyberattacks, like ransomware attacks, companies can find compromised systems, implement best practices, integrate the best cybersecurity tools and technologies, and create strong remediation procedures by exchanging threat intelligence.

7.1.3. Challenges of Threat Intelligence Sharing

- **Building Trust:** It makes sense, both practically and theoretically, to share threat intelligence. In actuality, though, a great degree of mutual trust is necessary. Establishing and maintaining partnerships based on mutual trust and understanding is imperative for organizations. Strongest trust bonds ensure that exchanging threat intelligence is seen as a collective duty that benefits all parties involved, as opposed to merely a duty. An ecosystem that facilitates the exchange of threat information must have trust.
- **Standardizing Shared Intelligence Pipelines:** Threat actors are starting to use AI to boost the strength and speed of their attacks, so organizations need to stay up to date. Automated systems and pipelines are needed to transmit threat intelligence in real time. Making sure that a wide range of organizations can generate, use, access, and read threat data from different sources, formats, and exchange protocols is the main challenge.
- **Legalities Around Sensitive Data:** Common components of threat intelligence include trade secrets, controlled unclassified information (CUI), and personally identifiable information (PII). Sensitive material that is unintentionally revealed or published may incur heavy fines and penalties, as well as legal costs from regulatory bodies. Therefore, it is essential to carefully disseminate threat intelligence.

7.2. THE IMPORTANCE OF SHARING THREAT INTELLIGENCE ACROSS ORGANIZATIONS AND SECTORS

The connected world of today makes cybersecurity threats more common and advanced than before. Rapid changes in the digital landscape have made it easier for cybercriminals to take advantage of weaknesses in a variety of industries, making it more challenging for individual organizations to protect themselves. To effectively combat these threats, sharing threat intelligence amongst organizations and sectors has become essential.

7.2.1. Enhancing Collective Cybersecurity Posture

Improving the group's cybersecurity posture is one of the main advantages of exchanging threat intelligence. It is impossible for one organization to foresee or defend against every cyberthreat. Organizations can gain from the experiences and insights of others by exchanging information about threats, vulnerabilities, and attack patterns. Entities are able to detect new threats faster and create stronger defenses thanks to this cooperative approach. Additionally, it permits resource pooling, which is advantageous for smaller businesses in particular, as they might not have the knowledge or resources to recognize and stop sophisticated attacks.

7.2.2. Early Detection and Proactive Defense

Sharing threat intelligence makes it easier for organizations to identify cyber threats early and implement a proactive defense strategy. Sharing information about a threat that has been detected in one organization with others enables them to spot similar trends and take action before the threat gets worse. The implementation of an early warning system is imperative in mitigating the impact of cyber incidents. It enables organizations to promptly patch vulnerabilities, implement suitable defenses, and prevent recurrence of the attack. In order to minimize the harm caused by cyberattacks, it is essential to have a proactive defense that is made possible by intelligence sharing. This can be achieved by reducing the amount of time between threat detection and response.

7.2.3. Building Trust and Collaboration Across Sectors

Transparency in threat intelligence promotes cross-sector trust and cooperation. Competitors may be reluctant to divulge information in many industries for fear of losing a competitive advantage or showing their weaknesses. But when it comes to cybersecurity, cooperation is crucial for the greater good. Organizations that share threat intelligence show that they are dedicated to ensuring the security of the whole, which can strengthen relationships and create a more robust ecosystem. In critical infrastructure sectors, where the failure of one organization can have a domino effect on others, trust is especially crucial. Organizations can cooperate to protect the security of the whole industry by creating a cooperative network.

7.2.4. Reducing the Cost and Impact of Cyberattacks

Cyberattacks can have catastrophic financial effects, resulting in long-term consequences like lost customer trust and reputational harm in addition to the immediate costs of incident response and remediation. Organizations can lower these costs by averting attacks or lessening their effects by exchanging threat intelligence. For instance, if a financial sector business discovers a novel kind of phishing attack, informing other businesses in the field can assist them in educating their staff and clients, consequently decreasing the possibility of successful attacks. In addition to safeguarding specific companies, this cooperative strategy helps to maintain the sector's overall stability.

7.2.5. Strengthening National and Global Security

Cyber threats are not limited by national borders, and state-sponsored actors or transnational criminal organizations are often the masterminds behind cyberattacks. Therefore, exchanging threat intelligence is essential to bolstering both national and international security. In order to facilitate the sharing of threat intelligence across national boundaries and industry sectors, governments and international organizations frequently play a key role. By taking part in these initiatives, organizations can help promote coordinated responses to cyber threats and advance a better understanding of the threat landscape. In order to effectively mitigate the complex and multifaceted nature of cyber threats, which frequently call for coordinated efforts, global collaboration is imperative.

7.2.6. Encouraging Innovation and Resilience

Innovation in cybersecurity techniques and technologies can also be fostered by the process of exchanging threat intelligence. Organizations build up a knowledge base that other organizations can use to strengthen their own defenses by exchanging information about the threats they face and the solutions they have developed. The creation of fresh instruments, methods, and approaches to counter cyberattacks may result from this intellectual interchange. Additionally, organizations can foresee future threats and create more resilient systems by understanding the strategies employed by attackers. The ongoing development of threat intelligence sharing procedures guarantees that organizations maintain their flexibility and ability to adjust to the constantly shifting terrain of cyber threats.

7.2.7. Overcoming Challenges and Barriers to Sharing

Organizations face numerous obstacles and hurdles in their efforts to effectively share threat intelligence, despite the obvious advantages. The lack of trust amongst organizations is one of the main challenges, which can be made worse by worries about data privacy, legal liability, and possible misuse of shared information. To solve these problems, it is critical to create explicit policies and procedures for sharing threat intelligence that safeguard private data and guarantee its appropriate use. This could involve the use of contracts, safe data sharing platforms, and anonymization strategies.

The technical intricacy of exchanging threat intelligence presents an additional obstacle. To efficiently gather, examine, and disseminate threat data, organizations need to be equipped with the right tools and knowledge. Smaller businesses with fewer resources may find this especially challenging. Bigger businesses, governmental organizations, and trade associations can help break down this barrier by offering assistance, instruction, and resources to promote the sharing of threat intelligence. Standards and collaborative platforms like TAXII (Trusted Automated Exchange of Indicator Information) and STIX (Structured Threat Information Expression) protocols can also aid in standardizing and improving the accessibility of threat intelligence exchange.

7.2.8. The Role of Government and Policy

Promoting the sharing of threat intelligence amongst organizations and sectors is a crucial role for governments. Information sharing can be encouraged or required by law, especially in fields like energy, finance, and healthcare that are crucial to national security. By offering venues and platforms where groups can exchange information in a safe and regulated setting, governments can also help organizations share threat intelligence. Additionally, government agencies frequently possess unique threat intelligence that can be extremely helpful to private sector companies, especially when it comes to state-sponsored cyber threats.

Governments can assist in mitigating the legal and regulatory obstacles linked to the sharing of threat intelligence, in addition to promoting information exchange. They can offer advice, for instance, on how businesses can exchange threat intelligence while abiding by data protection regulations and averting antitrust issues. In order to combat international cyberthreats, governments should collaborate with foreign partners to encourage the cross-border exchange of threat intelligence.

7.3. PRIMARY THREAT INTELLIGENCE SHARING

Primary Threat Intelligence Sharing, a crucial cybersecurity practice, entails sharing information amongst different organizations, stakeholders, or sectors about potential or current threats. Enhancing collective security through early warning systems, threat detection, and proactive measures is the primary goal. This procedure is crucial in an environment where cyberthreats are becoming more complex, well-organized, and widespread.

7.3.1. Unidirectional Threat Intelligence Sharing

The process of sending threat intelligence in a one-way flow from one entity to another is referred to as unidirectional threat intelligence sharing. By using this technique, it is made impossible for the recipient to return information to the source and yet be able to receive and act upon the shared intelligence. This approach's main objective is to improve the recipient's security posture while preserving the integrity and confidentiality of the data from the source.

7.3.1.1. Mechanisms of Unidirectional Sharing

Unidirectional sharing can be achieved through various mechanisms, including:

- **Data Diodes:** A data diode is a hardware device that enforces a one-way data flow between two networks. It allows information to pass from the source network to the recipient network while preventing any data from flowing back in the opposite direction. Data diodes are commonly used in environments where high-security levels are required, such as military or critical infrastructure networks.
- **One-Way APIs:** Application Programming Interfaces (APIs) can be designed to allow data to be pulled from a source without enabling any data to be sent back. These APIs provide a secure method for organizations to access threat intelligence feeds without risking the exposure of their own systems.
- **Physical Media Transfer:** In some cases, threat intelligence may be shared via physical media, such as USB drives or hard disks. The media is delivered to the recipient, who can then use the information without establishing any direct connection with the source.

7.3.1.2. Benefits of Unidirectional Sharing

The primary benefits of unidirectional threat intelligence sharing include:

- **Enhanced Security:** By ensuring that data only flows in one direction, organizations can mitigate the risk of exposing their networks to potential threats. This is particularly important in scenarios where the recipient may be less secure than the source.
- **Regulatory Compliance:** Many industries are subject to strict data protection regulations. Unidirectional sharing can help organizations

comply with these regulations by minimizing the risk of unauthorized data exposure.

- **Reduced Complexity:** Unidirectional sharing simplifies the sharing process by eliminating the need for complex bidirectional communication protocols. This can reduce the time and resources required to implement threat intelligence sharing.

7.3.1.3. Use Cases and Applications

Unidirectional threat intelligence sharing is particularly valuable in scenarios where there is a significant disparity in the security levels of the participating organizations. Some common use cases include:

7.3.1.3.1. Critical Infrastructure Protection

The energy, water, and transportation sectors are among the most vulnerable to cyberattacks because of their vital role in maintaining national security. Without exposing their own networks, unidirectional sharing enables these sectors to obtain threat intelligence from governmental organizations or other reliable sources. Maintaining the security and uninterrupted provision of vital services requires this.

7.3.1.3.2. Supply Chain Security

Cybercriminals are increasingly focusing on supply chains as a means of breaking into larger organizations by taking advantage of weaknesses in smaller suppliers. Large organizations can share pertinent threat intelligence with their suppliers to strengthen their defenses without putting their own systems at risk by implementing unidirectional threat intelligence sharing.

7.3.1.3.4. Government and Military Networks

Government and military networks are prime targets for state-sponsored cyberattacks because they frequently handle extremely sensitive data. These organizations can obtain threat intelligence from outside sources, like for-profit cybersecurity companies, thanks to unidirectional sharing, which also protects the security of their own data.

7.3.1.4. Challenges and Limitations

Despite its benefits, unidirectional threat intelligence sharing is not without challenges and limitations. Some of the key issues include:

7.3.1.4.1. Limited Feedback

The absence of feedback is one of unidirectional sharing's main drawbacks. A bidirectional sharing arrangement allows the recipient to comment on how accurate or useful the shared intelligence was, which can enhance the quality of intelligence that is shared in the future. This feedback loop is missing in a unidirectional setup, which could eventually cause the shared intelligence's relevance and accuracy to decrease.

7.3.1.4.2. Potential for Misuse

There is a chance that the recipient will abuse the shared intelligence, even in a unidirectional sharing arrangement. An organization might, for instance, employ threat intelligence more for offensive than defensive purposes, which could escalate online conflicts. Organizations must carefully screen recipients and set precise policies for the use of shared intelligence in order to reduce this risk.

7.3.1.4.3. Technical Implementation Challenges

Unidirectional sharing mechanisms, like data diodes, can be expensive and technically difficult to implement. To avoid any unintentional data leakage, organizations must make sure that these mechanisms are set up and maintained correctly. Furthermore, considerable customization might be needed for the integration of unidirectional sharing with the current threat intelligence platforms.

7.3.1.5. Best Practices for Unidirectional Threat Intelligence Sharing

To maximize the effectiveness of unidirectional threat intelligence sharing, organizations should consider the following best practices:

7.3.1.5.1. Establish Clear Objectives

Establishing clear goals is a prerequisite for organizations to participate in unidirectional sharing. This entails specifying the categories of threat intelligence to be disseminated, the people to whom it is intended, and the results that are anticipated. The sharing process will be guided by clear objectives, which will also guarantee that it is in line with the organization's overall cybersecurity strategy.

7.3.1.5.2. Vet Recipients

Potential recipients of threat intelligence should be thoroughly screened by organizations to make sure they have the skills and intentions to use the information responsibly. This entails evaluating the recipient's regulatory compliance, industry reputation, and security posture.

7.3.1.5.3. Implement Robust Security Controls

Strong security measures, like encryption and access controls, should be put in place by organizations to safeguard the integrity of the sharing process. By implementing these controls, it will be possible to avert unwanted access to the shared intelligence and guarantee that it is only utilized for the intended reason.

7.3.1.5.4. Monitor and Evaluate

Organizations should keep an eye on the use of shared intelligence and assess its efficacy even in a one-way sharing arrangement. This may entail performing routine audits of the sharing procedure and getting recipient input through oblique methods like surveys or evaluations by outside parties.

7.3.1.5.5. Collaborate with Industry Partners

Unidirectional sharing ought to be regarded as a component of a more comprehensive plan for cybersecurity cooperation. Companies should collaborate closely with other stakeholders, government organizations, and partners in the industry to make sure they are getting the most recent and pertinent threat intelligence. In addition to fostering a culture of shared cybersecurity responsibility, collaboration can help build trust.

7.3.1.6. Future Trends in Unidirectional Threat Intelligence Sharing

As the cybersecurity landscape continues to evolve, unidirectional threat intelligence sharing is likely to become more sophisticated and widespread. Some future trends to watch for include:

7.3.1.6.1. Automation and AI Integration

The integration of automation and artificial intelligence (AI) into unidirectional sharing processes will likely enhance the speed and accuracy of threat intelligence dissemination. AI-driven analytics can help organizations identify and prioritize the most relevant threats, while automation can streamline the sharing process.

7.3.1.6.2. Expansion of Sharing Networks

As more organizations recognize the benefits of unidirectional sharing, we can expect to see the expansion of sharing networks. These networks may include a wider range of participants, from small businesses to large multinational corporations, all working together to combat cyber threats.

7.3.1.6.3. Enhanced Regulatory Frameworks

Regulators may introduce new frameworks or guidelines to govern unidirectional threat intelligence sharing. These frameworks could address issues such as data privacy, cross-border sharing, and the ethical use of shared intelligence. Compliance with these frameworks will be critical for organizations seeking to engage in unidirectional sharing.

7.3.2. Bidirectional Threat Intelligence Sharing

Bidirectional threat intelligence sharing involves the mutual exchange of threat data, including information about indicators of compromise (IoCs), attack vectors, threat actors, and vulnerability reports. The goal is to provide both parties with actionable intelligence that can be used to preemptively defend against attacks or respond more effectively when an incident occurs.

7.3.2.1. Mechanisms of Bidirectional Sharing

Bidirectional sharing can be facilitated through several mechanisms, each with its own advantages and considerations:

- **Automated Threat Intelligence Platforms:** These platforms, such as Threat Intelligence Platforms (TIPs) or Security Information and Event Management (SIEM) systems, enable organizations to share threat data in real-time. These systems often include APIs that allow for the seamless integration of threat feeds from multiple sources, enabling automated analysis and response.
- **Cyber Threat Intelligence (CTI) Sharing Communities:** Organizations often participate in formal or informal threat intelligence sharing communities, such as Information Sharing and Analysis Centers (ISACs) or industry-specific consortia. These communities facilitate the exchange of threat data, best practices, and response strategies among members, often through secure communication channels.
- **Direct Peer-to-Peer Sharing:** In some cases, organizations may establish direct relationships with peers or trusted partners for

the exchange of threat intelligence. This could involve secure communication channels, such as encrypted emails or dedicated VPNs, where threat data is shared and discussed.

7.3.2.2. Benefits of Bidirectional Sharing

Bidirectional threat intelligence sharing offers several key benefits:

- **Enhanced Situational Awareness:** By exchanging threat data with peers or partners, organizations can gain a broader perspective on the threat landscape. This enhanced situational awareness enables them to identify emerging threats, trends, and patterns that may not be apparent from their own data alone.
- **Improved Incident Response:** The continuous exchange of threat intelligence allows organizations to respond more effectively to incidents. For example, if one organization detects a new type of malware, sharing this information with partners can help them update their defenses before they are targeted.
- **Collaborative Defense:** Bidirectional sharing fosters a sense of community and collaboration among organizations. By working together, they can collectively improve their defenses and reduce the overall risk of cyberattacks.
- **Feedback Loops:** Unlike unidirectional sharing, bidirectional sharing allows for feedback loops where recipients can provide insights or additional context to the shared intelligence. This can lead to more accurate and actionable threat data over time.

7.3.2.3. Use Cases and Applications

Bidirectional threat intelligence sharing is particularly valuable in environments where timely and accurate information is critical to maintaining security. Some common use cases include:

7.3.2.3.1. Financial Services

The financial services industry is a prime target for cybercriminals due to the high value of the data and assets involved. Bidirectional sharing within financial ISACs allows institutions to quickly share information about fraud attempts, phishing campaigns, or malware targeting financial systems. This collaborative approach helps institutions stay ahead of threats and protect customer data.

7.3.2.3.2. Healthcare Sector

The healthcare sector faces unique challenges, including the need to protect sensitive patient data and maintain the availability of critical medical services. Bidirectional sharing among healthcare providers, insurers, and government agencies enables the rapid exchange of intelligence on ransomware attacks, data breaches, and vulnerabilities in medical devices, enhancing the sector's overall security posture.

7.3.2.3.3. National Security and Defense

Government and defense organizations often engage in bidirectional sharing with both domestic and international partners to protect national security interests. This includes the sharing of intelligence on state-sponsored cyberattacks, espionage activities, and critical infrastructure threats. The ability to rapidly exchange and act on this intelligence is vital to national defense.

7.3.2.4. Challenges and Limitations

Despite its benefits, bidirectional threat intelligence sharing presents several challenges and limitations that organizations must address to be effective:

7.3.2.4.1. Trust and Data Sensitivity

One of the primary challenges in bidirectional sharing is establishing trust between participating organizations. There is often a concern that shared data could be mishandled, leaked, or used for competitive advantage. Additionally, organizations must be cautious about sharing sensitive or proprietary information that could expose them to additional risks if compromised.

7.3.2.4.2. Data Standardization and Quality

For threat intelligence to be useful, it must be accurate, timely, and presented in a standardized format that can be easily interpreted by the recipient. Inconsistent data formats, varying levels of detail, and differing definitions of threats can complicate the sharing process and reduce the effectiveness of the shared intelligence.

7.3.2.4.3. Legal and Regulatory Compliance

Organizations must navigate a complex landscape of legal and regulatory requirements when sharing threat intelligence. This includes ensuring compliance with data protection laws, such as the General Data Protection Regulation (GDPR) in the European Union, which imposes strict rules on the sharing of personal data. Failure to comply with these regulations can result in significant penalties.

7.3.2.4.4. Resource Constraints

Sharing threat intelligence effectively requires dedicated resources, including personnel, technology, and infrastructure. Smaller organizations may struggle to allocate the necessary resources to participate fully in bidirectional sharing initiatives, limiting their ability to benefit from the shared intelligence.

7.3.2.5. Best Practices for Bidirectional Threat Intelligence Sharing

To maximize the effectiveness of bidirectional threat intelligence sharing, organizations should consider the following best practices:

7.3.2.5.1. Establish Trust and Legal Agreements

Before engaging in bidirectional sharing, organizations should establish formal agreements that outline the terms of the sharing relationship. This includes defining the types of data that will be shared, the frequency of sharing, and the security measures that will be implemented to protect the shared data. Legal agreements, such as non-disclosure agreements (NDAs), can help build trust and protect sensitive information.

7.3.2.5.2. Standardize Data Formats

To facilitate effective sharing, organizations should adopt standardized formats for threat intelligence data. Frameworks such as Structured Threat Information eXpression (STIX) and Trusted Automated eXchange of Indicator Information (TAXII) are widely used for this purpose. Standardization ensures that shared data is easily interpretable and actionable by all participants.

7.3.2.5.3. Implement Robust Security Controls

Security is paramount when sharing threat intelligence. Organizations should implement robust security controls, including encryption, access controls, and secure communication channels, to protect the integrity and confidentiality of the shared data. Additionally, regular audits should be conducted to ensure compliance with security policies.

7.3.2.5.4. Prioritize Data Quality

The quality of shared threat intelligence is critical to its effectiveness.

Organizations should prioritize the accuracy, relevance, and timeliness of the data they share. This includes validating the sources of intelligence, ensuring that the data is up-to-date, and providing sufficient context for recipients to understand and act on the information.

7.3.2.5.5. Foster a Collaborative Culture

Bidirectional sharing is most effective when organizations embrace a collaborative culture. This involves not only sharing data but also actively participating in discussions, providing feedback, and offering assistance to partners. By fostering a spirit of collaboration, organizations can build stronger relationships and enhance the overall security of the community.

7.4. THREAT INTELLIGENCE AND SHARING FOR COLLABORATIVE DEFENSE

Because new threats are constantly emerging and getting more sophisticated, cybersecurity is a moving target. Because of this, cybersecurity's goal is ever-changing. Businesses are searching for new ways to fortify their defenses and improve the security of their systems, data, and users due to the constantly changing nature of the threats that they must contend with. This is due to the constantly changing nature of the threats themselves. Spreading information about potential network threats and defensive tactics is the most efficient way to improve network security. To address potential threats more successfully than taking individual combat, several organizations pool their people, resources, and expertise into a cooperative defense strategy. A single company cannot defend itself against every possible cyberthreat; however, by banding together, several companies may be able to strengthen their defenses and lessen their vulnerability to attacks. This is the way of thinking that guides this tactic. The term "threat intelligence" describes the information-gathering, information-analysis, and information-sharing process that goes into identifying potential threats or attacks. Two examples of the data types included in this category are indicators of compromise (IOCs) and knowledge of the tactics, techniques, and procedures (TTPs) used by threat actors. "Threat actor data" refers to both of these categories of information. ". Threat information greatly facilitates the process of identifying and prioritizing hazards and developing workable solutions.

The fundamental block diagram of threat intelligence is shown in Figure 7.1, and sharing threat intelligence is the process by which companies talk to each other and exchange information about possible threats. Either a formal setting with predetermined standards and protocols, or an informal one with a trusted group of peers, can be used for this. By increasing the awareness of and capacity to counter threats, the sharing of threat intelligence aims to strengthen the security posture of all parties involved. It is possible to carry out this action regardless of the manner in which threat intelligence is disseminated. Over the past several years, the threat landscape has progressively grown more sophisticated and complex, necessitating increased defense cooperation and threat intelligence sharing. The threat environment's degree of sophistication and complexity has gradually increased in recent years. Businesses that are a part of larger ecosystems—like those in the same sector or area, for example—are starting to realize how important it is to share threat intelligence and engage in collaborative defense. This is as a result of these organizations' integration into bigger ecosystems.

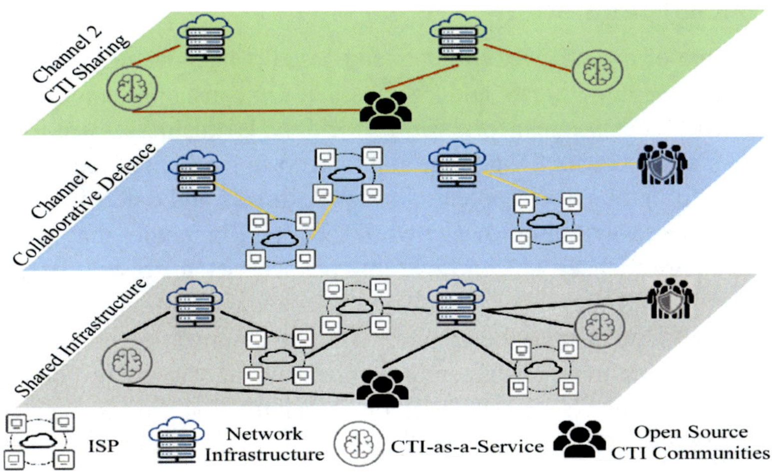

Figure 7.1. *Basic block diagram of threat intelligence and sharing for collaborative defense.*

Source: https://encrypted-tbn0.gstatic.com/images?q=tbn:ANd9GcTok6q45aBXC Ptp5QcEPXB1H6XSfmu7_aswbw&s.

By sharing threat intelligence and coordinating their defenses, the organizations that are a part of these ecosystems are able to better defend themselves against potential attacks and lessen the harm that would be caused by attacks that are successful. While there are many advantages to exchanging threat intelligence and coordinating defenses, there are drawbacks as well. For starters, companies may be hesitant to divulge private information to rivals for a number of reasons, such as concerns about confidentiality and trust. This is a result of the perception that rival companies pose a risk to their company.

When trying to distribute threat intelligence, a variety of logistical and technical problems could arise. Among these difficulties are differences in the standards or data formats that are used. Despite these challenges, it is anticipated that sharing threat intelligence and cooperating on defense will become more and more important in the future years as the threat landscape continues to change. Businesses that prioritize collaboration and information sharing are more likely to succeed when it comes to safeguarding their users, data, and systems from unforeseen and novel threats. The characteristics necessary for threat intelligence sharing and collaborative defense are examined in the following, along with some of the opportunities and difficulties associated with putting such strategies into practice.

7.4.1. Background Study

The landscape of cybersecurity threats and assaults is constantly changing to accommodate the new threats and assaults that are constantly emerging. As a result, in order to stay one step ahead of their rivals, businesses are forced to maintain a state of constant vigilance and to keep strengthening their defenses. Spreading information about potential network threats and defensive tactics is the most efficient way to improve network security. Companies may be able to strengthen their defenses and improve internet security for people of all ages and backgrounds if they band together. The theory underlying collaborative defense is that while it is challenging for a single organization to defend itself against every cyberthreat, businesses can enhance their security by cooperating to counter these attacks. By exchanging threat intelligence, businesses can better prepare for potential attacks and gain a deeper understanding of the threat landscape. Because it helps these organizations to better prepare, it is therefore an essential part of joint defense. Although sharing threat intelligence is not a new practice, in recent years it has become increasingly important due to the complexity and level of sophistication of contemporary threats. For companies that are a part of larger ecosystems, like those that operate in the same market or region, exchanging threat intelligence has become an increasingly important practice. By exchanging threat intelligence and coordinating their defenses, the organizations that are a part of these ecosystems can better defend themselves against potential attacks and lessen the harm that would be caused by attacks that are successful. While some options call for more formal arrangements with mutually agreed-upon standards and procedures, others entail informal information sharing among a group of trustworthy peers. By increasing the awareness of and capacity to counter threats, the sharing of threat intelligence aims to strengthen the security posture of all parties involved. It is possible to carry out this action regardless of the manner in which threat intelligence is disseminated. While there are many advantages to exchanging threat intelligence and coordinating defenses, there are drawbacks as well. For starters, companies may be hesitant to divulge sensitive information to rivals for a number of reasons, such as privacy and trust issues. This is a result of the perception that rival companies pose a risk to their company. When trying to distribute threat intelligence, a variety of logistical and technical problems could arise. Discrepancies in the data form are two instances of these difficulties.

7.4.2. Existing Methodology

Organizations can work together on defense and share threat intelligence with the help of a variety of strategies and tools. For example:

- ISACs are dependable channels via which companies can coordinate their security measures and share threat intelligence. Companies are frequently invited to join one of the several ISACs that cater to particular industries and regions if they fulfill certain requirements for cybersecurity maturity and information sharing.
- Threat Intelligence Platforms (TIPs) are platforms that gather, store, and analyze threat intelligence. Utilizing the visualization tools and additional features found in TIPs, organizations can gain a deeper understanding of the threat intelligence gathered from various sources.
- Open-Source Intelligence, or OSINT, is the term for information gathered from publicly available sources and used to identify possible attackers or threats. Open-source intelligence (OSINT) can paint a more comprehensive picture of a possible threat when used in conjunction with more conventional techniques of intelligence collection.
- One widely recognized way for businesses to exchange indicators of compromise (IOCs) is through Automated Indicator Sharing (AIS). By automating the process of exchanging IOCs, AIS aims to reduce the amount of time required to identify and address possible threats.
- The activity of actively searching within an organization's computer systems and networks for vulnerabilities and other indications of compromise is known as "threat hunting," or "hunting for security risks.". To look for indications of malicious activity, this may entail examining log files, network traffic, and other data sources.
- Red teaming is the act of feigning an attack on a company to identify its vulnerabilities and security gaps. Red teaming is advantageous to organizations because it helps identify potential risks and develop effective countermeasures.

Table 7.1. *Comparative Study of Various Existing Techniques*

Methodology	Description	Benefits
Information Sharing and Analysis Centers (ISACs)	ISACs are trusted forums for organizations to share threat intelligence and coordinate their defenses.	- Provides a trusted forum for organizations to share threat intelligence - Enables organizations to coordinate their defenses and collaborate on incident response - Can help organizations to better understand the threat landscape
Threat Intelligence Platforms (TIPs)	TIPs are software tools that enable organizations to collect, store, and analyze threat intelligence.	- Can automate the process of collecting and analyzing threat intelligence - Provides visualization tools and other features to help organizations make sense of the data - Enables organizations to more effectively defend against potential threats
Automated Indicator Sharing (AIS)	AIS is a standardized protocol for sharing IOCs between organizations.	- Can reduce the time it takes to detect and respond to potential threats - Can enable organizations to more effectively defend against emerging threats - Supports the automation of threat detection and response
Red Teaming	Red teaming involves simulating a real-world attack against an organization to identify vulnerabilities and weaknesses in the organization's defenses.	- Can help organizations to identify potential threats and to develop effective countermeasures - Provides a realistic view of an organization's security posture - Enables organizations to improve their defenses and better protect against potential attacks

Source: https://www.kalaharijournals.com/resources/MAY_200.pdf.

Cyber Threat Intelligence (CTI) feeds are real-time, or nearly real-time, feeds of threat intelligence data that can be incorporated into an organization's security architecture. IOCs, TTPs, and other types of threat intelligence data may be found in CTI feeds, which can be used to automate threat detection and response (Table 7.1).

Companies can choose from a range of resources and strategies designed to promote coordinated defense and the sharing of threat intelligence, as shown in the above table. Organizations must assess their unique needs and top priorities in order to decide which tactics and resources will work best.

7.5. COLLABORATIVE THREAT INTELLIGENCE FRAMEWORK FOR IOT SECURITY

In this section, we present a comprehensive architecture aimed at enhancing the security of Internet of Things (IoT) ecosystems. Our approach leverages a synergistic combination of blockchain, ML, and an iOS control center, with the crucial role of human expertise. Real-time threat detection and response are made possible by the framework's ability to learn and adapt continuously to address new safety concerns. Important CTIF-IoT components are displayed in Figure 7.2. The deployment of IoT devices, which create the network of interconnected devices across multiple domains, is the first step in the framework. Because these devices are networked, they produce data and may be subject to security risks. The ML models are the first essential part of the framework. These models are trained in real-time to recognize patterns, recognize threats, and categorize security incidents using pertinent datasets, like the IoT23 dataset.

The iOS application serving as a control center is the second part. The program offers an easy-to-use interface for interacting with the ML models and reporting threats. Users can report threats they detect by providing crucial details like the threat type, source, and timestamp. To guarantee prompt threat detection and response, the application also makes use of features like secure communication channels and push notifications. The use of blockchain technology is the third essential element. Information is exchanged between the ML models and the iOS application upon threat detection and classification by the ML models. In the event that the ML models identify a threat, smart contracts are used to securely transfer the threat data and device information to the blockchain network. The blockchain network serves as an immutable, decentralized repository for threat data, guaranteeing its integrity and promoting cooperation amongst various stakeholders.

The collaborative nature of threat intelligence is emphasized by the CTIF-IoT. The collective repository created by the shared threat data kept on the blockchain network helps to continuously improve the efficacy and accuracy of the ML models. By using the shared intelligence, the ML models can learn from a larger variety of threat scenarios, adjust to new threats, and deal with false negatives. The shared threat data from the blockchain network is used by the CTIF-IoT iterative process to update and retrain the machine learning models on a regular basis. This enables the models to continuously enhance their detection abilities and stay current with changing threat landscapes. In order to improve IoT security, the CTIF-IoT creates a cooperative ecosystem that combines blockchain technology, ML models, IoT devices, and the iOS application. In the end, it contributes to the overall security of IoT systems by enabling secure data transmission, effective threat reporting, real-time threat detection, and ongoing model improvement.

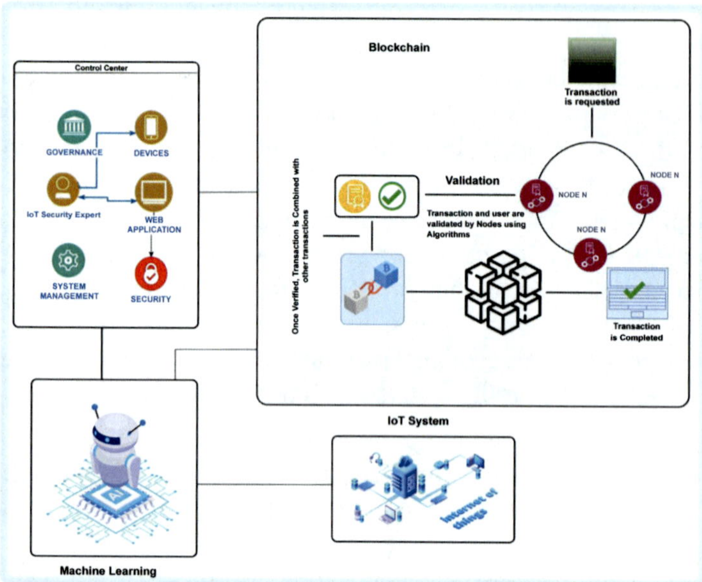

Figure 7.2. *Conceptual framework of proposed framework.*

Source: https://www.sciencedirect.com/science/article/pii/S1319157824000284#:~:text=This%20collaborative%20threat%20intelligence%20framework,adapt%20to%20emerging%20threats%20effectively.

7.5.1. Main Components of Framework

7.5.1.1. IoT Security Ecosystem

Our framework is based on the IoT Security Ecosystem, which stands for the wide range of networked devices and systems that make up the Internet of

Things. This covers everything from industrial machinery and driverless cars to smart home appliances and sensors. Assuring the security and integrity of data and operations is the main concern within this intricate network. A strong security framework must be in place since threats can range greatly, from data breaches to unauthorized access.

We explore the many tiers of the IoT security ecosystem in our study, which is fully depicted in Figure 7.3. The User Layer, which consists of end users, devices, and their digital environments, initially appears as the main interface. In order to strengthen the authentication and authorization procedures against potential vulnerabilities like unauthorized device interactions or unintentional misconfigurations, our novel approach introduces Blockchain for its inherent transparency and indelibility. In addition, machine learning provides a perceptive understanding of user behavior by instantly identifying and reacting to deviations.

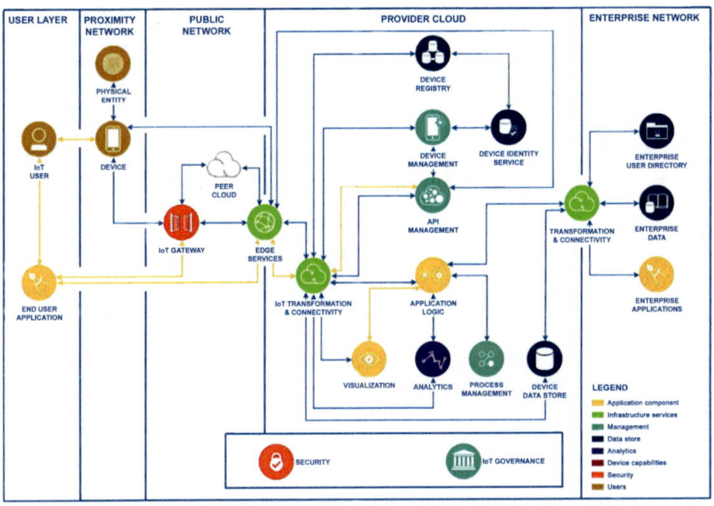

Figure 7.3. *IoT ecosystem.*

Source: https://www.sciencedirect.com/science/article/pii/S1319157824000284#:~:text=This%20collaborative%20threat%20intelligence%20framework,adapt%20to%20emerging%20threats%20effectively.

The Proximity Network facilitates short-range connections such as Bluetooth and Wi-Fi by acting as a hub between user devices and large networks. Under the auspices of our research, this bridge uses Blockchain to carefully verify and authenticate information exchanges. ML enhances this by identifying trends and averting possible security breaches. Similar to a huge global web, the Public Network requires reliable communication channels and strict encryption, both of which Blockchain enables. Strict security protocols are required for the Provider Cloud, which serves as central repositories for IoT data. Here, Blockchain guarantees data integrity and transparency while ML continuously monitors access patterns and flags any anomalies. While ML continuously learns from and corrects any network inconsistencies to ensure system integrity, blockchain guarantees the legitimacy of the device.

7.5.1.2. Machine Learning Layer

The ML Layer, which is central to CTIF-IoT, is in charge of continuously observing the data flow within the ecosystem for IoT security. This layer analyses trends and abnormalities in real-time using a wide range of machine learning algorithms. Its job is to spot possible security risks by looking for variations from known data patterns. When it comes to threat detection, ML is the first line of defense.

7.5.1.3. iOS Control Center

Acting as the central hub for system communication, the iOS Control Center is a crucial link between the ML Layer and human expertise. The ML Layer promptly sends out an Apple push notification alert in the event that it finds a possible security threat. In order to guarantee that security incidents are quickly brought to the attention of human experts, this notification is sent to the assigned IoT security expert researcher. According to Table 7.2.

Table 7.2. *Role of iOS App in the Framework and Advantages*

Role of iOS App in the Framework	**Advantages of Using the iOS App**
Real-Time Notification Receiver	Real-Time Response
Receives Apple push notifications	Immediate response to threats.
Alerts IoT security expert researcher	Reduced response times.
Provides access to alarm information	Simplified validation process.

7.5.1.4. Blockchain Technology

The framework gains transparency, immutability, and security from the Blockchain Technology component. It functions as a tamper-proof decentralized ledger that logs verified security incidents. This ledger is an indispensable tool for gathering professional opinions and keeping a permanent log of all security incidents in the IoT ecosystem. It guarantees that security incident history is unaltered and impervious to manipulation. Information is enumerated in Table 7.3.

Table 7.3. *Role of Blockchain in IoT Security Framework*

Blockchain Benefits in IoT Security	Description
Data Integrity and Immutability	Blockchain ensures the immutability and integrity of data records, preventing unauthorized alterations and deletions. This feature ensures the trustworthiness of security incident records.
Transparency and Trust	Blockchain's decentralized and transparent ledger fosters trust among IoT stakeholders. All participants can access and verify security incident details, ensuring transparency and accountability.
Security Incident History	Blockchain maintains a comprehensive historical record of security incidents and expert validations. This data is essential for trend analysis and threat detection.
Decentralization and Resilience	Decentralized blockchain networks enhance system resilience by eliminating single points of failure. Even if some nodes are compromised, the blockchain's integrity remains intact.
Smart Contracts for Automation	Blockchain platforms support smart contracts, enabling automated responses to security incidents. This feature enhances response times and system efficiency.

7.5.1.5. Human Expertise

Human Expertise is the framework's representation of the IoT security specialists who are essential in confirming security alerts. These professionals have extensive domain knowledge and are skilled at spotting and mitigating security risks. When the iOS Control Center warns them, they carefully look into the possible threat to ascertain its veracity. Their knowledge is essential for separating real security threats from false positives.

7.5.1.6. Feedback Loop

The Feedback Loop acts as a link between blockchain technology and human expertise. IoT security specialists can use it to log their verified security events on the blockchain. This action is necessary to maintain an exhaustive log of security incidents and professional evaluations. The feedback loop makes sure that human experts' knowledge and insights are incorporated into the system without any problems.

7.5.1.7. Machine Learning Enhancement

The ML Enhancement module makes use of the abundance of feedback that has amassed within the blockchain. To get better and adjust, ML algorithms examine this input in a methodical manner. The algorithms are able to identify real threats with greater accuracy while reducing false alarms thanks to the iterative process. This improvement is essential to improving the performance of the ML Layer.

7.5.2. Information Routing within the Framework

A well-coordinated information flow is essential to the Next-Generation IoT Security Framework because it facilitates smooth communication and cooperation between all of its essential parts. By combining ML, an iOS Control Center, blockchain technology, and human expertise, this framework aims to improve IoT security. Here, we clarify the complex information flow that exists within this ever-changing ecosystem.

Large volumes of data and network traffic are produced by a variety of devices within the IoT Security Ecosystem, which is where the data flow starts. The foundation of the framework is this data stream, which acts as the main source of information about possible dangers. This data is quickly transferred into the ML Layer after being continuously gathered. In this case, a wide range of algorithms take the lead and analyze incoming data instantly. Their two-pronged task involves spotting deviations from established data patterns and potential security threats hidden within the data.

Table 7.4. *Flow of Data Within the IoT Security Framework*

Source	Destination
IoT Security Ecosystem (Data and Network Traffic)	Machine Learning Layer
Machine Learning Layer (Alert)	iOS Control Center

iOS Control Center (Push Notification)	IoT Security Expert Researcher
IoT Security Expert Researcher (Validation)	Feedback Loop (Blockchain)
Feedback Loop (Blockchain)	Machine Learning Layer
Machine Learning Layer (Model Improvement)	Machine Learning Layer

The ML Layer initiates a cooperative chain reaction by sounding an alert as soon as it detects a potential threat. This notification quickly reaches the iOS Control Center, which functions as the framework's central communication point. In this instance, the iOS Control Center wears many hats and serves as a liaison between the virtual and physical worlds. It quickly creates an Apple push notification and fills it with pertinent details about the possible threat, like its nature and origin. With this notification, the designated IoT security expert researcher takes over as the new leader. Figure 7.5 depicts the data flow process in detail whereas Figure 7.4 illustrates the characteristics of the IoT Security Framework.

Algorithm 1 Flow of Data Handling Algorithm

```
procedure HandleDataFlow
    Receive data from IoT Security Ecosystem
    Analyze data in Machine Learning Layer
    if Potential threat detected then
        Trigger alert
        Formulate push notification in iOS Control Center
        Send push notification to IoT security expert researcher
        IoT security expert researcher validates threat
        Record findings in Feedback Loop (Blockchain)
        Improve machine learning models
    end if
end procedure
```

The IoT security expert researcher sets out on an investigation after receiving the push notification. The iOS Control Center is crucial because it gives users access to pertinent information and background on the possible threat. Using their domain knowledge and experience, the human element determines whether the security alarm is legitimate. This crucial step ascertains whether the threat is real or a false positive, guaranteeing a prompt and precise response.

After validation, the researcher with expertise in IoT security logs their results into the system, indicating a crucial step towards the Feedback Loop. By acting as a conduit, this loop directs human knowledge and understanding toward blockchain technology. It ensures that verified security incidents are safely recorded on the blockchain by acting as their guardian. In turn, the blockchain is essential because it acts as a permanent record of security events, improving accountability and transparency.

The verified security incident and expert assessment database stored on the blockchain is more than just an historical record. ML algorithms carefully review this collected input, feeding their development with it. They are always analyzing, evolving, and adapting to enhance their threat detection skills. By using an iterative learning process, ML models are guaranteed to improve their ability to distinguish between genuine threats and false alarms.

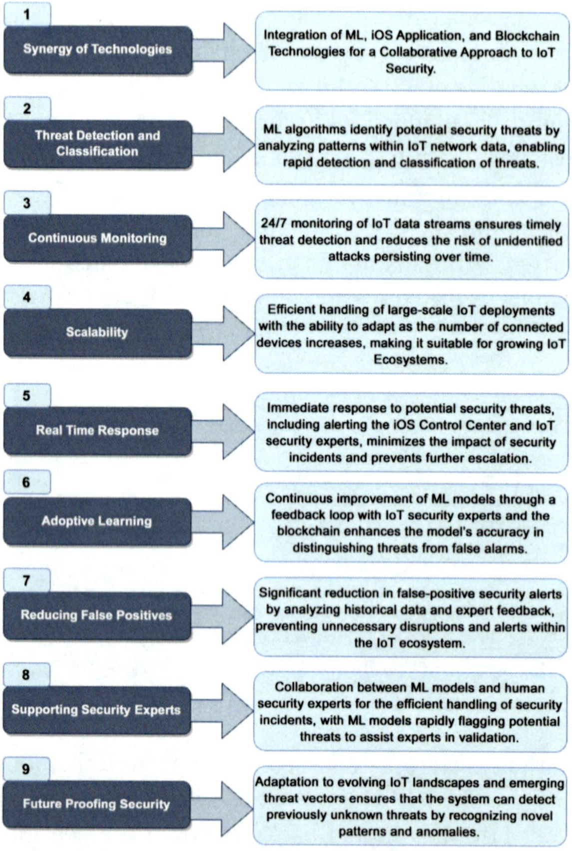

Figure 7.4. *Features of proposed framework.*

Source: https://www.sciencedirect.com/science/article/pii/S1319157824000284#:~:text=This%20collaborative%20threat%20intelligence%20framework,adapt%20to%20emerging%20threats%20effectively.

Improvements made to these ML models cascade back to the ML Layer as they are improved and polished via the feedback loop. Here, they are incorporated into the algorithms to improve their precision and hone their ability to identify real threats. The security posture of the framework is strengthened by the proactive threat identification that is made possible by the evolution of ML models.

Essentially, this ongoing information flow and the iterative development of machine learning models support the framework's overall security evolution. As time goes on, the system gets better at bolstering IoT security, and false alarms become less common. The dynamic interplay among machine learning, human judgment, blockchain technology, and an iOS control center serves as an example of how the framework can be used to safeguard the rapidly growing IoT Security Ecosystem.

Algorithm 2 Advanced IoT Security Enhancement Framework

```
Input: Anomaly scores S from machine learning classifiers, IoT security expert E, blockchain technology B, iOS control center C.
Output: Enhanced IoT security, refined machine learning models M.
procedure OperateFramework
    while System operates in real-time do
        Calculate anomaly score s_i for incoming data stream D_i.
        if s_i exceeds threshold T then
            A = AnomalyDetection(D_i)
            if A is True then
                DispatchAlert(C)
                E investigates the alarm and retrieves data context DC from D_i.
                Compute severity score SS based on s_i and DC.
                if SS exceeds critical threshold CT then
                    Expert E logs insights onto the blockchain B.
                    B becomes a transparent, immutable record of security incidents.
                else
                    Feedback is recorded for model refinement.
                end if
            end if
        end if
        Gather all feedback F from blockchain B.
        UpdateModel(M, F)
        Recompute threshold T based on new model M.
    end while
    Blockchain system B integrates expert feedback into ongoing learning processes.
    Machine learning models M adapt using both historical and real-time data.
    Framework optimizes T and minimizes false alarms, enhancing IoT security.
end procedure
function AnomalyDetection(D_i)
    Compute features f from D_i.
    Return True if s_i(f) > T, else return False.
end function
function DispatchAlert(C)
    Use push notification system of C to alert E.
end function
function UpdateModel(M, F)
    Incorporate F to retrain M.
end function
```

Algorithm 2 presents a systematic approach to improve security in Internet of Things networks. It is real-time and utilizes multiple basic inputs, such as an iOS control center, blockchain technology, input from an IoT security specialist, and ML classifiers for anomaly detection. Whenever they detect an anomaly, the ML classifiers promptly notify the iOS control center. After that, the alarm is investigated by the IoT security expert. If it is determined that the anomaly poses a genuine security risk, the expert's observations are appended to the blockchain ledger, offering a transparent and unchangeable record of the security incident. Over time, the blockchain system takes this feedback into account to improve continuous learning.

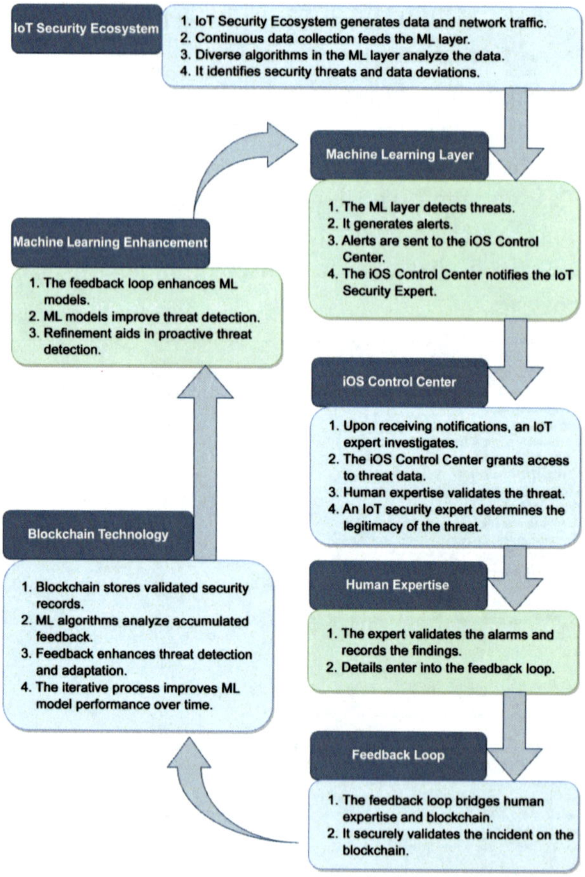

Figure 7.5. *Flow of data within IoT security frame work.*

REFERENCES

1. Ahuja, R., Kumar, A., & Sood, S. K. (2017). Collaborative defense using threat intelligence sharing. *International Journal of Computer Science and Mobile Computing, 6*(2), 76–83.
2. Graf, R., & King, R. (2018). Neural network and blockchain based technique for cyber threat intelligence and situational awareness. In *Proceedings of the 2018 10th International Conference on Cyber Conflict (CyCon)* (pp. 409–426). IEEE.
3. Graves, J. (2019). Reactive vs. proactive cybersecurity: 5 reasons why traditional security no longer works.
4. Kaiafas, G., Varisteas, S., Lagraa, R., State, C. D., Nguyen, T., Ries, M., & Ourdane, M. (2018). Detecting malicious authentication events trustfully. In *2018 IEEE/IFIP Network Operations and Management Symposium, NOMS 2018* (pp. 1–6).
5. Kim, E., Kim, K., Shin, D., Jin, B., & Kim, H. (2018). CyTIME: Cyber threat intelligence management framework for automatically generating security rules. In *Proceedings of the 13th International Conference on Future Internet Technologies, CFI 2018* (pp. 1–5). ACM.
6. Kreutz, D., Ramos, F., et al. (2014). Software-defined networking: A comprehensive survey. *arXiv preprint arXiv:1406.0440.*
7. Kure, H., & Islam, S. (2019). Cyber threat intelligence for improving cybersecurity and risk management in critical infrastructure. *JUCS—Journal of Universal Computer Science, 25*(12), 1478–1502.
8. McMahon, D., Rohozinski, R., & Bell Canada. (2013). The dark space project–Defence research reports.
9. Mohaisen, O. Al-Ibrahim, et al. (2017). Rethinking information sharing for threat intelligence. In *Proceedings of the Fifth ACM/IEEE Workshop on Hot Topics in Web Systems and Technologies* (p. 6). ACM.
10. Mutemwa, M., Mtsweni, J., & Mkhonto, N. (2017). Developing a cyber threat intelligence sharing platform for South African organisations. In *Proceedings of the 2017 Conference on Information Communication Technology and Society (ICTAS)* (pp. 1–6). IEEE.
11. Nazir, A., Wajahat, A., Akhtar, F., Ullah, F., Qureshi, S., Malik, S. A., & Shakeel, A. (2020). Evaluating energy efficiency of buildings using artificial neural networks and K-means clustering techniques. In *2020 3rd International Conference on Computing, Mathematics and Engineering Technologies (ICoMET)* (pp. 1–7).

12. Pourmajidi, W., & Miranskyy, A. (2018). Logchain: Blockchain-assisted log storage. In *2018 IEEE 11th International Conference on Cloud Computing (CLOUD)* (pp. 978–982). IEEE.
13. Sahoo, D., Liu, C., & Hoi, S. C. H. (2017). Malicious URL detection using machine learning: A survey. *CoRR, abs/1701.07179.*
14. Skopik, F., et al. (2016). A problem shared is a problem halved: A survey on the dimensions of collective cyber defense through security information sharing. *Computers & Security.*
15. Takahashi, T., & Miyamoto, D. (2016). Structured cybersecurity information exchange for streamlining incident response operations. In *Proceedings of the NOMS 2016—2016 IEEE/IFIP Network Operations and Management Symposium* (pp. 949–954). IEEE.
16. Tounsi, W., & Rais, H. (2018). A survey on technical threat intelligence in the age of sophisticated cyber attacks. *Computers & Security, 72*, 212–233.
17. Webster, D., Harris, R. L., et al. (2018). Sharing is caring: Collaborative analysis and real-time enquiry for security analytics. In *iThings* (pp. 1402–1409). IEEE.
18. Yang, W., & Lam, K. Y. (2020). Automated cyber threat intelligence reports classification for early warning of cyber attacks in next generation SOC. In *Proceedings of the International Conference on Information and Communications Security (ICICS 2019)* (pp. 145–164). Springer International Publishing.

CHAPTER 8

MACHINE LEARNING AND AI IN THREAT INTELLIGENCE

Contents

INTRODUCTION

Machine learning (ML) and artificial intelligence (AI) are revolutionizing the field of threat intelligence, providing advanced tools and methodologies to enhance the detection, analysis, and mitigation of cyber threats. As cyber threats become more sophisticated and widespread, traditional methods of threat detection and response are often inadequate. ML and AI offer significant advantages by automating the analysis of vast amounts of data, identifying patterns and anomalies that may indicate potential threats, and enabling faster, more accurate responses.

At the core of AI-driven threat intelligence is the ability to process and analyze large datasets in real time. Machine learning algorithms can sift through vast amounts of network traffic, logs, and other data sources to detect unusual activities that may signal a security breach. These systems can learn from past incidents to improve their accuracy over time, adapting to new types of threats as they emerge. This capability is particularly crucial in the current landscape, where zero-day attacks and advanced persistent threats (APTs) are increasingly common.

AI also enhances threat intelligence by enabling predictive analytics. By analyzing historical data, AI systems can forecast potential security incidents, allowing organizations to take proactive measures to protect their assets. This predictive capability extends to identifying vulnerabilities within systems before they can be exploited, significantly reducing the risk of successful attacks.

Furthermore, AI and ML contribute to more effective threat intelligence by automating routine tasks, such as malware classification and threat prioritization, freeing up human analysts to focus on more complex and strategic issues. This not only improves the efficiency of threat intelligence operations but also reduces the likelihood of human error.

Machine learning and AI are transforming threat intelligence by providing powerful tools for detecting, analyzing, and mitigating cyber threats. Their ability to process large datasets, learn from past events, and predict future threats makes them indispensable in the fight against increasingly sophisticated cyber attacks. As these technologies continue to evolve, they will play an even more critical role in safeguarding digital infrastructures.

8.1. THE ROLE OF MACHINE LEARNING IN THREAT INTELLIGENCE

In the domain of threat intelligence and cybersecurity, machine learning has emerged as an indispensable instrument. It is now essential to take a proactive approach to identifying and reducing cyber threats due to their growing intricacy and sophistication. Machine learning algorithms can give organizations a proactive security posture by allowing them to recognize and address threats in real-time. Machine learning can be used to detect and address threats before they have a chance to cause harm. It can assist organizations in recognizing behavioral patterns that may be suggestive of malicious activity.

Here are some ways in which machine learning can be used in threat intelligence:

- **Predictive Analytics:** Machine learning algorithms can enable organizations to predict threats before they occur. By analyzing historical data and identifying patterns, machine learning algorithms can predict the likelihood of future attacks and provide early warnings to *security teams*. For example, some organizations are using machine learning to predict potential phishing attacks by analyzing *email data* and identifying *suspicious patterns*.
- **Anomaly Detection:** *Machine learning* can help to detect anomalies in network traffic or user behavior that could indicate a threat. By analyzing large volumes of data, machine learning algorithms can identify patterns of behavior that are outside of the norm and flag them for further investigation. For example, if a user suddenly starts accessing *sensitive data* outside of their normal working hours, this could be an indication of *a security breach*.
- **Automated Response:** *Machine learning* can enable organizations to automate their response to threats. By using machine learning algorithms to identify threats, organizations can trigger automated responses that can neutralize the threat before it can cause harm. For example, if *a machine learning algorithm* detects a ransomware attack, it could trigger an automated response that isolates *the infected machine* and prevents the spread of the malware.
- **Threat Hunting:** Machine learning can help security teams to hunt for threats that may have gone undetected. By analyzing large volumes of data and identifying patterns of behavior, machine learning algorithms can identify potential threats that may have been missed by other security tools. For example, security teams can use machine learning to analyze network traffic and identify *unknown threats* that may be using *new and novel attack vectors*.

Machine learning has the ability to revolutionize threat intelligence and give businesses a proactive approach to cybersecurity. Organizations can improve their security posture by identifying and mitigating threats in real-time by utilizing machine learning algorithms.

8.2. CYBER THREAT INTELLIGENCE USING AI AND MACHINE LEARNING APPROACHES

Cyber threats present serious risks to people, organizations, and nations across the globe in today's interconnected digital landscape. Due to the ever-changing nature of cyberattacks and the growing sophistication of adversaries, traditional cybersecurity techniques are no longer sufficient to protect against contemporary threats. As a result, creative solutions that can adjust to shifting threat landscapes and enable defenders to keep up with cybercriminals are desperately needed.

This introduction lays the groundwork for discussing how machine learning (ML) and artificial intelligence (AI) are transforming cybersecurity and revolutionizing cyber threat intelligence (CTI). Organizations can improve their defensive capabilities by utilizing AI and ML techniques, which will allow them to identify, evaluate, and respond to cyber threats more quickly, accurately, and effectively.

The increasing frequency and intensity of cyberattacks are highlighted in the introduction, highlighting the vital role that proactive threat intelligence plays in reducing these risks. It highlights how outdated signature-based defenses against cunning and sophisticated threats are becoming less and less effective, calling for a paradigm change in favor of AI-driven solutions.

The introduction then gives a summary of AI and ML technologies, explaining their fundamental ideas and offering examples of how CTI can benefit from their use. AI enables machines to mimic human intelligence, giving them the ability to see, think, and act on their own. Without explicit programming, machines can learn from data, identify patterns, and make predictions thanks to ML algorithms, a subset of artificial intelligence.

CTI is crucial for protecting against new and emerging cyberthreats, as acknowledged by researchers and practitioners in the field of cybersecurity. While some of the traditional approaches to CTI, like rule-based systems and signature-based detection, have proven effective, the fast growth of complex and multifaceted threats is posing a growing threat. The application of ML and AI approaches to improve CTI capabilities has gained traction in response to these difficulties.

The use of AI and ML in CTI has been the subject of numerous studies, which have shown how revolutionary these technologies could be for threat detection, analysis, and response. Supervised learning algorithms, which use labeled data to train models to classify threats based on predefined categories, are a prominent area of research. Support Vector Machines (SVMs) and neural networks, for instance, have proven effective when used for CTI tasks, demonstrating high levels of malware detection and classification accuracy. In CTI, unsupervised learning techniques have also become popular, especially for spotting new and developing threats. By grouping related cyber events or entities, clustering algorithms like k-means and hierarchical clustering make it easier to identify unusual patterns that could be signs of impending threats. Algorithms for anomaly detection, such as Autoencoders and Isolation Forests, improve the capacity to identify departures from typical behavior and identify possible security issues that conventional approaches might miss.

Furthermore, reinforcement learning—which lets security systems pick up on and modify their defensive tactics in response to input from the outside world—has become a viable method for adaptive cyber defense. Reinforcement learning-based systems can effectively mitigate evolving threats and lessen the impact of cyberattacks by continuously improving their threat response mechanisms.

Notwithstanding the potential advantages of AI and ML in CTI, a number of obstacles and restrictions need to be overcome in order to fully realize their potential. Problems with data quality, like unbalanced datasets and noisy inputs, can impair machine learning model performance and result in false positives or negatives. Adversarial attacks are a serious risk to the integrity and dependability of AI-driven CTI systems because they involve adversaries manipulating data in order to trick machine learning algorithms. Furthermore, the uninterpretability of intricate machine learning models could impede comprehension of decision-making procedures, consequently restricting cybersecurity experts' ability to trust and utilize AI-powered solutions.

Researchers support strong data preprocessing methods, feature engineering approaches, and model validation procedures that are adapted to the particular needs of CTI tasks in order to lessen these difficulties. Furthermore, to create comprehensive and successful AI-driven CTI solutions, interdisciplinary cooperation between cybersecurity specialists, data scientists, and AI researchers is crucial.

Numerous real-world case studies and useful applications have shown how AI and ML can be used to improve CTI capabilities in a variety of sectors and industries. AI-driven CTI systems have demonstrated promise in improving cyber resilience and reducing security risks, from threat detection and incident response to threat hunting and vulnerability management.

AI-driven CTI has a bright future ahead of it thanks to continuous developments in data analytics, cybersecurity, and AI algorithms that will strengthen defenses against new online threats. To meet changing challenges and guarantee the efficacy and dependability of AI-driven CTI solutions in a constantly shifting threat landscape, ongoing research, innovation, and cooperation will be necessary.

8.2.1. Theoretical Framework for AI and Machine Learning Approaches to Cyber Threat Intelligence

Several fundamental ideas and concepts from the domains of cybersecurity, artificial intelligence, and machine learning are included in the theoretical framework for AI and machine learning approaches to cyber threat intelligence (CTI). This framework offers a theoretical foundation for comprehending the practical applications of AI and ML techniques to improve CTI capabilities.

8.2.1.1. Cyber Threat Intelligence (CTI)

CTI is the process of gathering, evaluating, and sharing information about cyber threats and vulnerabilities so that organizations can reduce risks and make well-informed decisions. Understanding the cyber threat landscape, including the goals, strategies, and tactics used by threat actors, is essential to understanding the theoretical underpinnings of CTI.

8.2.1.2. Artificial Intelligence (AI)

Artificial Intelligence (AI) is the simulation of human intelligence in machines, allowing them to carry out tasks like learning, reasoning, and problem-solving that normally require human cognition. Theoretical foundations of artificial intelligence (AI) span a number of disciplines, such as computer vision, natural language processing, and machine learning.

8.2.1.3. Machine Learning (ML)

Developing algorithms and models that can learn from data and make predictions or decisions without explicit programming is the focus of machine learning (ML), a subset of artificial intelligence. Deep learning, reinforcement learning, supervised learning, and unsupervised learning are all part of the machine learning theoretical framework.

8.2.1.4. Supervised Learning

ML models are trained on labeled data through supervised learning, wherein input data is matched with corresponding output labels. Algorithms like support vector machines (SVMs), decision trees, and neural networks, which are used for classification and regression tasks in CTI like malware detection and threat categorization, are part of the theoretical framework of supervised learning.

8.2.1.5. Unsupervised Learning

Unsupervised learning is the process of training machine learning models on unlabeled data with the intention of finding hidden structures or patterns in the data. Clustering algorithms like k-means and hierarchical clustering, along with anomaly detection techniques, are part of the theoretical framework of unsupervised learning. These techniques are used in CTI to detect anomalous behavior and identify new threats.

8.2.1.6. Reinforcement Learning

ML models are trained to make sequential decisions through reinforcement learning, whereby they interact with an environment and receive feedback in the form of incentives or penalties. Concepts like Markov decision processes (MDPs) and Q-learning, which are applied in CTI for adaptive defense tactics and dynamic threat response, are part of the theoretical framework of reinforcement learning.

8.2.1.7. Adversarial Machine Learning

The goal of adversarial machine learning is to comprehend and counteract machine learning (ML) attacks, in which malicious parties alter input data to trick ML models. Techniques like adversarial training, robust optimization, and model interpretability are all part of the theoretical framework of adversarial machine learning, and they are crucial factors to take into account in AI-driven CTI in order to guarantee the dependability and security of ML-based defenses.

8.2.2. Recent Methods in AI and Machine Learning for Cyber Threat Intelligence

In order to improve threat detection, analysis, and response capabilities, recent approaches in AI and machine learning for CTI have concentrated on using cutting-edge algorithms, data processing strategies, and model architectures. Here are some recent methods that have gained prominence in the field:

- **Deep Learning Architectures:** Deep learning techniques, particularly convolutional neural networks (CNNs) and recurrent neural networks (RNNs), have shown promise in CTI for their ability to learn complex patterns and representations from raw data. Recent advancements include the development of deep learning architectures tailored to specific CTI tasks, such as malware detection, network intrusion detection, and phishing detection.
- **Transfer Learning:** Transfer learning has emerged as a powerful

approach to leverage pre-trained models and knowledge from related domains to enhance the performance of CTI tasks with limited labeled data. Recent research has explored transfer learning techniques for fine-tuning deep learning models on CTI datasets, enabling more effective threat detection and classification with reduced training time and resource requirements.

- **Graph-Based Representations:** Graph-based representations have gained traction in CTI for modeling complex relationships and interactions among entities in cyber environments, such as IP addresses, domains, and malware samples. Recent methods utilize graph neural networks (GNNs) and graph embedding techniques to learn latent representations of cyber entities and identify anomalous patterns indicative of cyber threats, facilitating more comprehensive threat intelligence analysis and visualization.
- **Adversarial Defense Mechanisms:** With the rise of adversarial attacks on ML-based CTI systems, recent research has focused on developing robust defense mechanisms to mitigate the impact of adversarial perturbations. Techniques such as adversarial training, defensive distillation, and ensemble learning have been proposed to enhance the resilience of ML models against adversarial manipulation and improve their generalization performance in real-world scenarios.
- **Explainable AI (XAI):** Explainable AI has garnered attention in CTI for enhancing the interpretability and transparency of ML models, enabling security analysts to understand the reasoning behind model predictions and decisions. Recent methods employ techniques such as attention mechanisms, feature attribution, and modelagnostic explanations to provide insights into the underlying factors influencing threat intelligence outcomes, thereby fostering trust and confidence in AI-driven CTI systems.
- **Federated Learning:** Federated learning has emerged as a privacy-preserving approach to collaborative model training across distributed data sources, making it well-suited for CTI applications where sensitive data must be protected. Recent research has explored federated learning frameworks for aggregating threat intelligence from diverse sources while preserving data privacy and confidentiality, enabling organizations to collectively enhance their CTI capabilities without sharing raw data.
- **Meta-Learning and AutoML:** Meta-learning and automated machine learning (AutoML) techniques have been applied to

CTI to automate the process of model selection, hyperparameter tuning, and feature engineering, thereby reducing the burden on security analysts and accelerating the deployment of AI-driven CTI solutions. Recent advancements in meta-learning algorithms and AutoML platforms have facilitated the development of scalable and adaptive CTI systems capable of continuously learning and evolving in response to emerging cyber threats.

8.2.3. Significance of AI and Machine Learning Approaches to Cyber Threat Intelligence

The potential of artificial intelligence (AI) and machine learning techniques to transform cybersecurity procedures and enable enterprises to successfully counteract emerging cyberthreats is the significance of these approaches to CTI. Several key aspects highlight the significance of this topic:

- **Rapidly Evolving Threat Landscape:** The cyber threat landscape is constantly evolving, with adversaries employing increasingly sophisticated tactics, techniques, and procedures (TTPs) to exploit vulnerabilities and infiltrate networks. Traditional cybersecurity approaches, such as signature-based detection and rule-based systems, are often inadequate in detecting novel and stealthy threats. AI and machine learning offer the promise of adaptive defenses capable of learning from data and adapting to emerging threats in real-time.
- **Data Deluge and Complexity:** The volume, velocity, and variety of data generated by digital systems present significant challenges for cybersecurity practitioners. Traditional methods struggle to analyze and interpret vast amounts of data effectively, leading to missed opportunities for threat detection and response. AI and machine learning techniques enable automated analysis of large-scale datasets, uncovering hidden patterns, correlations, and anomalies that may indicate potential security incidents or vulnerabilities.
- **Proactive Threat Intelligence:** CTI plays a crucial role in proactive cybersecurity by providing organizations with timely and actionable insights into emerging threats and vulnerabilities. AI-driven CTI systems can continuously monitor and analyze diverse sources of threat intelligence, including network traffic, endpoint logs, open-source intelligence (OSINT), and dark web forums, enabling security teams to identify, prioritize, and mitigate risks before they escalate into full-fledged attacks.

- **Enhanced Detection and Response Capabilities:** AI and machine learning enable more accurate and efficient detection of cyber threats across various attack vectors, including malware, phishing, insider threats, and advanced persistent threats (APTs). By leveraging advanced analytics and anomaly detection algorithms, organizations can detect subtle indicators of compromise and anomalous behavior that may evade traditional security controls. Furthermore, AI-driven incident response capabilities enable rapid containment, investigation, and remediation of security incidents, minimizing the impact of breaches and reducing dwell time.
- **Resource Optimization and Scalability:** AI and machine learning technologies offer the potential to automate routine cybersecurity tasks and augment the capabilities of human analysts, enabling more efficient resource allocation and scalability of security operations. By automating repetitive tasks such as log analysis, threat hunting, and incident triage, organizations can free up valuable human resources to focus on high-value activities, such as threat intelligence analysis, strategic planning, and threat hunting.
- **Continuous Innovation and Adaptation:** The dynamic nature of cyber threats requires continuous innovation and adaptation in cybersecurity defenses. AI and machine learning enable adaptive defenses that can learn and evolve over time, leveraging insights from past incidents to improve future decision-making and response strategies. Furthermore, AI-driven CTI systems can leverage advanced analytics techniques, such as predictive modeling and trend analysis, to anticipate emerging threats and proactively strengthen defenses.

8.2.4. Limitations and Drawbacks

While artificial intelligence (AI) and machine learning (ML) approaches to cyber threat intelligence (CTI) have many advantages, there are a number of restrictions and disadvantages that businesses need to be aware of.

- **Data Quality and Bias:** AI and ML models are highly dependent on the quality, relevance, and representativeness of training data. Biases present in training data, such as imbalances, inaccuracies, and missing values, can lead to biased or skewed model predictions, undermining the effectiveness of CTI systems. Moreover, adversarial attacks aimed at poisoning training data or manipulating ML models can introduce vulnerabilities and compromise the integrity of threat intelligence outcomes.

- **Overfitting and Generalization:** ML models trained on historical data may suffer from overfitting, where the model learns to memorize patterns specific to the training data but fails to generalize well to unseen data. Overfitting can result in poor performance and inflated accuracy metrics, leading to false confidence in the reliability of CTI systems. Conversely, underfitting occurs when the model fails to capture underlying patterns in the data, resulting in suboptimal performance and missed opportunities for threat detection.
- **Lack of Interpretability:** Complex ML models, such as deep neural networks, often lack interpretability, making it challenging for security analysts to understand the rationale behind model predictions and decisions. The blackbox nature of ML algorithms hinders transparency and accountability in CTI, limiting the ability to validate model outputs, troubleshoot errors, and interpret findings. As a result, trust and adoption of AI-driven CTI systems may be compromised, particularly in high-stakes environments where explainability is critical.
- **Scalability and Resource Requirements:** Training and deploying ML models for CTI tasks can be computationally intensive and resource-demanding, requiring substantial computational resources, storage capacity, and expertise. As the volume and velocity of data continue to increase, organizations may face scalability challenges in processing and analyzing large-scale datasets in real-time. Additionally, maintaining and updating ML models over time incurs ongoing costs and operational overhead, which may pose financial and logistical constraints for resource-constrained organizations.
- **False Positives and Negatives:** ML-based CTI systems may generate false positives (incorrectly identifying benign activities as threats) or false negatives (failing to detect actual threats), leading to alert fatigue, wasted resources, and missed opportunities for threat mitigation. Balancing the trade-off between false positives and false negatives is a significant challenge in CTI, as overly conservative or aggressive thresholds may impact the efficiency and efficacy of security operations.
- **Ethical and Legal Considerations:** The use of AI and ML in CTI raises ethical and legal concerns related to privacy, transparency, and accountability. Collecting, storing, and analyzing sensitive data for CTI purposes must adhere to regulatory requirements, data protection laws, and ethical guidelines to safeguard individual privacy rights and prevent unauthorized use or misuse of personal

information. Moreover, bias and discrimination in ML models must be addressed to ensure fair and equitable treatment of diverse user populations and minimize unintended consequences.

- **Dependency on Human Expertise:** While AI and ML technologies can automate certain aspects of CTI, human expertise remains indispensable for contextualizing findings, validating results, and making informed decisions. Security analysts play a crucial role in interpreting model outputs, conducting threat assessments, and formulating effective response strategies based on domain knowledge and situational awareness. Therefore, AI-driven CTI systems should complement, rather than replace, human intelligence and judgment in cybersecurity operations.

8.3. APPLICATIONS OF MACHINE LEARNING AND AI IN THREAT INTELLIGENCE

Modern threat intelligence now includes machine learning (ML) and artificial intelligence (AI), which provide cutting-edge methods for more effectively detecting, analyzing, and responding to cyber threats. Traditional approaches of threat detection and response are no longer adequate due to the exponential increase in the complexity and volume of cyber threats. Here are key applications of ML and AI in threat intelligence:

8.3.1. Anomaly Detection

In threat intelligence, one of the most popular uses of machine learning is anomaly detection. It entails spotting behavioral anomalies that could point to possible security problems.

In artificial intelligence, anomaly detection is a method for locating oddities or outliers in a dataset that differ from the norm.

These anomalies may indicate an issue with digital system performance, an unforeseen system malfunction, security breaches, or an interesting but uncommon occurrence. Large volumes of data collected with particular meta tags, labels, and other properties are typically processed using AI and machine learning algorithms in anomaly detection to automatically identify such anomalies. These artificial intelligence (AI) models and algorithms can be trained to identify what is deemed "normal" and to alert users to any deviations from this baseline. This is especially helpful in sectors where early anomaly detection can avert more problems or losses, like enterprise networking, cybersecurity, finance, healthcare, and manufacturing.

The complexity and dynamic nature of contemporary network environments are addressed by the integration of artificial intelligence (AI) into anomaly detection. The volume, velocity, and variety of data generated by enterprise networks, including cloud orchestration and management systems and security platforms, make traditional methods of identifying outliers—which frequently rely on predefined thresholds and rules—increasingly insufficient.

8.3.1.1. Processing Large Datasets in Real-Time

In order to ensure that businesses can recognize and react to anomalies as they arise and maintain optimal digital systems, artificial intelligence (AI) necessitates the efficient processing, labeling, and categorization of massive datasets in real-time performance (network connectivity).

8.3.1.2. Automated, Real-Time Detection

Artificial intelligence (AI) makes automated, real-time anomaly detection possible by continuously observing and analyzing patterns, which enables AI to identify anomalies as soon as they arise. The impact of any disruptions is significantly lessened by this instant anomaly detection, giving organizations crucial time to address the anomaly before it gets worse.

8.3.1.3. Effective Pattern Recognition

AI's capacity for pattern recognition, made possible by a range of machine learning (ML) techniques built into its architecture, is one of the main reasons it functions in anomaly detection. Big datasets with complex behavior that traditional systems might find difficult to discern are produced by enterprise networks. Nonetheless, AI-powered systems that depend on a strong data architecture are superior at spotting trends, picking up on them, and precisely detecting any abnormalities or deviations.

8.3.1.4. Proactive Anomaly Management

Anomalies were traditionally dealt with reactively, frequently following a disruption. AI-powered systems alter this strategy by making it possible to detect anomalies proactively and use predictive maintenance strategies to automate closed-loop resolution. AI's predictive powers enable businesses to stop disruptions from negatively affecting their network service by predicting possible anomalies based on noticed changes in patterns.

8.3.1.5. How Does Anomaly Detection Work?

Anomaly detection identifies objects, occasions, or observations that stand out from the bulk of the data and give rise to suspicions. The exact steps involved in anomaly detection vary depending on the techniques employed, but these general steps are typically involved in most methods.

8.3.1.5.1. Data Collection and Preprocessing

Gathering pertinent information is the first step in the anomaly detection process. This could be any kind of data, including transactional records, sensor outputs, and network logs. Following collection, this data is cleaned and prepared for analysis through a process known as preprocessing. The basis for AI's comprehension of "normal" behavior is this extensive dataset.

8.3.1.5.2. Feature Selection

After the data is prepared, the next stage is to identify the informative characteristics, or "features," within the dataset. These particular characteristics point to certain patterns of behavior. By concentrating on these characteristics, the AI speeds up and improves the accuracy of the anomaly detection process.

8.3.1.5.3. Modeling

The creation of a dynamic baseline or "normal" behavior model is the foundation of the anomaly detection process. This frequently entails using statistical or machine learning algorithms on the chosen features. The goals and system requirements of the organization determine the best approach, be it density, clustering, or another methodology.

8.3.1.5.4. Anomaly Identification

Once the model is established, it is used for comparison with freshly received data. Every notable departure from the model is classified as an anomaly. It's crucial to remember that not every anomaly points to a problem. They might be the outcome of insignificant statistical fluctuations. But prompt detection is essential when they indicate underlying problems like fraud or errors.

8.3.1.5.5. Post-Processing

A post-processing stage follows the identification of anomalies. Based on how much they deviate from typical behavior, how likely they are to have an effect, and how confidently they were detected, the anomalies are assessed and ranked. Companies are able to allocate their resources more efficiently thanks to this ranking.

8.3.1.5.6. Interpretation

The detected anomalies and their rankings are translated into useful insights in the last stage. Depending on the details, this can entail additional research, remedial measures, or even system enhancements to stop similar anomalies in the future. This step's lessons can be applied to improve the anomaly detection process as a whole.

8.3.1.6. Models of Anomaly Detection

There are various models used for anomaly detection. Here are some of the most widely used models:

8.3.1.6.1. Statistical Anomaly Detection Models

Anomaly detection statistical models are based on the law of large numbers. These models postulate that a stochastic process, which offers a statistical foundation for identifying patterns, can be used to represent "normal" behavior. Any departure from the standard may be categorized as an anomaly.

8.3.1.6.2. Density-Based Anomaly Detection Models

Density-based models take into consideration the distribution of data within a dataset. The idea here is that data points in low-density regions are anomalies, while data points in high-density regions indicate "normal" behavior. When outliers are easily distinguished from typical patterns, this method is especially helpful.

8.3.1.6.3. Clustering-Based Anomaly Detection Models

These models create clusters out of related data instances. Anomalies are data instances that are too distant from their nearest clusters or that cannot be grouped within any cluster, while normal data instances are part of a specific cluster. This model works best with data sets that have clear categories, like a particular kind of location.

8.3.1.6.4. Classifier-Based Anomaly Detection Models

The foundation of classifier-based models is the division of data instances into "normal" and "anomalous" categories. In order to distinguish between normal and anomalous behavior, the model is trained on labeled data using supervised machine learning. This method provides a high level of accuracy and control.

8.3.1.6.5. Neural Network-Based Anomaly Detection Models

When working with high-dimensional data or in situations involving complex patterns, models like autoencoders are employed. These neural network models are an effective tool for anomaly detection because they are able to identify even minute departures from the norm.

8.3.1.6.6. Time-Series Anomaly Detection Models

Time-series data is the target audience for these models. ARIMA (AutoRegressive Integrated Moving Average) and LSTM (Long Short Term Memory) networks are two well-known examples. These models work well in scenarios like network performance monitoring where data is time-dependent.

8.3.1.6.7. Support Vector Machine (SVM) Anomaly Detection Models

In a high-dimensional space, SVM models are able to draw boundaries that distinguish normal instances from anomalies. Because of this, they work especially well with complicated datasets where it can be difficult to tell the difference between normal behavior and anomalies.

8.3.1.7. Different Techniques of Anomaly Detection

Anomaly detection employs a number of approaches, each with unique uses and benefits.

Here are some of the most popular techniques:

8.3.1.7.1. Statistical-Based Techniques

Statistically based methods find anomalies in a dataset by applying statistical rules. They typically consider that the data follows a normal distribution, and any data point that deviates from a predetermined range is regarded as abnormal. Anomalies are typically found within a range of three standard deviations from the mean.

8.3.1.7.2. Density-Based Techniques

The density of data points in a dataset is the basis for anomaly detection using density-based algorithms such as Local Outlier Factor (LOF). Anomalies are data points that are out of the ordinary because they are located in areas that are relatively low in density.

8.3.1.7.3. Clustering-Based Techniques

The idea behind clustering techniques like K-means clustering is to group data instances that are similar. Anomalies are defined as data points that show a significant deviation from a cluster center, indicating dissimilarity.

8.3.1.7.4. Supervised & Semi-Supervised Learning

These methods make use of past data that has labels designating "normal" and "anomalous" observations. These labels are used by the implemented algorithm to create a predictive model that can identify anomalies.

8.3.1.7.5. Unsupervised Learning

Algorithms for unsupervised learning, such as neural networks and deep learning, autonomously recognize and categorize anomalous data points. They become independent of pre-labeled data by finding patterns and correlations within the data.

8.3.1.7.6. Ensemble Techniques

By combining several anomaly detection algorithms, these methods produce a single, all-inclusive model. The benefit is improved performance as a result of combining different algorithms.

8.3.1.7.7. Support Vector Machines (SVM)

In a multi-dimensional space, SVMs look for a hyperplane that can clearly categorize data points. It works particularly well in situations where there is an obvious distinction between anomalies and regular data points.

8.3.1.7.8. Time Series Analysis

A technique called time series analysis is used to look at time-sequence data by finding irregularities in seasonal patterns or trends. Anomalies can be identified by any abrupt changes in identifiable patterns.

8.3.1.7.9. Isolation Forest

By choosing a feature at random and then choosing a split value between the feature's maximum and minimum values, the Isolation Forest algorithm divides observations. The reasoning behind this is that anomaly observations are simpler to identify because they deviate greatly from the bulk of the data.

8.3.1.7.9. Autoencoders

Artificial neural networks called autoencoders are used to efficiently encode data. Reconstruction errors increase when they are trained to reconstruct "normal" data, which makes it difficult for them to recreate anomalies. Anomalies are identified as those instances that produce these high errors.

8.3.2. Malware Detection and Classification

When it comes to detecting new and sophisticated malware variants, traditional signature-based malware detection techniques are becoming less and less effective. AI and ML provide more flexible and dynamic approaches.

There are two types of malware detection techniques: behavior-based and signature-based. Before using either of the two malware analysis methodologies—static or dynamic—it is imperative to understand their underlying principles. As the name suggests, static analysis is carried out "statically," that is, without running the file, whereas dynamic analysis is carried out via virtual machine execution. To infer the behavioral characteristics of a file, static analysis can be compared to "reading" the source code of the malware. Various techniques used in the static analysis:

- **File Format Inspection** Metadata in files can be particularly useful. For instance, PE (portable executable) files may offer a plethora of data regarding build time, functions that are imported and exported, and more.
- **String Extraction** is the process of scrutinizing software output (e.g., status or error messages) and extracting information about malware operation.
- **Fingerprinting Entails** performing cryptographic hash computations and locating environmental artifacts such as hardcoded usernames, filenames, and registry strings.
- **AV Inspection Scanners** will identify any well-known malware in the examined file. Although it might seem trivial, antivirus and sandboxes commonly employ this kind of detection to "confirm" their findings.
- **Disassembly** involves translating machine code into assembly language to deduce the logic and intents of the software. The most popular and reliable approach of static analysis is this one.

Another kind of analysis is dynamic analysis. Unlike static analysis, the behavior of the file is observed during execution, and the characteristics and intentions of the file are inferred from that information.

The file is typically run in a virtual environment, such as a sandbox. All behavioral characteristics, such as opened files and mutexes created, can be found using this type of analysis. In comparison to static analysis, it is also faster.

An example of a Training Phase is provided below to illustrate the process of teaching the machine learning model to predict the output.

8.3.2.1. Training Phase of the Algorithms

A specific pipeline, depicted in the below figure, is followed in order to solve the malware detection problem using machine learning techniques. For the training process, a collection of malware-free and benign binaries is utilized to train an ML model. Before feeding the machine learning model with this information, a feature extractor analyzes these binary files to extract details about them, like file size and section statistics (Figure 8.1).

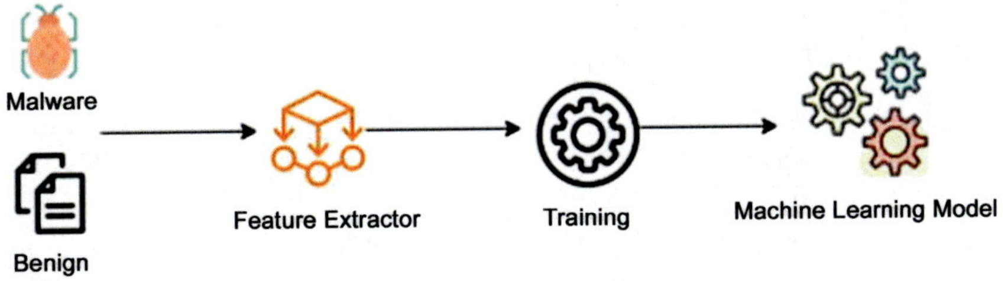

Figure 8.1. *Training phase of the algorithms.*

Source; https://www.einfochips.com/wp-content/uploads/2023/02/Training-Phase-image-source.webp.

8.3.2.2. Machine Learning Works in Malware Detection

To identify whether a file is malicious, machine learning models examine its properties and actions. Deep learning techniques, for example, can identify malware by looking at a file's structure, its execution patterns, and network activity. AI systems can also categorize malware into various groups (e.g. , ransomware, and trojans) according to its characteristics, facilitating quicker detection and action (Figure 8.2).

The capacity to provide defense against the most recent, unseen malware has improved thanks to machine learning. Windows Defender AV can offer real-time protection against a variety of threats because these expert systems give real-time visibility and context into attacks.

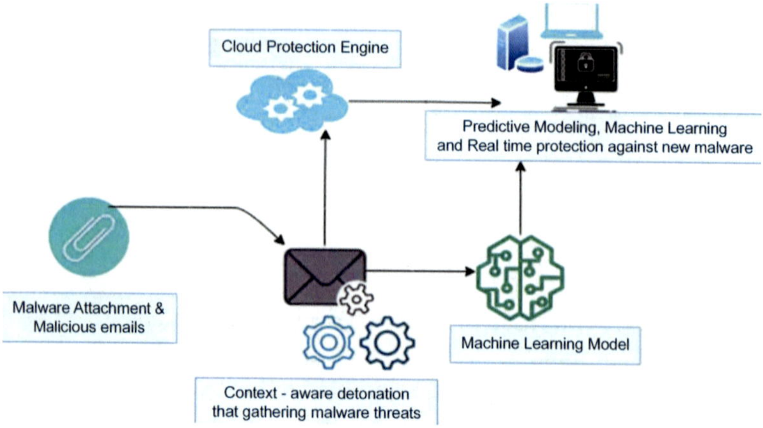

Figure 8.2. *How machine learning works in malware detection in antiviruses.*

Source: https://www.einfochips.com/wp-content/uploads/2023/02/How-Does-Machine-Learning-Work-in-Malware-Detection.webp.

Context-aware detonation systems examine millions of possible malware samples to gather enormous amounts of threat intelligence. This threat knowledge is fed into cloud security engines, allowing for real-time attack detection and prevention. Windows Defender looks for payloads in addition to Java malware; these are usually online banking Trojans (like Banker and Banload) or Java remote access Trojans (like Jrat and Qrat). ".

To protect themselves from cyberattacks, organizations need to continuously monitor and correlate millions of internal and external data elements from their user base and infrastructure. It's difficult to manually monitor and process such a massive amount of data, so it's easier said than done. Machine learning is particularly useful in these kinds of scenarios because it can quickly spot patterns and anticipate threats in a variety of data sets. By automating the analytical process, cyber teams can detect risks more quickly and distinguish situations that require a more in-depth human investigation.

For threat modeling, VAPT (Vulnerable Assessment Penetration Testing) devices, OS/firmware, web/mobile applications, data, and cloud workloads, Einfochips offers comprehensive cyber security services. Machine learning techniques, such as signature-based algorithms, feature extraction, static analysis, and dynamic analysis, are used to detect and classify malware. In addition, numerous tools such as Regshot, Wireshark, Procmon, Process monitor, Virustotal, etc. are employed to categorize various forms of malware, including rootkits, trojans, backdoors, and various viruses and worms. In the end, this strategy helps clients deploy safe products in public spaces, which helps shield goods from malicious software.

In order to comply with security industry standards, rules, and guidelines like NIST (National Institute of Standards and Technology), ENISA (European Network and Information Security Agency), OWASP (Open Web Application Security Project), MITRE (Massachusetts Institute of Technology Research and Engineering), and IoT Security Foundation, eInfochips has assisted businesses in the development, deployment, and management of security solutions on a global scale through strategic, transformative, and managed operations techniques.

8.3.3. Phishing Detection

One of the most popular attack vectors is phishing, and conventional detection techniques frequently can't keep up with phishing attempts that get more and more complex.

Phishing attacks have changed dramatically over time, starting as simple attempts to trick people and progressing to intricate plans aimed at particular companies or people. It is essential to comprehend the principles underlying these attacks in order to create effective defenses.

8.3.3.1. Traditional Tactics

Phishing attacks were initially designed to fool a large audience in the hopes that a small percentage would fall for it. They were intended to be general and indiscriminate. These tactics often involved:

- **Generic Emails:** Mass emails sent to thousands of users, impersonating reputable organizations, usually containing urgent requests to update personal information or confirm account details.
- **Fake Websites:** Cloning legitimate websites to trick users into entering their personal information, such as login credentials or financial data.
- **Attachment Scams:** Emails with attachments that, once opened, install malware on the user's device to steal information or monitor activities.

8.3.3.2. Evolution into Spear Phishing and Whaling

As cybersecurity measures improved, so did the sophistication of phishing attacks. This led to the development of more targeted approaches:

- **Spear Phishing:** Unlike the scattergun approach of traditional phishing, spear phishing targets specific individuals or organizations. Cybercriminals gather detailed information about their targets to craft convincing emails, often mimicking the tone, style, and type of communication the target expects to receive from trusted sources.
- **Whaling:** A more refined form of spear phishing, whaling targets high-profile individuals within organizations, such as executives or senior management. These attacks are meticulously planned, with emails that often involve requests for financial transactions or sensitive information, making them appear as legitimate business inquiries.

Whaling and spear phishing both mark a dramatic change in strategy by emphasizing quality over quantity and necessitating a thorough knowledge of the target to be successful. The necessity for sophisticated detection and prevention techniques that use AI and ML to examine behavior patterns and identify anomalies suggestive of such focused attacks is highlighted by this evolution.

Emails and messages can be analyzed by AI and ML for signs of phishing, such as dubious URLs, odd sender behaviors, and linguistic patterns. In this regard, natural language processing (NLP) is especially useful since it enables systems to comprehend and analyze email content in order to accurately identify phishing attempts. AI is able to identify, for instance, minute differences in domain names or peculiar wording that could point to a phishing attempt.

8.3.3.3. How Does Artificial Intelligence (AI) Detects Phishing Attacks?

As everyone is aware, artificial intelligence (AI) can speed up and improve the accuracy of email analysis. However, the key question that needs to be addressed in this context is how precisely AI detects and stops phishing.

8.3.3.3.1. Looking for Anomalies and Warning Signals

An effective artificial intelligence and machine learning system searches the entire email, from the metadata to the message content, for anomalies and warning signs of phishing. For example, this comprises alerts based on email behavior (e.g. falsified senders) and message purpose (e.g., pressing subjects).

The urgency of the message is one of the primary indicators that it is a phishing attempt. The warning signal is activated if the email you received contains words that indicate urgency and calls for immediate action. Next, artificial intelligence (AI) attempts to identify and comprehend the message's context, determining whether it is a typical spam message, a phishing attempt, or a genuine message.

Consider the term "publicity" as an example. The word itself might raise red flags already. An AI system, on the other hand, aims to determine with greater accuracy whether or not the email poses a threat and how serious it is. This makes it easier to distinguish between terms like "Fill in your card number right now to participate in the publicity" and "Urgent: 30% OFF publicity," which in this instance indicate a straightforward spam and a phishing scam, respectively.

The cautionary indicators in the email header follow the same reasoning. For example, AI recognizes instances of forged senders in emails, misspelled domains, and other forms of spoofing. The system greatly expands the threat detection capabilities when used in conjunction with conventional engines like DMARC, DKIM, and SPF.

8.3.3.3.2. Analyzing the Message Context

AI is one of the strongest defenses against phishing because, among other crucial features, it can analyze a message based on its context. This analyses an email holistically rather than just comparing it to other phishing scams that are currently active.

The system will consider a number of factors, such as whether or not there has been prior communication, any information that the sender may be requesting in the email, and the relationship between the subject line and the body of the message.

In addition, AI-based email protection continuously learns from the data as well as the input from administrators and users to provide an extremely accurate analysis.

8.3.3.3.3. Understanding How Users Communicate

These days, it is difficult to identify frauds using conventional email detection tools and security solutions. In particular, it can be difficult to identify the kind of fraud that harms businesses the most nowadays. This is because it doesn't contain any of the usual components of a malicious email.

The hacker can send convincing emails to the target or person until they are persuaded to take the desired action by opening a dialogue channel one at a time. For example, sending confidential, sensitive, or SATA data; paying bills; transferring money through a bank; or downloading malware or malicious files. Artificial intelligence (AI) algorithms are essential for stopping and identifying these sophisticated scams that can comprehend user communication. For example, being aware of their usual actions, their textual habits, and whether the messages make sense in context.

For example, if someone tries to mimic the company's CEO, the system needs to be able to spot shifts in the executive's communication style and stop the attack before it can do any harm.

8.3.3.3.4. Ways Artificial Intelligence (AI) Can Take on Phishing Attacks

The only time machine artificial intelligence fails is when it ceases to adapt. Since technological advancement is always changing, it is helpful to take note of the following details in order to close the knowledge gap and fend off attacks.

- To identify real-time threats, one should introduce Artificial Intelligence (AI) algorithms on every mobile phone, even on offline devices.
- To deduct the unnecessary hassle of unsecured passwords, these algorithms can help strengthen the security of mobile phones and double as an employee identification card.
- The evaluation of the efficacy of a cyber security strategy will be based on an enterprise's ability to predict, comply, and deter threats.
- One should increase cyber security protection in a predictive manner. It is necessary to study the data from endpoint devices and predict any possibility instead of analyzing things after they have been executed. This will help to prevent any sophisticated breaching attempts at the right time.

8.3.4. Threat Hunting

Security teams use a proactive strategy called "threat hunting" to look for potential dangers hidden inside an organization's network. This process is now much more effective and efficient thanks to AI and ML.

Algorithms using AI and machine learning search through massive amounts of data in real time for threats. Using past data, they pinpoint anomalous activity patterns and possible dangers. This lowers the possibility of data breaches and operational interruptions while enabling security teams to respond swiftly.

8.3.4.1. Benefits and Challenges of Automated Threat Hunting

Automated threat hunting has several advantages:

- **Improved Detection:** Advanced algorithms can analyze complex data with remarkable precision, enhancing the accuracy of threat identification.

- **Faster Response:** Automated systems can quickly detect and address threats in real time, reducing the window of vulnerability.
- **Cost-Effective:** Organizations can optimize their resources and lower operational expenses by automating repetitive tasks.

Notwithstanding these advantages, there are still drawbacks, including algorithmic bias, worries about data privacy, and the dynamic nature of cyberthreats. To get beyond these obstacles, automated threat-hunting systems must be carefully put into place and constantly improved.

8.3.4.2. Components of an Automated Threat Hunting System

An effective automated threat-hunting system comprises several key components:

- **Data Collection:** This process gathers various data sources, such as logs, network traffic, and endpoint information, to provide a thorough understanding of the digital environment.
- **Analytics Engine:** This engine employs advanced algorithms, including AI and machine learning, to identify anomalies and suspicious patterns within the collected data, enabling real-time threat detection.
- **Threat Intelligence Integration:** This process incorporates threat intelligence feeds to enhance the analysis and prioritize alerts based on known threats and attack tactics.
- **Incident Response Workflow:** This workflow streamlines the response process, facilitating prompt action upon threat detection by integrating with existing incident response procedures.

8.3.4.3. Integration with Existing Security Operations

Smooth collaboration is necessary to integrate automated threat hunting with the security operations that are in place. This entails coordinating processes, distributing knowledge amongst groups, and establishing connections with security information and event management (SIEM) platforms. This gives you full visibility and the ability to respond.

8.3.4.4. Best Practices for Implementation

To maximize the effectiveness of automated threat hunting, organizations should follow these best practices:

- **Continuous Training:** Regularly update AI models with new threat information and adapt to changing attack methods.
- **Cross-Team Collaboration:** Encourage collaboration between security analysts, data experts, and IT professionals to leverage diverse knowledge.
- **Regular Audits and Assessments:** Conduct periodic evaluations to identify areas for improvement and ensure compliance with regulations.

8.3.4.5. How It Works

Massive volumes of data, such as logs, network traffic, and endpoint activity, can be sorted through by ML algorithms to find patterns that might point to a security breach. Artificial Intelligence (AI) can suggest possible threats to human analysts and automate the process of searching for Indicators of Compromise (IOCs). This enables security teams to recognize threats and take appropriate action before they inflict serious harm.

8.3.5. Automated Threat Response

In order to respond to threats, speed is essential. The time it takes to minimize possible harm can be decreased by using AI and ML to automate responses to specific threats.

8.3.5.1. How It Works

AI-powered systems can be configured to react automatically, based on pre-established criteria, to particular threats. An AI system could, for instance, automatically isolate impacted systems, block malicious IP addresses, or restore infected files to a safe state if it detects an outbreak of malware. As a result, attackers have a smaller window of opportunity and the damage is limited.

8.3.6. Threat Intelligence Enrichment

A thorough grasp of the threat landscape is typically attained through the analysis and correlation of data from several sources, a process known as threat intelligence.

8.3.6.1. How It Works

AI systems are able to compile and correlate information from social media, dark web monitoring, threat intelligence feeds, and other sources to give a more comprehensive picture of possible threats. Threats can then be prioritized and dealt with more skillfully thanks to this enhanced intelligence.

8.3.7. Predictive Threat Modeling

One effective use of AI and ML in threat intelligence is the ability to anticipate possible threats before they materialize.

8.3.7.1. How It Works

To forecast possible future threats, machine learning models can examine historical events, present threat patterns, and a variety of environmental variables. This enables businesses to take action before an attack happens by fixing vulnerabilities and strengthening security procedures.

8.3.8. Adversarial Attack Detection

Cybercriminals are increasingly using AI and ML techniques to launch adversarial attacks, where they manipulate inputs to evade detection.

8.3.8.1. How It Works

AI systems are being developed to detect these adversarial attacks by analyzing the subtleties in input data that might indicate manipulation. This helps in identifying attacks that are designed to fool traditional security systems.

8.3.9. Incident Response Automation

After detecting a threat, the incident response process can be labor-intensive and time-consuming.

8.3.9.1. How It Works

AI can automate various stages of incident response, from triage to containment and remediation. For example, AI can automatically prioritize incidents based on severity, suggest appropriate response actions, and even execute those actions, such as isolating affected systems or deploying patches.

AI and ML are driving significant advancements in threat intelligence, providing more efficient, accurate, and scalable solutions for detecting and responding to cyber threats. As these technologies continue to evolve, their applications in threat intelligence will become even more sophisticated, helping organizations stay ahead of increasingly complex cyber threats.

8.4. AI-DRIVEN THREAT DETECTION AND PREDICTION

Artificial intelligence has become a vital tool in the quickly changing field of cybersecurity. By using machine learning and advanced AI algorithms, organizations automate the crucial processes of detecting, evaluating, and proactively mitigating cybersecurity threats. By sorting through large data sets, these sophisticated algorithms enable security teams to find hidden risks and detect threats early on, improving overall security measures.

8.4.1. Why is AI Important in Modern Threat Detection?

Decision-making in cybersecurity now heavily relies on AI systems. These systems automate highly accurate incident response strategies and handle a wide range of threats with skill. This evolution is essential for managing the enormous volumes of threat intelligence inputs along with the rapidly changing nature of cyber threats.

Although AI-powered threat detection is very successful, hackers are always changing their attack techniques to circumvent it. They use cutting-edge tactics like polymorphic malware, zero-day exploits, and phishing attacks with generative AI to build on one another and launch more vicious cyberattacks.

Artificial intelligence (AI)-based threat detection aims to stop dynamic threat strategies that are hard to identify and counter, like growing attack vectors like IoT devices, cloud deployments, and mobile devices. Its goal is to combat the growing frequency and amplitude of cyberattacks, ransomware in particular.

8.4.2. The Evolution of Threat Detection

Technological advancements have always been adopted; this is evident in the way threat detection methodologies have evolved. In order to combat increasingly complex cyber threats, the integration of AI represents a major advancement by enhancing human intelligence with cutting-edge algorithms.

As technology has developed, it has become more and more important for threat detection. Using automation, real-time data analysis, and predictive tools are some examples of this. The continuous competition between threat actors and security measures is the cause of this evolution. Threat actors create ever-more-advanced strategies to get around security technology with every advancement.

8.4.2.1. Initial Threat Detection: the Rule-Based System

A rule-based system that identified known threats was the foundation for threat detection in the 1970s. This approach, though, could have been more successful in thwarting cutting-edge cyberattacks.

8.4.2.2. The Signature-Based Approach

The development of a signature-based approach occurred in the 1980s due to the necessity of automated threat detection. It was able to neutralize known cyberthreats, but it was unable to detect zero-day ones.

8.4.2.3. Heuristic-Based Threat Detection

In order to battle newly emerging viruses and malware, heuristic-based threat detection first appeared in the late 1980s and early 1990s. By looking at questionable code properties, it finds malware variations and zero-day threats.

8.4.2.4. Anomaly Detection Systems

Threat detection was enhanced and manual monitoring was done away with the introduction of anomaly detection systems in the late 1990s and early 2000s. In order to determine baseline behavior and identify deviations as possible threats, they evaluate system activities and network traffic.

8.4.2.5. AI-Powered Solutions

Since the late 2000s, threat hunting has been transformed by AI. AI-powered solutions have been adopted by security teams to strengthen their security posture. AI plays a key role in threat detection, providing teams with a substantial advantage over even the most proficient adversaries.

8.4.3. AI Capabilities to Fortify Cybersecurity Defenses

Machine learning is one example of an artificial intelligence functionality that uses massive amounts of data to process and analyze threat intelligence gathered by security teams and human analysts in order to address complex and dynamic threats.

The unique capabilities that AI-powered systems provide to fortify cybersecurity defenses are:

- Adaptive learning uses machine learning models in AI systems to continuously improve threat detection capabilities for responding to evolving threats.
- Advanced pattern recognition identifies attacker patterns and anomalies within vast amounts of data, including subtle signs of

malicious activity that human analysts cannot detect.

- AI algorithms process and analyze vast amounts of data for threat detection at a scale and speed impossible for human analysts
- Automated responses mitigate threats
- Predictive analytics proactively identify future threats and refine threat-hunting work by analyzing trends and patterns in data.
- Reduced false positives eliminate time-consuming threat assessments for security teams by understanding the difference between benign and malicious activities

8.4.4. Core Concepts of AI in Threat Detection

It's helpful to understand how AI improves threat detection and how it modifies our search for and response to possible threats. These are the main AI techniques and instruments that replace antiquated threat detection with more advanced, swift, and futuristic security strategies.

8.4.4.1. Machine Learning Algorithms

Machine learning algorithms can aid in the prompt detection of novel and intricate threats. These algorithms can identify patterns and predict possible threats by examining data from previous incidents, which increases the precision and speed of threat detection.

Machine learning can be applied in two ways: supervised and unsupervised. In supervised learning, a labeled dataset is used to train the model to differentiate between benign and malevolent activity. Based on input-output mapping, the model gains the ability to forecast results.

Conversely, unsupervised learning does not make use of labeled data. Rather, the model gains the ability to recognize relationships, patterns, and anomalies. By detecting deviations from standard baselines of what is deemed normal, it can identify new or unknown threats.

With the use of current intelligence, sophisticated AI algorithms, like deep learning and neural networks, can gradually enhance their predictive abilities by sifting through enormous data sets in search of questionable patterns.

8.4.4.2. Data Handling and Processing

In order to identify potential threats, handling and processing data for threat detection entails gathering, sanitizing, and evaluating enormous volumes of data. This procedure involves applying AI algorithms, normalizing data, and filtering noise in order to find any anomalies or patterns that might point to ransomware or malware, security lapses, or other malicious activity.

Data collection sources include:

- Network traffic logs;
- System event logs;
- User activity records.

Real-time monitoring, API integrations, and automated data scraping technologies are used to gather threat intelligence data. The data must be cleaned and standardized through preprocessing. By locating pertinent data, eliminating unnecessary information, and creating new features to enhance model performance, feature selection and engineering optimize machine learning and artificial intelligence algorithms.

8.4.4.3. Threat Detection AI Model Development and Training

The process of creating an AI model for threat detection is intricate and iterative, requiring knowledge of both machine learning and threats. The quality of the data and the model's ongoing adaptation to new and changing threats are major factors in its efficacy.

Several key steps are involved, each critical to ensuring the effectiveness and accuracy of the final system. Here's a simplified overview of the process:

- Define the Problem: Decide what kind of threats the AI should detect.
- Collect and Prepare Data: Gather data related to these threats and clean it for use.
- Select Features: Choose essential parts of the data the AI will focus on.
- Choose an AI Model: The right AI algorithm suits your problem.
- Train the Model: Use your data to teach the AI to detect threats.
- Test and Improve: Evaluate the AI's performance and adjust to improve it.
- Implement and Update: Put the AI into use and keep updating it with new data to stay effective.

Ongoing validation and testing procedures, which compare models against unobserved data to guarantee accuracy and dependability, are the means by which model optimization and problem solving are accomplished. Testing evaluates the model's final performance in a changing threat landscape, whereas validation modifies the model during training.

8.4.5. Threat Detection Implementation Strategies

A multifaceted cybersecurity strategy is required to identify possible threats. Potential threats need to be tracked, analyzed, and responded to by both human analysts and sophisticated AI systems. Updating frequently is necessary to combat emerging and zero-day cyberthreats.

8.4.5.1. Integration with Existing Cybersecurity Systems

To increase threat detection, AI systems need to integrate seamlessly with current security systems. We also need to modify new threat detection systems to interface with outdated systems in order to accomplish this. To facilitate data exchange and communication between the various systems, middleware or APIs can be used. Improving threat detection while keeping the current system intact is our main goal.

AI is combined with already-established techniques like rule-based systems and machine learning in hybrid threat detection models. This makes it easier for us to recognize threats and quickly adjust to changing circumstances. We achieve the best of both worlds by combining the advantages of various strategies.

8.4.5.2. Real-Time Processing and Analysis

Monitoring data streams to identify possible threats is a key component of real-time threat processing and analysis. Security teams can quickly identify suspicious activity thanks to machine learning algorithms and AI models, which provide them with the threat intelligence they need to counteract evolving cyberthreats. There are two methods for doing this: edge computing and stream processing.

8.4.5.3. Scalability and Performance Optimization

Scalability and performance optimizations are necessary for AI threat detection systems to handle and compute data efficiently. Accurate threat detection depends on robust data processing techniques, scalable storage solutions, and efficient resource utilization.

8.4.6. Predictions of Artificial Intelligence (AI) in Cybersecurity

From a promising idea to an essential instrument for spotting, assessing, and averting cyberattacks, artificial intelligence (AI) has emerged as a major force in cybersecurity. AI in cybersecurity is expected to play a bigger part in threat detection and response in the future. Machine learning and AI tools will be used to identify sophisticated cyberthreats early on. It also highlights the use of generative AI to create predictive models, which improves security teams' capacity to promptly detect malicious activity and trigger automated reactions, thus cutting down on the amount of time needed to react to threat actors and stop cyberattacks.

Artificial intelligence has advanced in cybersecurity faster than anticipated, and it is now a vital tool for detecting and neutralizing cyberthreats and lowering associated risks. Decisions are being altered by AI models, which allow cybersecurity professionals to greatly enhance security procedures through the processing and real-time analysis of massive volumes of data.

The fundamental concepts and technologies for AI in cybersecurity that CISOs and security leaders should understand include:

- **Enhanced Threat Detection:** AI can quickly analyze data and identify potential threats by detecting patterns and anomalies, such as unusual network traffic or suspicious user behavior, often indicating malware, phishing, or other cyber attacks.
- **Proactive Security Posture:** AI predicts and identifies potential threats before they cause harm, enabling proactive security measures.
- **Automation of Repetitive Tasks:** AI automates routine cybersecurity tasks, freeing humans to focus on strategic activities. This includes patch management, network traffic monitoring, and sorting through false alarms.
- **Improved Incident Response:** AI can help coordinate and execute rapid responses to security incidents. It can automate responses to common threats and provide recommendations for mitigating more complex issues, thereby reducing the time it takes to resolve incidents and minimizing potential damage.
- **Adaptive Security Measures:** Cyber threats constantly evolve; what works today may not work tomorrow. AI systems can learn and change based on new data and threats, thereby continually adapting their defense mechanisms.
- **Scalability:** As organizations grow, so does the complexity and volume of their data and security needs. AI systems can scale to handle increased data without compromising performance or accuracy, making them indispensable for large, data-intensive environments.
- **Cost Efficiency:** By automating many aspects of cybersecurity, AI helps reduce the labor costs associated with monitoring and responding to threats. Additionally, by preventing attacks and

quickly mitigating those that occur, AI can save organizations significant amounts in potential losses and recovery costs.

In general, AI improves cybersecurity by bringing speed, efficiency, and proactive capabilities, which aid in thwarting increasingly complex and automated cyberattacks. This is especially important in the digital age, since cyberattacks are becoming more frequent and sophisticated.

8.4.6.1. Data Analytics in Cybersecurity

The fundamental component of artificial intelligence for cybersecurity is data analytics, which offers the insights required to successfully detect and mitigate cyberattacks. In order to identify anomalies and patterns suggestive of threat actors, it entails gathering, processing, and evaluating enormous volumes of data.

Real-time threat detection, improved incident response, and predictive analytics for vulnerability identification are all made possible by data analytics. Additionally, it supports vulnerability risk assessments and compliance monitoring for security teams.

8.4.6.2. Network Security and AI

Artificial intelligence has had a significant impact on network security in cybersecurity, as many CISOs had predicted. AI tools can detect anomalies that were previously unthinkable by analyzing network traffic patterns. Security teams can automate real-time monitoring, minimize false positives, and anticipate future cyber threats thanks to AI technologies' threat detection and response capabilities and vulnerability alerts.

8.4.6.3. Cryptography and AI

Early forecasts indicated that artificial intelligence would transform cryptography by enhancing encryption techniques with novel cryptographic algorithms and features to protect digital communications from ever-more-advanced cyberattacks.

Predictions about cybersecurity also centered on threat actors leveraging AI to subvert current encryption techniques through cyberattacks based on quantum computing. The development of next-generation encryption techniques that employed AI to produce quantum-resistant cryptographic methods allayed concerns about anticipated cyberattacks against encrypted files and systems. It is anticipated that encryption will develop to fully utilize artificial intelligence breakthroughs.

8.4.6.4. AI Threat Detection and Risk Mitigation

As expected, artificial intelligence proves to be highly proficient in detecting threats and pinpointing obscure hazards. Additionally, it makes it easier to mitigate cyber risks that serve as attack vectors for cyberattacks.

8.4.6.4.1. AI Vulnerabilities

Artificial intelligence (AI) tools in cybersecurity reduce risks by giving security teams automated vulnerability detection and the flexibility to adjust to and reduce the constantly changing threats that cybercriminals create.

8.4.6.4.2. Mitigation Strategies

Machine learning is a tool that AI-powered cybersecurity solutions use to reduce risk in ways that other technologies or people cannot. Artificial intelligence (AI) tools can automatically plan quick incident response, provide predictive threat intelligence, and analyze large data sets for anomalies. By improving network security through ongoing monitoring and using cutting-edge machine learning algorithms to inform proactive defense strategies that reduce risks, these AI systems also support security teams.

8.4.6.4.3. AI in Incident Response

AI-powered cybersecurity systems quickly identify and evaluate threats in the event of an incident, giving real-time actionable insights to speed up responses and simplify forensic investigations. Furthermore, all incident-related data is continuously used to train machine learning models, which improve incident response tactics and drastically cut down on response times and manual labor.

8.4.7. AI-Driven Threat Detection Tools

Artificial intelligence (AI) can greatly improve detection capabilities by utilizing machine learning algorithms in specialized tools. Large volumes of data, such as logs, network traffic, and code repositories, can be analyzed by these tools to find patterns and anomalies that might point to security flaws or risks.

AI-powered solutions are able to instantly notify security teams of any activity and monitor it continuously. We'll examine a few cutting-edge AI-driven solutions below, many of which offer strong API analysis and security features and can assist in identifying and resolving security issues.

8.4.7.1. Panoptica

Panoptica uses AI and graph-based technologies to prioritize and manage risks in multi-cloud environments. It offers all-inclusive API security solutions, such as risk prioritization to concentrate on the most serious threats, real-time protection via API scanning and fuzz testing, and graph-based analysis to spot departures from typical behavior. For enterprises that operate in multi-cloud environments, Panoptica is especially helpful because it improves accuracy and resilience in protecting various ecosystems.

8.4.7.2. Akamai-API Security

Machine learning algorithms are used by Akamai-API Security to track activity over time, spot irregularities, and pinpoint possible threats. By quickly identifying and addressing risks, it helps organizations maintain a secure API environment. It offers comprehensive insights into usage patterns and security vulnerabilities. It is perfect for companies that need to guarantee API security through ongoing monitoring and in-depth usage pattern analysis.

8.4.7.3. Aptori

The AI-driven application security testing tool Aptori was created especially with API security in mind. It increases the efficacy of security testing by utilizing semantic reasoning technology. Before an application's production release, developers can thoroughly examine and identify any flaws in the business logic of the application thanks to Aptori's AI-powered platform, which can simulate user behavior and create test scenarios for every possible API usage sequence. Because of this, Aptori is especially useful for developers who need to thoroughly test every API to make sure there are no vulnerabilities before release.

8.4.7.4. Traceable AI

AI is used by traceable AI to keep an eye on activities, spot irregularities, and pinpoint possible threats. By issuing security severity warnings, it assists organizations in setting priorities for remediation efforts. Unusual patterns in API usage are recognized by traceable AI, which also highlights the most important vulnerabilities and creates thorough documentation for problems that are found. For businesses looking to improve their capacity to identify and address API security risks, this tool is extremely helpful.

8.4.7.5. Salt Security

AI and machine learning are used by Salt Security to recognize and reduce security threats. Real-time monitoring and insights into API usage patterns are offered by the platform. Its features include attack severity ranking to rank threats according to severity, user intent detection to distinguish between benign and malicious activities, and a fast investigation mode to identify the most malicious attack events. Businesses that need to lower false positives and guarantee accurate detection of real threats should consider Salt Security.

8.4.7.6. 42Crunch

42Crunch provides an AI-powered platform for activity analysis, anomaly detection, and risk identification. Continuous security is ensured throughout the development lifecycle by integrating it into workflows for development. The platform offers security severity warnings to notify users of critical vulnerabilities, comprehensive API inventory and analysis, and API cataloging. For development teams that need to monitor security issues continuously and keep a secure development environment, 42Crunch is a great option.

8.4.7.7. Cequence Security

AI is used by Cequence Security to detect and reduce security threats. Real-time monitoring and insights into API usage patterns are provided by the platform. It includes a feature called Unified API Protection (UAP), which combines API discovery, monitoring, and security. Additionally, it offers custom security testing to customize security test plans to specific business needs and machine learning-driven threat detection (ML-driven security testing) to identify and neutralize threats. Cequence Security works especially well for enterprises that need to maintain strong security protocols and guard against sophisticated API attacks.

8.4.7.8. Darktrace

Darktrace provides a full range of AI-powered security solutions that are intended to detect and reduce security threats. Their platform provides real-time threat intelligence, analyzes network traffic, and looks for anomalies using machine learning. Advanced threat detection, automated reaction, and ongoing monitoring are some of Darktrace's AI features that offer protection against a variety of online threats. Through proactive threat mitigation and comprehensive insights into potential vulnerabilities, the platform assists organizations in maintaining a strong security posture. For enterprises that require in-depth analysis of network activity and up-to-date threat intelligence, Darktrace is extremely helpful.

REFERENCES

1. Abadi, M., Barham, P., Chen, J., Chen, Z., Davis, A., Dean, J., & Kudlur, M. (2016). TensorFlow: A system for large-scale machine learning. In *12th USENIX Symposium on Operating Systems Design and Implementation (OSDI 16)* (pp. 265–283).
2. Anderson, H. S., & Kharkar, A. (2019). *Machine Learning for Cybersecurity Cookbook: Over 80 Recipes to Get Smarter with the Latest Techniques in Cyber Security* (2nd ed.). Packt Publishing Ltd.
3. Apruzzese, G., Colajanni, M., Ferretti, L., Guido, A., & Marchetti, M. (2018). On the effectiveness of machine and deep learning for cybersecurity. In *2018 10th International Conference on Cyber Conflict (CyCon)* (pp. 371–390). https://doi.org/10.23919/CYCON.2018.8405026.
4. Bhattacharya, A. A., & Kalita, J. K. (2017). A survey of network anomaly detection techniques. *Journal of Network and Computer Applications, 83*, 104–120.
5. Buczak, A. L., & Guven, E. (2016). A survey of data mining and machine learning methods for cybersecurity intrusion detection. *IEEE Communications Surveys & Tutorials, 18*(2), 1153–1176. https://doi.org/10.1109/COMST.2015.2494502.
6. Chio, C., & Freeman, D. (2018). *Machine Learning and Security: Protecting Systems with Data and Algorithms*. O'Reilly Media. ISBN: 978-1491979907.
7. Goodfellow, I., Bengio, Y., & Courville, A. (2016). *Deep Learning* (Adaptive Computation and Machine Learning series). MIT Press.
8. Goodman, B., & Raghavan, V. (2017). Why machine learning is the future of cybersecurity. *Harvard Business Review*. Retrieved from: https://hbr.org/2017/05/why-machine-learning-is-the-future-of-cybersecurity (accessed on 9 October 2024).
9. Huang, J., & Ling, Z. (2019). *Adversarial Machine Learning: Foundations, Theories, and Methods*. CRC Press.
10. Kim, H. C., & Suresh, M. (2018). *Practical Machine Learning for Computer Security*. Packt Publishing Ltd.
11. Kolias, C., Kambourakis, G., Stavrou, A., & Voas, J. (2017). DDoS in the IoT: Mirai and other botnets. *Computer, 50*(7), 80–84.
12. Kumar, S. (2016). Credit Risk Modeling with Big Data Analytics: Regulatory compliance and data analytics in credit risk modeling. *International Journal of Transcontinental Discoveries*, *3*(1), 33–39.
13. Kumar, S. (2021). The role of deep learning in enhancing threat intelligence.

Security Magazine. Retrieved from: https://www.securitymagazine.com/articles/95037-the-role-of-deep-learning-in-enhancing-threat-intelligence (accessed on 9 October 2024).

14. LeCun, Y., Bengio, Y., & Hinton, G. (2015). Deep learning. *Nature, 521*(7553), 436–444.
15. Marr, B. (2018). How AI and machine learning are transforming cybersecurity. *Forbes*. Retrieved from: https://www.forbes.com/sites/bernardmarr/2018/09/17/how-ai-and-machine-learning-are-transforming-cybersecurity/ (accessed on 9 October 2024).
16. McCallie Jr., R. (2020). *Introduction to Cybersecurity for Non-Technical Managers*. Springer.
17. Nagaraj, B. K., Manikandan, et al. (2021). Predictive modeling of environmental impact on non-communicable diseases and neurological disorders through different machine learning approaches. *Biomedical Signal Processing and Control, 29*.
18. Pala, S. K. (2017). Advance analytics for reporting and creating dashboards with tools like SSIS, Visual Analytics, and Tableau. *International Journal of Operations and Production Engineering (IJOPE), 5*(2), 34–39. Available at: https://ijope.com/index.php/home/article/view/109 (accessed on 9 October 2024).
19. Pala, S. K. (2021). Databricks analytics: Empowering data processing, machine learning, and real-time analytics. *Eduzone: International Peer Reviewed/Refereed Multidisciplinary Journal, 10*(1), 76–82. Retrieved from: https://www.eduzonejournal.com/index.php/eiprmj/article/view/556 (accessed on 9 October 2024).
20. Papernot, N., McDaniel, P., Sinha, A., & Wellman, M. (2018). SoK: Towards the science of security and privacy in machine learning. *arXiv preprint arXiv:1802.06285*.
21. *Paul, S. L. (2016). International Journal of Transcontinental Discoveries*. Retrieved from: https://internationaljournals.org/index.php/ijtd/article/view/97 (accessed on 9 October 2024).
22. Russomanno, D. J., & Oliveira, J. M. (2020). *Reinforcement Learning Algorithms and Applications in Cyber Security*. Springer.
23. Sari, A. (2019). Artificial intelligence and machine learning in cybersecurity. In *Cyber Security and Threats: Concepts, Methodologies, Tools, and Applications* (pp. 1–23). IGI Global. https://doi.org/10.4018/978-1-5225-7347-0.ch001.
24. Sculley, D., Holt, G., Golovin, D., Davydov, E., Phillips, T., Ebner, D., &

Young, M. (2015). Hidden technical debt in machine learning systems. In *Proceedings of the 28th International Conference on Neural Information Processing Systems–Volume 2* (pp. 2503–2511). ISBN: 978-1510829182.

25. Shen, C., & Zhang, T. (2019). Deep learning-based intrusion detection system for advanced persistent threats. In *2019 IEEE International Conference on Intelligence and Security Informatics (ISI)* (pp. 70–75). https://doi.org/10.1109/ISI.2019.8823355.
26. Sommer, R., & Paxson, V. (2010). Outside the closed world: On using machine learning for network intrusion detection. In *2010 IEEE Symposium on Security and Privacy* (pp. 305–316). https://doi.org/10.1109/SP.2010.25.
27. Vyas, B. (2021). Ensuring data quality and consistency in AI systems through Kafka-based data governance. *Eduzone: International Peer Reviewed/Refereed Multidisciplinary Journal, 10*(1), 59–62.
28. Vyas, B. (2022). Ethical implications of generative AI in art and the media. *International Journal for Multidisciplinary Research (IJFMR), 4*(4). E-ISSN: 2582-2160.
29. Vyas, B. (2022). Integrating Kafka Connect with machine learning platforms for seamless data movement. *International Journal of New Media Studies: International Peer Reviewed Scholarly Indexed Journal, 9*(1), 13–17.
30. Vyas, B. (2022). Optimizing data ingestion and streaming for AI workloads: A Kafka-centric approach. *International Journal of Multidisciplinary Innovation and Research Methodology, 1*(1), 66–70. ISSN: 2960-2068.

CHAPTER 9

AUTOMATED THREAT INTELLIGENCE MANAGEMENT

Contents

INTRODUCTION

Threat intelligence management is the methodical gathering, examination, and sharing of data regarding possible risks and threats to an organization's cybersecurity. It includes procedures and tools for obtaining information from multiple sources, including dark web surveillance, open-source intelligence, and internal security instruments. After that, this data is examined to find new threats, weak points, and attack trends. Threat intelligence provides insights that are used to improve security posture, guide decision-making, and proactively reduce risks. Organizations can fortify their defenses, stay ahead of cyberthreats, and fend off potential cyberattacks with the help of effective threat intelligence management.

9.1. THREAT INTELLIGENCE MANAGEMENT

Your tactical advantage in combating cyberattacks is threat intelligence management. It involves putting insights into practice to safeguard the digital assets of your company. This section will guide you through the essential components of threat intelligence management, from data collection to actionable defense, assisting you in maintaining a proactive posture against cyber risks. But what does this entail, and how can it be effectively executed?

9.1.1. Threat Intelligence Management Definition

Threat intelligence management is essentially the methodical gathering, examination, and distribution of data regarding possible cyberthreats and risks to a company. It is a methodical process that entails the painstaking gathering, evaluating, and sharing of data about possible risks and cyberthreats to an organization.

Threat intelligence data is used by security teams to anticipate and neutralize cybercriminals. However, there are obstacles along the way. One of the biggest challenges is the overwhelming amount of threat data from various sources and formats. To overcome this, methods and tools that can separate meaningful insights from noise must be used.

Proactive risk mitigation is made easier and decision-making is informed by cyber threat intelligence. Cyber threat intelligence, as used here, is the process of obtaining and evaluating data regarding possible dangers to the digital assets of a company. The process of managing threat intelligence, which includes the threat intelligence lifecycle, helps organizations navigate digital threats and establish a safe online presence.

9.1.2. The Three Pillars of Threat Intelligence Management

The cornerstones of threat intelligence management support the structure's resilience to threats, much like the foundation of a secure system. The following series of factors support this stronghold of cybersecurity are:

- strategic planning;
- data collection;
- analysis;
- the creation of actionable insights.

Every component is essential to the integrity of the fortress.

We'll dissect how each of this system's essential parts functions to repel online attacks as we examine each one in detail.

9.1.2.1. Structuring the Planning Phase

The plan for our defense is created during the planning stage. Here, goals are established, influencing the kind of information gathered and the overall path of the threat intelligence management procedure. The architect uses closed-ended questions as a tool to carefully and focusedly shape the information needs. These inquiries serve as the basis for both the gathering and use of intelligence. The foundation for a successful intelligence management operation is established during this phase, guaranteeing that the later stages are constructed on a strong and clear basis.

9.1.2.2. Optimizing Data Collection Tactics

Multifaceted and adaptable data collection strategies are necessary for effective threat intelligence. These consist of specialized monitoring services, internal security alerts, and open-source intelligence (X. Liao, et al., 2016). The canvas is further expanded by tools like our own Intelligence Graph, which keeps an eye on less obvious areas like the dark web and looks for minute indications of data leaks and human error. Since new threats are always emerging, it is imperative to stay informed and flexible in response to the changing threat landscape.

9.1.2.3. Enhancing Analysis for Actionable Intelligence

Raw data that has been gathered is examined to provide actionable threat intelligence. This entails weeding out the unnecessary and analyzing the environment and circumstances that breed dangers. By analyzing this data, a cohesive story that highlights possible dangers and establishes the highest priority courses of action can be told.

Equipped with the knowledge gleaned from this threat intelligence analysis, proactive threat hunting improves detection capabilities and identifies sophisticated threats, such as fileless malware, that more conventional approaches might miss.

9.1.3. Building an Adaptive Threat Intelligence Platform

Security experts plan their defenses from a command center provided by a strong threat intelligence platform. It offers:

- Centralized collection of threat data;
- Singular source of truth for security investigations;
- Enhanced visibility across the attack surface;
- Aggregation and operationalization of intelligence;
- Integration with security team workflows for optimal utilization of threat intelligence platforms.

In order to strengthen collective response strategies, collaboration is also essential. Secure platforms facilitate real-time sharing and discussion of threat intelligence. Organizations are able to react swiftly and precisely to new threats because of the platforms' ability to balance people, procedures, and technology.

9.1.4. Streamlining Threat Intelligence Data Processing

The operational efficiency of processing threat intelligence data has increased dramatically with the introduction of automation and artificial intelligence. Automated platforms find patterns in large datasets and add intelligence to alerts by offering context and metadata.

Once a laborious and manual process, the normalization and prioritization of threat data can now be customized with minimal human involvement to meet a company's unique security requirements. By analyzing text-based data and applying reasoning algorithms to generate well-informed recommendations, machine learning and artificial intelligence (AI) further improve decision-making. To guarantee that the automated systems stay in line with the changing threat landscape, analysts continue to be crucial, managing the scoring and prioritization process.

9.1.5. Integrating Threat Intelligence Across the Security Posture

It is ensured that intelligence is not only gathered but also actively used to strengthen the digital battlements by integrating threat intelligence throughout an organization's security posture. Security teams are able to improve the efficacy of security measures and increase efficiency through automated actions that are based on threat intelligence.

- Respond to threats with unprecedented speed;
- Identify critical alerts that might be missed;
- Reduce response efforts and delay;
- Decrease the risk of successful attacks.

Beyond incident response, threat intelligence is also used to identify vulnerabilities, inform security strategies, and match security policies to the threat actor's current TTPs. Having a single, integrated threat intelligence platform serves as the cornerstone for improved workflows, faster response times, and departmental collaboration.

9.1.6. Tactical Approaches to Threat Actor Profiling

Half the fight is won when one understands the opposition. Threat actor profiling using a tactical approach digs deep into adversaries' minds to identify their TTPs in order to predict and thwart potential attacks. Security teams can strengthen their defenses by using tactical threat intelligence to customize defensive postures and security practices to their unique technology environments. This is achieved by providing detailed information on threat actors, malware, vulnerabilities, and behaviors. Organizations that possess this strategic knowledge are better equipped to modify their security protocols in response to new threats and to keep up a strong defense against even the most determined attackers.

9.1.7. Proactive Defense: From Threat Hunting to Incident Response

The art of anticipation, or being ready for attacks before they happen, is proactive defense. The development of preventative measures and quick detection are accelerated by threat intelligence management. This proactive approach is strengthened by AI-driven systems, which use predictive analytics to identify possible threats and trigger automated reactions.

The role of threat hunting is crucial, as it:

- Scours the digital landscape for indicators of compromise (IOCs);
- Sets the stage for an efficient and focused incident response;
- Enables faster action;
- Feeds back into strengthening security measures;
- Reduces the time adversaries remain undetected.

Maintaining a strong security posture is made possible by the invaluable insights obtained through threat hunting.

9.1.7.1. The Impact of Threat Intelligence Reports

Just as important as gathering threat intelligence is disseminating it. Using tailored strategies when creating threat intelligence reports guarantees that technical staff or executives will find them interesting. The clarity and efficacy of the intelligence shared are maximized through secure communication channels and a variety of formats that accommodate diverse preferences.

A culture of informed proactivity is fostered by keeping stakeholders informed and involved through regular training initiatives and updates. This makes every employee in the organization a watchful sentinel against cyber threats.

9.1.8. Leveraging External Expertise for Enhanced Threat Visibility

Sometimes, the perimeter of one's stronghold opens up to reveal a wider range of threat intelligence. Outside cybersecurity experts increase the visibility of security teams and provide defense against ever-more-advanced cyberthreats. Their profound comprehension of the dynamic threat landscape enables them to proficiently detect weaknesses and strengthen an organization's security protocols. These professionals can optimize the use, interpretation, and implementation of threat intelligence as a member of security operations teams, improving business operations and bolstering customer confidence (M. Verma et al., 2018).

9.1.9. Adapting to the Evolving Cyber Threat Landscape

It's critical to adjust to the constantly shifting landscape of cyber threats. Recognizing and reacting to the most recent CVEs and threats requires constant monitoring and updating threat intelligence management strategies. Lack of knowledge about current cybersecurity trends can expose systems, making them more inviting to cybercriminals searching for a simple target. To guarantee that their defenses against the threat of cyberattacks never weaken, companies must thus make a commitment to the ongoing development of their defenses.

9.1.9.1. The Role of the Community in Threat Intelligence

There is strength in unity. The community of cybersecurity experts is a powerful ally in the fight against cyberattacks. Through the exchange of threat intelligence within the broader security ecosystem, organizations enhance their ability to effectively mitigate threats. Collaboration lowers human error, a major source of cybersecurity threats, and improves the identification and mitigation of security risks.

While an isolated strategy may result in blind spots, a cooperative approach guarantees complete visibility and a strong defense against vulnerabilities that are missed.

9.2. THE BEST PRACTICES FOR STORING AND MANAGING THREAT INTELLIGENCE DATA

In order for incident response teams to identify, evaluate, and react to cyberattacks, threat intelligence data is essential. But gathering, keeping, and managing this data can be difficult, particularly when there are a lot of different sources, a lot of data, and ever-changing threats. You will discover some best practices for securely and efficiently storing and handling threat intelligence data in this section.

9.2.1. Define Your Objectives and Requirements

Determine your goals and needs before you begin collecting, storing, and handling threat intelligence data. These questions will help you determine the best storage and management solutions for your threat intelligence data. What are the objectives and scope of your incident response program? What kinds and sources of threat intelligence data do you need? How will you use and share this data with your stakeholders? How will you measure and evaluate the quality and value of this data?

9.2.2. Choose a Suitable Storage Format and Location

Depending on your requirements and preferences, threat intelligence data can be stored in a variety of formats and locations. Structured data (like XML, JSON, or STIX), unstructured data (like text, photos, or videos), and hybrid data (like CSV or PDF) are a few common formats. Cloud storage, databases, and local or network drives are a few examples of common locations. It is advisable that you select a storage format and location that satisfy your needs regarding compatibility, scalability, accessibility, and security. For instance, you should use a secure and encrypted storage location if you need to store confidential or classified data. A quick and dependable storage location is what you should use if you frequently need to access or query your data.

9.2.3. Implement a Data Governance Framework

The policies, practices, roles, and duties that specify how you keep and handle your threat intelligence data are called a data governance framework. It assists you in guaranteeing the accuracy, consistency, safety, and conformance of your data. Data ownership, classification, retention, disposal, backup, recovery, encryption, auditing, and reporting are just a few of the topics that should be covered by a data governance framework. A data governance framework should be put into place that is in line with your organization's and industry's best practices, standards, and objectives.

9.2.4. Use a Threat Intelligence Platform

Software that assists you in organizing and managing your threat intelligence data is called a threat intelligence platform (TIP). It enables you to gather data from multiple sources and formats, combine it, normalize it, enhance it, analyze it, and visualize it. Additionally, it makes it possible for you to integrate your data with other programs and platforms, like incident response platforms (IRP), endpoint detection and response (EDR), and security information and event management (SIEM). A TIP can improve the usability and value of your data while automating and streamlining your data management and storage procedures.

9.2.5. Update and Validate Your Data Regularly

Data from threat intelligence is dynamic. Over time, it shifts and changes as new threats appear, current threats change, and former threats vanish. As a result, in order to guarantee the timeliness, accuracy, and relevance of your data, you must constantly update and validate it. Keep an eye out for updates and changes in your data sources and feeds, and make the appropriate adjustments to your data. Additionally, you should check your data for any mistakes, irregularities, or inconsistencies and fix them as soon as you find them. Your incident response efforts may be jeopardized by out-of-date, erroneous, or misleading data, which can be avoided by routinely updating and validating your data.

9.2.6. Share and Collaborate with Your Peers

Data pertaining to threat intelligence should not be handled and stored separately. It is intended to be shared and worked on in conjunction with colleagues, researchers, security analysts, and other incident response teams. Gaining additional insights, viewpoints, and comments on your data can be facilitated by sharing and working together with your peers. Additionally, it can assist you in maximizing the combined expertise and experience of your peers to raise the caliber and value of your data. Using safe and reliable channels, like threat intelligence sharing platforms (TISP), threat intelligence communities (TIC), or TIPs, you should share and work together with your peers.

9.3. AUTOMATED THREAT INTELLIGENCE: HOW IT HELPS SECURE ORGANIZATIONS

In this infinite cybersecurity landscape, there is an ongoing arms race between cybercriminals and security defenders. The need for a proactive and clever defense strategy has grown more critical as cyber threats adapt and change at an alarming rate. This is the main moment for threat intelligence.

Threat intelligence is the proactive collection, examination, and sharing of data about possible cyberthreats, giving organizations the early warning they need to strengthen their defenses. Is threat intelligence sufficient, though?

The dynamic and sophisticated nature of contemporary cyberattacks frequently renders manual approaches to threat intelligence inadequate. We must investigate automated threat intelligence solutions that change how businesses detect, evaluate, and handle cyberthreats in light of this reality.

9.3.1. Automated Threat Intelligence

The process of gathering and analyzing data about possible or existing risks to an organization's cybersecurity is known as threat intelligence. It's a crucial component of contemporary security tactics, offering thorough insights into the possible risks associated with stalking in the digital sphere. It also covers the methods, instruments, and procedures used to recognize, evaluate, and address security risks. Security teams can customize their defensive tactics by using the information that threat intelligence teams provide them about the characteristics of threats.

9.3.2. The Urgent Need for Automation in Threat Intelligence

Because of the overwhelming amount and intricacy of cyberthreats, as well as the quick development of attack methods, traditional approaches find it difficult to be as flexible and responsive. Despite its indisputable value, manual threat intelligence collection and analysis methods are frequently hampered by the following issues:

- **Limited IOC Volume Handling:** It is difficult for security teams to handle and evaluate a high number of IOCs efficiently. Due to this restriction, organizations are more susceptible to malicious activity that goes unnoticed and makes it more difficult to identify and mitigate potential threats.

- **The Noise Dilemma:** Envision conversing in a packed room while everyone is yelling at the same time. Threat intelligence is not any different from the rest of the noisy digital world. Security teams find it challenging to differentiate between genuine threats and false positives due to the constant barrage of unnecessary information and repeated alerts.
- **The Correlation Conundrum:** Even when pertinent threat intelligence is gathered, it is frequently dispersed among various formats and sources. It can take a lot of time and effort to correlate and prioritize this data, which makes it difficult for security teams to stay on top of the constantly changing threat landscape. It's similar to attempting to assemble a puzzle without the necessary parts and without a clear idea of how it should look.
- **The Silos of Secrecy:** Although threat intelligence is a global concern, it is frequently compartmentalized within specific organizations. This lack of cooperation and sharing impedes our ability to understand threats as a group and reduces the potency of our defenses.
- **Lack of Integration with Security Infrastructure:** Winning half the fight requires gathering and evaluating threat intelligence. Making this intelligence actionable and integrating it into security infrastructure is the real challenge. Threat intelligence is useless without adequate integration; it is just another piece of data that cannot be used to build strong defenses.
- **The Manual Manner of Actioning:** Using threat intelligence manually can be laborious and prone to mistakes. This makes organizations more open to attacks and delays the deployment of security countermeasures.

9.3.3. How Automated Threat Intelligence Drives Security Success

- **Scalability:** Large volumes of data can be processed and analyzed far more quickly by automated systems than by manual ones. In the context of cybersecurity, where there is an overwhelming volume of threats and data that needs to be analyzed, this is vital. Organizations can scale their threat intelligence capabilities with automation to keep up with the ever-intricate threat landscape.

- **Increased SecOps Efficiency:** SecOps teams can defend their organizations from cyber threats to a greater extent thanks to automated threat intelligence. It frees up analyst time for more strategic endeavors like security planning and proactive threat hunting.
- **Better Prioritization of Threats:** Automated threat intelligence systems are capable of evaluating threats according to preset standards for both relevance and seriousness. As a result, security teams are able to concentrate their response efforts on the most serious and pressing threats. This guarantees that resources are allocated where they are most needed while also strengthening the security posture overall.

In addition to these benefits, automated threat intelligence helps organizations to:

- Reduce the time to detect and respond to threats;
- Improve the accuracy of threat detection;
- Reduce the risk of false positives;
- Improve compliance with security regulations.

9.4. AUTOMATION OF THREAT INTELLIGENCE LIFECYCLE

The framework for organizing and converting unstructured security data into decision-supporting, actionable intelligence is provided by the threat intelligence lifecycle. Although there are numerous iterations of the intelligence lifecycle, they all have the same goal and essential components. The procedure directs the cybersecurity team in the development and implementation of a successful threat intelligence plan. The dynamic nature of cyber threats makes developing a threat intelligence strategy difficult because organizations need to quickly adjust to the changing threat landscape. Teams can respond to sophisticated threats and optimize resources by using the threat intelligence lifecycle framework.

Analytical methods developed over many years by military and government organizations serve as the foundation for threat intelligence. The six distinct phases that comprise the "intelligence cycle" are the focus of traditional intelligence.

- Direction;
- Collection;
- Processing;

- Analysis;
- Dissemination;
- Feedback.

The six phases are aligned with threat intelligence, as seen in Figure 9.1.

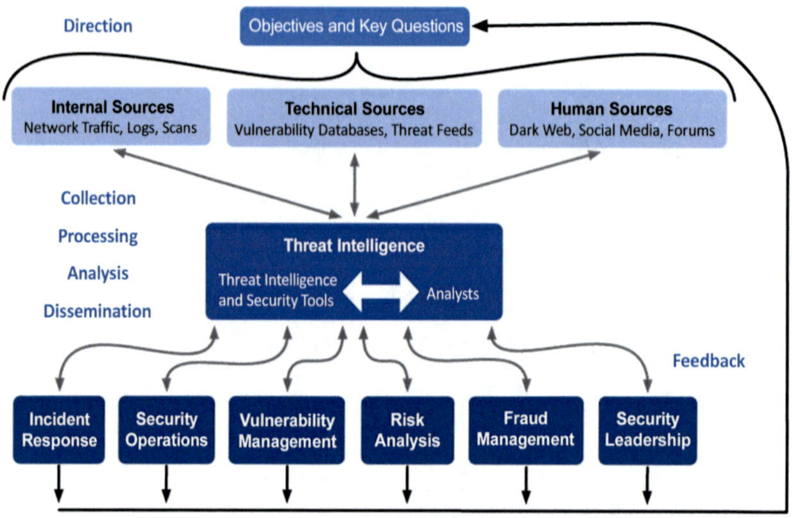

Figure 9.1. *Threat intelligence and the six phases of the intelligence lifecycle.*

Source: https://cms.recordedfuture.com/uploads/threat_intelligence_lifecycle_phases_1_dd3b3df8c3.png.

9.4.1. Direction

Setting objectives for the threat intelligence program takes place during the direction phase of the lifecycle. This calls for comprehending and expressing:

- The information assets and business processes that need to be protected;
- The potential impacts of losing those assets or interrupting those processes;
- The types of threat intelligence that the security organization requires to protect assets and respond to emerging threats;
- Priorities about what to protect.

Following the identification of high-level intelligence requirements, a company can create inquiries that focus information needs into specific requirements. One reasonable question to ask, for instance, if one's objective is to identify potential enemies, would be, "Which threat actors on underground forums are actively soliciting data concerning our organization?"

9.4.2. Collection

Information is gathered through the process of collection in order to fulfill the most crucial intelligence needs. Information can be gathered naturally in a number of ways, such as:

- Pulling metadata and logs from internal networks and security devices;
- Subscribing to threat data feeds from industry organizations and cybersecurity vendors;
- Holding conversations and targeted interviews with knowledgeable sources;
- Scanning open source news and blogs (a common OSINT practice);
- Scraping and harvesting websites and forums;
- Infiltrating closed sources such as dark web forums.

Usually, a combination of raw data—such as malware signatures or compromised credentials on a paste site—and completed intelligence information—such as intelligence reports from cybersecurity experts and vendors—will be included in the data collection.

9.4.3. Processing

The process of converting gathered data into a format that the organization can use is known as processing. Nearly all of the raw data that is gathered needs to be processed, either by machines or people. Various methods of collection frequently call for various processing techniques. It could be necessary to rank, correlate, deconflict, and verify human reports.

An illustration could be taking IP addresses out of a report provided by a security vendor and putting them into a CSV file that can be imported into an SIEM (security information and event management) program. Processing in a more technical context might entail taking indicators out of emails, adding to them with additional data, and then interacting with endpoint security tools to automate blocking.

9.4.4. Analysis

The human process of analysis transforms processed data into knowledge that can guide choices. Depending on the situation, decisions may need to be made about how to improve security controls, whether to look into possible new threats, what steps to take right away to stop an attack, or how much money to spend on extra security.

Particularly crucial is the format in which the data is provided. Information should not be gathered, processed, and then delivered in a format that the decision maker cannot comprehend or utilize. This is both wasteful and useless. To communicate with non-technical leaders, for instance, your report needs to:

- Be concise (a one-page memo or a handful of slides);
- Avoid confusing and overly technical terms and jargon;
- Articulate the issues in business terms (such as direct and indirect costs and impact on reputation);
- Include a recommended course of action.

For a variety of audiences, intelligence may need to be presented in multiple formats, such as a PowerPoint presentation or a live video feed. Not every intelligence must be analyzed and reported in writing. Proficient cyber threat intelligence groups consistently furnish other security units with technical reports that offer external context concerning indicators of compromise (IOCs), malware, threat actors, vulnerabilities, and threat patterns.

9.4.5. Dissemination

Delivering the completed intelligence output to the appropriate locations is known as dissemination. Threat intelligence can help at least six teams in the majority of cybersecurity organizations.

For each of these audiences, you need to ask:

- What threat intelligence do they need, and how can external information support their activities?
- How should the intelligence be presented to make it easily understandable and actionable for that audience?
- How often should we provide updates and other information?
- Through what media should the intelligence be disseminated?
- How should we follow up if they have questions?

9.4.6. Feedback

Understanding your overall intelligence priorities and the needs of the security teams that will be using the threat intelligence is, in our opinion, extremely important. They inform you and direct every stage of the threat intelligence lifecycle with their needs.

- What types of data to collect;
- How to process and enrich the data to turn it into useful information;
- How to analyze the information and present it as actionable threat intelligence;
- To whom each type of intelligence must be disseminated, how quickly it needs to be disseminated, and how fast to respond to questions.

To ensure that you comprehend each group's needs and that you adapt as their priorities and requirements change, you need regular feedback.

9.4.7. Tools and People

Tools are necessary to support and expedite analysis as well as automate the phases of the intelligence lifecycle that involve gathering, processing, and disseminating information. Analysts will never have time for actual analysis if they are not equipped with the proper tools and must dedicate all of their time to the mechanical parts of these tasks.

Most mature threat intelligence groups leverage two types of tools:

- Threat intelligence solutions that are designed to collect, process, and analyze all types of threat data from internal, technical, and human sources.
- Existing security tools, such as SIEMs and security analytics tools, which collect and correlate security events and log data.

Human analysts are just as significant, if not more so. In order to interview security experts and sift through closed dark web forums, you can't rely on tools. Instead, you need people to analyze and synthesize intelligence for the security organization's and management's benefit.

It is not necessary for the analysts to be part of a centralized, elite threat intelligence unit. We have seen many successful organizational structures, but someone still needs to take an organization-wide view of the threat intelligence function, make decisions about resources and priorities, and monitor progress. A small group within the incident response (IR) or security operations center (SOC) organizations, or a central group with specialized threat intelligence analysts, could be your options. As an alternative, individuals within the various cybersecurity teams may be in charge of doing threat intelligence analysis on behalf of their peers.

9.5. THREAT INTELLIGENCE FOR SECURITY OPERATIONS

The vast amount of alerts generated by the networks they monitor has taken over most Security Operations Center (SOC) teams. These alerts require too much time to prioritize, and many go uninvestigated. Analysts who experience "alert fatigue" may not give alerts the serious consideration they merit. Threat intelligence offers a solution to address a number of these issues. It can be used, among other things, to expedite triage, reduce false alarms, and streamline incident analysis.

9.5.1. Responsibilities of the SOC Team

On paper, the responsibilities of the SOC team seem simple:

- Monitor for potential threats;
- Detect suspicious network activity;
- Contain active threats;
- Remediate using available technology.

The SOC team looks into any suspicious events and collaborates with other security teams to lessen the attack's impact and severity. As seen in Figure 9.2, you can compare the roles and responsibilities of emergency services teams responding to 911 calls to those within a SOC.

Stage	Role	Responsibilities
Triage	Operator (911 Center) Security Analyst (SOC)	Determine the relevance and urgency of each incoming alert. Decide if the alert is legitimate and should be escalated.
First Response	First Responder (911) Incident Responder (SOC)	Determine the scope of the incident. Identify affected and vulnerable systems. Recommend actions to contain the effects.
Investigation	Detective (911) Threat Hunter (SOC)	Determine root causes and weaknesses in defenses. Recommend actions to prevent recurrences.

Figure 9.2. *The roles and responsibilities of emergency services teams and SOC teams are similar.*

Source: Chris Pace. The Threat Intelligence Handbook. CyberEdge. ISBN: 978-0-9990354-6-7.

9.5.2. The Overwhelming Volume of Alerts

The majority of businesses have upgraded their networks with new threat detection technologies over the last few years. Every tool that detects unusual or suspicious activity sounds the alarm. These tools have the potential to produce a symphony of security alerts when combined. Security analysts can't possibly look through, sort through, and look into every one of these alerts on their own. They frequently ignore alerts, chase false positives, and make mistakes as a result of alert fatigue.

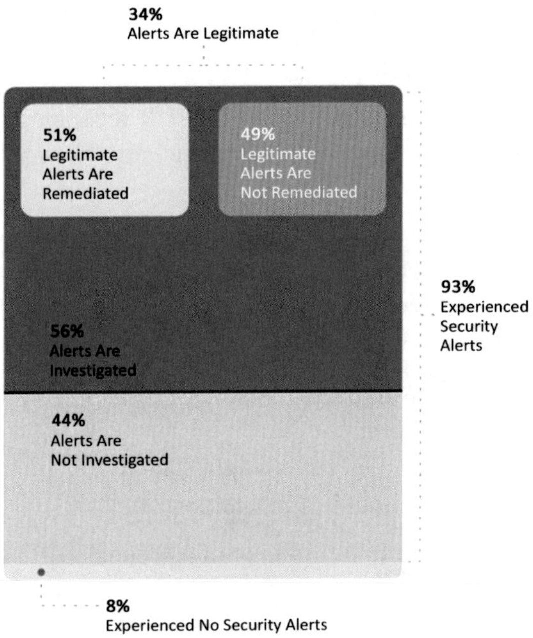

Figure 9.3. *Many threat alerts are not investigated or remediated.*

Source: Chris Pace. The Threat Intelligence Handbook. CyberEdge. ISBN: 978-0-9990354-6-7.

Studies validate the extent of these issues. When asked what their largest security operations challenge was, 35% of cybersecurity professionals cited "keeping up with the volume of security alerts," according to industry analyst firm ESG. According to SIEM provider Exabeam's 2018 State of the SOC report, 45% of professionals who work in SOCs believe they are understaffed, and 63% of those professionals believe they could use two to ten more employees. According to Cisco's 2018 Security Capabilities Benchmark study, only 56%

of security alerts that organizations receive on a daily basis can be investigated, and only 34% of those alerts that are investigated are found to be legitimate (Figure 9.3).

9.5.3. Context Is King

Fundamentally, threat intelligence for the SOC is about adding external data and context to internal alerts so that decisions can be made based on risk. Context is essential for both scoping and containing incidents, as well as for quick triage.

9.5.3.1. Triage Requires Lots of Context

The majority of a typical SOC analyst's workday is devoted to handling alerts from internal security systems, like SIEM or EDR technologies. Internal data sources are essential for spotting potentially dangerous network activity or data breaches.

Regretfully, it is frequently challenging to understand this data on its own. Gathering pertinent data (context) from a range of internal system logs, network devices, security tools, and external threat databases is necessary to evaluate if an alert is pertinent and urgent (Figure 9.4). It takes a long time to search through all of these threat data sources to find the background information on each alert.

Figure 9.4. *Key aspects of security monitoring and internal sources of context.*

Source: Chris Pace. The Threat Intelligence Handbook. CyberEdge. ISBN: 978-0-9990354-6-7.

9.5.4. Improving the 'Time to No'

One could argue that the ability to quickly rule out false alarms is even more crucial for SOC analysts than the ability to obtain information about real threats more quickly and accurately. Threat intelligence gives SOC staff the extra details and context they need to quickly and efficiently prioritize alerts. It can save analysts hours of time spent following up on alerts based on:

- Actions that are more likely to be innocuous rather than malicious;
- Attacks that are not relevant to that enterprise;
- Attacks for which defenses and controls are already in place.

A large portion of this filtering is done automatically by certain threat intelligence solutions, which modify risk feeds to reject or downgrade alerts that don't meet organization- and industry-specific standards.

9.5.5. Beyond Triage

Threat intelligence can assist SOC teams in expediting triage and streamlining incident analysis and containment. For example, the SOC team can begin closely monitoring financial applications and focus on further evidence of that type of attack by revealing that a particular piece of malware is frequently used by cybercriminals as the first step in an attack.

9.6. HOW TO INCREASE INCIDENT RESPONSE EFFICIENCY WITH SECURITY INTELLIGENCE

Security intelligence is more important than ever for incident response (IR) teams, who are at the forefront of cyber defense, to help them cut through the noise and react swiftly to genuine threats.

A constant onslaught of poor-quality alerts from threat data feeds and across numerous, disconnected systems means too much information and not enough time to thoroughly investigate it all in security operations center (SOC) environments where minutes count.

Teams are left to struggle through mountains of redundant information and false positives in the absence of crucial context regarding which alerts represent genuine security incidents. This reduces team output and causes diligent analysts to almost burn out. In actuality, false-positive rates of 50% or more affect almost half of SOC teams. Additionally, the typical organization loses 424 to 286 hours a week just looking into false positives.

If you picture yourself spending half of your working day following leads that make you work harder and longer just to stay afloat, you can understand why security analysts frequently leave their positions within the first one to three years of employment due to exhaustion, stress, and job dissatisfaction.

The entire security organization is impacted by this reactive approach to cybersecurity and ongoing turnover. According to an ESG report, 41% of security personnel are compelled to devote an excessive amount of time to incident response, which takes away from crucial time allotted for important planning, strategy, and training initiatives.

When intelligence is used effectively, it can give security analysts the context they need to concentrate their efforts, increase their impact, and improve the effectiveness of the security team as a whole. Using security intelligence also supports teams' transition to a more proactive, holistic approach, which is essential for empowering an engaged, productive workforce and drawing in and keeping top talent.

9.6.1. Threat Intelligence for Incident Response

Perhaps the most under pressure of any security group are incident response teams. One of the causes is:

- Cyber incident volumes have increased steadily for two decades.
- Keeping up with the constantly changing threat landscape has become a significant task in and of itself. Threats have also grown more complex and difficult to analyze.
- Analysts are compelled to invest a significant amount of time in manually verifying and sharing data from various sources when responding to security incidents.
- Containment of attacks and eradication of vulnerabilities continually grows more difficult.

Because of this, incident response teams frequently face extreme time constraints and are unable to quickly contain cyber incidents.

9.6.2. Continuing Challenges

There is no denying that the volume of cyberattacks is increasing quickly, even though it is difficult to pinpoint the exact number of incidents that a typical organization experiences. SonicWall reports that just in 2017, there was an increase in malware attacks globally of over 18%. Every year, the volume of other well-liked attack vectors, like phishing and encrypted traffic, also rises noticeably. Even though preventative technologies help to some extent to alleviate this increasing pressure, incident response teams are still under tremendous additional strain due to the following four factors:

9.6.2.1. A Skills Gap

Reaction to incidents is not a security function for beginners. It includes a wide range of abilities, such as digital forensics, reverse engineering, and analysis of both static and dynamic malware. It needs analysts who are dependable and have experience in the field of handling complicated tasks under time constraints.

Over the past ten years, the much-discussed cybersecurity skills gap has steadily widened. Nearly three-quarters of security professionals say their organization is impacted by the global skills shortage, according to a 2017 ISSA research report. According to Frost and Sullivan's most recent Global Information Security Workforce Study, by 2022, there will be a 11.8 million worker skills gap.

9.6.2.2. Too Many Alerts, Too Little Time

Incident response teams receive an overwhelming volume of alerts in addition to a shortage of personnel. Security teams should anticipate logging close to 17,000 malware alerts in a typical week, according to the Ponemon Cost of Malware Containment report. For a team that works around the clock, that is more than 100 alerts every hour. And those are just the malware-related alerts.

To put these numbers into perspective, security teams may need to expend over 21,000 man-hours annually investigating false positives as a result of all these alerts. That works out to 2,625 standard eight-hour shifts just to separate false positives from false positives.

9.6.2.3. Time to Response Is Rising

There's only one result when you have an excessive number of alerts and insufficiently trained staff: it will take longer to resolve actual security incidents. A recent Verizon Data Breach Investigations Report's source data was analyzed, and the results showed that although the median time to incident detection is a respectable four hours, the median time to resolution (MTTR) is more than four days.

Naturally, cybercriminals are not limited by time in this way. The time it takes to compromise a target network once an attacker gains traction is typically measured in minutes.

9.6.2.4. A Piecemeal Approach

The majority of organizations' security teams have expanded naturally as cyber risk has increased. They have therefore implemented security procedures and technologies piecemeal and without a strategic plan.

Although this ad hoc approach is perfectly acceptable, it requires a significant amount of time from incident response teams to compile information and context from threat feeds and a range of security technologies (such as firewall logs, SIEM, EDR, and logs from security events). This endeavor considerably lengthens response times and raises the possibility of errors.

9.6.3. The Reactivity Problem

To reduce cyber risk, an alert must be prioritized, addressed, and followed up on as soon as it is flagged.

Consider a typical incident response process:

- **Incident Detection:** Receive an alert from a SIEM, EDR, or similar product;
- **Discovery:** Determine what's happened and how to respond;
- **Triage and Containment:** Take immediate actions to mitigate the threat and minimize damage;
- **Remediation:** Repair damage and remove infections;
- **Push to BAU:** Pass the incident to "business as usual" teams for final actions.

Take note of this process's reactivity. Nearly all of the work required to resolve an incident is back-loaded for the majority of organizations, which means it cannot be finished until after an alert is raised. To a certain extent, this is unavoidable, but it is not ideal when incident response teams are already having trouble finishing investigations in a timely manner.

9.6.4. Minimizing Reactivity in Incident Response

Incident response teams need to become less reactive in order to shorten response times. Prioritization and the identification of potential threats are two areas where advanced planning can be very beneficial.

9.6.4.1. Identification of Probable Threats

An incident response team can create robust, reliable procedures to address the most frequent threats if they can anticipate them. This planning avoids errors, cuts down on the amount of time the team must spend handling individual incidents, and frees up analysts to deal with emerging and unanticipated threats.

9.6.4.2. Prioritization

Every threat is not created equal. Incident response teams can better allocate their time and resources if they know which threat vectors present the highest level of risk to their organization.

9.6.5. Strengthening Incident Response with Threat Intelligence

Our conversation thus far should have made it abundantly evident that security technologies by themselves are unable to alleviate the burden on human analysts. Threat intelligence can solve many of the problems we have been examining and lessen the load on incident response teams by:

- Automatically identifying and dismissing false positive alerts;
- Enriching alerts with real-time context from across the open and dark web;
- Assembling and comparing information from internal and external data sources to identify genuine threats;
- Scoring threats according to the organization's specific needs and infrastructure.

Put differently, threat intelligence stops the flood of false positives and irrelevant alerts that normally make incident response teams' jobs so hard by giving them the precise actionable insights they need to act more quickly and effectively.

9.6.6. Essential Characteristics of Threat Intelligence for Incident Response

It's time to look at the traits of a strong threat intelligence capability and how they help incident response teams with their biggest problems.

9.6.6.1. Comprehensive

Threat intelligence needs to be automatically gathered from as many sources as possible, including open sources, technical feeds, and the dark web, in order for incident response teams to benefit from it. If not, analysts will have to carry out independent, manual research to make sure nothing significant is overlooked.

9.6.6.2. Relevant

When attempting to identify and contain incidents, it is impossible to prevent all false positives. However, incident response teams should be able to swiftly identify and eliminate false positives produced by security technologies like SIEM and EDR products with the aid of threat intelligence.

There are two categories of false positives to consider:

- Alerts that are relevant to an organization but are inaccurate or unhelpful;
- Alerts that are accurate and/or interesting but aren't relevant to the organization.

The time spent by incident response analysts could be greatly wasted by either kind. Machine learning technology is now being used in advanced threat intelligence products to automatically identify and eliminate false positives and highlight the most significant and pertinent intelligence for analysts.

9.6.6.3. Contextualized

Not every threat is the same. Certain threat alerts, even those that are pertinent, will unavoidably be more critical and urgent than others. Even if an alert comes from a single source and is accurate and pertinent, it may not be given much priority. Context is crucial because it gives important hints about which alerts are most likely to be important to your organization.

Contextual information related to an alert might include:

- Corroboration from multiple sources that the same type of alert has been associated with recent attacks;
- Confirmation that the alert has been associated with threat actors known to be active in your industry;
- A timeline showing that the alert occurred slightly before or after other events linked with attacks.

The ability to analyze multiple sources simultaneously and prioritize which alerts are most critical to a given organization is provided by modern machine learning and artificial intelligence (AI) technologies (Atluri and Horne, 2021).

9.6.6.4. Integrated

Integrating a threat intelligence system with a wide range of security tools, such as incident response and SIEM solutions, and analyzing the alerts these tools produce are some of its most important features.

- Determine whether each alert should be dismissed as a false positive;
- Score the alert according to its importance;
- Enrich the alert with valuable extra context.

Analysts will no longer need to manually compare each alert to data from various security and threat intelligence tools thanks to this integration. What's even more significant is that automated processes and integration can eliminate a great deal of false positives without requiring human analyst verification.

This capability may be the most useful piece of threat intelligence for incident response teams because of the time and frustration it saves.

9.7. HOW SECURITY INTELLIGENCE ENABLES RISK-PRIORITIZED VULNERABILITY MANAGEMENT

Your company is vulnerable to external attacks. However, since new ones appear daily, it is impossible to fix everything. Security intelligence is essential for vulnerability management teams to swiftly assess and decide between the real-world threat posed by the vulnerability and the risk of possible disruption that comes with applying a patch.

Vulnerability management and battling fires are similar in this regard. Teams are battling against the clock in both situations, and the surroundings are ever-changing. A small, contained fire can quickly engulf large territories and cause unprecedented damage, as seen by the sobering headlines about the wildfires in Australia and California recently. Tools that were effective yesterday in containing the fires might not be sufficient to contain them today.

Comparably, a common vulnerability that you've seen a lot of times could be suddenly exploited, leading to serious problems that you've never had to deal with before. Alternatively, your vulnerability management team might find ten serious vulnerabilities in a single day from your vulnerability scan, in which case they would have to decide almost immediately which ones should be patched first due to their high risk. Even though it's not possible to patch every issue, choosing the wrong priority can have disastrous results.

Teams can concentrate efforts and maximize impact by using real-time intelligence to provide the external context, such as knowing whether a vulnerability is being actively weaponized. Teams can prioritize, measure, and mitigate the risk from vulnerabilities in a much more strategic and risk-based manner when they have visibility into specific evidence that indicates a CVE is being exploited. This section, which has been simplified and edited for clarity, looks at the difficulties that exist today in addressing vulnerabilities that are based on real risk. We also look at how operational aspects of vulnerability management can be made more efficient by using risk-based intelligence to provide insights into threat actor behavior.

9.7.1. Threat Intelligence for Vulnerability Management

Although vulnerability management isn't glamorous, it is one of the few proactive approaches to organizational security that you can take. Its significance as a function cannot be emphasized enough. The secret to successful vulnerability management is to get your security teams to stop patching everything and start making decisions based on risk. This is crucial because the teams in charge of identifying vulnerable assets and deploying patches are overwhelmed by the enormous amount of vulnerabilities that are revealed each year. Making effective, risk-based decisions also requires utilizing a greater variety of threat intelligence sources.

9.7.2. The Vulnerability Problem by the Numbers

Based on analysis by analyst firm Gartner, Inc. , over the previous ten years, about 8,000 vulnerabilities were revealed annually. Only about one in eight of them were truly exploited, and the number increased very little year over year. But at the same time, there was a massive increase in the quantity of new software being used, and there was also a sharp rise in the number of threats. Put another way, despite an increase in breaches and threats over the previous ten years, very few of them were caused by newly discovered vulnerabilities. "More threats are leveraging the same small set of vulnerabilities," according to Gartner.

9.7.2.1. Zero Day Does Not Mean Top Priority

Regularly, zero-day threats garner excessive attention. But the great majority of "new" threats classified as "zero day" are really just riffs on an existing theme, taking advantage of the same vulnerabilities in slightly different ways. Furthermore, the data reveals that only approximately 0.4% of all vulnerabilities exploited over the previous ten years were actually exploited on day zero.

It follows that identifying and patching vulnerabilities unique to the software your company uses, rather than concentrating on zero-day threats, is the most efficient way to manage vulnerabilities.

9.7.2.2. Time Is of the Essence

The speed at which threat actors exploit vulnerabilities has increased. Over the past ten years, the average time between the discovery of a vulnerability and the release of an exploit into the wild has decreased from 45 days to 15 days, according to Gartner.

This has two implications:

- You have roughly two weeks to patch or remediate your systems against a new exploit.
- If you can't patch in that timeframe, you should have a plan to mitigate the damage.

According to research, there is a statistically low chance that a vulnerability will ever be exploited if it is not used within two weeks to three months of being made public. Consequently, patching "old" vulnerabilities is typically not a top priority.

Based on all of these statistics, you should focus on identifying and addressing the threats that are most likely to be used against your organization rather than trying to patch every vulnerability or even zero-day threat.

9.7.3. Assess Risk Based on Exploitability

To use an analogy, you must determine which vaccinations are essential and which are not if patching vulnerabilities to keep your network secure is similar to receiving vaccinations to protect yourself from illness. If you want to stay healthy, you might need a flu shot every season, but unless you will be exposed to yellow fever or malaria, you don't need to continue getting shots against those diseases. You must conduct research because, among a threat intelligence solution's best benefits, it pinpoints the precise vulnerabilities that pose a risk to your company and provides you with information about how likely it is that they will be exploited.

The point is illustrated in Figure 9.5. Hundreds of the thousands of vulnerabilities that have been made public so far are being used maliciously. It's also true that your environment most likely contains at least some of those vulnerabilities. However, the only people who truly need to worry about are those who fall into the middle of those two groups.

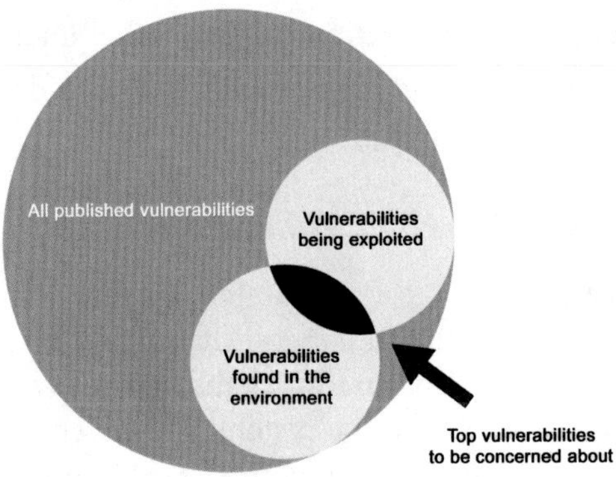

Figure 9.5. *The biggest risks are vulnerabilities that are present in your organization and currently being exploited.*

Source: Chris Pace. The Threat Intelligence Handbook. CyberEdge. ISBN: 978-0-9990354-6-7.

9.7.3.1. Severity Ratings Can Be Misleading

When managing vulnerabilities, it's common to concentrate on assigning a threat a severity level. Systems for ranking and classifying vulnerabilities, such as Common Vulnerabilities and Exposures (CVE) naming and Common Vulnerability Scoring Systems (CVSSs), do not consider the fact that threat actors may be actively exploiting vulnerabilities in your sector or geographical area at any given time. Depending only on the degree of vulnerability is akin to receiving a vaccination against the bubonic plague instead of a flu shot because the plague killed a greater number of people in the past.

9.7.4. The Genesis of Threat Intelligence: Vulnerability Databases

Vulnerability databases compile data on vulnerabilities that have been made public and assign an exploitability score. In actuality, the National Vulnerability Database (NVD) maintained by NIST was among the earliest sources of threat intelligence. It helped organizations determine whether they were likely to be impacted by centralizing information on vulnerabilities that had been disclosed. The NVD has gathered data on over 100,000 vulnerabilities over the course of more than 20 years, making it a priceless resource for information security specialists. China and Russia are among the other countries that have established vulnerability databases, following NIST's example.

However, there are two significant limitations to most vulnerability databases:

- They focus on technical exploitability rather than active exploitation.
- They are not updated fast enough to provide warning of some quickly spreading threats.

9.7.4.1. Exploitability Versus Exploitation

Virtually all of the information in vulnerability databases focuses on technical exploitability—a measure of the likelihood that a given vulnerability will be exploited to cause more or less harm to systems and networks. This is assessed in the NVD using the CVSS scoring system. However, there is a difference between technical exploitability and active exploitation. As long as you understand what the score means, CVSS base scores offer a measure that is both understandable and fairly accurate. However, a base score alone doesn't indicate whether a vulnerability is being exploited in the real world or how serious it is theoretically unless it is adjusted by a temporal score or an environmental score.

9.7.4.2. Next Week Versus Now

Timeliness is another issue with a lot of vulnerability databases. For instance, it takes an average of one week for 75% of vulnerabilities that are disclosed to surface on other websites before they do so in the NVD. As Figure 9.6 illustrates, this is a very serious issue because it hinders security teams in their race to patch before adversaries can exploit.

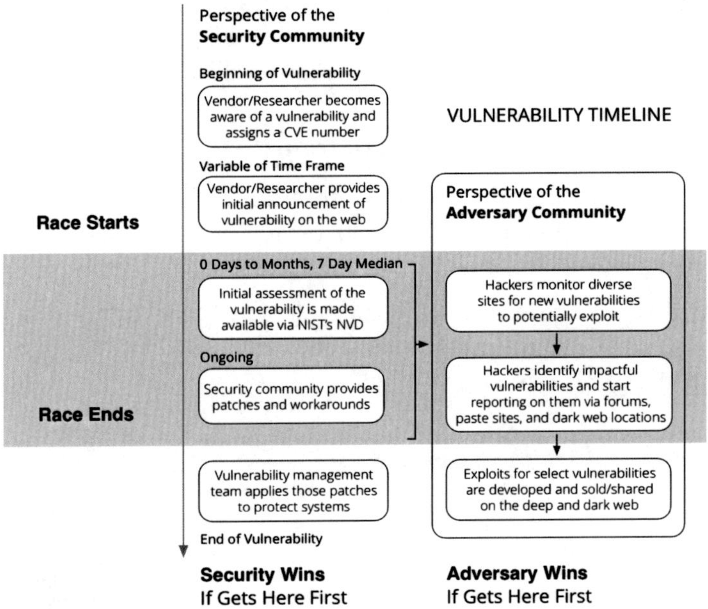

Figure 9.6. *The race between security professionals and adversaries.*

Source: Chris Pace. The Threat Intelligence Handbook. CyberEdge. ISBN: 978-0-9990354-6-7.

9.7.5. Threat Intelligence and Real Risk

Combining the following methods is the most efficient way to determine the actual risk of a vulnerability to your company.

- Internal vulnerability scanning data;
- External intelligence from a breadth of sources;
- An understanding of why threat actors are targeting certain vulnerabilities and ignoring others.

9.7.5.1. Internal Vulnerability Scanning

Nearly all vulnerability management teams scan their own systems for vulnerabilities, compare the findings with data from vulnerability databases, and use the findings to decide which vulnerabilities need to be patched. Even though we don't typically think of it that way, this is a fundamental application of operational threat intelligence.

Vulnerabilities that don't show up on your systems can be de-prioritized quite effectively with conventional scanning. Scanning, however, is insufficient on its own to reliably rank vulnerabilities that are discovered.

9.7.5.2. Risk Milestones for Vulnerabilities

Examining a vulnerability's evolution from first discovery to availability, weaponization, and commoditization in exploit kits is a useful method of determining its risk.

As the real risk crosses the milestones depicted in Figure 9.7, it increases significantly. Wide-ranging threat intelligence can show how a vulnerability is developing along this route.

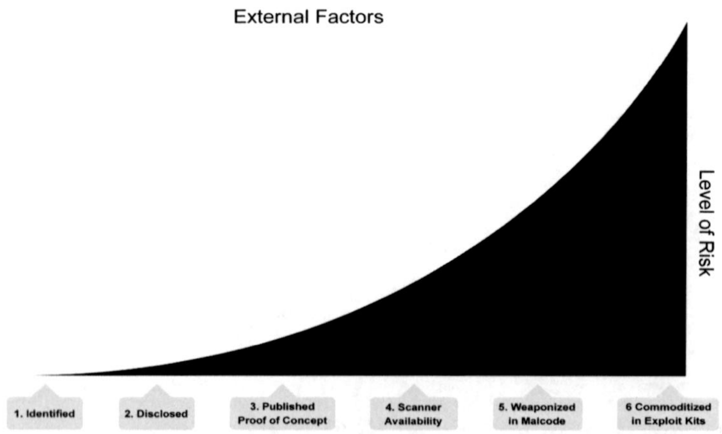

Figure 9.7. *Real risk rises dramatically when vulnerabilities progress to weaponization and commoditization.*

Source: Chris Pace. The Threat Intelligence Handbook. CyberEdge. ISBN: 978-0-9990354-6-7.

9.7.5.3. Understanding the Adversary

In addition to scores and statistics, good threat intelligence should offer a deeper understanding of the methods and motivations behind threat actors' targeting of some vulnerabilities while ignoring others.

9.7.6. Sources of Intelligence

Only the beginnings of information that can assist you in determining the risk of vulnerabilities can be found in asset scan and external vulnerability databases. If threat intelligence does not incorporate information from multiple sources, analysts run the risk of failing to identify new vulnerabilities before it is too late.

Valuable sources of information for assessing true risk to your business include:

- Information security sites, including vendor blogs, official disclosure information on vulnerabilities, and security news sites
- Social media, where link sharing provides jumping-off points for uncovering useful intelligence
- Code repositories such as GitHub, which yield insights into the development of proof-of-concept code for vulnerabilities
- Paste sites such as Pastebin and Ghostbin (sometimes wrongly defined as dark web locations), which often house lists of exploitable vulnerabilities
- The dark web, composed of communities and marketplaces with a bar to entry where exploits are developed, shared, and sold
- Forums with no bar to entry or requirement to be using specific software, where threat actors exchange information on vulnerabilities and exploits
- Technical feeds, which deliver data streams of potentially malicious indicators that add useful context around the activities of malware and exploit kits

9.7.7. Vulnerability Chatter on the Dark Web

For the reasons listed below, it is difficult to listen in on the channels used by threat actors to communicate and conduct business.

- Underground forums are difficult to find (after all, there's no Google for the dark web).
- Threat actors change locations whenever they feel their anonymity is at risk.

- Finding the crumb that might be relevant to your security is no small endeavor.
- There are likely to be bars to entry, either financial or kudos from the rest of the community.
- Many of these forums operate exclusively in local languages.

Here is where threat intelligence vendors come into play. They have experience gathering and analyzing intelligence from the dark web. They can give you context-rich information about vulnerabilities that are specifically related to your network from dark web forums.

9.7.8. Bridging the Risk Gaps Between Security, Operations, and Business Leadership

Two teams are usually in charge of guarding against vulnerabilities in organizations.

- The vulnerability management team runs scans and prioritizes vulnerabilities by potential risk.
- The IT operations team deploys patches and remediates the affected systems.

Vulnerability management approaches are sometimes approached "by the numbers" as a result of this dynamic. For instance, the security organization's vulnerability management team may decide that a number of vulnerabilities in Apache web servers represent a serious risk to the company and ought to be given top priority.

Nonetheless, it's possible that the IT operations group supports a lot more Windows machines than Apache servers. Team members have an incentive to continue concentrating on lower-priority Windows vulnerabilities if their performance is solely evaluated on the number of systems patched.

Understanding exploitability also helps your company find the right balance between patching weak systems and causing disruptions to regular business operations. Disrupting business continuity is something that most organizations strongly dislike doing. However, if you are aware that a patch will shield the company from an actual, pressing threat, then a brief disruption is entirely warranted.

Speaking with your security and operations teams, senior managers, and the board about the threat posed by a vulnerability is made much simpler by the risk milestones framework that was previously mentioned. Your entire organization's confidence in the security team will grow as a result of this degree of transparency into the reasoning behind decisions made regarding vulnerabilities. Introduce the risk of exploitability in order to close the gap between the IT operations and vulnerability management teams. Give the vulnerability management team more context-rich information regarding the likelihood of exploitability so they can identify fewer high-risk CVEs and place less pressure on the operations team. The operations team will then have time to focus on other objectives while giving that small number of critical patches top priority.

REFERENCES

1. Al-Fuqaha, A., Guizani, M., Mohammadi, M., Aledhari, M., & Ayyash, M. (2015). Internet of things: A survey on enabling technologies, protocols, and applications. *IEEE Communications Surveys & Tutorials, 17*(4), 2347–2376. https://doi.org/10.1109/COMST.2015.2444095.
2. Atluri, V., & Horne, J. (2021). A machine learning based threat intelligence framework for industrial control system network traffic indicators of compromise. In *SoutheastCon 2021* (pp. 1–5). https://doi.org/10.1109/SoutheastCon45413.2021.9401809.
3. Gascon, H., Grobauer, B., Schreck, T., Rist, L., Arp, D., & Rieck, K. (2017). Mining attributed graphs for threat intelligence. In *Proceedings of the Seventh ACM Conference on Data and Application Security and Privacy* (pp. 15–22). New York, NY, USA. https://doi.org/10.1145/3029806.3029811.
4. Liao, X., Yuan, K., Wang, X., Li, Z., Xing, L., & Beyah, R. (2016). Acing the IOC game: Toward automatic discovery and analysis of open-source cyber threat intelligence. In *Proceedings of the 2016 ACM SIGSAC Conference on Computer and Communications Security* (pp. 755–766). New York, NY, USA. https://doi.org/10.1145/2976749.2978315.
5. Verma, M., Kumarguru, P., Deb, S. B., & Gupta, A. (2018). Analyzing indicators of compromise for ransomware: Leveraging IOCs with machine learning techniques. In *2018 IEEE International Conference on Intelligence and Security Informatics (ISI)* (pp. 154–159). https://doi.org/10.1109/ISI.2018.8587409.

CHAPTER 10

FUTURE TRENDS AND EMERGING TECHNOLOGIES

Contents

INTRODUCTION

Cyber Threat Intelligence (CTI) automation is advancing quickly due to new technologies that improve threat detection and response times and accuracy. Combining artificial intelligence (AI) and machine learning (ML) to analyze massive amounts of data in real-time and spot patterns and anomalies that point to possible threats is one important trend. By automating the gathering, processing, and distribution of CTI, these technologies are being utilized more frequently. This lowers the need for manual intervention and speeds up response times to new threats. Furthermore, unstructured data from various sources, including social media, forums, and dark web sites, is being sorted through using natural language processing (NLP) in order to extract actionable intelligence. The emergence of blockchain technology is particularly significant because it provides immutable, secure ledgers for the exchange of threat intelligence amongst enterprises, fostering better cooperation while safeguarding private data. Automation platforms are getting more advanced; they are combining CTI with SIEM (security information and event management) systems and using SOAR (security orchestration, automation, and response) tools to orchestrate responses. As these technologies develop further, they should be crucial in building cybersecurity frameworks that are more proactive, adaptable, and able to fend off ever-more-sophisticated cyberattacks.

10.1. EMERGING CYBER-SECURITY THREATS AND TECHNOLOGIES

10.1.1. Artificial Intelligence and Machine Learning

Artificial intelligence (AI) is the application of computational thinking and self-correcting systems to make computers think and behave like humans (Michalski et al., 2013). The main idea is to represent logical connections and then use machine learning (ML) algorithms to solve complex problems based on these representations. Artificial intelligence's machine learning (ML) field enables computers to learn from data, identify patterns, and anticipate outcomes on their own without human intervention (Cioffi et al., 2020). Machine learning (ML) techniques have gained popularity in many fields to extract intelligence from data as a result of the exponential growth in both the amount and types of data in the digital age.

Cybersecurity is using AI and ML more and more to automate threat detection, analysis, and response (Shah, 2021). The ever-evolving strategies, techniques, and procedures of advanced threat actors pose a challenge for rule-based security tools. Cyber defense systems may now quickly identify outliers that might indicate an attack by using advanced machine learning techniques like supervised, unsupervised, and deep learning. These techniques enable cyber defense systems to learn average trends from large datasets. 2015). AI-driven solutions provide security measures like adaptability, speed, and the capacity to grow as needed because threats are constantly changing (Figure 10.1).

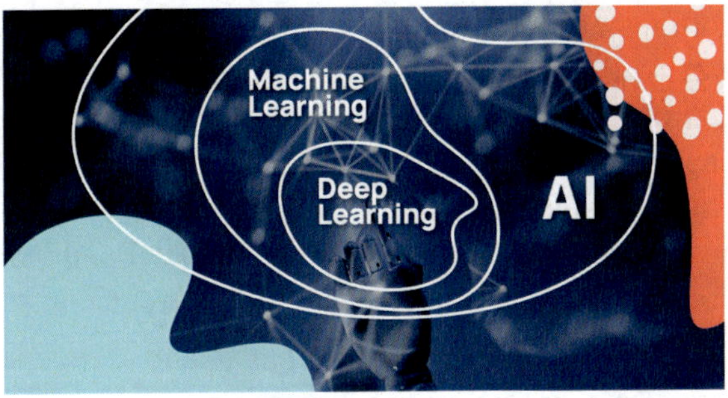

Figure 10.1. *Machine learning and AI.*

Source: https://lh4.googleusercontent.com/proxy/NMybxZe1eKmL1TeTCklX_gI-2kruQZTAJp2RB8ixWyac27lwvDugun7f973nqynpFqFkwKhJ9q6V3IxX488oxAQ-toLU7jDrUoSrzaKD0E3d03-WoV-RWkdhhtxPeTj08.

Malware detection is a crucial application of machine learning in defense (Shah, 2021). By examining thousands of examples of malware artifacts and behavior patterns, machine learning models are able to identify malicious code with high accuracy. This is accurate even in cases where incorrect code is concealed by mutations or encryption. In order to train classifiers to identify malware variants and zero-day attacks that haven't been observed previously, features such as file/registry actions, system calls, network connections, and API hooks are removed. Approximately 90% of novel strains and more than 99% of malware that has previously been studied can be detected by ML algorithms, according to research (Shah, 2021). This eliminates the needless but laborious task that was previously completed by humans utilizing signature-based definitions.

Similarly, machine learning (ML) is critical for detecting network intrusions by identifying odd patterns in traffic (Das et al., 2015). Over time, TCP/IP becomes accustomed to its typical operation, so any modifications to protocols, ports, or data transfers that indicate a potential breach can be detected right away. Unsupervised techniques, like clustering, assist in identifying outliers without immediately labeling cases. By using this method, new threat trends that circumvent signature-based rules are captured. These insights can be used by threat-finding teams to locate compromised assets and hidden attackers within networks. The scale and speed of AI analysis enable constant monitoring of both external and internal IT environments.

Simultaneously, AI is assisting in preventing threats from occurring by anticipating attacks and vulnerabilities (Ullah et al., 2020). Machine learning (ML) collects data from open sources, closed platforms, and the dark web to identify vulnerabilities and outdated software, easily exploitable settings, and unprotected servers—all of which are common targets for cybercriminals. In order to prevent exploitative changes before they occur, predictive algorithms assist in allocating priorities for patch management, access control hardening, and security testing. Businesses are also utilizing machine learning (ML) for user and object behavioral analytics to identify unusual employees who might be intentionally or unintentionally attempting to harm the company.

By controlling bots, cleaning up inputs, and preventing IPs from attempting to attack, machine learning strengthens web application defenses at the application layer to safeguard websites and portals (Cioffi et al., 2020). Mobile apps can be automatically reverse engineered to look for potential backdoors or data leaks. Additionally, spam emails, fake information on social media, and online deception networks that can be used to gain access to a system are screened using natural language processing. These programs provide proactive protection against emerging threats and assist in preventing damage from occurring from the initial point of compromise. Machine learning is used by malware analysis and digital forensics systems to support ongoing investigations and incident response. Advanced neural networks can decipher the obfuscation techniques used by advanced persistent threats to obtain telltale signs of compromise, attack strategies, and malware samples' objectives (Shah, 2021). By automatically classifying resource handling, command-and-control channels, encryption procedures, and patterns in code, machine learning (ML) facilitates effective sorting to accelerate response times. Experts claim that research can be completed up to ten times more quickly than by hand (Shah, 2021). Moreover, graph-based learning assists in assembling the kill chain and creating a map of all the breaches. This facilitates the process of identifying issues and following the correct legal procedures.

AI can alter threat intelligence by utilizing massive amounts of relationship-based, behavioral, and textual security data. ML constructs intelligence models that incorporate patterns discovered in millions of historical events worldwide rather than depending on the experiences of a single expert (Michalski et al., 2013). Contemporary neural networks are highly effective at deciphering critical information from surveillance traffic, well-organized logs and reports, and conversations on the dark web. Research indicates that machine learning (ML) can identify relationships between threat actors to create a map of those actors' objectives, surroundings, and behavior (Ullah et al., 2020). AI platforms are able to consistently identify cyber trends, actors, and behaviors ahead of analysts because they are able to draw conclusions from existing data and continuously update themselves based on new observations.

Table 10.1. *Machine Learning in Cybersecurity*

Application	Description
Malware Detection	ML models can accurately detect malware by analyzing features like system calls, network connections, and file/registry actions, even for new and unseen malware variants.
Network Intrusion Detection	ML can identify anomalous trends in network traffic that may indicate a breach, using unsupervised methods like clustering to detect outliers.
Threat Modeling and Prediction	ML helps model potential attacks and vulnerabilities by gathering data from sources like the dark web, enabling predictive patch management and security hardening.
Web Application Security	ML enhances application layer defenses by managing bots, sanitizing inputs, blocking malicious IPs, and detecting backdoors or data leaks.
Digital Forensics and Incident Response	ML assists in analyzing malware, breaking down obfuscation tactics, identifying attacker behavior patterns, and reconstructing the kill chain for investigations.
Threat Intelligence	ML can uncover hidden insights and connections from vast security data sources like dark web forums, traffic logs, and reports, revealing threat actor behavior and motives.
Automated Security Operations	ML enables the automation of security tasks, moving towards proactive and predictive cybersecurity capabilities at scale.

Source: https://jsaer.com/download/vol-11-iss-5-2024/JSAER2024-11-5-100-112.pdf.

By transforming unintelligent data into insightful information representations and potent reasoning tools, machine learning (ML) is driving innovation in cybersecurity at a faster rate. Security tasks are becoming more fully automated, proactive, and predictive as AI improves at solving problems involving skills, speed, and scale. AI has definite advantages over sophisticated threats when combined with automation. Companies are beginning to realize that the future of strong and dependable defenses required in today's digitally connected world is intelligence-driven protection. Although there is still much to learn and experience in order to fully realize AI's potential to make everyone safer online (Table 10.1).

10.1.2. Blockchain Technology

A sophisticated distributed ledger system called blockchain enables decentralized, transparent, and secure business without the need for middlemen (Zheng et al., 2017). Blockchain is made up of digital records of information stored in an increasing number of blocks that are cryptographically secure (Sarmah, 2018). Every block includes proof-of-work to demonstrate that it was added to the chain, transaction data, and an encrypted hash of the previous block (Zheng et al., 2017). This generates a time-stamped, permanent public record that is visible to all users on the blockchain (Figure 10.2).

Figure 10.2. *Block chain.*

Source: https://www.cyberbahnit.com/wp-content/uploads/2017/11/blockchain.jpg.

Blockchain is immutable because it is computationally impossible to change records without permission, open and honest because all copies of the ledger remain in sync without a central authority, and trustworthy because it lacks a central authority (Pilkington, 2016). According to Zheng et al., decentralized peer networks securely and anonymously record transactions. 2017). They use proof-of-work and proof-of-stake as their consensus mechanisms. In ways that ledgers couldn't, this innovative technology is encouraging many fields to create decentralized cooperation (Yli-Huumo et al., 2016).

Personal data sharing and decentralized identity management may be beneficial (Pilkington, 2016). Because they don't use centralized systems that can be hacked, people with blockchain-linked digital identities have complete control over private data, including medical records, credentials, financial information, and personal accounts (Pilkington, 2016). Cryptographic signatures guarantee that specific attributes can only be changed or accessed by credential holders. This approach improves privacy, resolves problems with centralized databases, and simplifies e-governance and Know Your Customer checks.

By tracking asset origin and history without a single point of failure, blockchain enhances supply chain operations (Andoni et al., 2019). Blockchain makes complicated supply networks between companies and nations more transparent by permanently recording every transaction, including the origin of an item, the person holding it, its condition, and the destination of the transfer (Sarmah, 2018). The digitalized paper trail of goods facilitates better logistics, rule enforcement, handling of recalls, prevention of fakes, and simplification of customs fees. There have been significant rollouts in the food, jewelry, pharmaceutical, luxury goods, and even energy sectors.

Blockchain has become more popular in the financial services industry as a clearing and settlement network that enables real-time transactions without requiring reconciliation (Zheng et al., 2017). Early large-scale use cases for distributed ledger-based cryptocurrency systems, such as Bitcoin, were to securely transfer digital currencies without the need for middlemen and related fees (Pilkington, 2016). To modernize overburdened payment architectures, central banks are also investigating digital fiat currencies based on blockchain technology. The implementation of programmed negotiations and smart contracts to automate process fulfillment is revolutionizing the financial derivatives markets and transactional legal frameworks.

Blockchain specifically helps address major risks in cybersecurity. Because any tampering is visible when comparing global ledger copies, the inherent transparency discourages deceit and manipulation (Yli-Huumo et al., 2016). Without depending on outside repositories, private blockchain also permits organizations to securely share threat intelligence and indicators (Andoni et al., 2019). One day, homomorphic encryption may become widely used in decentralized computing frameworks, enabling affordable confidential analytics between silos. Scalability issues persist since most public networks have transaction speed restrictions that prevent widespread commercial use cases (Zheng et al., 2017). Different protocols and data models also lead to interoperability problems between different ledgers. Furthermore, blockchain dependability can still be jeopardized by human behavior inconsistencies and contingencies resulting from consensus algorithms, even though transparency tries to lower trust risks (Pilkington, 2016). But developments indicate that distributed ledgers could revolutionize legacy architectures in the fields of finance, healthcare, energy, government, and more by facilitating efficient coordination in the absence of centralized overseers and the systemic risks and bottlenecks they bring with them (Yli-Huumo et al., 2016). As blockchain's full potential is discovered through experience and research, its security applications are expected to expand.

10.1.3. Cloud Security

Cloud computing is a widely used online business model that offers scalable service models for computing, storage, and application tools via the internet (Kandukuri and Rakshit, 2009). However, moving data and assets outside of the conventional on-premises perimeter security introduces additional risks that impede cloud adoption (Coppolino et al., 2017). Application programming interface security vulnerabilities, incomplete identity verification, improperly configured activity tracking, and weaknesses in web, mobile, and Internet of Things services that expose clouds to risk are some of the major issues regarding cloud security (Rizvi et al., 2018). Ensuring privacy, integrity, and availability of systems is crucial, regardless of whether deployment methods are public, private, or hybrid.

Making sure they have strong identity and access management controls over their data, apps, and tools is one issue that many businesses run into when they migrate to the cloud (Kandukuri and Rakshit, 2009). To authenticate users and grant them specific access to cloud-based services, a strong identity federation system comprising cloud platforms and on-premises directories is required (Coppolino et al., 2017). If entry permissions are too loose or unclear, privacy is at risk in the event that credentials are stolen. It is essential to have multi-factor authentication, well-defined permission policies, and frequent access reviews. But maintaining clean credentials is the responsibility of both clients and providers. Users who receive regular security knowledge training are more responsible for their identities.

One of the biggest risks in cloud environments, where multiple users work on the same infrastructure, is still application vulnerabilities (Kandukuri and Rakshit, 2009). It's critical to write code according to security best practices, use fuzz testing to check functions for buffer overflows, and monitor vulnerabilities throughout the life of software (Coppolino et al., 2017). Other strategies to reduce software supply chain risks include tracking software origins, performing quality assurance tests prior to deployment, and utilizing a third-party risk manager (Rizvi et al., 2018). You can reduce your exposure risk by using runtime protections, automatic source code analyzers, and web application firewalls (Kandukuri & Rakshit, 2009). Penetration testing by qualified evaluators enhances responsible software development practices.

Without safeguards, data could become private due to malware and intrusions that target cloud platforms (Coppolino et al., 2017). Traditional perimeter-based defenses must be supplemented by network-level and host-based attack prevention suited to cloud infrastructure and multi-tenancy requirements (Rizvi et al., 2018). Both insiders attempting to cause harm and external attackers posing as authorized users can be identified through behavioral monitoring and anomaly detection (Kandukuri and Rakshit, 2009). People are prevented from switching between compromised customer accounts through the use of software-defined networking and containerization, which isolates individual accounts from one another. Frequent vulnerability scans help keep things safe by collaborating with investigators and preventative measures.

Clouds with web and mobile services, as well as natural language interfaces, increase attack surfaces that users might not be able to control but nevertheless have an impact on security (Coppolino et al., 2017). Using social engineering, injection flaws, or account takeovers, malicious individuals are attempting to gain access to these entry points and the platforms that facilitate them (Rizvi et al., 2018). By ensuring that the processes for input validation, output encoding, session management, and account recovery operate properly, exploitation vectors can be reduced to a minimum (Kandukuri and Rakshit, 2009). Defenses across disaggregated clouds become stronger when customers, third-party providers, and cloud systems collaborate. Because of this, it is less important to rely too heavily on outdated models with perimeters that aren't suitable for adaptable cloud-native designs.

The privacy and confidentiality benefits of the cloud—which include improved regulatory compliance—are severely jeopardized by data breaches brought on by insufficient access controls or by data that isn't encrypted while it's being sent or stored (Coppolino et al., 2017). Flexible cloud operations security is a special challenge for industries that adhere to regulations like GDPR and PCI DSS to protect private data (Rizvi et al., 2018). To counter threats from both insiders and outsiders, the bare minimum is to use encryption, key management, data loss prevention technologies, and strict access rules (Kandukuri and Rakshit, 2009). You should also investigate more sophisticated techniques that include managing consent, tracking data usage, and anonymizing data, depending on your level of risk tolerance (Table 10.2).

Table 10.2. *Key Cloud Security Issues and Mitigation Strategies*

Security Issue	**Mitigation Strategy**
Identity and Access Management	Robust identity federation, multi-factor authentication, clear access permissions, regular access reviews, security awareness training
Application Vulnerabilities	Secure coding practices, fuzz testing, vulnerability management, web application firewalls, source code analysis, penetration testing
Malware and Intrusions	Network and host-based intrusion prevention, behavioral monitoring, anomaly detection, isolation techniques, vulnerability scanning
Web, Mobile, and IoT Attacks	Input validation, output encoding, session management, secure account recovery, collaboration across providers and customers
Data Privacy and Compliance	Encryption, key management, data loss prevention, access controls, data usage tracking, consent management, data anonymization
Availability and Continuity	Redundancy, failover, disaster recovery, workload migration, service level agreements, pre-production testing
Governance and Shared Responsibility	Clear security roles and responsibilities, alignment with standards (e.g., ISO 27001), regular audits, continuous monitoring and adaptation

Source: https://jsaer.com/download/vol-11-iss-5-2024/JSAER2024-11-5-100-112.pdf.

Threats to availability increase as more and more embedded devices, actuators, connected sensors, and vital infrastructure depend on the cloud. Information security, economics, and safety are all negatively impacted by these threats (Coppolino et al., 2017). Applications that are vital to missions must be dependable because even a single failure could cause them to cease. (Rizvi et al., 2018). Redundancy, failover, disaster recovery, workload migration, and other techniques are required to keep things operating smoothly, according to service level agreements and continuity responsibilities (Kandukuri and Rakshit, 2009). Before going into production, organizations must still conduct extensive testing to make sure that the anticipated uptime levels can be reached. Finally, a common issue with cloud security is insufficient governance. In complex multi-tenant environments, the roles of customers, providers, and partners are distinct (Coppolino et al., 2017). Establishing unambiguous information security guidelines, responsibilities, and roles in accordance with ISO 27001 standards guarantees that all dispersed IT systems possess identical fundamental controls (Rizvi et al., 2018). Peace of mind is provided by routine reviews of contractual obligations, continuous security monitoring, adapting defenses to new threats, and patching system vulnerabilities to maintain control over time (Kandukuri and Rakshit, 2009). Collaboration is facilitated by strategic partnerships that emphasize risk mitigation and compliance, which is crucial for long-term cloud security. For cloud security to function, accountability must be shared by all. Appropriate access controls, network security, governance guidelines, and a cautious identity and access management culture can all help achieve this. Standards, vigilant control monitoring, and continuous investments in new security measures can help cloud services reduce associated risks while safely delivering on the promised benefits of scalability and agility.

10.1.4. Threat Intelligence

Threat intelligence (TI) is current information that is gathered and assessed to find out about adversaries' tools, strategies, and objectives in order to protect against known threats (Conti et al., 2018). This method detects new cyberthreats by fusing open-source data with technical indicators of improper behavior (Tounsi and Rais, 2018). Policies and security measures prevent threats, but a proactive, anticipatory strategy based on useful intelligence thwarts invaders before they can cause harm (Conti et al., 2018).

TI feeds from reputable and unofficial sources are essential for important information. Tools and techniques are shared by dark web forums, intrusion detection logs, and firewall alarms. Nonetheless, social media, news, and official records aid in our understanding of the motivations behind people's behavior. Information Sharing and Analysis Centers and commercial threat intelligence systems provide organized data. Regarding state-sponsored threat actors and their evolving TTPs, government agencies frequently reveal and issue warnings (Tounsi and Rais, 2018). Utilize cyber threat intelligence technologies to make sure information is consistently gathered, handled, and shared from these numerous sources. The primary cyber death chain information model is called ATT&CK, or MITRE Adversarial Tactics, Techniques, and Common Knowledge. In order to plan tactical and strategic responses, it connects enemy behaviors observed through IOCs to plans and tactics. STIX and TAXII forms for ATT&CK are created using the Diamond Model of Intrusion Analysis and Lockheed Martin's Intelligence Driven Computer Network Defense (Conti et al., 2018,).

Through the use of intelligence models and technological security measures, commercial cyber threat intelligence platforms (CTIPs) automatically identify, neutralize, and respond to threats. They can detect patterns and connect attacks across platforms and victims thanks to AI/ML-powered analysis and visualization of feeds from numerous sources (Tounsi and Rais, 2018). Beyond updates, threat detection logic can be obtained directly from CTIP data by firewalls, endpoint security, IDS/IPS, and SIEM. Playbooks are used by SOAR systems to automate threat-data-based fixes (Conti et al., 2018). Cyber threat information aids in the early detection of active attackers targeting your company. Before victims were notified, almost real-time Dark Web behavior analysis identified breaches and data theft, enabling prompt action (RAICU, 2015). Critical assets are the focus of MITRE ATTandCK adversary profiles, which threat models and red teams work to protect. Constant vulnerability monitoring, patching, user awareness, and historical intelligence reduce attacker entry (Tounsi and Rais, 2018). Proactive discovery and containment prior to damage can prevent attack chains from starting.

Predictive analysis, which arises from strategic knowledge, facilitates the anticipation of novel threats. Monitoring the relationships, adaptations, and opportunistic actions of persistent threat groups can provide insight into their long-term goals and capabilities (Conti et al., 2018). This makes it easier for risk assessments and resilience strategies to focus on the future rather than the past. The actions of state actors brought to light vulnerabilities that might permit influence operations to take place before they are discovered. Their knowledge of protected democracy is greater (RAICU, 2015). Observing how people use underground hacker sites allows us to discover new exploits even during testing (Tounsi and Rais, 2018). When problems are resolved right away, threats vanish.

Deepfakes are a novel threat to TI that calls for cooperation to counter. Fake news created by AI undermines trust by disseminating lies online (Jones, 2020). Commercial platforms, academics, and ethical hackers work together. Datasets educate people how to spot false information and prevent it from spreading. Evaluations of credibility expose falsehoods before they cause harm to society (Tounsi and Rais, 2018). Cyber TI benefits from AI as well since it can automatically link and enhance indicators, expedite intelligence combinations, locate anomalies in large amounts of time series data, and forecast danger scenarios with generative models such as GANs (Kadel et al., 2022). These developments offer scale analysis, speed, and context that humans cannot.

Cyber threat intelligence is useful for tracking down your adversaries and their strategies at all times (Conti et al., 2018). A strategy that considers adversaries can identify, lessen, and eliminate cyberthreats that surpass technology-driven defenses. Senior decision-makers, security engineers, and intelligence teams frequently work together to integrate insights into risk management and strategic asset management. Everyone is prepared because online threats are always evolving. Cyber threat intelligence will transform security by enabling proactive and predictive defense globally, while artificial intelligence is opening up new domains.

10.1.5. Emerging Technologies

Emerging technologies include novel, cutting-edge concepts that have the potential to profoundly impact society, science, and technology globally in the medium to long term (Rotolo et al., 2015). They present opportunities never before seen, but they also carry risks that should be carefully weighed in order to obtain the best and least harmful outcomes. If ethical concepts of responsibility, security, and justice aren't taken into consideration, some new technologies have the potential to significantly impact cybersecurity, for better or worse (Moor, 2005). Many computers can work on the same problem at once thanks to quantum computing, which makes use of the random behavior of quantum bits (qubits), which can exist in superposition (Veletsianos, 2010). This creates a lot of opportunities to address problems that are currently unsolvable in fields like artificial intelligence, materials science, medicine, and logistics. However, once an errorcorrected universal quantum computer is created, algorithms like Shor's can quickly break RSA and elliptic curve encryption, posing a threat to the cryptographic systems that support digital security (Moor, 2005). Far before this occurs, it is imperative to move to post-quantum security standards involving lattices and codes in order to protect financial and trust systems from grave dangers. Other safe multiparty techniques that are impervious to quantum attacks are being researched by scientists. Embedded sensors, software, and network connectivity connect actual machines when the Internet of Things (IoT) and operational technology (OT) are integrated, resulting in new efficiencies in industries like manufacturing, healthcare, and smart cities (Rotolo et al., 2017). 2015. You, however, disregard communication channels and endpoint security. Under those circumstances, it would be simple for these unpatched devices to be used in deadly distributed denial of service attacks or to interfere with safety devices (Moor, 2005). Guidelines for device protection, identity management, update cadence, and zero trust network access that restricts lateral movement are crucial as the number of devices in use worldwide continues to rise rapidly. Deepfakes use neural networks trained on real data to create phony images, videos, and audio recordings. Although they seem remarkably realistic in appearance and sound, they have not yet been located through the use of technical means (Veletsianos, 2010). While nonconsensual images and disinformation campaigns can empower marginalized groups and foster creativity, they can also be detrimental to society if they spread widely. The intention is to prevent improper use of joint datasets, identification techniques, licenses, legal frameworks, and media literacy (Moor, 2005). One day, blockchain-based Proof of Personhood techniques may produce online identities that can be verified through cryptography. Regulations should promote responsibility without outlawing certain tools. Systems designed to covertly manipulate users and their outcomes in public discourse, marketing, or employment are referred to as deceptive intelligence (Rotolo et al., 2015). These systems appear to be helpful, honest, and harmless. When we use them without protection, we feel guilty about responsibility, transparency, and privacy (Moor, 2005). Before malicious apps become widely used, open, interdisciplinary research employing strategies such as the constitutional AI technique can help prevent harm, whether intentional or unintentional (Veletsianos, 2010). Standards that instruct system designers on how to grant users the authority they rightfully possess aid in preventing power disparities that facilitate widespread deception and social engineering.

Cyber-physical systems are becoming increasingly complex and self-governing, fusing digital networks with tangible tools. Defense systems, energy grids, and self-driving automobiles all employ them (Rotolo et al., 2015). However, growing interconnectedness increases the likelihood of attacks, which extend beyond risks to financial security and privacy (Moor, 2005). When lives depend on systems, balancing functional optimization and security requirements is essential to prevent catastrophic breakdowns. This can be achieved by integrating robustness testing, redundancy, and human oversight from the beginning of the design process (Veletsianos, 2010). All things considered; you must exercise caution while remaining receptive to novel concepts if you hope to fully benefit from the potential of emerging technologies (Table 10.3).

Frameworks for responsible creation and adoption must be continuously monitored and evaluated due to the rapid pace of change. Policies and guidelines ought to be grounded in the perspectives of diverse individuals and should uphold the general principles of responsibility, ability, and safety (Rotolo et al., 2015). Prioritizing long-term well-being over short-term goals is achieved through a helpful and transparent public discourse that brings together the knowledge of numerous interested parties. New technologies must be managed cautiously but optimistically, guaranteeing that people and society come first, even though big changes may be flawless (Moor, 2005). Their development offers more opportunities, better lives, and greater prosperity for everyone on the planet when ethical stewardship is exercised pro-actively.

Table 10.3. *Emerging Technologies, Their Potential Impacts, and the Key Considerations*

Emerging Technology	Potential Impacts	Key Considerations
Quantum Computing	Revolutionize fields like medicine, materials science, AI, and logistics. Potential to break current encryption algorithms.	Transition to post-quantum cryptography standards. Explore quantum-safe multiparty computation methods.
Internet of Things (IoT) and Operational Technology (OT)	Increased efficiency in manufacturing, healthcare, and smart cities.	Ensure device security, identity management, update mechanisms, and zero-trust network access to limit lateral movement.
Deepfakes	Enabler of creativity and empowerment. Potential for nonconsensual media and disinformation campaigns.	Develop detection methods, establish credentials and regulations, promote media literacy. Explore blockchain-based identity verification.
Deceptive AI	Potential for manipulation and control in public discourse, marketing, and hiring.	Open and cross-disciplinary research, user control standards, and ethical design principles to avoid power imbalances and social engineering.
Cyber-physical Systems	Applications in defense, energy grids, and autonomous vehicles.	Integrate robustness testing, redundancy, and human oversight from the design stage to balance functionality and security, especially for life-critical systems.

Source: https://jsaer.com/download/vol-11-iss-5-2024/JSAER2024-11-5-100-112.pdf.

10.2. NON-TECHNICAL ASPECTS OF CYBERSECURITY

10.2.1. Governance, Risk, and Compliance

Strong governance models that clearly define roles, responsibilities, and industry-compliant procedures are necessary for cybersecurity to function well. Both

ISO 27001 and the NIST Cybersecurity Framework (CSF) provide a framework for identifying risks, prioritizing them, allocating treatment responsibilities, and establishing guidelines for fundamental controls. Independent audits and frequent reports to the board serve to uphold accountability. You must set up an information security management system (ISMS) in order for risk management to function more efficiently. Tools for both quantitative and qualitative risk analysis, like COSO ERM, are useful in determining how much risk an individual is willing to take and how to approach it. Regularly verifying that controls and assets remain strong in the face of emerging risks and regulatory obligations is crucial. Laws like the CCPA and GDPR mandate the protection of private information and privacy.

10.2.2. Policies and Implementation

Businesses create comprehensive security policies that cover everything from identity and access management, patches and configurations, encryption protocols, data retention and destruction, incident handling, and more. Depending on the degree of risk, separate policies can be created for data and systems with critical and general use. Stakeholder consultations ensure that roles and responsibilities are clearly defined and that policies cover real-world use cases. Automated policy enforcement tools can help achieve scalable compliance. However, due to technological issues and cultural disparities, change management is still difficult. It's critical to be transparent about the dangers, the accountability, and the advantages of safe behavior in order to gain support. Additionally, policies are reinforced by lessons learned from errors and near misses. Enforcement is aided while maintaining efficiency requirements by least privilege access, logging, and auditing.

10.2.3. Skills

Culture and Metrics You need continual training, simulated exercises, and constructive criticism to create a strong security environment where everyone knows their role and is accountable. Processes should be continuously improved based on KPIs and lessons learned, and their efficacy should be assessed using metrics from tools and audits. Metrics such as the amount of awareness training provided, the number of vulnerabilities discovered and fixed, the speed at which patches are applied, the frequency of policy violations, and the average response time to threats could all be monitored using these metrics. Above all, concentrating on outcomes rather than merely marking off compliance boxes ensures long-term security that aligns with corporate objectives. Success communities that are closely knit both within and between businesses accelerate.

10.2.4. Security Education and Training Awareness (SETA)

SETA seeks to enhance the non-technical human elements that are frequently involved in leaks. Beyond technology, SETA provides an additional line of defense by educating staff members on cyber awareness and best practices. A manufacturing plant's click-through rates fell from 35% to less than 5% in less than two years, and customized awareness campaigns reduced the time it took an airline to report phishing attacks by 90% Such data emphasizes the importance of ongoing SETA for business (Hu et al., 2022; Alyami and colleagues. 2023). Success, though, hinges on how well the plan of action takes into account the current circumstances. The needs assessment examines the ecosystem, functions, threat model, and compliance requirements of the organization in order to identify pertinent and interesting content that can be delivered in the most effective way through a variety of techniques, including workshops and simulations, based on the preferred learning style of each individual. Sentiment analysis continuously monitors the outcomes, including security culture reviews and awareness metrics, to make sure the findings remain applicable as risks evolve over the course of the program. It is simpler to offset the cost savings realized by educating human cyber defenders to perform their duties more effectively and with greater impact thanks to this continuous evaluation and improvement process.

Effective implementation also requires organized support. With executive support, funding is secured and SETA and technical controls are given priority. The organization as a whole then starts to hear this message. Setting priorities, managing delivery logistics, and effectively allocating resources are made possible by the appointment of capable, independent security coordinators. Their control sets the tone for context-specific content curation and facilitation. User-centered program management includes:

- Online dashboards for tracking compliance.
- Places to store paperwork.
- Ways to reward people who go above and beyond to use what they have learned.

People finish more quickly when they use blended formats that fit into their busy schedules. Continuous skill development via initiatives like train-the-trainer guarantees that strict service requirements are fulfilled. Role-based structures, which assign modules to the appropriate individuals automatically, also facilitate compliance. Long-term behavioral changes are maintained by repeated warnings, and simulations raise awareness. SETA can be made simpler and more seamless to integrate into daily life, which helps address issues like time and resource constraints. Last but not least, SETA's basic principles include being proactive and flexible, which increases its resistance to unknown threats. The emphasis shifts to helping people adopt security-conscious mindsets that enable them to make wise decisions. The technical staff gains knowledge on how to set up and assess controls in a safe manner. This culture of shared security risks and responsibilities is kept alive by regular training programs and open lines of communication. This strengthens the human firewall in response to technological advancements. Along with meticulous program reviews, a well-designed SETA operating system applied across an organization's lifecycle enhances the non-technical aspects of the people and process layers that make up the foundation of cybersecurity.

10.3. PREDICTIVE THREAT INTELLIGENCE SERVICES

Cyberattacks are becoming more sophisticated and metamorphic, and there is a significant risk that businesses will be targeted. Threat intelligence encompasses both the proactive identification of possible threats and the reactive handling of authorized ones. It entails examining large amounts of data to identify trends that could indicate an attack. Numerous companies offer predictive threat intelligence services that are specialized in gathering, evaluating, and interpreting security data to assist organizations in staying ahead of constantly changing cyber threats.

10.3.1. Challenges of Conventional Threat Intelligence

When it comes to anticipating novel attack sources, traditional threat intelligence frequently fails. Even though sophisticated services promise low false positive rates and high accuracy, problems still exist.

- **Accuracy and Capacity:** While advanced services have minimal false positives and high accuracy, traditional providers might struggle.
- **Reactive Mindset:** Security teams often react to ongoing attacks, leaving them vulnerable to novel threats.
- **Threat Landscape Complexity:** Keeping ahead of the curve is difficult due to the constantly changing cyber landscape and the dearth of cybersecurity talent.
- **Data Integration and Analysis:** PTI uses a variety of data sources, necessitating strong integration and analytical skills.
- **Standardization Gap:** A "one-size-fits-all" framework is needed to facilitate the sharing of threat intelligence across organizations.

These difficulties show that in order to effectively identify and stop cyber threats, proactive predictive threat intelligence services are required.

10.3.2. Need to Predictive Threat Intelligence Services

Threats were always evolving, and traditional cybersecurity techniques could not keep up. Attackers took advantage of flaws before remedies could be implemented. Early threat intelligence lacked predictive capabilities and instead concentrated on disseminating attack history. Predictive threat modeling with historical data was made possible in the 2010s by the merging of machine learning and data analytics. Social media and dark web monitoring saw a spike in data volume in the late 2010s, which fueled the development of truly predictive PTI services. PTI is essential for businesses today because it allows for proactive defense against changing threats. These services enable organizations to anticipate, prioritize, and strengthen their resilience against future attacks by utilizing data and analytics.

In order to protect themselves from cyber threats and attacks, industries handling sensitive customer data—such as FinTechs, insurance providers, and others in the BFSI—as well as those in the healthcare sector, need predictive threat intelligence in particular. Financial institutions use it to protect sensitive data and prevent fraud. PTI helps safeguard patient safety and data integrity in the healthcare industry by thwarting attacks on medical records and devices. These services are used by other industries, such as telecom, XaaS, retail, CPG, e-commerce, mobility, and gaming, to reduce the risk of disruptions and infrastructure vulnerabilities. On the endpoints, Movate has installed advanced security tools in collaboration with Palo Alto Networks. These tools make use of behavioral analysis, data leak prevention, secure browsing, AI/ML-led malware protection, and remote software deployment.

Movate has installed advanced security tools on the endpoints in collaboration with Palo Alto Networks. These tools make use of behavioral analysis, remote software deployment, data leak prevention, secure browsing, and AI/ML-led malware protection.

1.3.3. The Future of Predictive Threat Intelligence Services

Predictive threat intelligence services have the potential to completely transform cybersecurity by replacing reactive defense tactics with proactive ones. These services will use cutting-edge technologies like artificial intelligence (AI), machine learning, and big data analytics to predict and mitigate attacks before they happen as cyber threats become more complex and widespread. With the help of AI-powered algorithms, predictive systems will be able to identify vulnerabilities and anticipate potential breaches with an unprecedented level of accuracy. These algorithms will be able to learn continuously from an ever-expanding pool of data, including threat patterns, attacker behavior, and global cyber trends. This evolution will enable automated responses that can instantly neutralize threats in addition to improving the efficacy and speed of threat detection.

Predictive threat intelligence will become more individualized in the upcoming years, with solutions catered to the unique risk profiles and operational settings of different organizations. With the proliferation of IoT devices, cloud computing, and remote work adding layers of complexity to cybersecurity, this customization will become increasingly important as the digital landscape continues to expand. Furthermore, industry collaboration will be prioritized more in the future, as shared intelligence platforms support a collective defense strategy. Businesses will both add to and gain from a global threat intelligence pool, enhancing the digital ecosystem's overall resilience.

Predictive threat intelligence will be seamlessly integrated into current cybersecurity frameworks, providing scalable and adaptable solutions that change in tandem with new threats. These services will become increasingly important in protecting sensitive data, preserving business continuity, and protecting vital infrastructure as they advance in sophistication. Predictive threat intelligence will ultimately play a significant role in the next wave of cybersecurity, helping businesses to keep one step ahead of cybercriminals and lessening the impact of attacks globally.

1.3.4. The Benefits of Predictive Threat Intelligence Services

In the intricate threat landscape of today, taking the initiative is crucial. Predictive threat intelligence services excel in this, offering key benefits:

- **Proactive Defense:** Anticipate, prevent attacks, and reduce the impact of breaches effectively.
- **Enhance Efficiency:** By prioritizing the most serious threats, you can decrease the amount of time wasted on false alarms and diversions and boost productivity.
- **Visibility Into Emerging Threats:** Identify emerging threats, attack vectors, and malware to improve your defense plan.
- **Reduced Risk:** Mitigate the potential impact of successful attacks, protecting data and reputation.
- **Enhanced Decision-Making:** Gain actionable insights to make informed security investments and allocate resources effectively.

- **Streamlined Response:** Anticipate possible attacks in advance to facilitate quicker and more effective incident response.

Organizations can gain a significant cybersecurity edge by utilizing predictive intelligence to safeguard assets and fortify themselves against ever-changing threats.

10.4. THREAT LANDSCAPE

The most concerning development is the growing number of global breaches, as reported by Symantec, FireEye, and Verizon. These breaches pose a serious risk to every country in the world. Both the corporate suites of large corporations and governmental leaders around the world are extremely concerned about the cost of intellectual property loss and information system damage. Due to the growing number of breaches, scarce resources are being reallocated from new research initiatives to strengthening cybersecurity defense programs. The plethora of attack tools and exploit techniques that are all too readily available for free from the Internet or for sale from cybercriminals and hactivists has led to an evolution and increase in the breaches that have happened over time. We think that threat landscape analysis offers an organizational framework of great value, even with the thousands of variations in computer and network attacks that have been created and employed since the identification of the first computer attack tools in 1981.

10.4.1. Traditional Threats

10.4.1.1. Worm

- A stand-alone malware program that replicates itself;
- Harms networks by consuming bandwidth;
- A lateral attack vector that can ex-filtrate data.

10.4.1.2. Trojan

- Typically masquerades as a helpful software application;
- Can be initiated by spam mail, social media, or a game application;

10.4.1.3. Computer virus

- Is a malicious code that attaches itself to a program or file, enabling it to spread from one computer to another, leaving infections as it travels.

10.4.1.4. Spyware

- Covertly gathers user information without the user's knowledge, usually for advertising called "Adware".

10.4.1.5. Botnet

- Is a collection of compromised Internet-connected computers on which malware is running command and control servers; can launch distributed denial-of-service (DDoS) attacks using these botnets;

10.4.2. Social Engineering Threats

10.4.2.1. Social Engineering Attacks

- Phishing is one instance, where the goal is to acquire credit card numbers, social security numbers, usernames, and passwords.
- The user is led to enter personal information on a phony website that nearly looks identical to a genuine website after clicking on a (seemingly innocent) hyperlink.

10.4.2.2. Spear Phishing

- Targets a specific person within an organization.

10.4.2.3. Whaling

- Is directed specifically toward senior executives and other high profile targets.

10.4.2.4. Baiting

- A thief willfully and carelessly drops a CD-ROM or USB thumb drive in a cybercafé or parking lot. To attract the attention of whoever finds it, the drive is clearly labeled with terms like "Executive Compensation" or "Company Confidential.". Malware is installed on the victim's computer when they access media files.

10.4.3. Buffer Overflow and Structured Query Language Injection

10.4.3.1. Buffer Overflow

A memory buffer is overwritten by the hacker with more data than it is intended to contain. A portion of the data overflows into nearby memory, resulting in the desktop or web application crashing or executing arbitrary code with elevated privileges.

10.4.3.2. Structured Query Language (SQL) Injection

Uses a website or web-based application to attack databases. To get the web application to send the rogue SQL command to the database, the attacker inserts SQL statements into a web form. Passwords, social security numbers, credit card numbers, and other database content can be accessed by a successful SQL injection attack.

10.4.4. Next-Generation Threats

10.4.4.1. Polymorphic Threats

- A cyberattack that is impossible to detect by signature-based defenses, such as a virus, worm, spyware, or Trojan that is always changing (morphing).
- Manufacturers of signature-based security products have an ongoing obligation to develop and disseminate fresh threat signatures.

10.4.4.2. Blended Threats

An attempt to increase the severity of damage caused by a cyberattack that incorporates elements of several different malware types and typically uses multiple attack vectors (different attack paths and targets). Examples include the Conficker virus, Code Red virus, and Nimda virus.

10.4.4.3. Zero-Day Attack

A cyberattack on an application or an unidentified publicly accessible operating system application vulnerability is known as a "zero-day threat," so named because the attack is launched on or before the "day zero" of the vulnerability's public awareness.

10.4.4.4. APTs

Sophisticated network attacks wherein an unauthorized user enters a network and remains hidden for a considerable amount of time. Rather than causing harm, the APT seeks to exfiltrate data.

The APT attack process is as follows:

- Stage 1—Initial intrusion through system exploitation.
- Stage 2—Malware is installed on the compromised system.

- Stage 3—Outbound connection initiated.
- Stage 4—Attack spreads laterally.
- Stage 5—Compromised data are extracted via tunneling and encryption.
- Stage 6—Attacker covers their tracks—remains undetected.

APT attacks, according to Eric Cole, are focused on data, targeted, and aim to obtain valuable information and intellectual property from the target organization. The organization will suffer a great deal of harm if the APT attack is successful. According to Cole's report, the APT attack is characterized by its nonstop nature, making signature analysis an ineffective means of defense against it. Once they have access, attackers won't just enter and depart; instead, they want permanent access and will stay for as long as they can. Researchers have found that attacks typically take 243 days to be discovered and reported, with some attacks taking up to 4 years. This information pertains to the APT attack. Cole also notes that the APT attack is not based on a lone hacker or small hacker group, but rather on a highly structured and well-organized organization with a highly sophisticated and detailed attack protocol and methodology. Cole adds that turning our greatest strength into our biggest weakness is one of the APT's most terrifying characteristics. The attacker creates an outbound tunnel from the targeted victim's organization to their site using encryption, which was created to protect and prevent attackers from accessing critical information. This allows the attacker to exfiltrate data virtually undetected because most security devices are unable to read encrypted packets.

10.4.5. Attacker's Need for Information

Information is the one thing that an attacker needs in order to succeed, regardless of the kind of computer attack or exploit techniques they intend to employ. The servers at the targeted victim's company would be the attacker's source of information. Since ports are the point of entry into a computer system, the attacker will be searching for open ports in order to obtain this information. The attacker also needs an Internet protocol (IP) address. In the end, a system must have a vulnerability for an attacker to compromise it, and the attacker will look for this vulnerability. The attacker will locate the domain's name servers through a Whois search in order to obtain the IP information. The attacker will use Nslookup to find the IP address after determining the identity of the name servers. The IP address of the organization will be found using Nslookup, and if it is a U.S address, the target will be able to obtain the address range from the American Registry for Internet Numbers (ARIN). After gaining knowledge of the IP range, the attacker will use tools like NMap and Zenmap, which are both software tools used as security scanners to find hosts or services on a computer network, to scan the range for visible IP addresses and open ports. Finding vulnerabilities is the next stage of an attack on a targeted organization, and the attacker will use a vulnerability scanner like OpenVas to find exposures or vulnerabilities. The attacker's next move will be to use a tool like Core Impact, which can actually identify system vulnerabilities and, if found, exploit the service to grant the attacker access to the system. In order to strengthen their own security, Eric Cole advises an organization to use the same methodology to find and identify their exposure points.

Typical Phase of the Computer Attack

- Phase 1—Reconnaissance;
- Phase 2—Scanning;
- Phase 3A—Gaining Access at the Operating System and Application Level;
- Phase 3B—Gaining Access at the Network Level;
- Phase 3C—Gaining Access and Denial-of-Service Attacks;
- Phase 4—Maintaining Access;
- Phase 5—Covering Tracks and Hiding.

Their book makes an outstanding contribution, particularly in its thorough explanation of every attack phase and the tools and strategies employed at each one. According to Eric Cole, APT attacks are a revolutionary threat to our conventional cybersecurity programs, systems, and products. For instance, although worms and viruses evolved over time, their basic mechanisms stayed the same. The APT is now an organized adversary that is a person, group, or nation that will not give up until they obtain or ex-filtrate the information or intellectual property they are seeking, rather than software that is programmed to perform a specific function. You won't find a product that will safeguard your company from an APT attack, for this reason. Rather, a strategy that employs a range of adaptable solutions will need to be developed in order to be ready for any future shifts in the APT threat. We now need a proactive security approach that goes beyond the simple allowed or denied choice, and this new approach must be more than the previous reactive security approach. These days, social media, cloud computing, BYOD (bring your own device), machine-to-machine (M2M-IoT), and big data are all part of our cybersecurity environment. These are all domains where varying degrees of access and trust are necessary. Access must therefore be determined by total risk rather than by rigid rules. The general truth is this: you will be the target of attacks regardless of your size—you are an individual, small business, large corporation, government agency, or academic institution.

10.5. PREPARING FUTURE GENERATIONS FOR CYBERSECURITY TRANSFORMATIONAL CHALLENGES

Because there are so many new fundamental security vulnerabilities brought about by the IoT, cloud computing, and big data era, cybersecurity professionals face both deep and long-term challenges. The threat landscape is still expanding, making it challenging to detect and stop breaches in real time or almost real time. The rise of big data has made it necessary to conduct more research on the theoretical underpinnings of big data. In addition to conducting more research in the area of correlation analysis, the disciplines of engineering, computer science, and statistics will need to address the research issues surrounding inferential algorithms.

In order to build the academic instructional areas in security analytics, data analytics, decision science, predictive analytics, and correlation analysis, our universities will need to find and hire professors and researchers who can provide the necessary foundations. In order to provide both a robust research program and skilled and educated workers for the next generation, the university's role in research collaborations with governmental agencies and the DoD will only increase.

The actions taking place in the cyberspace environment have had a significant impact on the fundamental role that defense of our country plays. The ongoing advancements in digital technology have permanently altered the nature of war. These days, cyberweapons are real and can destroy even the most developed countries. The majority of countries' current defense plans fall short of the capacity to create and develop cyberweapons. Governments and nations will need to make patient, well-informed decisions to navigate the growing challenges of international law and individual privacy issues.

In order to get ready for new scientific discoveries and inventions, there will need to be more collaboration between our universities, research centers, and businesses. Last but not least, a strength that offers our kids unparalleled chances for development and success is our country's dedication to an educational system that aims to push the frontiers of science, technology, and knowledge. The commitment of the faculty at our colleges and universities, along with the instructors in our elementary and secondary school systems, is to produce the next wave of innovative and civic leaders for our country. It would be wise for our country to keep funding education at all societal levels as we prepare our children for the future and the revolutionary challenges they will face. A vital component of our legacy is the persistence and sustainability of our country's dedication to these principles, objectives, and the highest standards.

REFERENCES

1. Alyami, A., Sammon, D., Neville, K., & Mahony, C. (2023). The critical success factors for security education, training, and awareness (SETA) program effectiveness: A lifecycle model. *Information Technology & People, 36*(8), 94–125.
2. Andoni, M., Robu, V., Flynn, D., Abram, S., Geach, D., Jenkins, D., & Peacock, A. (2019). Blockchain technology in the energy sector: A systematic review of challenges and opportunities. *Renewable and Sustainable Energy Reviews, 100*, 143–174.
3. Cioffi, R., Travaglioni, M., Piscitelli, G., Petrillo, A., & De Felice, F. (2020). Artificial intelligence and machine learning applications in smart production: Progress, trends, and directions. *Sustainability, 12*(2), 492.
4. Conti, M., Dargahi, T., & Dehghantanha, A. (2018). Cyber threat intelligence: Challenges and opportunities. In *Advances in Information Security* (pp. 1–6). Springer International Publishing.
5. Coppolino, L., D'Antonio, S., Mazzeo, G., & Romano, L. (2017). Cloud security: Emerging threats and current solutions. *Computers & Electrical Engineering, 59*, 126–140.
6. Craigen, D., Diakun-Thibault, N., & Purse, R. (2014). Defining cybersecurity. *Technology Innovation Management Review, 4*(10).
7. Das, S., Dey, A., Pal, A., & Roy, N. (2015). Applications of artificial intelligence in machine learning: Review and prospect. *International Journal of Computer Applications, 115*(9).
8. Djenna, A., Harous, S., & Saidouni, D. E. (2021). Internet of things meet internet of threats: New concern cyber security issues of critical cyber infrastructure. *Applied Sciences, 11*(10), 1–30.
9. Hu, S., Hsu, C., & Zhou, Z. (2022). Security education, training, and awareness programs: Literature review. *Journal of Computer Information Systems, 62*(4), 752–764.
10. Jasim, K. F., Ghafoor, K. Z., & Maghdid, H. S. (2022). Analysis of encryption algorithms proposed for data security in 4G and 5G generations. In *ITM Web of Conferences* (Vol. 42, p. 01004).
11. Jones, V. A. (2020). Artificial intelligence enabled deepfake technology: The emergence of a new threat (Doctoral dissertation, Utica College).
12. Kadel, R., Shrestha, H., Shrestha, A., Sharma, P., Shrestha, N., Bashyal, J., & Shrestha, S. (2022). Emergence of AI in cyber security. *IRJMETS.*
13. Kandukuri, B. R., & Rakshit, A. (2009). Cloud security issues. In *2009*

IEEE International Conference on Services Computing (pp. 517–520). IEEE.

14. Kemmerer, R. A. (2003). Cybersecurity. In *25th International Conference on Software Engineering, 2003. Proceedings* (pp. 705–715). IEEE.
15. Mansoor, R., Hamood, D. N., & Farhan, A. K. (2023). Image steganography based on chaos function and randomize function. *Iraqi Journal for Computer Science and Mathematics, 4*(1), 71–86.
16. Michalski, R. S., Carbonell, J. G., & Mitchell, T. M. (2013). *Machine Learning: An Artificial Intelligence Approach*. Springer Science & Business Media.
17. Moor, J. H. (2005). Why we need better ethics for emerging technologies. *Ethics and Information Technology, 7*(3), 111–119.
18. Nahi, A. A., Ghaib, A. A., & Ali, A. A. A. A. (2023). Metaverse applications and its use in education. In *International Multi-Disciplinary Conference-Integrated Sciences and Technologies* (pp. 61–80). Cham: Springer Nature Switzerland.
19. Pilkington, M. (2016). Blockchain technology: Principles and applications. In *Research Handbook on Digital Transformations* (pp. 225–253). Edward Elgar Publishing.
20. Raicu, R. (2015). The emergence of social media intelligence. *Romanian Intelligence Studies Review, (14)*, 181–196.
21. Rizvi, S., Ryoo, J., Kissell, J., Aiken, W., & Liu, Y. (2018). A security evaluation framework for cloud security auditing. *The Journal of Supercomputing, 74*, 5774–5796.
22. Rotolo, D., Hicks, D., & Martin, B. R. (2015). What is an emerging technology? *Research Policy, 44*(10), 1827–1843.
23. Sarker, I. H., Kayes, A. S. M., Badsha, S., Alqahtani, H., Watters, P., & Ng, A. (2020). Cybersecurity data science: An overview from machine learning perspective. *Journal of Big Data, 7*, 1–29.
24. Sarmah, S. S. (2018). Understanding blockchain technology. *Computer Science and Engineering, 8*(2), 23–29.
25. Shah, V. (2021). Machine learning algorithms for cybersecurity: Detecting and preventing threats. *Revista Espanola de Documentacion Cientifica, 15*(4), 42–66.
26. Tarter, A. (2017). Importance of cyber security. In *Community Policing—A European Perspective: Strategies, Best Practices and Guidelines* (pp. 213–230).

27. Tounsi, W., & Rais, H. (2018). A survey on technical threat intelligence in the age of sophisticated cyber attacks. *Computers & Security, 72*, 212–233.
28. Ullah, Z., Al-Turjman, F., Mostarda, L., & Gagliardi, R. (2020). Applications of artificial intelligence and machine learning in smart cities. *Computer Communications, 154*, 313–323.
29. Untawale, T. (2021). Importance of cyber security in digital era. *International Journal for Research in Applied Science and Engineering Technology, 9*(8), 963–966.
30. Veletsianos, G. (2010). *Emerging Technologies in Distance Education.*
31. Yamin, M. M., Ullah, M., Ullah, H., & Katt, B. (2021). Weaponized AI for cyber attacks. *Journal of Information Security and Applications, 57*, 102722.
32. Yli-Huumo, J., Ko, D., Choi, S., Park, S., & Smolander, K. (2016). Where is current research on blockchain technology?—A systematic review. *PLOS ONE, 11*(10), e0163477.
33. Zheng, Z., Xie, S., Dai, H., Chen, X., & Wang, H. (2017). An overview of blockchain technology: Architecture, consensus, and future trends. In *2017 IEEE International Congress on Big Data (BigData Congress)* (pp. 557–564). IEEE.

INDEX

D

E

F

G

H

I

K

L

M

N

V

W

Printed in the United States
by Baker & Taylor Publisher Services